THEORIES OF INTERNATIONAL ECONOMICS

International economic theories emerged within particular social, economic and political frameworks and were developed as solutions to particular economic problems. In order to understand the increasingly complex and interdependent state of today's international economy, we need to realize the importance of those theories that came before. However, many international economics textbooks do not place the theories they discuss within this historical context.

Theories of International Economics aims to redress the balance by taking a pluralistic approach, presenting with authority both orthodox and heterodox international economic theories. Each chapter shows the necessarily interdependent nature of schools of international economic theories by including an historical component that shows how each school of thought developed, why it developed and what it has to say about the contemporary world. This text examines a wide range of theories, with an emphasis on the benefits of a pluralistic approach, addressing schools of thought including Mercantilist and Neo-Mercantilist, Classical and Neoclassical, Keynesian, Austrian, Institutional, Post Keynesian, Marxian and Feminist Economics, alongside—and in relation to—each other. This approach allows the scholarly value of each approach to be understood and appreciated, and in doing so enables a greater understanding of the world economy.

This book is suitable for use as either a core or supplementary text for international economics and international political economy courses.

Peter M. Lichtenstein is Professor Emeritus of Economics at Boise State University, USA. He was a Fulbright Scholar in China and also taught in Vietnam, specializing in international economics and heterodox economic theory.

THEORIES OF INTERNATIONAL ECONOMICS

Peter M. Lichtenstein

LONDON AND NEW YORK

First published 2016
by Routledge
2 Park Square, Milton Park, Abingdon, Oxon OX14 4RN

and by Routledge
711 Third Avenue, New York, NY 10017

Routledge is an imprint of the Taylor & Francis Group, an informa business

© 2016 Peter M. Lichtenstein

The right of Peter M. Lichtenstein to be identified as author of this work
has been asserted by him in accordance with sections 77 and 78 of the
Copyright, Designs and Patent Act 1988.

All rights reserved. No part of this book may be reprinted or reproduced or
utilised in any form or by any electronic, mechanical, or other means, now
known or hereafter invented, including photocopying and recording, or in
any information storage or retrieval system, without permission in writing
from the publishers.

Trademark notice: Product or corporate names may be trademarks or
registered trademarks, and are used only for identification and explanation
without intent to infringe.

British Library Cataloguing in Publication Data
A catalogue record for this book is available from the British Library

Library of Congress Cataloging in Publication Data
  Names: Lichtenstein, Peter M., 1944–
  Title: Theories of international economics : a pluralistic approach /
    Peter M. Lichtenstein.
  Description: New York : Routledge, 2016.
  Identifiers: LCCN 2015036726| ISBN 9781138911543 (hardback) |
    ISBN 9781315692562 (ebook) | ISBN 9781138911550 (pbk.)
  Subjects: LCSH: International economic relations. | International trade. |
    Keynesian economics. | Marxian economics.
  Classification: LCC HF1359 .L545 2016 | DDC 337.01--dc23
  LC record available at http://lccn.loc.gov/2015036726

ISBN: 978-1-138-91154-3 (hbk)
ISBN: 978-1-138-91155-0 (pbk)
ISBN: 978-1-315-69256-2 (ebk)

Typeset in Bembo
by Servis Filmsetting Ltd, Stockport, Cheshire

Printed and bound in the United States of America by Publishers Graphics,
LLC on sustainably sourced paper.

To Wang Juan, my partner in life,
and to my yet-to-be-named grandson.

CONTENTS

List of figures	*xi*
List of tables	*xiii*

1 Introduction

1

What is international economics? 1
The historical context of international economic theory 2
International economic theory: orthodoxy and heterodoxy 3
International economics and economic pluralism 7
Plan of the book 9
Conclusions 10
References 11

2 Mercantilism and neo-Mercantilism

12

Introduction 12
The historical background of early Mercantilism 13
Early mercantilist economic principles 17
Early British Mercantilism: the case of Thomas Mun 19
Early French Mercantilism: the case of Jean Baptiste Colbert 21
Other early examples of Mercantilism 22
Neo-Mercantilism 23
Two neo-Mercantilist models 24
Neo-mercantilist theory: John Maynard Keynes and Joan Robinson 27
Conclusions 30
References 32

viii Contents

3 Classical trade theory: Smith and Ricardo — 34

Introduction 34
Adam Smith on international trade 34
Ricardo on international trade 38
Ricardo's theory of surplus and the wage–profit relation 38
Ricardian trade theory: assumptions and analytical tools 41
The basic Ricardian model: autarky 45
The basic Ricardian model: from autarky to free trade 51
Extensions to the Ricardian model 54
Empirical studies of Ricardian comparative advantage 57
A critical summary of Ricardian trade theory 58
Conclusions 60
References 62

4 Neoclassical trade theory — 63

Introduction 63
The Neoclassical model: autarky 64
Neoclassical equilibrium: autarky to free trade 68
Five Neoclassical trade theorems 72
Extensions of the Neoclassical trade model 75
Is free trade really better? 79
Conclusions 81
References 84

5 The New Orthodoxy: trade theory recast — 86

Introduction 86
A note on scale economies 87
External scale economies and trade 88
Scale economies: internal 93
The Baumol-Gomory Global Conflict Model 99
Conclusions 105
References 108

6 Classical and Keynesian international economics — 109

Introduction 109
An overview of macroeconomics 109
Elements of Classical international macroeconomics 114
The Keynesian open economy model 118
Global Classicism: Neoliberalism 132
Global Keynesianism 134

Contents **ix**

Conclusions 137
References 139
Appendix 6A: diagrammatic presentation of the Classical model 140
Appendix 6B: diagrammatic presentation of the Keynesian model 142

7 Austrian international economics 144

Introduction 144
The methodology of Austrian economics 145
Austrian macroeconomics 152
Austrian international monetary economics 154
Austrian international production theory 157
Austrian theories of international entrepreneurship 162
Austrians and global institutions 167
Conclusions 171
References 172

8 Institutionalist international economics 174

Introduction 174
Methodology of Institutional economics 175
Overview of institutional-international economic theory 184
Network analysis 184
Transactions analysis and the firm 187
Transnational corporations 189
Institutional economic policy 192
Conclusions 196
References 198

9 Post Keynesian international economics 200

Introduction 200
An overview of Post Keynesian economics 200
Robinson's critique of Neoclassical trade theory 204
Michał Kalecki: income distribution and macroeconomics 209
Kaleckian open economy model 211
Hyman P. Minsky and global financial instability 222
Global instability and financialization 224
Post Keynesian views on the international monetary system 227
Conclusions 231
References 234

x Contents

10 Marxian theories of imperialism and capitalist development 236

Introduction 236
Marx on free trade 237
Economic imperialism: Marxism and Leninism 239
Economic imperialism: Neo-Marxism 242
Austrian counterpoint: Joseph Schumpeter on imperialism 247
Globalism or imperialism? 248
Conclusions 249
References 250

11 Marxian and Sraffian theories of unequal exchange 252

Introduction 252
International value theory: prelude to unequal exchange theory 252
Unequal international exchange theory I: Henryk Grossman 255
Unequal international exchange theory II: Arghiri Emmanuel 256
Unequal international exchange theory III: Piero Sraffa 259
Empirical evidence of Marxian theory 263
Conclusions 267
References 268
Appendix 11A: an overview of Marx's theory of value and price 270
Appendix 11B: an overview of Sraffian economics 279

12 Gender and Feminist trade theory 284

Introduction 284
The trade–gender connection: competitive advantage 286
The trade–gender connection: structural context 286
Global gender gaps in employment and earnings 291
Gender, orthodox economics and international trade theory 294
Heterodox Feminist theories of international trade 299
Conclusions 307
References 308

Index 311

FIGURES

3.1	Production possibilities frontier	43
3.2	Three scenarios	44
3.3	Production frontiers A-Land and B-Land	46
3.4	Indifference curves A-Land and B-Land	48
3.5	A-Land marginal rate of substitution	49
3.6	Equilibrium solution	50
3.7	Terms of trade	53
4.1	Production possibilities frontier	67
4.2	A-Land's production possibilities frontier	68
4.3	A-Land equilibrium	69
4.4	A-Land factor markets	69
4.5	Autarky equilibrium	70
4.6	Final terms of trade	71
4.7	Free trade equilibrium	71
4.8	Taste bias model	76
4.9	A-Land trade equilibrium	79
4.10	Is free trade better?	80
5.1	Constant and increasing returns to scale	88
5.2	Adjustments toward optimality	89
5.3	Cost and demand curves for computers	90
5.4	Trade among unequals	91
5.5	Three nation case	92
5.6	Firm demand curve	95
5.7	Shifting demand curve	95
5.8	Average costs	96
5.9	Output share graph for given distribution	100
5.10	Output share graph for all possible distributions	100

xii Figures

5.11	A-Land's share of world income	101
5.12	B-Land's share of world income	102
5.13	When conflict over trade exists	103
5.14	World income	104
6.1	IS-LM-BOP equilibrium	122
6.2	Swan diagram	124
6.3	Expansionary monetary policy: floating rates	126
6.4	Expansionary fiscal policy: floating rates	126
6.5	Expansionary monetary policy: fixed rates	127
6.6	Expansionary fiscal policy: fixed rates	128
6.7	The Classical model	140
6.8	Mundell-Fleming model	142
6.9	Balance of payments relationships	143
7.1	Time structure of production: A	160
7.2	Time structure of production: B	160
7.3	Time structure of production: C	161
8.1	One link of an export chain	186
8.2	A chain of transfers for one transaction	186
9.1	Aggregate supply and demand	212
9.2	Income redistribution	215
9.3	Trade balance	216
9.4	Interest rates and exchange rates	217
9.5	LM curve	218
9.6	General open economy model	218
9.7	Change in foreign profit share	221
11.1	Wages in rich and poor nation when $r = 10\%$	261
11.2	Wage and profit relation	282
12.1	Gender Inequality Index	288
12.2	Time spent on domestic work	290
12.3	Male and female unemployment rates	292
12.4	Female labor force participation rates	293

TABLES

3.1	Scenario #1	44
3.2	Hypothetical production data	46
3.3	World production and consumption: autarky	50
3.4	World output: specialization and free trade	52
3.5	Unit labor requirements	56
3.6	Rank-ordered unit labor requirements	56
4.1	The Leontief Paradox	74
5.1	Payoff matrix: Boeing and Airbus	98
5.2	New payoff matrix	98
6.1	Summary table: fixed and floating rates	128
7.1	Entrepreneurship in selected countries	166
11.1	Marxian value ratios example #1	253
11.2	Marxian value ratios example #2	254
11.3	Marxian value ratios example #3	254
11.4	Emmanuel model	257
11.5	Profits, wages and prices for rich and poor nation	261
11.6	Distribution of global surplus	262
11.7	Simple reproduction (a subsistence economy)	279
11.8	A surplus-producing economy with labor	280
11.9	Equilibrium prices with alternative wage–profit distributions	281
11.10	Percentage wage and profit shares	283
12.1	Gender–employment ratios by sector	292
12.2	Gender participation rates by sector, 2012	295

1

INTRODUCTION

What is international economics?

International economics is the study of trade in produced goods, natural resources and financial assets between nations and regions. Trade has three dimensions: the *volume* of trade (the total amount of exports and imports of all kinds), the *composition* of trade (the kinds of commodities and assets traded) and the *direction* of trade (who trades with whom). These three dimensions constitute what we call the *pattern of trade* between nations.

One approach to the study of trade is to focus on a nation's availability of human, natural and produced resources relative to other nations. Relative resource abundance influences relative costs of production which, in turn, determines which industries, and which resource owners, benefit the most from international trade. This general approach is customarily called *international microeconomics* and the emphasis is on relative rather than absolute magnitudes.

Another approach to the study of trade patterns is to focus on a nation's aggregate economic performance. This involves analyzing the interaction between international trade and aggregate output, income, employment and inflation. This interaction is strongest when a nation's economy is "open," which means that goods and financial assets can flow freely in and out. Economists typically call this approach *open economy macroeconomics* or *international macroeconomics*.

Beyond these two approaches, international economics also tries to answer questions such as "How are the benefits and costs of trade shared among social classes?" "Does trade result in dependence on other nations?" "Does trade enhance or impede economic development?" "Should trade be regulated or left free?" "What is the connection between growing global inequality and the spread of capitalism around the world?" These are open-ended questions for which researchers have devoted a great deal of energy to answer.

2 Introduction

Finally, international trade occurs in a social, cultural, political and institutional context. This context includes values, beliefs and attitudes. It also includes relations with other nations and with regional and multinational institutions. These contextual factors are always in a state of flux and vary widely around the world. They are an important part of the study of international economics because they directly affect, and are affected by, trade patterns.

The study of international economics can be narrow in scope, or it can be wide ranging, comprehensive and multi-disciplinary. It can be empirical or theoretical. It can be mathematically precise, or it can be qualitative, focusing instead on historical, cultural and institutional factors. There are indeed many roads that one can follow in studying the world economy.

The historical context of international economic theory

Today there are close to 200 sovereign nation states in the world, each with a particular endowment of natural and human resources. Each has unique economic and political institutions as well as distinct geographies, histories and cultures. A century or more ago, however, there were only half as many sovereign nation states as there are now. Most lands and territories were colonies of one or another European nation. In fact, the entire African continent, most of Southeast Asia and almost all of South America were colonized by a handful of European nations. And if we go back even further in time we will find no nation states at all, at least not as we know them today. There were only kingdoms, dynasties, empires, principalities, and, of course, their possessions and protectorates. Some scholars say that the nation state today is becoming irrelevant, that the "nation" as an analytical category has been superseded by large transnational corporations (TNCs) and global and regional organizations that dominate world economic affairs and act like nation states.

Alongside the proliferation of nation states has been the emergence and worldwide diffusion of capitalism, its philosophies and ideologies, its social structures, and its institutions. The capitalist way of thinking and doing things is relatively new, having begun in the late Middle Ages. Since then, capitalism has grown to dominate most of the world, especially since the collapse and transformation of the former communist nations.

The faces of capitalism

Capitalism is a distinct kind of economic system, and international economics is ultimately about global capitalism and its expansion. While capitalism is, broadly speaking, a single idea, it has many faces and bears the stamp of each society in which it has been practiced. That is to say, the essence of capitalism has many forms, depending on when and where it occurs.

Capitalism, therefore, differs according to time and place. Historically, capitalism has evolved in the last four or five hundred years from *merchant capitalism* in the late medieval Italian city states, to *industrial capitalism* in 19th-century Europe and

North America and, more recently, to *financial capitalism*, its current global manifestation. Each variation has had a well-defined logic and dynamic force.

If instead we look at capitalism contemporaneously, we find variations in the way it is practiced on different continents. For example, there is North American capitalism, European capitalism, Chinese capitalism and Japanese capitalism. We can even identify variations within each of these regional categories. For example, European capitalism includes Swedish, German, French and Italian capitalism, all of which have very distinct features.

It doesn't matter if we look at capitalism historically or contemporaneously. All the many forms of capitalism have the same essential ingredients. These ingredients include (1) private ownership of the means of production by a minority of the population; (2) a property-less class that includes a majority of the population who must sell their labor to make a living; and (3) market allocation of resources and commodities.

History and economic ideas

As the novelist L. P. Hartley once famously said, "The past is a foreign country: they do things differently there." We might add, "People also think differently there." The same applies to economic reasoning and theorizing. Economic ideas about capitalism closely correspond to the particular historical and social circumstances in which they arise. And as capitalism has evolved, so too have economic ideas about capitalism.

The world today is a far different place than it was three hundred years ago when economics first came into existence as an academic discipline. The 18th-century world of Adam Smith was far different from the 19th-century world of Karl Marx, and Marx's world was far different from the 20th-century world of John Maynard Keynes. Each of these economists, separated by several generations, faced radically different domestic and international economic problems. These differences are reflected in the theories they advanced to address these problems.

The point is that theories of international economics are rooted in particular historical and social conditions. We must therefore be cautious about generalizing any one of these theories and making them universally applicable. What may be true today may not be true in another era or another place. Therefore, international economic theory is necessarily tentative and contingent: no theory can be absolutely true and universally valid.

International economic theory: orthodoxy and heterodoxy

One would think that the field of international economics welcomes competing views and approaches. Unfortunately, this has not been the case. For more than a century, a distinct methodology and theoretical framework has monopolized intellectual activity in the field of international economics. We call this the *economic orthodoxy*. For decades this orthodoxy has dominated university teaching, research

4 Introduction

and publication, and many of its adherents have an almost religious devotion to its principles. Some prefer the term *mainstream economics* to orthodoxy. We favor the latter term over the former because it insinuates a more dogmatic attachment to established principles.

Nevertheless, there are other schools of thought that reject the domination of economic orthodoxy and offer in its place alternative methodologies, perspectives and theories. This is the world of the *economic heterodoxy*. Seldom taught at colleges and universities, these alternative approaches view global capitalism very differently. The heterodoxy is a collection of independent schools of thought, each with roots going back a century or more. Yet there is no central core methodology or theoretical framework that everyone accepts. Diversity and dissent from orthodoxy are the heterodoxy's common attributes.

What is the economic orthodoxy?

The economic orthodoxy emerged in the latter part of the 19th century. Its rise to dominance coincides, more or less, with the rise of Marxism, socialism and revolutionary socialist movements in Europe and Russia. The latter exposed capitalism's abuses and challenged its moral legitimacy. The economic orthodoxy played, and continues to play, an instrumental role in defending capitalism against these critiques and in demonstrating capitalism's alleged superiority over socialist alternatives.

Five central principles make up the core of orthodox economic theory. These principles are employed in international economics.

The first principle is that a capitalist economy with unfettered competitive markets and well-defined private property rights efficiently allocates its scarce resources to their highest valued (i.e., best possible) uses. This is the *economic efficiency principle*.

The second principle is that markets are self-correcting. This means that prices and quantities will always adjust, automatically, to achieve equilibrium between supply and demand. This is the *equilibrating principle*.

The third principle is that the capitalism system can be understood best by first describing its individual elements, namely the individual consumer and the individual producer. Each of these individual entities behaves rationally by maximizing utility and profits subject to budget and cost constraints. This is all that is really necessary to understand how the entire capitalist economy works. This is the *individual rationality principle*.

The fourth principle is the belief that, in a perfectly competitive economy, income results from hard work and thrift and not from exploitation or oppression. Income and wealth are therefore the rewards for productive contributions to the economy which, in turn, derive from diligence, self-improvement, entrepreneurship and ingenuity. Moreover, if talents, abilities and ambitions are unequally distributed among the population then it stands to reason that income and wealth will also be unequally distributed. Inequality simply reflects the attributes of individuals and their choices to work and save. This idea provides a theoretical and moral defense of the unequal distribution of wealth and privilege that distinguishes capitalism. This is the *economic justice principle*.

The fifth principle is that any attempt by government to interfere with this rational self-correcting system will undermine economic efficiency. This is the *laissez-faire principle*. The idea is that a government should play a neutral and unobtrusive role in the economy.

There are two main branches of the contemporary economic orthodoxy, each building on these five principles. One branch is Neoclassical microeconomics and the other is Classical-Keynesian macroeconomics. Neoclassical microeconomics is an outgrowth of Classical economics. It redirected scholarly attention away from the Classical theory in which *social classes* (capitalists, workers and farmers) competed against each other for national income, toward a theory in which *individuals* collaborate with each other in production to share the national income. In Neoclassical microeconomics, capitalism is a harmonious social system and not a system rooted in class conflict.

The second branch of economic orthodoxy is Classical-Keynesian economics, which is the foundation for modern macroeconomics. A key proposition of Classical-Keynesian economics is that a capitalist economy, if left alone, will always seek a long-run supply–demand equilibrium in which there is full employment. This full employment equilibrium is capitalism's natural state, and, in the long run at least, the government can do little to improve upon it. Classical-Keynesian economics represents a rightward shift in the economics profession and actually stands Keynes on his head by making both discretionary fiscal and monetary government policies ineffectual if not perverse.[1]

What is the economic heterodoxy?

Economic heterodoxy is a collection of distinct schools of thought. Each school has a distinctive history, methodology, theoretical framework and policy orientation. Economic heterodoxy is an umbrella term; there is no single approach to which all schools subscribe. We therefore cannot provide a list of principles that all heterodox schools can accept. We can, however, provide a list of some of the ideas which heterodox economists reject.

First of all, heterodox economists would reject the five principles we enumerated above. Except perhaps for the Austrians,[2] heterodox economists would say that the individual as a category of economic analysis should not be the starting point. Further, capitalism is not a harmonious, efficient and self-equilibrating system. The competitive free market ideal is therefore a delusion.

Second, the heterodoxy rejects the orthodoxy's unqualified reliance on abstract, axiomatic and deductive reasoning and mathematics. While heterodox economists occasionally use these techniques, they also apply a large dose of historical, institutional and qualitative analysis.

Third, according to the heterodoxy, there is much more to capitalism than rational individuals and firms interacting in perfect markets. The rationality assumption of

6 Introduction

orthodox economics reduces human behavior to robotics. And the assumption that only markets matter ignores a great deal of human experience. These assumptions capture only a part of real world capitalism. Non-market interactions and social institutions play an equally important role in heterodox economics.

When it comes to international economics, the heterodoxy is highly skeptical of any portrayal of the world economy as a well-oiled machine in which nations freely, rationally and efficiently trade, producing an optimal outcome for everyone. Things are far too complex to reduce to a single set of propositions.

This book includes six main heterodox schools of international economics: Mercantilism and neo-Mercantilism, Austrian, Institutional, Post Keynesian, Marxian and Feminist international economics. There are other heterodox traditions, such as ecological economics and evolutionary economics. But these traditions have not yet had much to say about the topics that concern us in this book.

A majority of colleges and university courses are taught from the orthodox perspective. The major national and international economic research institutions are also orthodox in the work they do. The heterodoxy is far from being a threat to the privileged position of mainstream economics. However, there is a growing number of institutions that are friendly to heterodox ideas and that offer diverse academic programs where students are encouraged to study heterodox economic theory. The *Heterodox Economics Directory* lists 51 undergraduate programs and 31 graduate programs that offer students coursework in heterodox economics. There are also about 45 academic associations based on Austrian, Institutionalist, Post Keynesian, Marxian and Feminist ideas. While struggling for attention, the heterodoxy still is vibrant and prolific.

Orthodoxies and heterodoxies: hedgehogs and foxes

The philosopher Isaiah Belin once wrote that there are two types of people in the world, foxes and hedgehogs (Berlin, 1953). The analogy comes from an ancient Greek poet who wrote, "The fox knows many things, but the hedgehog knows one big thing." According to Berlin's interpretation of this line, the hedgehog is a person who relates "everything to a single central vision, one system, less or more coherent or articulate, in terms of which they understand, think and feel—a single, universal, organizing principle in terms of which alone all that they are and say has significance. . ." The fox, on the other hand, is someone who pursues "many ends, often unrelated and even contradictory, connected, if at all, only in some de facto way . . . related to no moral or aesthetic principle."

We can think of the orthodoxy and heterodoxy as hedgehogs and foxes. Orthodoxy aspires to be an axiomatically based science. Its theories reflect a unitary vision of reality that is held to be universally true and everywhere applicable. The "one big thing" that orthodox economists believe is the set of self-evident principles outlined above. On the other hand, we can think of the heterodoxy as foxes. Their theories are diverse and operate on many different levels of abstraction. It is

Introduction **7**

hard to identify, for any one heterodox school of thought, a unitary vision of reality that all participants accept as universally true.

Berlin admits that his categorization of people is a great oversimplification and might seem absurd. Likewise, it is hard to drive all orthodox economists into a single corral, so to speak. But Berlin suggests that the dichotomy "offers a point of view from which to look and compare, a starting-point for genuine investigation." Neither the hedgehog nor the fox is wrong. They just have different perspectives. We suggest that this dichotomy is a useful way to begin the study of international economics.

International economics and economic pluralism

As we have noted, international economics is dominated by a single economic way of thinking. Some call this "monism," which is the belief that there is only one set of inviolable economic principles or laws that describe reality. It is the hedgehog's view of the world.

Pluralism is the opposite of monism. It is the fox's view of the world. Pluralism in economics is an appeal for diversity. It argues that all schools of thought offer compelling explanations of reality and therefore have scholarly value, including the orthodoxy. After all, the world is a complex place and it is not possible to use only a few universal principles to explain it. Each of the orthodox and heterodox approaches offers important insights into international economics and none should be dismissed out of hand.[3]

This book takes a pluralistic approach to international economics. One consequence of a pluralist approach is that we do not presume that free trade is sacrosanct, although it might under certain circumstances be an appropriate system. Nor do we regard the principle of comparative advantage, the centerpiece of orthodox theory, as indisputable, although it can often be a useful tool.

A pluralistic approach justifies a detailed examination of all the schools of thought, orthodox and heterodox, that contribute to our understanding of the world economy.

The pluralist movement in economics

The movement for pluralism in economics began in 1992 with the publication of a petition titled "A Plea for a Pluralistic and Rigorous Economics." It was sponsored by economists Geoffrey Hodgson, Uskali Mäki and Donald McCloskey in the *American Economic Review*, the profession's leading journal. The full text of the petition is a follows:

> We the undersigned are concerned with the threat to economic science posed by intellectual monopoly. Economists today enforce a monopoly of method or core assumptions, often defended on no better ground that it constitutes the "mainstream". Economists will advocate free competition, but will not practice it in the marketplace of ideas.

8 Introduction

> Consequently, we call for a new spirit of pluralism in economics, involving critical conversation and tolerant communication between different approaches. Such pluralism should not undermine the standards of rigor; an economics that requires itself to face all the arguments will be a more, not a less, rigorous science.
>
> We believe that the new pluralism should be reflected in the character of scientific debate, in the range of contributions in its journals, and in the training and hiring of economists.
>
> *(Hodgson, Mäki and McCloskey, 1992: xxv)*

The petition was signed by many famous economists including four Nobel laureates.

In 1993, a year after publication of the "plea," the International Confederation of Associations for Pluralism in Economics (ICAPE) was founded. ICAPE is a consortium of 30 scholarly associations that fosters pluralism in economics. Then, in June 2000, several economics students in Paris circulated a petition calling for the reform of their economics curriculum. They complained that Neoclassical economics was not giving them sufficient understanding of real-life economies and they called for introducing diversity and critical dialogue into the university curriculum. Their demands spread to the United Kingdom and then to Europe and North America. It led to the formation of the International Student Initiative for Pluralism in Economics, a collaboration of 65 associations of economics students from 30 countries around the world. The opening paragraph of the students' initiative states,

> It is not only the world economy that is in crisis. The teaching of economics is in crisis too, and this crisis has consequences far beyond the university walls. What is taught shapes the minds of the next generation of policymakers, and therefore shapes the societies we live in. We . . . believe it is time to reconsider the way economics is taught. We are dissatisfied with the dramatic narrowing of the curriculum that has taken place over the last couple of decades. This lack of intellectual diversity does not only restrain education and research. It limits our ability to contend with the multidimensional challenges of the 21st century—from financial stability, to food security and climate change. The real world should be brought back into the classroom, as well as debate and a pluralism of theories and methods. Such change will help renew the discipline and ultimately create a space in which solutions to society's problems can be generated.
>
> *(International Student Initiative for Pluralism in Economics, n.d.)*

Two more recent outgrowths of the pluralist movement are the student-led Manchester Post-Crash Economics Society ("The world has changed, the syllabus hasn't.") and Rethinking Economics. These were prompted in part by the inability of orthodox economics to explain the 2008 worldwide economic recession and the desire to reform economics curricula to include alternative schools of thought.

Clearly, the pluralism in economics movement is not a transient phenomenon. As the world becomes increasingly complex and interdependent we will hear more and more voices demanding that economists learn and teach the whole range of orthodox and heterodox theories; hiding the heterodoxy from view is no longer acceptable.

Plan of the book

This book emphasizes the historical context of international economic theory. We are particularly concerned with how different historical epochs give rise to different theories of international economics. We are equally concerned with how the various schools of thought developed and what problems they have been trying to solve. Our intention is to display the contingent nature and context of international economic theory.

We begin in Chapter 2 ("Mercantilism and neo-Mercantilism") with the history of Mercantilism from its origins in the 16th century to the present. Mercantilism, in its earliest expressions, is the soil from which Classical and Neoclassical trade theories grew. But Mercantilism is not just an artifact of history. It continues to exist in a contemporary variation that we call neo-Mercantilism. In either case, Mercantilism proposes a larger role for the government in controlling international trade and thus serves as a counterpoint to the free trade ideology of orthodox economics. For this reason, we consider Mercantilism to be part of the economic heterodoxy.

In Chapter 3 ("Classical trade theory: Smith and Ricardo") we examine Adam Smith's and David Ricardo's formal theories of trade. Their ideas about trade addressed the particular concerns and issues of Britain in the 18th and 19th centuries. Smith was among the first to describe capitalism as a dynamic social, political and economic organism regulated by inherent natural forces. And Ricardo was the author of the famous theory of comparative advantage, later to become the foundation of orthodox international economics.

As capitalism evolved in the late 19th century, so too did international economic theory. Faced with the challenges posed by Marxism, anarchism and other revolutionary movements occurring in Europe, economists wanted a theoretical framework that could defend capitalism against these challenges. The result was Neoclassical trade theory, which became, and still is, the modern economic orthodoxy. It is based on an elaboration of Ricardo's theory of comparative advantage and on the ideology of free trade. We discuss these topics in Chapter 4 ("Neoclassical trade theory").

Today, not all orthodox economists agree that comparative advantage is the best model to use to understand trade patterns. They would argue that the world today is a far cry from the standard assumptions of perfect competition, constant returns to scale and zero externalities that make up the foundation of Neoclassical theories. The world economy is instead characterized by market imperfections

10 Introduction

and these imperfections make comparative advantage irrelevant. These economists have developed an alternative approach called New Trade Theory which assumes imperfect competition, economies of scale and externalities. We introduce these ideas in Chapter 5 ("The New Orthodoxy: trade theory recast").

Later contributions to economic orthodoxy, mainly after the Second World War, incorporated trade theory into Classical and Keynesian macroeconomics. There we see how trade affects, and is affected by, national output and income, employment and inflation. This approach is referred to as open economy macroeconomics. We introduce these topics in Chapter 6 ("Classical and Keynesian international economics").

Despite the immense influence that the orthodoxy has had in the economics discipline, its challengers—the heterodoxy—have not gone away. They have always been standing close by, and their critical voices could always be heard, if only scholars had chosen to listen. However, beginning in the rebellious years of the 1960s and 1970s there emerged a renewed interest in alternative methodologies and doctrines. Among these alternatives are Austrian (Chapter 7), Institutionalist (Chapter 8), Post Keynesian (Chapter 9), Marxian (Chapters 10 and 11) and Feminist (Chapter 12) economics. Together these constitute the economic heterodoxy which we introduce in the remainder of the book.

The purpose of including historical perspectives and alternative theories and doctrines is to provide a context for the study of international economics. Without such a context we deprive ourselves of the tools needed to think critically about the received conventional wisdom and about the established order of things. Neither could we even begin to think of new ways of understanding the world economy in the 21st century.

Conclusions

We conclude this introductory chapter with three cautionary notes. The first is that the boundaries separating the different schools of thought presented in this book are not as sharply drawn as the above discussion might suggest. The landscape of economic ideas is actually quite murky. For example, economists often span two or more schools of thought. Thus, we find many cross-overs between Marxists, Post Keynesians, Institutionalists and Feminists as well as between Austrians, Institutionalists and the orthodoxy. Moreover, none of the heterodox schools of thought is homogenous. Each has many subdivisions that display significant methodological and theoretical differences. While not perfect, we nonetheless conclude that the orthodoxy–heterodoxy distinction that we make in this book is a first approximation that helps us to understand the existing state of affairs in modern international economics.

Second, the standard Neoclassical model that serves as the foundation for modern microeconomics is not the only model orthodox economists use. There are also behavioral economics, bounded rationality, evolutionary economics, experimental economics, game theory, happiness theory, network theory, new institutional economics and transactions cost theory. All of these introduce new and novel ways of modeling the economy. Yet most of them still rely on the orthodox assumptions of rationality, individualism and equilibrium.

Finally, taking a pluralist approach requires evenhandedness and value transparency (deliberately making our values known). It does not, and cannot, require that we always be neutral and objective. Neutrality and objectivity are impossible, except as a disingenuous pose. Economists always lean in one direction or another. To this end, in the interest of transparency, the reader should be aware that this textbook leans decidedly toward the heterodoxy, especially to the Post Keynesian and Marxian schools of thought.

Notes

1   The appearance of the word "Keynesian" is an historical curiosity. It suggests that this branch of orthodoxy is a synthesis of Classical and Keynesian economics. This is misleading, however, because Keynes's ideas play only a small role. In fact, there is little that is recognizably Keynesian in Classical-Keynesian theory. We will explain this in detail in later chapters.
2   While Austrians are in every way heterodox, and severely critical of the orthodoxy, they nonetheless adopt an "individualistic" methodology. We describe this in Chapter 7.
3   For a survey of pluralism in economics see Garnett, Olson and Starr (2010).

References

Berlin, I. (1953). The Hedgehog and the Fox. Retrieved August 30 2014, from http://press.princeton.edu/chapters/s9981.pdf.

Garnett, R., Olson, E. K. & and Starr, M. (Eds). (2010). *Economic Pluralism*. New York: Routledge.

Heterodox Economics Directory (2013). Retrieved July 21 2014, from http://heterodoxnews.com/directory/hed5.pdf.

Hodgson, G., Mäki, U. & McCloskey, D. (1992). "A Plea for a Pluralistic and Rigorous Economics." *American Economic Review, 82*(2), xxv.

International Confederation of Associations for Pluralism in Economics (n.d.). Retrieved 21 July 2014, from http://www.icape.org/Home.

International Student Initiative for Pluralism in Economics (n.d.). Retrieved July 21 2014, from http://www.isipe.net/open-letter/.

Post-Crash Economics Society (n.d.). Retrieved July 24 2014, from http://www.post-crasheconomics.com/.

Rethinking Economics (n.d.). Retrieved July 24 2014, from http://www.rethinkeconomics.org.

2

MERCANTILISM AND NEO-MERCANTILISM

Introduction

The word "mercantilism" comes from the Latin word *mercantem*, which means either trade or merchant. Mercantilism proposes that a nation must grow trade surpluses in order to expand its wealth and power. And to accomplish this, a nation can use some combination of: (1) import restrictions; (2) export subsidization and promotion; (3) exchange rate controls; (4) special trading privileges and rules; and (5) regulation of capital flows. These policies result in an excess of exports over imports and hence an accumulation of bullion and species which at one time filled state coffers with funds to finance wars and to provide exotic luxuries for Europe's aristocracy.[1]

However, any restriction on imports from another nation is simultaneously a restriction on the other nation's exports. Trade is thus a zero–sum game: one nation's gain is another's loss. This contrasts sharply with free trade doctrine which, as we will see in the next chapters, claims that trade is a positive sum game because everyone who participates benefits (although not equally).

Mercantilism, some say, is nationalistic and autarkic.[2] It is nationalistic because it favors the wellbeing of the nation over all other nations. Mercantilism leans toward autarky because it promotes economic self-sufficiency, especially in key economic sectors such as national defense. The argument here is that a nation ought not to rely on other nations for critical commodities even if such trade would make both parties better off.

Mercantilism finds ethical legitimacy in the subordination of private interests to the national interest, however we choose to define this. This means that the state can justifiably constrain or prohibit the pursuit of self-interest by certain economic agents if there is a higher national purpose in doing so. Restrictions on the export of arms is an example. However, in the 16th and 17th centuries, when mercantilist writings first appeared, this conflict between private and public interests would not have been a problem, since the idea of a "private" sphere, as distinct from a "public" sphere, had not yet taken root in intellectual discourse. Today, the distinction is fundamental to the ideological separation between schools of economic thought.

Finally, we must be careful how we classify Mercantilism. Mercantilism is not actually a cohesive school of thought, if by this we mean that its adherents share a uniform methodology and analytical framework. While mercantilists typically recommend some form of state intervention in international economic affairs, their overall aims and policies are quite diverse, and it would be an overstatement to regard them as a single school with a unified set of principles.[3]

Today, orthodox economists generally dismiss Mercantilism and "neo-Mercantilism," its modern-day version, as misguided, quaint, and lacking theoretical substance. As one economist exclaimed, somewhat hysterically, "The neo-mercantilist concept is simply neo-socialist apologetics for neo-bureaucracy, neo-regulation and (ultimately) neo-totalitarianism" (Ekelund, 1995: 880). Another economist more soberly wrote, "Mercantilism was essentially a folk doctrine, evolved in the light of the prevailing historical circumstances and values by simple inference from apparent facts. It was a doctrine of practical men not given to subtle economic analysis . . ." (Viner, 1991: 263).

This chapter departs from the usual treatment of Mercantilism. It does this in three ways: (1) by stressing the diversity of mercantilist ideas; (2) by extending the historical range of Mercantilism to include not only early Mercantilism but also contemporary Mercantilism, or neo-Mercantilism; and (3) by challenging the categorical rejection of Mercantilism by orthodox economists.

The historical background of early Mercantilism

Mercantilism in history

Times were changing rapidly in Europe in the first three centuries (1500–1800) when the first mercantilist writers appeared on the scene. These are some of the most important changes that were taking place:

- capitalism was replacing feudalism, resulting in a complete makeover of the class structures of Europe; an influential merchant capitalist class, and later an industrial and financial capitalist class rose to prominence, replacing the old feudal order;
- the power and authority of organized religion was declining; society was becoming more secular and worldly;
- the constitutional nation state was becoming the dominant political institutional form; an elected parliament vied with the royalty for power;
- joint stock companies were emerging as powerful social and political institutions;

14 Mercantilism and neo-Mercantilism

- sophisticated financial markets were developing in London and on the European continent;
- colonialism and global empires were growing, as were the volume of imports of luxuries and raw materials from exotic places such as China and India;
- a new rationalistic approach to life was introduced that was centered on market exchange.

Given these extraordinary transformations, it is understandable that early mercantilist writers held diverse and often contradictory views about what was going on. There was no prior generally accepted theoretical doctrine for them to fall back on, and the principles that governed economic life were changing almost every day. Mercantilists certainly wanted to see trade flourish, merchants prosper, domestic industry grow and employment expand. Who wouldn't have? Yet, the competitive nature of international commerce, particularly between Britain, Holland, France, Spain and Portugal, led most observers of the time to believe that some strategic state control over trade was essential to protect the national interest. Free trade, it was believed, was just too reckless and dangerous a policy to pursue.

Early Mercantilism and the public space

Today, ideas about economics (theories and analyses, empirical studies, policy advice, narratives and opinions) are widely disseminated throughout the world. Most of these ideas originate and develop within academia where university scholars each year write and publish thousands of articles in hundreds of periodicals intended mainly for other scholars. University presses, non-profit think tanks and government research institutes disseminate economic ideas in the form of monographs, studies and reports. Beyond this academic literature, there are commercial publishing houses as well as newspaper and magazine presses that popularize economists' interpretations of economic events and issues. Noted economists such as Milton Friedman, Paul Samuelson and Paul Krugman have even attained popstar status with their op-ed pieces in major newspapers and news magazines. Moreover, computer information technologies have allowed economists to investigate, empirically, every imaginable economic relationship and hypothesis, the results of which they report in the academic and popular literature. Finally, internet websites, blogs and email have enabled the circulation of an enormous amount of economic ideas and have created a worldwide community of scholars.

None of these institutions and technologies existed four or five hundred years ago. The community of scholars then was small and limited to clergy, literate nobles, aristocrats and a handful of private citizens. Books and documents were either handwritten and copied or printed with carved wooden blocks, and their circulation was very limited.

All this changed when, around 1450, Johannes Gutenberg, a German goldsmith, invented typographic printing, a technology that revolutionized the production and distribution of knowledge.[4] It facilitated social, political, economic and religious change in Europe and enabled the European Enlightenment. The expansion of the number of printers and booksellers helped to create a form of public scholarship that began to have commercial value. Private citizens wrote the earliest mercantilist manuscripts and distributed them in the form of pamphlets, handbills, small books and broadsheets. Merchants also privately distributed their personal correspondences and journals, reporting on commercial opportunities and the perils of international trade. As worldwide commerce grew, so too did the value of this "news."

The emerging importance of such printed materials had much to do with the rise of European nation states. Statecraft was becoming increasingly public in nature as parliaments and legislative bodies were replacing monarchs in making social and economic policy. Mercantilist writings thus became an invaluable instrument for publicizing the policies, regulations and laws of governments. Hoping to influence state economic policymaking, mercantilist writers began to address economic issues relating to commerce and finance and, later on, industry. Their publications were usually polemical and dealt with a large variety of concrete economic problems that legislators were actively debating in Parliament.

Mercantilist writers were mostly unknown and often remained anonymous. Some only used pseudonyms. Among the better-known early mercantilists were Thomas Mun (1571–1641), Gerard de Malynes (1586–1641) and Sir William Petty (1623–1687) in Britain; Jean Baptiste Colbert (1619–1683) and Anne-Robert-Jacques Turgot (1727–1781) in France; Friedrich List (1789–1846) in Germany; and Alexander Hamilton (1755–1804) in the United States.

The importance of this growing mercantilist print culture was that it created a "public sphere" in which critical debate took place among literate citizens who were unattached either to the state or to the monarchy. The published word became all-powerful, just as an independent and educated middle class—a *bourgeoisie*—arose and as the old courtly and feudal society was breaking up. The bourgeoisie attended concerts and theaters, frequented coffee houses and social clubs, and debated public policy; they constituted a readership that was becoming interested in economic affairs and that had a personal stake in the development of commerce and industry.

The rise of nation states

Modern international economics presumes the existence of "nation states" and hence a division between the domestic sphere and the international sphere. A nation state is an autonomous sovereign entity with distinct borders. Historically, it is a relatively new kind of political and social organization, different from the kingdoms, dynasties and empires of earlier ages.

The territorial reorganization of kingdoms and empires into autonomous nation states occurred at about the same time as the emergence of Mercantilism, especially in Europe and parts of Eurasia. The Austro-Hungarian, Russian and Ottoman empires each had multi-ethnic populations, yet one group, whose language became the *lingua franca* of the empire, dominated politically. Wars and post-war agreements resulted in the complete restructuring of these empires into

16 Mercantilism and neo-Mercantilism

nation states. Citizens of these states came to accept a communal identity and consciousness. Benedict Anderson argues that this identity gave rise to nationalism and to the creation of "imagined communities." (Anderson, 1991) These communal identities are "imagined" in the sense that citizens do not actually know one another; they only imagine that they belong to a common community. The new print culture, together with the growing system of market capitalism, tied citizens to one another, enabling the creation of imagined national communities.

These developments were most advanced in Britain. The Revolution of 1688 and passage of the Bill of Rights brought to an end monarchical absolutism and transferred power from the king to Parliament. These changes effectively located the power to tax and spend, and to raise and finance armies, in the "public space." That is to say, economic affairs became public, and the king no longer had a monopoly over the power to make economic decisions. Economic affairs then became increasingly important as the British textile industry and the slave trade mobilized the nation's financial capital, putting it to work around the world in the production, distribution and accumulation of wealth. The British nation state had become a genuine economic power with which other European nations states now had to reckon. Given these events, it is not surprising that the British mercantilist writers were the first to rise to prominence.

Elsewhere in Europe, things developed somewhat differently and at a different pace. Around 1600, the unified territories that once constituted France were, like Britain, also shedding their feudal roots and were becoming a strong centralized nation state. This culminated in 1792 with the creation of the First French Republic. A unique form of Mercantilism, Colbertism, dominated French thought at this time. Named after Jean Baptiste Colbert (1619–1683), the French finance minister under King Louis XIV, Colbertism became what many regard as the highest form of Classical Mercantilism. Germany, on the other hand, did not become a unified nation state until 1871. Until that time, Germany consisted of many individual principalities, each with its own culture and religion.

These transformations were not peaceful. The new nation states of Europe and Britain seemed to be in a perpetual state of war, mainly over territory and markets. In this kind of environment, economic relations between nations understandably appeared to mercantilist writers as nasty and cutthroat. It was not unreasonable at the time to suppose that trade was a zero-sum game.

The German economist Gustav Schmoller (1838–1917) summarized the connection between Mercantilism and the rise of the nation state as follows:

> The essence of [Mercantilism] lies not in some doctrine of money, or of the balance of trade; not in tariff barriers, protective duties, or navigation laws; but in something far greater:—namely, in the total transformation of society and its organisation, as well as of the state and its institutions, in the replacing of a local and territorial economic policy by that of the national state.
>
> *(Schmoller, 1895: 50–51)*

Early mercantilist economic principles

Early mercantilist writers promoted trade policies that increased the nation's wealth and its military might. They believed that building a prosperous economy required extensive international commerce and a strong foreign demand for its own products. Mercantilists believed that by restricting imports and encouraging exports a nation would experience a net inflow of bullion and species. Economists call this idea "bullionism." The nation could then use that money to pay for its military expenditures.

Mercantilists focused on the *current account* of the balance of payments rather than the *financial account*.[5] This was reasonable to do in a competitive commercial world where exchange rates were fixed and where gold was used to settle international accounts. It was not until the late 18th century, when London became the financial capital of the world, and when global financial markets began to develop more fully, that the financial account also became the focus of attention.

In the early mercantilist era, raw materials destined for domestic production, and luxury goods destined for Europe's upper classes, flowed abundantly into and out of countries. Capital and labor were largely immobile. Not until colonialism and the Industrial Revolution did capital begin to migrate. Labor, on the other hand, remained immobile due to restrictions on immigration and emigration. Exceptions, of course, were the slave trade and the large-scale migrations and resettlements of people following wars, famines and political and ethnic struggles. The early mercantilist world thus differed substantially from today's world in which everything freely and rapidly circulates around the globe.

Many early mercantilists believed that when individual capitalists imported commodities that other domestic capitalists would have produced at home, the nation as a whole suffered and economic development slowed. This understandably led to support for import restrictions, especially when imports competed with homemade products. This was especially true in agriculture as most nations restricted the import of grain that competed with domestically produced grain.

The calico trade

An example of an issue that occupied the attention of early mercantilists was the calico trade. During this time, calico became an exceptionally important commodity that was traded between India and Europe. Calico is a finely woven cotton fabric that was first produced in Calicut, India, around the 11th century. Merchants started to import calico into Britain in the early 1600s. Predictably, many in Britain were afraid that unrestricted imports of calico would undermine the British cotton industry, create unemployment and cause a loss of bullion and species. They called for government restrictions on calico imports.

Opponents of restrictions argued that only those engaged in the cotton industry would benefit, while everyone else would have to pay higher prices for cotton goods. Prices would be higher because import restrictions would curtail supply.

18 Mercantilism and neo-Mercantilism

Opponents of restrictions believed it was "unnatural" to sustain a particular industry if it could not survive on its own. Should the private interests of the domestic cotton manufacturers and cotton workers override the general public's interest in low-priced textiles? It was another matter if the state wished to cultivate a domestic cotton industry, in which case it may have been appropriate to temporarily protect such a nascent industry. But what if the industry already exists?

The shipping industry

Shipping was particularly important, especially to Britain, France and the Netherlands. Most believed at the time that control of the seas was vital to a nation's economic and military power. Thus, the French placed heavy duties on all vessels of foreign origin entering French ports. They also subsidized domestic shipbuilders, allowing them to compete against foreign shipbuilders. The English, too, passed the Navigation Laws of 1650 and 1651, which prohibited any foreign vessel from engaging in trade with England. The laws stipulated that only British ships could carry goods between England and her colonies. Regulation of shipping went even further with passage of the Staple Act in 1663, which required all exports to Europe from British colonies to first pass through English ports. These 17th-century laws were aimed primarily at England's chief competitors, the Dutch and the French.

Protection of home industry

The economic policies pursued by governments, especially in Britain and on the European continent, generally tried to protect home businesses and industries. Domestically, the government often provided capital to new industries and exempted other industries from regulations and taxes. The government established trade monopolies, especially for colonial trade, and granted special privileges to successful businesses. Governments imposed tariffs, quotas and outright prohibitions on the import of foreign-made commodities that competed with local manufacturers. Other import restrictions targeted luxury goods and goods deemed unnecessary to the development of domestic industry. Also forbidden was the export of equipment that foreign firms might use to compete with domestic manufacturing. Export of homemade goods was encouraged, however.

Which imports to restrict, which exports to encourage?

Two general principles underlay mercantilist doctrines. One was the need to maintain a favorable trade balance. There was a political justification for this: trade earnings could directly finance wars. There was a second economic justification: carefully selected import restrictions would encourage development of certain key domestic industries by protecting them from foreign competition until they matured and became globally competitive. In addition, the net inflow of money that resulted from a positive trade balance increased the domestic money supply and helped to keep interest rates low (although it might also be inflationary).

Which commodities should be subject to import restrictions? Which commodity exports should be encouraged? The usual answer was this:

1. Encourage the export of domestically produced manufactured goods by using bounties (i.e., rewards) and special trade dispensations.
2. Encourage the import of raw materials needed for the production of these exported goods by granting tariff exemptions.
3. Discourage the export of raw materials needed for production at home.
4. Discourage the import of manufactured goods that compete with home production.
5. Discourage the import of luxuries and "superfluities."

These economic objectives presumably would lead to a favorable trade balance, increase the domestic production of high value-added goods, and generate employment.

Early British Mercantilism: the case of Thomas Mun

In his famous monograph, *England's Treasure by Foreign Trade, or The Balance of Our Foreign Trade is The Rule of our Treasure*, published posthumously in 1664, Thomas Mun endeavored to demonstrate "the general means whereby a Kingdom may be enriched" (Mun, 1664: 1). In this book, Mun begins by spelling out the role of the merchant in expanding the state "treasure": it was the merchant who was the "steward of the Kingdom's stock." It was the merchant who would supply the princes and aristocracies of a nation with the riches to which they had been accustomed. The perfect merchant, said Mun, must be a scholar, a diligent observer of best business practices, perfectly knowledgeable of all domestic and foreign prices, duties and taxes, skilled in navigation and, of course, a linguist. Only such a merchant can serve as the principal agent of the Kingdom's global commerce.

The best way for a nation to accumulate wealth is through foreign trade. The object of foreign trade, said Mun, was to "to sell more to strangers yearly than we consume of theirs in value" (Mun, 1664: 7). A positive balance of trade, in other words, is what leads to the accumulation of wealth and economic development.

But, Mun asked, what policies might a nation adopt to realize a positive trade balance? One set of policies entails reducing imports. To do this, tariffs could be imposed on imported commodities that could be produced domestically. This is called an import substitution policy: the product made at home substitutes for the product made abroad. Additionally, a nation could restrict its imports of unwanted or unneeded luxuries and fashions. Mun called these "superfluities."

Another set of policies involves expanding exports of domestically produced commodities, but only after domestic demand for these commodities has been satisfied. Where would the resources come from with which to produce these

20 Mercantilism and neo-Mercantilism

exported commodities? They could come from currently unemployed resources and by reducing waste and inefficiencies.

Mun also favored a strategy of re-exporting: importing commodities from one foreign market and then exporting them to another. To Mun, the bullion used to do this was like seed corn: it would produce even more corn after it was sown. Lastly, exports should be carried in the nation's own ships, which would boost the domestic shipping industry and related industries such as insurance.

Of course, in order to do all this, merchants would need extensive knowledge of both domestic and foreign elasticities of demand for their products. They would also have to be flexible in their pricing policies, selling their goods at the lowest possible prices in order to remain globally competitive. The best situation is to export commodities for which international demand is price inelastic. This would allow exporters to receive higher prices and at the same time expand their revenues.

Another of Mun's noteworthy contributions to international economics was his idea that Britain's trade balance should be measured not bilaterally but multi-laterally. That is, it was the aggregate balance that mattered, not the balance with a given trading partner. And that aggregate balance ought to be positive. Mun, however, was not a bullionist: he argued that a nation's wealth should be measured in terms of the net amount of *real* goods acquired, not just in terms of how much money, or bullion, was left over after foreign payments were settled. Moreover, the money that accumulates through positive trade balances must not sit around idly—it must be put to work by engaging in further foreign trade. This is the only way a nation could get rich.

One problem with Mun's mercantilist trade doctrine is that it might be infla-tionary. After all, a trade surplus results in a net increase in the money supply, or species. And wouldn't domestic prices rise as the supply of species increases? In other words, wouldn't an increase in the domestic money supply increase aggre-gate demand and push up prices? This is what the quantity theory of money would predict. Higher prices for domestic goods would also make domestic products less attractive to foreign buyers, thereby discouraging exports.

Economic historians still debate this problem in Mun's doctrine, but several answers are possible. First, inflation might be avoided, claimed Mun, if merchants immediately reinvested the increased money supply to further expand exports. But if exports expand more rapidly than imports, then the inflow of species would simply rise further, adding to inflationary pressures. This is not a satisfactory answer. Second, inflation might just be the sacrifice a nation would have to make if it wished to grow. This is also an unsatisfactory answer. Third, the expanding money supply might lower interest rates, thereby expanding investment and aggregate output. If output grows faster than aggregate demand, then inflation would be curbed. This answer is in the spirit of Keynesian economics. Fourth, also in the spirit of Keynesianism, unemployment levels might be high enough to reduce any inflationary tendencies.

It is uncertain what exactly Mun had in mind and it seems he never resolved these problems. Contemporary observers claim that these issues would not have arisen if Mun had had a better understanding of economics. Of course this is not a very useful criticism.

Early French Mercantilism: the case of Jean Baptiste Colbert

Perhaps the highest form of early Mercantilism was Colbertism, named after Jean Baptiste Colbert, the famous French Minister of Finance during the reign of the Sun King, Louis XIV. Colbertism is an early example of how a state's authority can be used to manage a nation's internal and external trade and domestic manufacturing. The overall goal was to secure a steady flow of tax revenues to meet the consumption demands of the royalty and also to finance France's military. At the time there was yet little faith in the invisible powers of the free market and in what later came to be called economic liberalism. Instead, the visible powers of the state were thought to be better suited to accomplish France's goals.

In the 17th century, France was experiencing severe financial crises due to the enormous expenses of war and also to the extravagant consumption spending by the king and the royalty, especially on luxuries imported from abroad. To pay the bills, taxes and public debt rose, which, together with a cumbersome and overburdened system of taxation, spelled economic disaster for France.

In response to these crises, Colbert sought to strengthen the French economy, especially in the areas of public finance and taxation, manufacturing, trade and shipping. One strategy was to build up France's colonial system. To this end, the government created the French East India Company in 1664 to compete with the British and the Dutch East India companies.

Another strategy, one that is most closely associated with Colbertism, was a vast array of laws regulating French manufacturing. These regulations controlled both the quality and the quantity of goods that French firms produced; they were so detailed that, in the textile industry for example, even the number of stitches per centimeter of cloth, as well as the range of permissible colors, were strictly controlled. The proliferation of uniform regulations, privileges, inspectors and administrative bureaus created a rigid economic environment that left little room for local variations in how goods were produced.

New industries were also created, and protected, especially in the production of luxury goods such as silks, glassware and tapestries. France in fact became well known for the production of these luxury goods. Not only would these new industries supply the needs of the self-indulgent royalty, but they would also expand the tax base.

It was believed that these strategies, together with a favorable trade balance achieved through high import tariffs and export promotion, would relieve France's financial difficulties and foster economic development.

The next generation of French economists, especially followers of Anne-Robert-Jacques Turgot, accused Colbert of relying too much on the visible hand of the state and set out to reverse "Colbertist" economic policies. Turgot, who had a strong influence on Adam Smith, insisted that policymakers trust the market

22 Mercantilism and neo-Mercantilism

mechanism and rely on the competitive spirit. Critics of Colbertism, just as contemporary critics of state-directed economic policy regimes, disagreed with the use of the interventionist visible hand. French mercantilists, the critics say, were irrational, and failed to recognize that state-imposed economic regulations undermine flexibility and that bureaucratic centralization of economic decision-making policy kills off entrepreneurship.

The problem with this liberal critique of Mercantilism is that it compared an abstract, ideal, theoretical model of free market competition with the complex, imperfect real world of French business and finance. As French historian Philippe Minard (2000) pointed out, there was a serious concern at that time in France with fraudulent buyers and sellers and middlemen, a problem that grew larger as the economy grew larger. Blind faith in the free market did little to dispel the fear of deceitful business practices. The regulations that were put into place and the bureaucracy of inspectors who policed the economy were rational responses that "secured the trust that was necessary for efficient and profitable commercial transaction" (Minard, 2000: 488).

Not much has changed in the last three hundred or more years; the same debate continues to divide economists and politicians. How much state control of the economy should there be? How much protection should there be for domestic businesses? Is pursuit of a favorable trade balance a reasonable strategy? Should exchange rates be fixed or flexible?

Other early examples of Mercantilism

Britain and France were, of course, not the only nations that adhered to mercantilist economic principles in the years leading up to the Industrial Revolution. The United States at this time was created within a mercantilist world and the nation's founders were understandably influenced by Mercantilism. Many Americans even envisioned building an American empire, similar to the empires of Europe. Empire, colonialism, Mercantilism were, after all, ideas and practices shared by most of the people living at this time. It was the dominant world view, at least until free trade and economic liberalism replaced it.

Among the early Americans most frequently mentioned as a proponent of Mercantilism and of protectionism was Alexander Hamilton, the first Secretary of the Treasury. Hamilton's preferred policy was to establish tariffs on imports of not more than 15% and to use the tariff revenues to subsidize domestic industry. Actual tariffs were in fact higher than what even Hamilton recommended, and the US Congress refused to subsidize domestic industry in the way Hamilton wanted.

Hamilton, like many other mercantilists, believed in free trade in theory, but only after a nation had become economically strong and politically unified. Universal free trade was an admirable goal, but in the meantime, Mercantilism was essential for an agricultural nation such as the US that was striving to industrialize: protecting "infant industries" was thus essential. Moreover, unilateral pursuit of a free trade policy by a weak nation, in a world where everyone else was pursuing mercantilist policies, would spell certain ruin. European nations were glad to export manufactured goods to the US but did not allow the free importation of American agricultural goods.

The German political economist Friedrich List was another famous mercantilist writer. Germany at his time was not yet unified into a single nation. It was divided into a league of 39 relatively sovereign states (the German Confederation). List argued, as did Hamilton, that protectionism was essential for Germany, at least until domestic trade had fully developed and Germany had become a more mature economy capable of competing with other more developed nations. Despite the fact that List saw himself as an economic liberal, he nonetheless believed that the state was ultimately responsible for managing a nation's economic development, especially when it came to industrial development. In this vein List's name is usually associated with his defense of "infant industry" protection. This was essential, claimed List, to enable a nation to catch up with its more industrially advanced competitors.

Political unity and industrialization were believed to be prerequisites for entering into the world of universal free trade. According to List, Britain's promotion of free trade in the early 1800s was self-serving and would only enrich Great Britain. To List, a universal global community, "a transcendent, universal human society of perpetual peace" governed by free trade, is utopian and would only work when nations of the world are more or less at the same level of economic and social development. Otherwise free trade would be exploitive and would result in the universal subjection of poor nations by rich nations.

Neo-Mercantilism

Early Mercantilism was a diverse set of ideas and policies centered on the goal of achieving a positive trade balance. It preceded, and subsequently came to challenge, the main precepts of free trade economic liberalism which came to dominate economic discourse in the 19th century. Both Mercantilism and liberalism arose at a time when capitalism was evolving from a simple system of international mercantile trade into a complex system of international production and finance based on colonialism and empire.

Mercantilism continues to be a diverse set of ideas about state-regulated trade, and it continues to challenge free trade economic liberalism. However, we will now use the modifier "neo" to describe contemporary versions of these older ideas. Thus, the expressions neo-Mercantilism and Neoliberalism describe the modern post-Second World War varieties of these earlier viewpoints. The modern versions now apply to a contemporary market-oriented, post-colonial world economy. It is an economy dominated by transnational corporations and a few rich and powerful nations. In fact, some argue that the transnational corporation itself must be viewed and analyzed as a nation state unto itself, albeit one without borders.

24 Mercantilism and neo-Mercantilism

Neo-Mercantilism is distinctive in at least three ways:

1. State-directed international trade and investment now are linked systematically to domestic macro- and microeconomic policy. This makes it hard to discuss Mercantilism alone, without also talking about domestic macroeconomic policymaking.
2. The world economy today has coalesced into a truly global competitive market system. The rules of the game of this system are so pervasive that a nation can ill afford not to abide by them. The pressures placed on nations to open their doors to free world trade and to conform to World Trade Organization trade regulations are overwhelming. This makes neo-Mercantilism far more difficult to practice than ever before.
3. More than traditional trade regulations (i.e., tariffs, quotas, etc.) are now at stake. Issues concerning the environment, public safety and health, labor standards, and the preservation of national cultural identities are now at the center of trade controversies. The terrain has shifted from more narrow concerns to broader social, moral and environmental concerns.

Despite the strong global trend toward economic Neoliberalism, however, mercantilist sentiments continue to endure. Many economists and politicians are reluctant to adopt the American-inspired model of freewheeling global capitalism, a model that, some claim, would surely benefit only those nations that were already prosperous. Friedrich List expressed the same reluctance, as did many other early mercantilists. This reluctance to adopt economic Neoliberalism not only characterizes Europe, but it also characterizes East Asia where neo-Mercantilism has played a major role in economic development.

The resiliency of Mercantilism has prompted the US and other allied economically advanced nations to use their political muscle to "open up" the relatively closed and regulated economies to free trade and investment. This battle over free access to global markets has been ongoing for fifty years or more and shows little sign of ending. Its most recent manifestation was the worldwide controversy over the Washington Consensus, a pro-free trade, Neoliberal movement in the 1990s that was advanced by the International Monetary Fund (IMF) and the World Bank in Washington, DC and by the United States. But sentiments favoring the Washington Consensus have faded, and the pendulum appears to be swinging back toward Mercantilism.

Two neo-Mercantilist models

We can try to make sense of the complexity of the postwar global economy by identifying two mercantilist models. Each represents certain common elements and is therefore only an approximation, or perspective. The two models are the European model and the East Asia model.

The European model: the case of France

The French state has undertaken an important role in directing economic affairs ever since the end of the Second World War. A system of "indicative economic planning" was adopted, something that the French call *dirigisme*. This entailed the use of economic incentives to coax business and industry to conform to long-range targets set by the state. The state channeled resources to these chosen sectors, provided them with credit and protected them from foreign competition. The state also nationalized many key industrial enterprises, a practice that was also adopted elsewhere in Europe.[6] This was more or less a typical mercantilist approach that was combined with state economic management of the domestic economy.

At first, the goal of planning was postwar economic reconstruction, and among the favored industries were coal and steel. By the 1970s, the emphasis of economic planning shifted toward nuclear energy and telecommunications. But in 1981 things began to change. In 1981 French voters elected a socialist-communist government that promised to expand further the role played by *dirigisme* and protectionism. But in 1983, in the face of a severe economic crisis, France did its famous U-turn. The government began to undo the planning institutions that it had so diligently built up in previous decades. Many nationalized corporations were privatized, price controls and credit rationing were discontinued and protectionist regulations lifted. France, it appears, had become much more of a decentralized, market-oriented economic system.

Also starting in the 1980s, the pressures of globalization were intensifying. Globalization, it seemed, was threatening to undermine the foundations of French political institutions and culture as well as its economic sovereignty. France became increasingly concerned about protecting the French way of life.

As the European Union (EU) and the World Trade Organization (WTO) drew France into a multilateral trading regime based on free trade, French policymakers responded by asserting a "cultural exception" by exempting France from free trade in cultural goods such as film, television and music. France even sought to protect agriculture from foreign competition on the grounds that it was preserving the French rural way of life (Meunier, 2000).

Two recent trade disputes involving France, the EU and the US clearly demonstrate the changing nature of the world trade system and its impact on France. One is the banana case in the late 1990s. France had prior preferential trade agreements with various African and Caribbean nations that were once part of France's colonial empire. Bananas imported from those regions were favored over US banana imports. The WTO ruled that this was discriminatory and the WTO allowed the US to impose retaliatory tariffs on French imports to the US. France and the EU then ran into trouble when it banned imports of hormone-treated US beef. They argued that this was done only for public safety reasons. The WTO ruled that this was indeed discriminatory and once again permitted the US to impose retaliatory tariffs on French imports.

These WTO rulings inflamed French public opinion about globalization and its influence on the French way of life. France became a voice of anti-globalization because many people there thought that corporate interests were overriding human and cultural interests. Economic Neoliberalism and free trade were inconsistent with human values. This debate over trade is now taking place all over the world. More than tariffs and quotas are now at stake as trade conflicts increasingly address issues concerning the environment, public safety and health, labor standards and the preservation of national identities.

It seems that France is moving away from Mercantilism and toward economic Neoliberalism. But this is too hasty a conclusion. State interventionism and the mercantilist sentiment remains strong although its focus has shifted away from industrial planning and protection of large industry toward protection of groups who suffer as a result of globalization, the so-called losers of economic Neoliberalism. This led political scientist Jonah Levy to refer to France as the Anesthesia State (Levy, 2008). The idea is that the French government has been relieving the "suffering" of certain industries in the same way a physician applies anesthesia to a suffering patient.

Thus, state-led social policy has replaced state-led industrial policy in France. The French state has become less concerned with trade regulation and more concerned with building competitiveness. It has done so by supporting the adoption of new advanced technologies and by encouraging innovation by small business. In other words, French Mercantilism has become more "market-led" than "market-steering" (Levy, 2008: 426–427).

The East Asia model

Economists debate whether the dramatic economic successes of East Asian nations (i.e., Japan, South Korea, Taiwan and China) have been due to the leading role played by governments in directing economic development, or to market-friendly policies that included trade and investment liberalization. Was it state-directed neo-Mercantilism, or was it market-directed economic Neoliberalism that explains their economic achievements?[7]

There is sufficient evidence to claim that the East Asian experience mimics the European and American experiences. That is, almost all successfully developing nations started out using state-directed mercantilist policies, and, after a significant level of economic strength had been achieved, they then shifted toward market-directed trade liberalization.

In the case of South Korea, for instance, the state has essentially socialized business investment. It did this by picking industries to support that it believed would become winners in the global market. These high-potential industries were then provided with investment subsidies and guarantees. Starting in the 1960s, the government also nationalized Korean banks and took over the function of allocating credit. The state also directly initiated the startup of new enterprises and organized private entrepreneurs to start new ventures. This is how the Korean steel, ship-building and automobile industries started out. As Amsden observed, "every major shift in industrial diversification ... was instigated by the state" (Amsden, 1989: 80).

Taiwan too can be described in terms of neo-Mercantilism, despite the fact that it has pursued a policy of trade liberalization and has become one of Asia's most open economies. Taiwan can be said to be neo-mercantilist because it has combined the management of trade and foreign investment with state-directed domestic strategies. Reviewing Taiwan's postwar trade history, Robert Wade observed that Taiwan has, for the past four decades, pursued a state-directed industrial strategy that both favors and discriminates against selected industries. It began in the 1960s by encouraging export-oriented labor-intensive lines of production, and then in the 1990s it moved on to capital- and technology-intensive lines of production. This strategy was complemented with foreign exchange controls, export promotion schemes such as tariff rebates and tax credits, export processing zones, and management of foreign direct investment. Wade concludes that the Taiwan state has interfered in trade not less, but differently, than in many other developing countries. As gatekeeper for the national economy, it has scrutinized inflows and outflows and affected the terms of transactions in line with national objectives. It has accomplished this by avoiding both free trade and high, unselective and unconditional protection, and by welcoming foreign investment while placing constraints on its role in the domestic economy (Wade, 2003: 57–58).

Even the Heritage Foundation, a conservative think tank, deducted 20 percentage points from Taiwan's "trade freedom" rating of 76% because of its high non-tariff barriers. The Foundation complained of Taiwan's non-tariff barriers, including "[p]rohibitive agriculture tariffs, import bans and restrictions, import taxes, export subsidies, burdensome standards and certification requirements, complex regulations, restrictive sanitary and phytosanitary rules, service market access barriers, and weak enforcement of intellectual property rights" (Heritage Foundation and *Wall Street Journal*, 2007).

We can tell a similar story about the other East Asian "miracle economies." Government intervention and protection, government selection of "winners," allocation of credit, establishment of strict standards and targets, exclusion of foreign imports and subsidization of exports—these were all tools East Asian states used to establish internationally competitive industries. Today, after having achieved considerable economic success, and after having been confronted with enormous pressure from Americans and Europeans to open their closed economies, the East Asian economies are growing out of their neo-mercantilist phase and entering an economic liberal phase.

Neo-mercantilist theory: John Maynard Keynes and Joan Robinson

In his famous book, *The General Theory of Employment, Interest and Money*, John Maynard Keynes observed that most "statesmen and practical men" believed that a positive trade balance is good and a negative trade balance is bad. The former balance results in a net inflow of money and the latter balance a net outflow.

28 Mercantilism and neo-Mercantilism

However, orthodox economists have believed the opposite, that international trade is a self-adjusting mechanism and that there need not be any concern with trade imbalances one way or the other. Overriding this mechanism would undermine the ability of society to take advantage of comparative advantage and the international specialization of labor. Keynes reversed this orthodox line of reasoning. Practically, he said, Mercantilism is dangerous and should be avoided as a long-run strategy. Theoretically, however, Mercantilism makes sense.

The orthodox theoretical argument against Mercantilism rests on the species flow mechanism first described by Richard Cantillon (1680–1734) and David Hume (1711–1776). This theory supposedly undermines the validity of mercantilist doctrines which, as we have seen already, have as their objective a continued net inflow of money (bullion and species). According to the species flow mechanism, if exports grow relative to imports, as intended by mercantilists, there will be a net inflow of money. This net inflow will cause two things to happen: (1) domestic prices will rise because the money supply increases and (2) the high demand for the nation's currency will cause its value to rise. These two forces will automatically curtail exports and stimulate imports, effectively eliminating the favorable trade balance. It is therefore theoretically impossible to pursue a mercantilist strategy.

This self-adjusting mechanism might be all well and good, especially if the economy is growing and running at full employment. But what if the economy is stagnating and has high rates of unemployment? Can a mercantilist policy effectively correct this situation? Keynes said, when he was a younger man, that to use Mercantilism to eliminate unemployment was a "Protectionist fallacy in its grossest and crudest form" (Keynes, 1936: 334). But he later discovered a theoretical basis for supporting the mercantilist solution, one that he presents in the *General Theory*. His argument goes like this.

Any laissez-faire, free market economy will inevitably experience periods when profitable investment opportunities decline or even disappear. This will cause an economic downturn and rising unemployment. Keynes called this phenomenon an "insufficiency of the inducements to new investment" (Keynes, 1936: 335). How can a nation get out of this situation?

Keynes demonstrated that the rate of interest governs investment: higher interest rates discourage investment, while lower interest rates encourage investment. However, market interest rates will not always be low enough to generate sufficient investment to bring about full employment. Here Keynes agreed with the mercantilists: "Mercantilist thought never supposed that there was a self-adjusting tendency by which the rate of interest would be established at the appropriate [full employment] level" (Keynes, 1936: 341). The solution? A favorable trade balance which results in net inflows of money. This increase in the money supply would lower interest rates, increase investment spending and expand economic activity. As Keynes concluded,

> At a time when the authorities [in the 17th and 18th centuries] had no direct control over the domestic rate of interest or the other inducements to home investment, measures to increase the favourable balance of trade were the

only *direct* means at their disposal for increasing foreign investment; and, at the same time, the effect of a favourable balance of trade on the influx of the precious metals was their only *indirect* means of reducing the domestic rate of interest and so increasing the inducement to home investment.

(Keynes, 1936: x)

Keynes warned, however, as did the mercantilists themselves, that such a course of action can be impractical, if not downright treacherous. He offered several reasons for this.

1. It can undermine the very real benefits derived from trade based on comparative advantage.
2. It might cause wage and price inflation.
3. It might provoke trading partners to retaliate, causing "senseless international competition."
4. It might lead to administrative incompetence among trade regulators, which could produce a result opposite from what was intended. Today economists would call this rent-seeking.

Keynes summarized his position on free trade and Mercantilism like this:

Thus, the weight of my criticism is directed against the inadequacy of the *theoretical* foundations of the *laissez-faire* doctrine upon which I was brought up and which for many years I taught;—against the notion that the rate of interest and the volume of investment are self-adjusting at the optimum level, so that preoccupation with the balance of trade is a waste of time. For we, the faculty of economists, prove to have been guilty of presumptuous error in treating as a puerile obsession what for centuries has been a prime object of practical statecraft.

(Keynes, 1936: 308)

Keynes was also suspicious of unbridled free trade on grounds of national security. In his 1933 essay, 'National Self-Sufficiency', written during the turmoil of the Great Depression, Keynes argued that the influence of foreign capitalists on a nation's economy, and its dependence on the erratic and unpredictable policies of other nations, undermines world peace. Keynes was no fan of globalization:

I sympathise, therefore, with those who would minimise, rather than with those who would maximise, economic entanglement between nations. Ideas, knowledge, art, hospitality, travel—these are the things which should of their nature be international. But let goods be homespun whenever it is reasonably and conveniently possible; and, above all, let finance be primarily national.

(Keynes, 1933: 758)

30 Mercantilism and neo-Mercantilism

Keynes's wish for world peace was dashed by the Second World War.

Joan Robinson (1903–1983), the Cambridge (England) economist who helped originate the Post Keynesian school of thought, brought the discussion of Mercantilism into the post-Second World War age. She wrote of how the postwar world of globalized free trade has constrained the ability of nations to use conventional mercantilist tools (tariffs, quotas, etc.). Other tools had to be invented, such as those used in Europe and East Asia: subsidizing selected export industries, tax and credit preferences, currency devaluations, keeping wages low, etc.

Robinson saw that free trade economics is after all "just a more subtle form of Mercantilism. It is believed only by those who gain an advantage from it" (Robinson, 1966: 24; see also Blecker, 2003). She was assailing the hypocrisy of many advanced nations who preach free trade on one hand but who on the other hand restrict imports from poorer developing nations when these imports jeopardize the wellbeing of established businesses. Robinson was also critical of a world financial system that favored rich nations and discriminated against poor nations.

In conclusion, Keynesians and Post Keynesians recognized that the pure theory of free trade Neoliberalism ignores, or assumes away, most of what is important to understand about the real world of international economics. They acknowledged the problematical nature of adopting free trade as a universal policy and gave priority to policies that promoted domestic economic growth and employment.

Conclusions

Mercantilism has been condemned by everyone from Adam Smith to contemporary orthodox economists. But it has also been defended by many reputable scholars, from Friedrich List to Gustav Schmoller to John Maynard Keynes to Joan Robinson. The historical record suggests that state control over domestic and international economic activity—Mercantilism and neo-Mercantilism—has been rarely irrational and usually has been rooted in reasoned attempts to promote economic development and economic welfare.

Despite this, the economically advanced nations of the world have been urging poor developing nations to liberalize their trading regimes. This means opening their doors to foreign goods and foreign capital, eliminating trade restrictions and trade protections, and adopting flexible exchange rates for their currencies. It also means pressuring these economies to adopt laissez-faire domestic institutions.

It is essential to reiterate that none of the rich advanced nations had adopted these laissez-faire policies when they themselves were poor and just beginning to set out on the road to economic progress. Britain heavily protected and subsidized its domestic industries, just as the United States had during most of its history. The US and European nations understood well that a generalized free trade policy works only *after* economic development has occurred, and that until this time subsidization and state intervention are needed.

Aside from the strictly economic justification, namely, that *dirigisme* can contribute to economic development after which time free trade then can be profitably adopted, there is another explanation for why many developing nations reject free trade: the legacy of colonialism. Wealthy nations were once their colonial masters. They had enslaved and massacred their peoples, de-industrialized their economies, and plundered their natural resources. Opening the doors of free trade and investment to these former colonialists is, understandably, pursued with considerable suspicion.

Since the mid-1990s, when the goal of establishing a World Trade Organization was finally reached, after 50 years of conflict and negotiation between rich and poor nations, free trade is once again pursued with great vigor. Elimination of protectionist barriers to trade in goods and financial capital and services, open access to national markets, and adherence to market-based institutions and standards of taxation and intellectual property rights have become the new basis for the world economy. Underlying these efforts is the belief that free trade is the best path toward economic development if not a panacea for poverty. These are clearly old ideas dressed up in new clothing, prescriptions offered by those nations that have already attained high levels of economic development using policy tools that are essentially mercantilist, not liberal.

In fact, *dirigistic* trade policies, especially stable exchange rates, low inflation, and selective controls over capital inflows and imports are more closely correlated with export growth and industrialization than is adherence to generalized free trade. The successes of South Korea, Japan, China, Taiwan can be attributed to a *dirigistic* trade orientation, while the failures of Argentina, Mexico and Chile can be attributed to attempts at comprehensive trade liberalization.

If *dirigisme* is more closely correlated with economic growth, can we be sure that economic growth then will contribute to poverty reduction? It has been assumed by orthodox theorists of trade that it will. However, trade liberalization has also been associated with rising income inequality; the gains from trade have enriched those near the top of the income ladder rather than those at the bottom. This would suggest that state control over income distribution is a corollary to trade policy *dirigisme*.

Notes

1   Bullion is gold and silver not minted into coins, while species refers to coins and other kinds of currency.
2   Autarky describes a closed economy, one that is entirely self-sufficient. There are few examples of autarkies, except perhaps modern-day North Korea.
3   In fact, the early mercantilists did not even refer to themselves as mercantilists, and the term was unknown until the French economist Marquis de Mirabeau reportedly first introduced it in 1763. A few years later, Smith popularized—and then dismissed—"the mercantile system" in his book, *The Wealth of Nations*.
4   Actually, the Koreans and Chinese had already invented movable type. Most believe Gutenberg invented it independently.
5   The current account records international transactions in which people buy or sell tangible goods and services. In a current account transaction, the seller's legal obligations to a buyer end once the transaction is completed. It is in this sense that we use the word "current." One party to the transaction sells, the other party buys, and that's the end of

it. The financial account, on the other hand, records international transactions of financial assets. Financial assets include bonds, stocks, foreign currencies, bank deposits, drafts, acceptances, notes, derivatives and every other imaginable kind of financial instrument. In these transactions the seller's legal obligation to the buyer continues long past the transaction date itself. This is because the seller agrees to make periodic payments in the form of dividends or interest. These income payments are recorded in a special subcategory of the current account.

6 Britain also nationalized many of its large industries, giving the British state a large role in private economic affairs. This came to end, however, in the 1980s when Margaret Thatcher became Prime Minister and Britain again moved toward economic liberalism. In fact, many mercantilist tendencies in Europe weakened in the 1980s.

7 See for example Johnson (1982); Wade (2003); Amsden (1989); World Bank (1993) and Ravenhill (2001).

References

Amsden, A. H. (1989). *Asia's Next Giant: South Korea and Late Industrialization*. New York: Oxford University Press.

Anderson, B. (1991). *Imagined Communities: Reflections on the Origin and Spread of Nationalism* (1983, revised ed.). London: Verso.

Blecker, R. A. (2003). "Global Keynesianism Versus the New Mercantilism: International Economics After Joan Robinson." *Paper prepared for the Joan Robinson Centennial Conference, University of Vermont*. Burlington VT.

Ekelund, J. (1995). "Book Review: Mercantilist Economics, Lars Magnusson, Editor." *Southern Journal of Economics*, *61*, 877–880.

Heritage Foundation and *Wall Street Journal* (2007). *Index of Economic Freedom*. Retrieved July 3 2007, from http://www.heritage.org/research/features/index/country.cfm?id= Taiwan.

Johnson, C. (1982). *MITI and the Japanese Miracle: The Growth of Industrial Policy, 1925–1975*. Stanford, CA: Stanford University Press.

Keynes, J. M. (1933). "National Self-Sufficiency." *The Yale Review*, *22*, 755–769.

Keynes, J. M. (1936). "Notes on Mercantilism, the Usury Laws, Stamped Money and Theories of Under-Consumption." In *The General Theory of Employment, Interest and Money*, (pp. 333–371). London: Macmillan.

Levy, Jonah D. (2008). "From the Dirigiste State to the Social Anaesthesia State: French Economic Policy in the Longue Durée." *Modern & Contemporary France*, *16*, 417–435.

Meunier, S. (2000). "France, Globalization and Global Protectionism." *Harvard University, Center for European Studies Working Paper Series*, *71*.

Minard, P. (2000). "Colbertism Continued? The Inspectorate of Manufactures and Strategies of Exchange in Eighteenth-Century France." *French Historical Studies*, *23*, 477–496.

Mun, Thomas. (1664). *England's Treasure by Foreign Trade, or The Balance of Our Foreign Trade is The Rule of our Treasure*. Retrieved June 14 2013, from http://babel.hathitrust.org/cgi/pt?id=nyp.33433023217304;view=1up;seq=19.

Ravenhill, J. (2001). "From National Champions to Global Partnerships: The Korean Auto Industry, Financial Crisis and Globalization." MIT Japan Program Working Paper.

Robinson, J. (1966). *The New Mercantilism: An Inaugural Lecture*. Cambridge: Cambridge University Press.

Schmoller, G. (1895). *The Mercantile System and its Historical Significance*. (W. J. Ashley, trans.) London: Macmillan.

Viner, J. (1991). *Essays on the Intellectual History of Economics*. Princeton, NJ: Princeton: Princeton University Press.

Wade, R. (2003). *Governing the Market: Economic Theory and the Role of Government in East Asian Industrialization*. Princeton, NJ: Princeton University Press.

World Bank (1993). *The East Asian Miracle: Economic Growth and Public Policy*. Washington, DC: World Bank Policy Research Report.

3

CLASSICAL TRADE THEORY

Smith and Ricardo

Introduction

The Classical period in economics begins in 1776 with the publication of Adam Smith's (1723–1790) *An Inquiry into the Nature and Causes of Wealth of Nations*. It ends in 1871 with the publication of William Stanley Jevons' (1835–1882) *Theory of Political Economy*.[1] Many historians give credit to Jevons for having started the Neoclassical (or "Marginal") revolution in economic thought, a revolution that established the current economic orthodoxy.

The centerpiece of both Classical and Neoclassical trade theory is the principle of comparative advantage. The development of this principle begins with Adam Smith's rudimentary theory of *absolute* advantage. Forty years after Smith, David Ricardo (1772–1823) expanded on Smith's idea with his own theory of *comparative* advantage.[2] So important was Ricardo's contribution that many call Classical trade theory "Ricardian trade theory."

Adam Smith on international trade

Adam Smith's two seminal books, *The Theory of Moral Sentiments* and *The Wealth of Nations*, presented for the first time a comprehensive theory of capitalism. This theory was, in fact, a new science of society that no one at the time had ever seen before. It is philosophically sophisticated, logically coherent, rich in historical and institutional detail and practical in its laissez-faire policy advice. The ideas of Smith continue to this day to inspire scholars and political leaders, and for this reason many regard him as the "father of economics."

Adam Smith's general theory

The Theory of Moral Sentiments is a philosophical treatise that establishes the moral foundation for *The Wealth of Nations*, which is a political-economic treatise. The two books, written on the eve of the Industrial Revolution, complement each other. *Moral Sentiments* shows how systems of morality naturally arise from social relationships and human interactions. It demonstrates how such moral systems prevent society from descending into chaos, especially if everyone pursues his or her self-interest with little or no restraint or regulation. The *Wealth of Nations* shows how laissez-faire capitalism expands human happiness and advances civilization. It also shows how the invisible hand guides "the private interests and passions of men." Both books reveal an optimistic and hopeful view of human nature and of capitalist society.

To Smith, society is an organism that has evolved in four stages: hunting, pastoral, agricultural, and commercial or capitalist. Unique forms of property ownership and of public and government institutions distinguish each stage. The drive for self-improvement, guided by self-interest and reason, pushes society from one stage to the other. Smith believed that European society was evolving toward the ideal and last historical stage, that of self-regulating market capitalism. This ideal capitalist order would provide happiness, harmony and relative equality and social justice.

Smith grounds his theory of capitalism on a system of classification that most Classical economists also adopted. In this system, capitalism consists of three social classes, three inputs and four economic sectors. The three social classes are workers, capitalists and landowners; the three inputs are labor, capital and land; and the four sectors are, in Smith's order of importance, agriculture, manufacturing, domestic commerce and foreign commerce. Using this taxonomy, Smith then constructs his theoretical system.

The first component of this system is a cost of production theory of value. According to this theory, the cost of producing a commodity determines its long-run "natural" price (or value). Daily market prices fluctuate around these natural prices in response to temporary variations in supply and demand. But these daily fluctuations trigger opposite reactions by producers and consumers that ultimately restore the natural price.

The three key elements of cost are workers' wages, capitalists' profits and landlords' rents. The cost of subsistence, especially the cost of food, determines wages, while profits and rents accrue to capitalists and landlords at rates that allow these two classes to preserve their privileged positions in society. Smith used this cost of production theory to make a crucial point: the way in which a nation allocates its resources between agriculture and manufacturing, and the way in which it shares the resultant annual income between wages, profits and rents, determines total output, the rate of economic growth and the path of economic development.

A second component of Smith's general theory is capital accumulation. Economic growth requires continued investment spending, the creation of new factories, new capital goods and new technologies. All these improve worker productivity and

36 Classical trade theory: Smith and Ricardo

speed up economic growth. The source of investment funds is capitalists' profits. This is where income distribution enters the picture. If wages rise as a proportion of total income, then the profit share falls and so too would investment and economic growth. The paradox here is that faster economic growth might actually increase capitalists' demand for labor, which would also push up wages and push down profits. How then can a growing nation keep wages low and profits high? Solutions might be population growth and expansion of the labor force, the discovery of new lands through colonization, or technological improvements in agriculture and manufacturing.

A third component of Smith's general theory is the division of labor. This is another way to promote economic growth and fend off stagnation. The division of labor really means specialization, and specialization promotes the productive powers of labor. The first type of specialization that emerges in history is between agriculture and manufacturing. Agriculture, of course, locates in rural areas while manufacturing tends to cluster in urban areas. Once domestic rural–urban specialization has progressed to a certain point, specialization can then spread internationally.

How far can specialization go in an economy? Increased division of labor clearly requires more opportunities to buy and sell the products made by specialized labor. Divided "specialized" labor means interdependent labor. To Smith, the extent of the market limits the division of labor and thus too economic growth. The wider the spread of the market, both domestically and internationally, the greater would be the division of labor and the faster would be economic growth. The expansion of international trade and colonialism, therefore, are two avenues along which a nation could promote its own economic development. Expanded international trade expands the reach of the market and permits greater division of labor, and colonialism provides cheaper resources to feed domestic economic development.

Adam Smith's theory of international trade: absolute advantage

Adam Smith's theory of international trade is part of his general theory of capitalist economic development. It is within this context that Smith developed his theory of absolute advantage. As we have seen in the previous section, absolute advantage compares the cost of making something in a foreign country with the cost of making that same thing at home. To Smith, it is far better for a nation to avoid producing things that foreign nations can produce more cheaply; the nation instead ought to focus its attention on producing things that can it can produce more cheaply at home.

Differences in "natural" advantages (e.g., climate, soil) as well as differences in "acquired" advantages (e.g., through technology, knowhow, education) explain differences in the costs of producing commodities internationally. Trading according to this principle of absolute advantage would cause no economic problems at home as resources simply would shift to other activities with unique advantages. As Smith put it,

Whether the advantages which one country has over another, be natural or acquired, is in this respect of no consequence. As long as one country has those advantages, and the other wants them, it will always be more advantageous for the latter, rather to buy of the former than to make.

(Smith, 1776/1904: Book IV, Chapter 2, Vol. I)

Smith identifies the benefits from trading according to absolute advantage. A nation engaging in international trade could sell more products to foreigners, products for which there is inadequate domestic demand. Put another way, sectors with an absolute advantage can expand and produce more than what is demanded at home. Smith calls this extra output, or surplus, "superfluities." The nation receives in exchange commodities for which its citizens have a greater desire. Trade thus expands the "home market" and encourages improvements in the nation's productive powers. It also increases society's revenues, incomes and wealth.

As noted above, international trade, together with the new opportunities presented by colonialism, extends the market system into new arenas and thereby enhances productivity and economic growth. Writing about the colonization of America, Smith said,

By opening a new and inexhaustible market to all the commodities of Europe, it gave occasion to the new divisions of labour and improvements of art, which, in the narrow circle of the ancient commerce, could never have taken place for want of a market to take off the greater part of their produce. . . A new set of exchanges, therefore, began to take place which had never been thought of before, and which should naturally have proved as advantageous to the new as it certainly did to the old continent.

(Smith, 1776; 1904: Book IV, Chapter 1, Vol. I;
see also Book IV, Chapter 7, Part III, Vol. II)

Smith concludes his analysis of global capitalism by asserting the superiority of free trade. Only in this way can a nation take advantage of its potential productive powers by spontaneously promoting the extent of the market, the division of labor, and capital accumulation.

A final note on Smith's contribution

Most orthodox economists criticize Smith's theory of international trade and, in particular, his theory of absolute advantage for being wrong if not naïve. They fault him for failing to take the next theoretical step in his analysis: comparative advantage. Because of this failure, Smith supposedly failed to address with sufficient analytic rigor questions of allocative efficiency and economic welfare. This is why most economists today regard Ricardo's theory of comparative advantage as a significant scientific advance over Smith, one that has led inevitably to the current Neoclassical orthodoxy.

38 Classical trade theory: Smith and Ricardo

But we should not be too anxious to dismiss Smith for failing to discover the theory of comparative advantage. There is, in fact, much to be said in favor of absolute advantage and absolute cost theory. Firms and industries in some nations do become more competitive by producing commodities more cheaply than in other nations. And nations that must compete in an open global economy may, in the real world, lose jobs and suffer from balance of payments crises if their own industries are the high-cost producers. Moreover, even if Smith's weakness was his theory of absolute advantage, then his strength was in placing international trade theory in the context of a broader moral and social theory of global capitalist economic development.

Ricardo on international trade

As did Adam Smith, David Ricardo analyzed international trade within the context of a general theory of capitalist economic development. Among Ricardo's most noteworthy contributions to political economy are (1) the law of diminishing returns; (2) the theory of rent; and (3) the principle of comparative advantage. Although we focus on the last of these, all three are related.

In Ricardo's framework of analysis, the law of diminishing returns says that population growth, which is driven by general economic development, pushes the use of agricultural land to more inferior land. This increases the value of superior land. As a result, those fortunate enough to own such superior land can demand higher rents. The problem with this is that higher rents take away from capitalists' profit income. It therefore curtails capital accumulation, and slows economic growth. This cumulative set of events results in a zero-growth steady state. The only way out of this dilemma is through international trade. This is where the theory of comparative advantage fits in. It demonstrates how a nation—Britain in this case—can gain from trade and thus offset the trend toward a steady state.

Ricardo's theory of surplus and the wage–profit relation

To Ricardo, the annual aggregate output of a capitalist economy consists of two portions, one *necessary* and one *surplus*. The necessary portion of aggregate output consists of two sub-categories: (1) wage goods used for workers' subsistence and (2) capital goods (fixed capital and other means of production) used to replace the capital that has been used up. If sufficient amounts of both types of goods are produced we say the economy is able to "reproduce" itself from one year to the next.

The second portion of aggregate output is a surplus or residual. It is what remains after businesses have paid workers their wages and after they have replaced the capital goods used up in production. This residual or surplus is the source of capitalists' profits and landowners' rents. Without it capitalists merely cover their costs of production (labor and capital costs) and provide nothing more for themselves.

What do capitalists and landowners do with their profit and rent incomes? According to Ricardian economics, capitalists reinvest their profits in expanding production. Landowners spend their income on luxuries. Profit reinvestment drives capital accumulation and economic growth. Rent income does not. It follows that a rise in either wages or rents reduces profits and hence slows economic growth. Furthermore, if rents are constant then there is an inverse relationship between wages and profits. Economic progress therefore requires that wages be low so that profits can be high.

By suggesting that wages be kept low, Ricardo did not mean that workers should live in poverty. He reasoned that wages would always tend toward a subsistence level. At this subsistence level workers could buy the wage goods they need in order to maintain their customary standard of living. This standard of living, to Ricardo, varies over time and across nations and is more than what is minimally required for physical survival.

Given this understanding of workers' subsistence, anything that lowers the prices of wage goods will: (1) lower the cost of workers' subsistence; (2) lower wages; and (3) raise profits. Lower prices for wage goods means lower prices of food, housing, clothing and other necessaries of life. Thus, if these prices fall, workers in the short term will not be worse off. In fact they will eventually benefit from the faster economic growth brought about by higher profits.

Labor theory of value

Ricardo believed, along with most Classical economists, that market prices of commodities are proportional to the amount of labor required to produce those commodities. For example, if a computer requires twice as much labor to produce as a bushel of wheat, then the long-run equilibrium price of a computer will be twice that of a bushel of wheat. Although actual market prices may deviate from these labor-determined prices in the short run, in the long run competition will drive them back again. Demand therefore is irrelevant in price determination since, assuming a competitive economy, it only determines how much of an item will be produced and sold and not the price at which it will sell.[3]

When we calculate the amount of labor needed to produce a commodity, we do more than just add up the number of people currently working. This is only the "direct" labor cost. We must also add up the indirect labor cost, which is the amount of labor used in the past to produce the fixed capital and the means of production currently used. In equation form we can say

$$\text{Price} = \text{Direct Labor Cost} + \text{Indirect Labor Cost} \qquad (3.1)$$

A theoretical complication

This way of calculating the value of a commodity introduces a controversial theoretical complication. Consider the fact that each industry most likely uses labor and means of production in different proportions. Some industries are capital intensive while others are labor intensive. Some of the capital goods used may be quite old,

40 Classical trade theory: Smith and Ricardo

while other capital goods may be new and may have a more recent vintage. In addition, some products take a long time to produce and bring to market, while others take very little time.

Now, imagine that wage rates change. This change only affects current or direct labor, not the labor already expended in the past to produce currently used fixed capital and means of production. If computer production is capital intensive and wheat production is labor intensive, then a change in wages would disproportionately affect the wheat industry since it uses *relatively* more labor than the computer industry. This implies that the strict proportionality between prices and labor breaks down. The total labor embodied in production cannot precisely predict market prices.

Ricardo apparently understood this dilemma, yet he defended the labor theory of value by saying that there is no need to attach much importance to the discrepancy, that practically speaking the theory is approximately correct. He believed that in the real world labor costs are the largest portion of the costs of production so that any change in wages will affect prices more or less proportionately. This argument has led some economists to say that Ricardo's theory was an empirical and not an analytical theory. George Stigler called it a "93% labor theory of value."

Ricardo and international trade

What does all this have to do with Ricardo's trade theory? These were Ricardo's three main conclusions about international trade:

1. Profits will rise only if real wages fall, and this can happen if a nation imports wage goods at prices cheaper than what are available domestically. The cost of subsistence then falls, allowing profits to rise. As Ricardo said in his *Principles*,

> the rate of profits can never be increased but by a fall in wages, and that there can be no permanent fall of wages but in consequence of a fall of the necessaries on which wages are expended. If, therefore, by the extension of foreign trade, or by improvements in machinery, the food and necessaries of the labourer can be brought to market at a reduced price, profits will rise. If, instead of growing our own corn, or manufacturing the clothing and other necessaries of the labourer, we discover a new market from which we can supply ourselves with these commodities at a cheaper price, wages will fall and profits rise; but if the commodities obtained at a cheaper rate, by the extension of foreign commerce, or by the improvement of machinery, be exclusively the commodities consumed by the rich, no alteration will take place in the rate of profits.
>
> *(Ricardo, 1817/1821: 137)*

2. The technical conditions of production in trading nations determine trade patterns. Said Ricardo,

Under a system of perfectly free commerce, each country naturally devotes its capital and labour to such employments as are most beneficial to each. . . By stimulating industry, by rewarding ingenuity, and by using most efficaciously the peculiar powers bestowed by nature, it distributes labour most effectively and most economically: while, by increasing the general mass of productions, it diffuses general benefit, and binds together by one common tie of interest and intercourse, the universal society of nations throughout the civilized world. It is this principle which determines that wine shall be made in France and Portugal, that corn shall be grown in America and Poland, and that hardware and other goods shall be manufactured in England.

(Ricardo, 1817/1821: 139)

3. Free trade improves the general welfare of society because it expands the aggregate volume of commodities available. As Ricardo put it,

[F]oreign trade will . . . very powerfully contribute to increase the mass of commodities, and therefore the sum of enjoyments.

(Ricardo, 1817/1821: 131)

These three conclusions constitute the essence of the Ricardian theory of comparative advantage. They also express the Enlightenment view that free international commerce would provide an essential bond between nations and create a world based on economic efficiency and reciprocity.

Ricardian trade theory: assumptions and analytical tools

What follows is a "modern retrospective" of Ricardian trade theory. That is, we explain Ricardo's theory with a degree of formal precision (i.e., abstract and mathematical) typical of contemporary Neoclassical economics, but not typical of Classical economics.

The Ricardian trade theory begins with the following nine assumptions:

1. There are only two nations, A-Land and B-Land, each producing two final goods, computers (C) and wheat (W). "Final" means that the good does not enter into the further production of anything else: they are consumed or used up.[4]
2. We consider only tradable goods, in this case computers and wheat. "Tradable" means that products made in one nation can be transported and sold in another nation. We assume all goods other than computers and wheat are non-tradable.
3. Labor productivity, and hence labor costs, alone influences prices. We exclude from consideration the costs of fixed capital and other produced means of production, the prices of which we assume remain constant. In addition, we assume that the ratio in which labor and non-labor inputs are used is everywhere the

42 Classical trade theory: Smith and Ricardo

same and fixed, including computers and wheat production. This implies that both nations use identical technologies.

4. Each nation has a fixed endowment of labor and non-labor resources and this endowment is different for each nation.

5. Labor, capital and means of production are perfectly mobile domestically, but perfectly immobile (i.e., non-tradable) internationally. This implies that wage and profit rates equalize throughout the domestic economy only.

6. Perfect competition prevails everywhere, and all transportation and transactions costs are zero. This assumption implies that the computers and the wheat produced in each nation are identical, or homogeneous. In addition, competition and the free domestic flow of resources will eliminate all domestic price, wage or profit differentials.

7. There are no scale economies, nor are there diminishing marginal returns. This means that the cost (i.e., labor cost) of producing a computer or a bushel of wheat remains constant over the entire range of possible output. However, these costs differ in A-Land and B-Land because labor productivity and labor costs differ.

8. Each economy fully employs its labor force. Without this assumption, a nation could produce more of one good without withdrawing resources from the production of the other good. That is to say, the opportunity cost would be zero.

9. Trade is balanced. This means that exports exactly pay for imports. There can be no lending and borrowing between nations, and hence no possibility to finance deficit and surplus trade balances. The exchange rate will always adjust, instantaneously, to bring about this trade balance.

These nine assumptions allow us to construct a hypothetical world economy in which only national differences in labor productivity and labor costs influence trade. *The model does not explain why these productivity differences exist in the first place.* Accordingly, trade allows each nation to take advantage of the relative productivity advantages held by the other nation, and hence to obtain commodities more cheaply than if they had produced those commodities themselves. People in trading nations thus can buy more commodities with their incomes than they otherwise could, making them "wealthier." Free trade is thus "welfare enhancing."

The distribution of advantages in production

Our analysis continues with the construction of simple models, or scenarios, that compare two nations, each producing two goods. The purpose is to demonstrate that, given the nine assumptions, trade is mutually advantageous no matter how we distribute the final gains among industries and nations.

The basic tool of analysis is the production possibilities frontier, or PPF. Figure 3.1 shows a PPF for a nation we call A-Land that has a labor force of

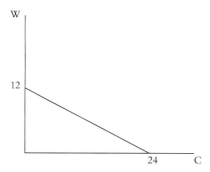

FIGURE 3.1 Production possibilities frontier

24 workers. These workers can produce either 12 bushels of wheat (W) or 24 computers (C) or any linear combination of each.

The amount of labor available, and labor productivity in each industry, determines the shape and position of the PPF. Thus, the equation describing the PPF is:

$$a_C^A C + a_W^A W = 24 \qquad (3.2)$$

The "a"s in equation (3.2) are unit labor requirements. These show the amount of labor used to produce one computer and one bushel of wheat in A-Land. The superscripts identify the variables as belonging to A-Land. The subscripts associate the employment of labor with either computer or wheat production. The variables C and W represent total computer and wheat output. The terms $a_C^A C$ and $a_W^A W$ therefore measure total employment in each of the two industries. Because we assume full employment, the two terms must sum to 24, which is the total number of workers available.

Solving for W, we can rewrite (3.2) as an equation for a straight line:[5]

$$W = \frac{24}{a_W^A} - \frac{a_C^A}{a_W^A} C \qquad (3.3)$$

The vertical intercept of the PPF line is $(24/a_W^A)$, which, as we see from Figure 3.1, has a value of 12. This value is maximum wheat output when A-Land produces no computers at all. The slope of the PPF is (a_C^A/a_W^A), which has a value of $-.5$. From (3.3) we can determine the unit labor requirements as $a_W^A = 2$, then $a_C^A = 1$.[6] Applying this information, we can write the equation for the PPF as:

$$1C + 2W = 24 \qquad (3.4)$$

Using equation (3.4), we construct in Table 3.1 of production data for A-Land. The unit labor requirements appear in columns (2) and (3). Labor productivity, or output per unit labor input, is simply the inverse of unit labor requirements and appears in columns (4) and (5).[7]

TABLE 3.1 Scenario #1

	Total labor available (1)	Unit labor requirements (# workers/unit output)		Labor productivity (output/unit labor input)		Opportunity costs	
		Computers (units) (2)	Wheat (bushels) (3)	Computers (units) (4)	Wheat (bushels) (5)	Computers (units) (6)	Wheat (bushels) (7)
A-Land	24	1	2	1	.5	.5	2

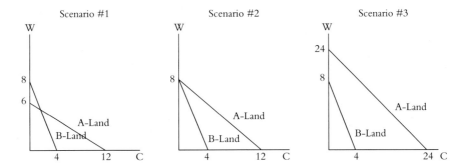

FIGURE 3.2 Three scenarios

Columns (6) and (7) show the opportunity costs.[8] This is the amount of one good we must sacrifice in order to produce an additional unit of the other good. To produce one more computer requires one more worker; if we get that worker from the wheat industry, we must sacrifice .5 bushels of wheat. Similarly, to get one more unit of wheat requires two workers; to get these workers we must sacrifice 2 computers. Notice that the absolute value of the slope of the PPF, which is .5, is also the opportunity cost of producing an additional computer. It follows that the flatter the PPF, the lower the opportunity cost of producing computers.

We now introduce another fictitious nation, B-Land, which also has 24 workers. Both nations can produce different combinations of the two goods. Figure 3.2 shows three different hypothetical scenarios for A-Land and B-Land, each of which distributes the advantages in different ways. The nation with the flattest PPF (i.e., where the absolute slope value is the smallest) has a comparative advantage in that good.

In Scenario #1, A-Land and B-Land have the same size labor force of 24 workers, but A-Land has an absolute advantage in computers since it can produce a maximum of 12 units as compared to B-Land's 4 units. B-Land has an absolute advantage in wheat since it can produce a maximum of 8 units of wheat as compared to B-Land's 6 units. We can also see that A-Land has a comparative advantage in computers since the absolute value of the slope of its PPF is 6/12 = .5 while that of B-Land is 8/4 = 2.0. The inverse of this proposition is also true: B-Land has a comparative advantage in wheat.

In Scenario #2, production conditions and labor supply for B-Land remain unchanged, but labor in A-Land's wheat industry becomes more productive. The same number of workers now can produce 8 units of wheat instead of 6. This erases B-Land's absolute advantage in wheat. A-Land continues to have an absolute advantage in computers. Despite this improvement in A-Land's wheat production, its comparative advantage still lies in computer production since the absolute value of the slope is now $8/12 = .67$, which is higher than before, but still less than in B-Land.

In Scenario #3, A-Land's 24 workers can produce more computers and more wheat so that A-Land now has an absolute advantage in both industries. Production conditions for B-Land remain unchanged. Moreover, computer and wheat prices in A-Land will be lower because the same number of workers can produce more computers and more wheat. Using the Ricardian labor theory of value, the amount of labor embodied in one computer and one bushel of wheat has decreased, and hence computer and wheat prices will be lower as well.

Ricardo's special concern was with Scenario #3. He posed the question of whether Britain could gain from trade even if it had no absolute advantages. That is to say, if other nations such as Portugal can produce *everything* more cheaply, could Britain still gain from trade? If all prices in A-Land are lower, how can B-Land possibly compete and benefit from trade? We will focus now on this particular question.

The basic Ricardian model: autarky

Our Ricardian model compares two hypothetical states of affairs. One is *autarky*, in which nations are strictly self-sufficient and engage in no trade. Residents of each nation can only consume what they themselves produce. The second state of affairs is *free trade*. Here, each nation specializes in producing what it does *relatively* best, consumes what it wants of this output, and then trades the rest for other commodities produced in the other nation. We retain the nine assumptions throughout the analysis. The procedure we follow entails calculating the gains derived by moving from autarky to free trade. We do not calculate the benefits, if any, of going from a little bit of trade regulation to a lot of trade regulation, or vice versa. We consider only the two extremes, no trade and free trade.

Autarky: production possibilities

We continue with our example of two nations, A-Land and B-Land. Each produces two final goods, computers and wheat, and each has 24 workers. Table 3.2 provides the hypothetical production data used throughout this section.

The two columns showing unit labor requirements indicate that, as compared to B-Land, A-Land is 6 times as productive in computer production, and only 1.5 (or 3/2) times as productive in wheat production as compared to B-Land. This is consistent with the fact that A-Land has a comparative advantage in computer

TABLE 3.2 Hypothetical production data

| | Labor supply (1) | Unit labor requirements (# workers/unit output) || Labor productivity (output/unit labor input) || Opportunity costs ||
		Computers (2)	Wheat (3)	Computers (4)	Wheat (5)	Computers (6)	Wheat (7)
A-Land	24	1	2	1/1 = 1.00	½ = .50	.5 bu wheat	2 computers
B-Land	24	6	3	1/6 = .17	1/3 = .33	2 bu wheat	.5 computers

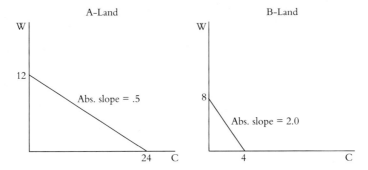

FIGURE 3.3 Production frontiers A-Land and B-Land

production: its productive advantage is that much greater in that industry. The cells in the last two columns show comparative advantages. Finally, A-Land has an absolute advantage in both goods, but a comparative advantage in only one.

With this data, we construct production possibilities frontiers (PPFs) for both nations in Figure 3.3. We know the PPFs are linear because labor costs are constant throughout the entire range of production (Assumption #7).

Combinations on the PPFs fully employ labor, while combinations inside the PPFs imply unemployment. Any computers–wheat combination on or below the PPF is feasible; combinations lying outside the PPFs are not feasible.

Each nation can trade off, at a fixed rate, production of wheat for production of computers. In A-Land, a sacrifice of 1 ton of wheat will always release enough labor to produce an additional 2 computers, while in B-Land a sacrifice of 1 ton of wheat will always release enough labor to produce an additional .5 computers. We say "always" because we have assumed constant costs. These two rates of trade-off, 1:2 in A-Land and 2:1 in B-Land, are the absolute values of the slopes of the two PPFs. They are also the respective opportunity costs shown in Table 3.2. We also call these slopes the *marginal rates of technical substitution*, or MRTS, where the term "technical" refers to the physical attributes of production.

The linear equations describing the two PPFs are:

$$1C^A + 2W^A = 24 \qquad (3.5)$$

$$6C^B + 3W^B = 24 \qquad (3.6)$$

where C and W represent the amount of computers and wheat actually produced in each nation, and the superscripts identify A-Land and B-Land. Because we assume full employment, the total amount of labor used in each nation must be equal to the total amount of labor available, which is 24.

We can generalize equations (3.5) and (3.6) as follows:

$$a_C^A C^A + a_W^A W^A = L^A \tag{3.7}$$

$$a_C^B C^B + a_W^B W^B = L^B \tag{3.8}$$

where the unit labor requirement coefficient, a, is the number of labor hours needed in A-Land and B-Land to produce one computer and one ton of wheat, respectively. L is the total labor available. The absolute values of the PPF slopes are $(a_C^A/a_W^A = 1/2 = .5)$ for A-Land, and $(a_C^B/a_W^B = 6/3) = 2$ for B-Land.[9] These slopes are the marginal rates of technical substitution, or MRTSs.

$$MRTS = \frac{a_C^A}{a_W^A} = \frac{1}{2} = .5 = \text{slope of PPF for A-Land} \tag{3.9}$$

$$MRTS = \frac{a_C^B}{a_W^B} = \frac{6}{3} = 2 = \text{slope of PPF for B-Land} \tag{3.10}$$

Prices, wages and unit costs in autarky

If the values for the "a"s represent the labor required to produce one unit of output, then the real cost of producing that unit of output is the wage rate per worker, or ω, multiplied by a. This is the only cost because labor is the only input that we count (Assumption #3), and the wage rate, which is uniform throughout the nation, is determined by workers' subsistence. Thus, the cost of one more unit of output is $a \cdot \omega$, which is also the unit cost, or marginal cost, MC. Since we have perfect competition throughout the two economies (Assumption #6), P = MC in both industries:

$$\text{Price} = \text{MC} = (\text{wage rate}) \times (\text{unit labor requirement}) = (\omega)\,(a)$$

We can put this all together by writing:

$$MRTS = \frac{a_C^A \omega^A}{a_W^A \omega^A} = \frac{MC_C^A}{MC_W^A} = \frac{P_C^A}{P_W^A} \tag{3.11}$$

$$MRTS = \frac{a_C^B \omega^B}{a_W^B \omega^B} = \frac{MC_C^B}{MC_W^B} = \frac{P_C^B}{P_W^B} \tag{3.12}$$

The absolute slope value of the PPF, or MRST, equals: (1) the ratio of unit labor requirements; (2) the ratio of marginal costs; and (3) the relative price of computers with respect to wheat:

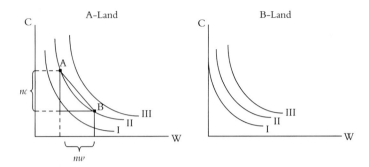

FIGURE 3.4 Indifference curves A-Land and B-Land

$$\text{PPF slope} = \text{MRTS} = \text{unit labor requirement ratio} = \text{MC ratio}$$
$$= \text{price ratio} \tag{3.13}$$

Put simply, market prices reflect only the productivity of labor, which is the only input factor we consider.

Autarky: consumption possibilities

How much of each good will people in both nations actually wish to consume? To answer this question, we describe residents of A-Land and B-Land as two different but unique "communities." Each community consists of residents with identical tastes and preferences. We describe these tastes and preferences using "community indifference curves." Figure 3.4 displays three representative indifference curves for A-Land and B-Land.

Community indifference curves have the following characteristics:

- Each point, or coordinate, along a community indifference curve represents consumption of a certain amount of wheat and of computers. Points A and B are two examples.
- Each point shows the subjective utility derived from this consumption.
- Points on a single indifference curve yield the same amount of subjective utility, while points on higher (lower) indifference curves yield more (less) utility. Thus, any combination along indifference curve III yields greater satisfaction than any combination along indifference II, and so on.
- There exist an infinite number of community indifference curves in each graphical space.
- Indifference curves are smooth and convex to the origin (i.e., bowed inward toward the origin with no discontinuities), signifying that each community experiences diminishing marginal utility from consuming computers and wheat.
- The shape and position of the indifference curves for A-Land will be different from B-Land, reflecting the differences in tastes and preferences of each community.

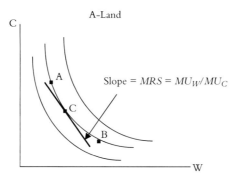

FIGURE 3.5 A-Land marginal rate of substitution

Comparing points A and B in Figure 3.4, we see that each point represents a different combination of wheat and computers: point A represents relatively large amounts of wheat and small amounts of computers, while point B represents just the opposite. However, each point lies on the same indifference curve II, meaning that A-Landers do not care which combination they have since each yields them the same amount of satisfaction. They are "indifferent" to all points along a given indifference cure. Stated differently, they would be willing to accept nw units of wheat to compensate them for a loss of nc units of computers. The rate at which they are willing to substitute one good for the other is the ratio nw/nc, which happens to be the slope of the line segment AB connecting the two points.

We can refine this result by observing what happens to the slope of the line segment AB as the two points A and B come closer and closer together. Eventually they will merge to point C. We show this in Figure 3.5 for A-Land.

The slope of a tangent line drawn at point C measures the "instantaneous" rate of substitution, or more properly, the marginal rate of substitution or MRS. MRS is the rate at which people are willing to substitute one commodity for the other *while remaining at the same level of satisfaction.*

Autarky: production and consumption equilibrium

Now we return to our story. How much of each commodity will each nation actually choose to produce and consume in autarky?

We know how many computers and how much wheat A-Land and B-Land are *able to* produce, and we know how much the two communities are *willing to* consume. People then will buy that combination of computers and wheat that maximizes their utility, or where the PPF reaches the highest community indifference curve. Figure 3.6 shows this "equilibrium solution" where we imagine that A-Land chooses point A, and B-Land chooses point B.

Point A implies that A-Land produces and consumes 16 computers and 4 bushels of wheat, while B-Land produces and consumes 3 computers and 2 bushels

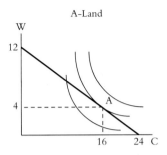
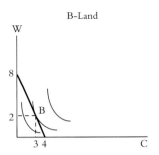

FIGURE 3.6 Equilibrium solution

TABLE 3.3 World production and consumption: autarky

	Computers	Wheat
A-Land	16	4
B-Land	3	2
World output	19	6

of wheat. At these two points, each nation employs all of its 24 workers. Table 3.3 summarizes these results:

Note that we added an extra row to show total world output for each commodity.

The equilibrium combination of computers and wheat occurs where MRTS = MRS. This means that everyone in each nation is satisfied with the assortment of products produced and the amount of these products consumed. More than being merely satisfied, their satisfaction is at a maximum: it can get no better than this in autarky.

Technically speaking, we have reached an equilibrium when the rate at which a nation's industries are able to substitute production of one good for another equals the rate at which residents are willing to substitute one good for another. If these rates are not equal, i.e., when MRTS ≠ MRS, people prefer another combination of output than what industry is producing. The competitive market system presumably will induce producers to change the composition of production to match the desires of the residents until they reach the combinations represented by points A and B in Figure 3.6.

We summarize the autarky equilibrium with the following relationship, which holds for each of the two nations:

$$MRTS^A = \frac{a_C^A}{a_W^A} = \frac{P_C^A}{P_W^A} = \frac{MC_C^A}{MC_W^A} = MRS^A \qquad (3.14)$$

$$MRTS^B = \frac{a_C^B}{a_W^B} = \frac{P_C^B}{P_W^B} = \frac{MC_C^B}{MC_W^B} = MRS^B \qquad (3.15)$$

However, the price ratios in A-Land and B-Land are not the same in autarky equilibrium. In fact, the price of computers in A-Land is lower than in B-Land so that $P_C^A < P_C^B$. Additionally, the price of wheat in B-Land is lower than in A-Land so that $P_W^A > P_W^B$. This implies:

$$MRTS^A = \frac{P_C^A}{P_W^A} < MRTS^B = \frac{P_C^B}{P_W^B} \tag{3.16}$$

The basic Ricardian model: from autarky to free trade

What would happen if producers in each nation discover that computer and wheat prices in the other nation are different? In our hypothetical model, computers in A-Land sell at a relative price of .5, and in B-Land they sell for a relative price of 2 (the reciprocal of the price of computers, or 1/.5):

$$\frac{P_C^A}{P_W^A} = .5 < \frac{P_C^B}{P_W^B} = 2 \tag{3.17}$$

These numbers come from Figure 3.6 where the slopes of the PPF lines represent price ratios.

It would make sense for A-Land computer producers to sell their computers in B-Land where they can fetch a much higher price. Their profits would certainly rise. In fact, if wheat producers were smart, they too would also get into the computer-making business. Because wheat prices are lower in B-Land, A-Land wheat producers would see no benefit in selling wheat in B-Land. Given that producers always pursue activities that promise the highest reward, we should expect a reallocation of resources to take place in A-Land, away from wheat production and into computer production.

The opposite reasoning applies in B-Land where wheat producers observe that wheat in A-Land sells for 2 (the reciprocal of the price of computers, or 1/.5), while domestically it only sells for .5. In other words,

$$\frac{P_W^A}{P_C^A} = 2 > \frac{P_W^B}{P_C^B} - .5 \tag{3.18}$$

A similar and opposite reallocation of resources would occur in B-Land as producers pursue the activity with the highest reward, which in this case is wheat production.

The principle here is that for trade to be beneficial, the relative prices of the commodities must be unequal. Otherwise, there would be no incentive for producers to sell in other nations' markets. Additionally, the principle does not say what *ought* to happen, but only what *would* happen in the theoretical world that we have constructed, a world in which factor productivities and prices differ. In Ricardian theory, each nation will specialize in the production of those goods in which they have a comparative advantage, not because anyone tells them to, but

52 Classical trade theory: Smith and Ricardo

TABLE 3.4 World output: specialization and free trade

	Computers	*Wheat*
A-Land	24	0
B-Land	0	8
World output – specialization	24	8
World output – autarky	19	6
Surplus	5	2

rather because they will do so on their own accord. This is an application of Smith's "invisible hand."

The reallocation of domestic resources from low profit to high profit activities continues so long as these price differentials exist. If autarky prices and wages remain constant in the face of these changes in the composition of production, then all firms in A-Land will end up specializing in computer production, and all firms in B-Land will end up specializing in wheat production. Once firms have met domestic demand for computers and wheat, they will then sell the excess in the other nation's market.

The gains from trade and their distribution

If A-Land specializes only in computers, and B-Land specializes only in wheat, then the 24 workers in each nation will produce the output shown in Table 3.4. We base these values on the assumed labor productivities of Table 3.1.

With specialization, world computer output rises from 19 to 24 and world wheat output rises from 6 to 8 bushels. The surplus in world production is 5 computers and 2 bushels of wheat.

How will the two nations share the surplus? All we can say here is that, whatever the final distribution of the gains from trade, it must prove beneficial to both nations or else trade would not occur in the first place. To be beneficial, everyone in A-Land and B-Land must receive at least as much of either computers or wheat as they did in autarky, *and* some more of the other good. Thus, referring once again to Table 3.3, A-Land residents must be able to consume either (1) 16 computers and more than 4 bushels wheat or (2) 4 bushels wheat and more than 16 computers. B-Land residents must be able to consume either (1) 3 computers and more than 2 bushels wheat or (2) 2 bushels wheat and more than 3 computers. The gains of trade will end up somewhere within these boundaries.

How will residents of each nation share the surplus? This is a question of income distribution, which community indifference curve analysis avoids entirely because it treats the entire population as a single entity. This severely limits the conclusion that trade is beneficial for everyone.

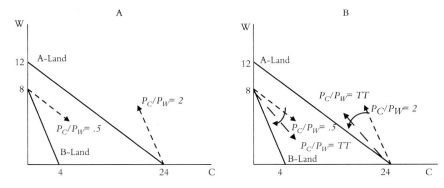

FIGURE 3.7 Terms of trade

Terms of trade

What happens to autarky prices when trade begins? The above equations showed that in autarky $P_C^A/P_W^A = .5 < P_C^B/P_W^B = 2$. Now, as A-Land exports computers to B-Land, the supply of computers in B-Land will increase and its price P_C^B/P_W^B will drop from its high of 2 down towards .5. Similarly, in autarky $P_W^A/P_C^A = 2 > P_W^B/P_C^B = .5$. Now, as B-Land exports wheat to A-Land, the supply of wheat there will increase and its price, P_W^A/P_C^A, will drop from its high of 2 down towards .5. Trade between the two nations will continue until the supply of computers equals the demand for computers, and the supply of wheat equals the demand for wheat.

The final equilibrium price ratio for *computers* will be:

$$\frac{P_C^A}{P_W^A} = \frac{P_C^B}{P_W^B} \quad (3.19)$$

and the price ratio for *wheat* will be the reciprocal:

$$\frac{P_W^A}{P_C^A} = \frac{P_W^B}{P_C^B} \quad (3.20)$$

We show this result graphically in Figure 3.7, panels A and B. The left-hand diagram displays each of the two PPFs together with the *other* nation's price line (the dashed lines). Each nation produces along their own PPF, specializing in their comparative advantage good, and then selling that good to the other nation at the price indicated by the dashed lines. B-Land will produce 8 units of wheat and then exchange some of that wheat for A-Land's computers at a price of .5 (along the dotted line with slope .5). A-Land will produce 24 computers and then exchange some of those computers for B-Land's wheat at a price of 2. This trade allows residents of each nation to consume outside their own PPFs. As they do so, the prices respond to the increased availability of the previously expensive good.

Eventually, as prices adjust to demand, a common price will emerge for both

54 Classical trade theory: Smith and Ricardo

computers and wheat. We call this price the *terms of trade*. The equilibrium terms of trade, TT, is a price ratio that lies somewhere between the original autarky prices. All we can say is that it will lie somewhere between .5 and 2. Where exactly within this range will the terms of trade lie? The answer depends on which nation has the strongest demand and the highest purchasing power (i.e., income and wealth). Unless we can provide detailed information about demand conditions in each nation, the answer remains indeterminate. Whatever the terms of trade wind up being, the international supply and demand of traded commodities balances and determines how trade will distribute the surplus world output between the two trading nations. It does *not* tell us how each nation will distribute the extra output among its residents.

Extensions to the Ricardian model

In this section, we extend the model in two ways. In the first extension we monetize the model by expressing costs and prices in terms of monetary units. Because our illustration describes trade between two nations, we need to introduce two currency units. The second extension introduces multiple traded commodities. In each case, the conclusions reached are logical deductions from the original Ricardian model.

Monetizing the Ricardian model

Suppose that A-Land uses the dollar (\$) and that B-Land uses the pound (£). Because P = MC = $a\omega$ for each commodity in each nation, the following autarky relationships will hold:

$$P_C^A = a_C^A\omega^A = (1.0)\omega^A$$

$$P_W^A = a_W^A\omega^A = (2.0)\omega^A \qquad (3.21)$$

$$P_C^B = a_C^B\omega^B = (4.0)\omega^B$$

$$P_W^B = a_W^B\omega^B = (3.0)\omega^A$$

These equations express all prices in terms of the money units of the respective nation.

If trade is to occur according to comparative advantage, then the price of computers in A-Land must be less than in B-Land, and the price of wheat in B-Land must be less than in A-Land. However, in order to compare the two prices, we first must convert dollars into pounds or pounds into dollars. If we let E stand for the rate at which pounds exchange for dollars, then

$$P_C^A < P_C^B \times E$$

$$P_W^A > P_W^B \times E \qquad (3.22)$$

We can also express these two conditions in term of wages:

$$1.0\omega^A < 7.0\omega^B E$$

$$2.0\omega^A > 3.0\omega^B E \qquad (3.23)$$

If we divide both sides of these two equations by $(\omega^B E)$ we get:

$$\frac{\omega^A}{\omega^B E} < 7.0 \qquad (3.24)$$

$$\frac{\omega^A}{\omega^B E} > \frac{3}{2}$$

In other words,

$$\frac{3}{2} < \frac{\omega^A}{\omega^B E} < 7.0 \qquad (3.25)$$

This means that the wage rate in A-Land will be higher than the wage rate in B-Land. It also means that A-Land's wage rate relative to B-Land's cannot be more than 6 times greater, nor can it be less than 3/2 times greater. If the relative wage rate lies outside these boundaries, trade will no longer be worthwhile.

To see that this is true, consider the fact that A-Land's computer workers are 6 times more productive than are B-Land's computer workers, and that A-Land's wheat workers are 3/2 times as productive as B-Land's wheat workers. If the wage rate in A-Land rises to (say) 7 times that of B-Land, then the autarky price of computers in A-Land will be higher than in B-Land. B-Land will then likely sell both products in A-Land when trade opens. A similar but opposite result obtains when the relative wage rate drops below 3/2.

Economists typically assert that wages in A-Land will be higher than in B-Land because labor is more productive. Using this model, they then claim that high wages will not prevent mutually beneficial trade. This conclusion is tenuous, however, because in the Ricardian model the cost of workers' subsistence determines wages, not labor productivity. The model says nothing about what constitutes wage goods, and until we specify this, we can say little about how wages will affect trade. Recall that Ricardo himself said that trade will be beneficial only if the imported commodities lower the prices of wage goods.

As with relative wage rates, the exchange rate could discourage trade. If the E in the denominator of (3.25) falls, implying that pounds exchange for fewer dollars, then the middle fraction could rise above 7. The result would be the same as if ω^A had risen.

In conclusion, trade will be mutually beneficial as long as relative labor productivity, relative wages (and hence the cost of subsistence), and exchange rates remain

56 Classical trade theory: Smith and Ricardo

within certain specified limits. Any change that pushes the values for these variables outside these limits will make trade infeasible.

The case of multiple traded commodities

What happens if there are many commodities traded among many nations? Does this change anything? One result is that the "strong" Ricardian principle no longer holds true; there will not be complete specialization. Instead, a "weak" Ricardian principle holds true. According to this weaker result, for each nation there will be a chain of commodities ranked according to their relative unit labor costs, of labor productivities. Each nation's exports will have lower unit labor costs, or higher productivities, than its imports.

To see this, suppose that A-Land and B-Land each produce five tradable commodities. Table 3.5 displays unit labor requirements for each good. The bottom row shows the relative unit labor requirements, a^A / a^B. Table 3.6 rank-orders the relative unit labor requirements.

The relative labor requirement must be less than the term $(\omega^A/\omega^B E)$ for a country to export a commodity. Thus, if $(\omega^A/\omega^B E)$ equals .67, then A-Land will specialize in and export wine and soybeans while B-Land will specialize in and export soybeans and toys. Both nations would likely produce wheat, since $a^A/a^B = \omega^A/\omega^B E = .67$. As with the 2-commodity case, labor productivity, exchange rates and wages (i.e., subsistence) will determine the pattern of trade between A-Land and B-Land.

Summary of main tenets

The Ricardian theory of comparative advantage purports to demonstrate that, given the nine assumptions, trade between nations with different labor productivities is mutually beneficial, even if one or more nations has an absolute advantage

TABLE 3.5 Unit labor requirements

	Wine	Soybeans	Computers	Wheat	Toys
A-Land	3	4	1	2	3
B-Land	9	4	6	3	1
a^A / a^B	0.33	1.00	0.17	0.67	3.00

TABLE 3.6 Rank ordered unit labor requirements

	Computers	Wine	Wheat	Soybeans	Toys
A-Land	1	3	2	4	3
B-Land	6	9	3	4	1
a^A / a^B	0.17	0.33	0.67	1.00	3.00

in producing all goods. The analysis begins with autarky, in which unit labor costs determine commodity prices. These costs, in turn, depend on labor productivity and on the nation's cost of subsistence. Production possibilities, and tastes and preferences, determine autarky output.

When trade opens, capitalists take advantage of autarky price differentials and specialize in the comparative advantage commodity. They export this commodity, and import the comparatively disadvantaged commodity. The final terms of trade, the international equilibrium price of the tradable goods, will lie somewhere between the original autarky prices, depending on the relative intensity of demand, relative wage rates, and the exchange rate. Note that the model does not attempt to explain how any of these variables are themselves determined.

Empirical studies of Ricardian comparative advantage

The opinion among most orthodox economists is that a model is good if it is simple and if it can predict well. Realism of a model's assumptions is not an important criterion for judging theories because realism is an unattainable goal. All models require assumptions, which effectively reduce realism. Accordingly, the best way to judge a model is to see if it can predict better than alternative models. This is a methodological approach derived from Milton Friedman's *Methodology of Positive Economics* (Friedman, 1953). It is mainly a research guide for orthodox economists and not a sophisticated and comprehensive philosophy of science.

The question put to Ricardian trade theory has been: do national variations in labor productivity explain variations in their exports and imports? An affirmative answer would verify the Ricardian theory. However, answering this question has been difficult because it requires that we adapt a labor-only, single factor model to a world in which many factors of production and many kinds of market imperfections influence trade.

There have been a number of important attempts to verify empirically the Ricardian hypotheses.[10] The first and most often cited study is that of MacDougall (1951 and 1952). He used 1930 data for American and British manufacturing industries and found that in 20 out of the 25 industries, covering 97% of the products included in these industries, there was a strong correlation between the relative exports to third countries and relative productivity differences. Said MacDougall: "where American output per worker was more than twice the British, the United States had, in general, the bulk of the export market, while for products where it was less than twice as high the bulk of the market was held by Britain" (MacDougall, 1951: 697–698).

Several similar studies in the 1950s and 1960s confirmed MacDougall's conclusions. Using data from 1950 and 1951, Stern (1962) and Balassa (1963) found positive and statistically significant correlations between relative costs and productivity and trade in terms of the volume and value of export and imports. They believed that other factors that might affect trade patterns, such as the influence of wages, were not important enough to reject the Ricardian result.

58 Classical trade theory: Smith and Ricardo

In a reversal of opinion, Bhagwati, in 1964, published a comprehensive and critical survey of trade theory. In that article, he concluded that the impressive empirical findings found by MacDougall, Stern and Balassa did not confirm the Ricardian theory of comparative advantage. Bhagwati offered his own empirical test of the studies, one that corrected several empirical flaws in the prior work, and concluded that his "results are seriously prejudicial to the usefulness of the Ricardian approach" (Bhagwati, 1964: 15). These econometric results proved "entirely hopeless" and disappointing: "[t]here is as yet no evidence in favor of the Ricardian hypotheses." A 1973 study by McGilvray and Simpson of trade between Ireland and Britain also failed to find any empirical support for the Ricardian theory of comparative advantage (McGilvray & Simpson, 1973).

As to whether comparative labor productivity and costs affect the terms of trade in any important way, we must reject this conclusion too. As Leamer and Levinsohn asserted in 1995, "We are inclined to think of this [conclusion] as a mathematical toy. It is great fun to have it in our play-pens but it has little to do with economics outside the play-pen" (Leamer, 1995: 1344).

To summarize, there seems to be little empirical support for the Ricardian theory of comparative advantage. While there appears to be a correlation between labor productivity and trade patterns, the evidence does not support the idealized Ricardian model, and we need better models with greater explanatory power to explain trade. We shall study some of these in the next chapter.

A critical summary of Ricardian trade theory

Ricardian trade theory makes three claims. First, trade will increase domestic profits and encourage economic growth, but only if a nation imports wage goods at prices cheaper than is available domestically. In our illustration, if wheat is a subsistence good in A-Land, then importing cheaper wheat from B-Land will lower wages and increase profits in A-Land. Similarly, if a computer is a subsistence good in B-Land, then importing cheaper computers from A-Land will lower wages and increase profits in B-Land. If computers and wheat are both elements of workers' subsistence, and if other non-tradable goods are also part of the subsistence bundle, then the well-known comparative advantage conclusions may break down altogether.

Unfortunately, contemporary presentations of Ricardian trade theory never specify whether the goods traded are wage goods or not. In a similar vein, they never say anything about profits; if wages are a basic form of income, then profits also must be a basic form of income. The typical textbook presentation of comparative advantage glosses over this omission of profit income by assuming that all production takes place in a labor-only economy, with "unassisted labor." This is nonsensical. First, there can be no workers if there are no capitalists, and vice versa. Second, in a labor-only economy, there can be no national differences in labor productivity without sneaking into the analysis some other non-labor factor of production that causes these differences in the first place. After all, what can cause labor to be more productive in one place than another? Ricardo did not approach

Classical trade theory: Smith and Ricardo **59**

the problem in this way, and the usual textbook presentation is an inaccurate representation of the Ricardo's trade model.

The second claim is that unit labor requirements in the production of computers and wheat determine who has a comparative advantage in which good. It also predicts who specializes in, and exports and imports, computers and wheat. This claim is incorrect if we introduce into the model (1) the payment of wages *and* profits and (2) methods of production that require more than one year to produce either computers or wheat.

To see this, suppose that both computers and wheat are subsistence goods and that workers' real wages, in both nations, consist of computers and wheat in varying proportions. Suppose, further, that it takes one year to produce a computer and a bushel of wheat in B-Land, and one year to produce a bushel of wheat in A-Land. Suppose, however, that it takes five years to produce a computer in A-Land. During each of these five years, the computer capitalists must advance their capital to pay their workers' wages. They also will charge an annual profit for the capital advanced, as they do not invest their capital without charge (i.e., for free). After five years, the price of a computer would be $P_C^A = a_C^A \omega^A (1 + r)^5$ where r is the going rate of profit and $a_C^A \omega^A$ is the capital advanced each year. The price will not be $P_C^A = a_C^A \omega^A$ as it was in our illustration. Depending on the nation's equilibrium rate of profit, r, the number of years it takes to bring a computer to market, and the proportions in which computers and wheat enter into the subsistence bundle, the relative autarky prices of computers and wheat will differ from the ratio of unit labor requirements that determine comparative advantage. In other words, A-Land might actually specialize in and export the commodity in which it has a comparative disadvantage!

The third claim is that free trade improves the general welfare of society because it expands the aggregate volume of commodities available. This claim may not be true either if wages and profits are paid out over several years and if one or both commodities are wage goods. In fact, in free trade, A-Land could easily wind up with a smaller bundle of commodities than they had in autarky.[11] Moreover, trade may fail to improve the aggregate welfare of society if some residents benefit from trade while others lose. Thus, the Ricardian model ignores the effect of trade on the distribution of income by introducing the fiction of community indifference curves, which assume all residents are alike.

Taken as a whole, the contemporary formulation of Ricardian trade theory is a considerable departure from the original aim of Ricardo (and other Classical economists), which was to examine how the international exchange of commodities affects the productive capacities of a nation, its standards of living, and its distribution of income. Rather than solving the above theoretical difficulties, contemporary comparative advantage models ignore these problems altogether by separating the analysis of exchange from the analysis of production. It does this by assuming that the commodities traded do not themselves enter into the production of other tradable and non-tradable commodities. Therefore, the comparative advantage model disconnects the exchange of commodities from the production of

60 Classical trade theory: Smith and Ricardo

commodities. Computers do not enter into the further production of wheat, and wheat does not enter into the further production of computers. The upshot is that, while there may be gains from trade, it is not clear at all how these gains translate into improved macroeconomic performance.

The Ricardian pure exchange theory of trade leaves us with the naïvely simple and unproblematic proposition that, if two nations exchange something, they will only do so if they benefit from the exchange; thus, if the exchange takes place, they will both benefit. This approach sheds very little light on the real world economy.

What can we conclude, then, about the Ricardian principle of comparative advantage and its corollaries of free trade and specialization? The inescapable conclusion is that, despite the overwhelming conviction that the principle is a universal truth, it is in fact theoretically narrow in scope, empirically unreliable, and limited in practical application.

Conclusions

Classical economics incorporated international trade theory into a broader, general theory of capitalism. The concerns of Classical economists were with a rapidly growing, expanding economic system that, by the time of Smith and Ricardo, stretched far and wide. Indeed, very little of the globe remained unaffected by the reach of European capitalism and European civilization. What did this global expansion mean for the welfare of European nations and for their prospects for continued growth and development? Would the economies of Europe continue to grow, or would they succumb to built-in forces that brought the capitalist engine to a halt?

International trade theory, and the theory of comparative advantage in particular, were part and parcel of the Classical economists' attempt to understand the dynamics of the society in which they lived, and they saw their society as part of an expanding global and colonial capitalist order.

The methods of analysis originally employed by Smith and Ricardo were not very abstract or mathematical, especially when compared to contemporary economics. They relied more on qualitative analyses and less on formal techniques and scientific precision. Most educated readers of Smith and Ricardo at the time were able to follow their arguments. Ricardo's treatise on political economy was certainly not as mathematical as it is in this chapter; the rigor we applied here to Ricardian theory is a modern retrospective that is more faithful to the ideological requirements of modern orthodox economics.

Smith and Ricardo, as well as most other Classical economists, understood capitalism as a dynamic social, political and economic organism that grows according to inherent natural forces, forces that political institutions could modify if they chose to do so. Smith was more of a social philosopher, while Ricardo was more of practical businessman-cum-scholar, yet both viewed international economics as belonging to a much larger scholarly endeavor.

In conclusion, it is important for us to keep in mind the historical context in which both Smith and Ricardo developed their ideas about international trade. For example, most of Europe at the time of Smith and Ricardo was embroiled in war. There was the Seven Years War from 1756 to 1763, and then the Napoleonic Wars from 1803 to 1815. In both wars, Britain and Portugal were allies fighting together first against Spain and then against France. While economists devote enormous energies to documenting the history of economic theory and to learning what Smith and Ricardo had specifically to say about trade theory, they often overlook the historical context of the theories they are studying. One would never know from reading economic analysis that these wars had been going on, and that perhaps this explains why Ricardo selected Portugal as an example for his theory of comparative advantage. Deeper consideration of the historical context might lead us to different conclusions about comparative advantage models. Joan Robinson pointed out what we miss by neglecting history and focusing only on abstract models:

> the models imply trade between countries of equal weight and at the same level of development. This rules out imperialism and the use of power to foster economic advantage. In Ricardo's example Portugal was to gain as much from exporting wine as England from exporting cloth, but in real life Portugal was dependent on English naval support, and it was for this reason that she was obliged to accept conditions of which trade wiped out her production of textiles and inhibited industrial development, so as to make her more dependent than ever.
>
> *(Robinson, 1974: 1)*

Notes

1 Identifying starting and ending dates is an imprecise endeavor. Smith began his career in Scotland decades before the 1776 publication of his path-breaking book, and his friend David Hume (1711–1776) influenced Smith's ideas at least 25 years prior to the appearance of *The Wealth of Nations*. Historians typically give credit to Jevons for having started the Neoclassical revolution in economic thought.
2 There is little agreement on who actually "discovered" the theory of comparative advantage. Some say it was Robert Torrens (1780–1864), others say it was James Mill (1773–1836), but most attribute the discovery to David Ricardo.
3 Thus, if there is an increase (or decrease) in demand, the market price will rise temporarily. This will create higher than normal profits and attract new firms. These new firms, together with heightened production by existing firms, will cause the market supply to rise and the market price to fall back down to its original level, assuming of course costs of production remain unaffected.
4 It is difficult to find an example of a "pure" final consumer good that does not itself enter into the production of something else. Most consumer goods enter into the "production" of labor in the sense that they provide for workers' subsistence and so regenerate, or reproduce, labor as a factor of production. This is certainly the case with wheat. Computers also enter as capital into the production of other commodities. Perhaps commodities such as sailing yachts and caviar are pure final consumer goods, but choosing these as examples reduces the theory to triviality.
5 A straight line is described by the equation $y = b + mx$ where b is the vertical intercept and m is the slope.

62 Classical trade theory: Smith and Ricardo

6 The intercept value is 12, so we can derive $a_W^A = 2$ from $24/a_W^A = 12$. This allows us to determine, $a_C^A = 1$ from $a_C^A/a_W^A = -.5$.

7 If one worker produces one bushel of wheat, then one bushel of wheat requires one worker. Likewise, if it takes two workers to produce one bushel of wheat, then .5 bushels of wheat require one worker.

8 This calculation was not in the original Ricardian analysis but was added by Gottfried Haberler in 1930. In so doing, Haberler deleted the labor theory of value from the theory of comparative advantage. Given the nine assumptions we made, however, this reformulation does not matter, and we can use either the Ricardian labor theory or the newer opportunity cost approach.

9 We derive the slope as follows. In either equation (3.7) or (3.8), first solve for W: $a_W W = L - a_C C$. Now divide through by a_W: $W = L/a_W - (a_C/a_W)C$. The slope is the coefficient of C, a_C/a_W.

10 There are three important surveys of empirical tests of the Ricardian hypotheses: (Bhagwati, 1964); (Deardorff, 1984); and (Leamer, 1995).

11 Steedman and Metcalfe (1979) have proven these three conclusions. We leave out the proofs for ease of exposition.

References

Balassa, B. (1963). "An Empirical Demonstration of Classical Comparative Cost Theory." *Review of Economics and Statistics*, *45*, 231–238.

Bhagwati, J. (1964). "The Pure Theory of International Trade: A Survey." *Economic Journal*, *74*, 1–84.

Deardorff, A. (1984). "Testing Trade Theories and Predicting Trade Flows." In R. W. Kenen, & P. B. Jones, *Handbook of International Economics* (Vol. 1, pp. 467–518). Holland: Elsevier Science Publishers.

Friedman, M. (1953). *Essays in Positive Economics*. Chicago: University of Chicago Press.

Leamer, E. E. (1995). "International Trade Theory: the Evidence." In G. Grossman, & K. Rogoff, *Handbook of International Economics* (Vol. 3, pp. 1339–1394). Holland: Elsevier Science Publishers.

MacDougall, G. D. (1951). "British and American Export: A Study Suggested by the Theory of Comparative Costs, Part I." *Economic Journal*, *61*, 697–724.

MacDougall, G. (1952). "British and American Export: A Study Suggested by the Theory of Comparative Costs, Part II." *Economic Journal*, *62*, 487–521.

McGilvray, J., & Simpson, D. (1973). "The Commodity Structure of Anglo-Irish Trade." *Review of Economics and Statistics*, *55*, 451–458.

Ricardo, D. (1817/1821). *On the Principles of Political Economy and Taxation*. London: John Murray.

Robinson, J. (1974). *Reflections on the Theory of International Trade*. Manchester, UK: Manchester University Press.

Smith, A. (1776/1904). *An Inquiry into the Nature and Causes of the Wealth of Nations* (5th ed.). (E. Cannan, Ed.) London: Methuen & Co., Ltd.

Steedman, I., & Metcalfe, J. S. (1979). "On Foreign Trade". In I. Steedman, & J. S. Metcalfe, *Fundamental Issues in Trade Theory* (pp. 99–109). London: Macmillan Press.

Stern, R. M. (1962). "British and American Productivity and Comparative Costs in International Trade." *Oxford Economic Papers*, *14*, 275–303.

4

NEOCLASSICAL TRADE THEORY

Introduction

Classical international trade theory tried to show that free trade promotes economic growth and development. Adam Smith, with the aid of the theory of absolute advantage, showed how free trade extends the market system, advances the division of labor and specialization and fosters economic growth and development. To David Ricardo, free trade also fostered economic growth and development by allowing the import of relatively cheaper wage goods, thereby encouraging capital accumulation. Ricardo's principle of comparative advantage was the centerpiece of his analysis and it plays a paramount role in Neoclassical trade theory.

The general orientation of economic theory changed significantly in the 20th century as Neoclassical economics replaced Classical economics as the new orthodoxy. The Classical economists built grand, visionary social theories showing how to improve the human condition. They reflected the realities of an evolving, class-based social economic system. Today, Neoclassical economists construct technically precise, formal and abstract theories which, despite their narrowness and distance from reality, claim to be universally valid and beyond reproach.

Neoclassical economists became especially critical of the labor theory of value employed by Smith and Ricardo. They saw that that theory potentially undermined the belief that capitalism is fundamentally a socially harmonious system. After all, if the value of all of society's annual output is attributable to labor, then why do capitalists and landowners get a share of that output? Don't the owners of society's means of production—the capitalist class—"exploit" the working class by expropriating a portion of their output as profit? This was how Karl Marx interpreted capitalism. Extending the application of the labor theory to international trade thus made global capitalism appear discordant and antagonistic, not harmonious and cooperative. Smith and Ricardo had faith in the intrinsic harmony and

64 Neoclassical trade theory

moral legitimacy of international free trade and capitalism; Marx believed international free trade extends class conflict globally and would not lead to mutually beneficial economic development.

Against this background, Neoclassical trade theory erased the labor theory of value and its corollary that antagonistic class differences exist in capitalism. It substituted a subjective theory of value founded on the psychology of individual choice and utility maximization. In this subjective theory, the value of produced commodities is determined not by the conditions under which goods are produced but rather by the sacrifices people make (i.e., pain) and the satisfaction individual decision makers (i.e., pleasure) receive. Neoclassical economics shifts attention entirely to pure exchange and reduces production to a series of exchange transactions.[1]

Pure exchange is, by definition, voluntary; it can never be exploitive or coercive. No one can force another to buy or sell. Extending this idea to international trade allows Neoclassical economists to characterize free trade as mutually beneficial for everyone who participates and to portray global capitalism as essentially harmonious and symbiotic.

The Neoclassical model: autarky

Neoclassical trade theory brings capital goods onto the stage where labor once stood alone. It dismisses the Ricardian labor theory of value and eliminates the assumption that all firms employ labor and capital in the same proportions. In Neoclassical theory, industries use differing amounts of capital and labor. Some industries are capital intensive, such as automobiles and oil refining, while others are labor intensive, such as some agriculture and textiles. Note that an industry is not inherently capital or labor intensive; it depends chiefly on the technologies adopted and on the initial endowments of capital and labor resources. Carpet making, for example, can be labor intensive, such as the hand-woven carpets from Asia, or capital intensive, such as those manufactured in the US. The capital–labor proportion adopted reflects the choices firms make, which in turn depends on the price of labor and capital.

There are two consequences of treating capital and labor in this way. First, resource endowments are important determinants of trade, as are labor and capital productivity. Second, shifting trade regimes from autarky to free trade entails a reallocation of resources between industries. The composition of a nation's output will change as it moves from autarky to free trade. This means some people will benefit and other people will lose. We cannot claim that a regime change from autarky to free trade is always "welfare enhancing" unless we make some heroic assumptions. We will discuss these assumptions later.

In this chapter, we continue to use computers and wheat, and A-Land and B-Land, to illustrate Neoclassical trade theory. Because we now have two factors of production (capital and labor) instead of one, we refer to our illustration as a "2 × 2 × 2" model: two goods, two nations, two factors of production. The model is intuitively simple yet analytically complex.

The concept of Neoclassical equilibrium

In our two-nation world, residents' tastes and preferences for computers and wheat determine the composition of national output. This is "consumer sovereignty" at work, as consumer demand, interacting with supply, dictates how many computers and how much wheat are produced. This desired output mix indirectly determines the demand for capital and labor by the computer and wheat industries. These "derived demands" for capital and labor then interact with the given supplies of capital and labor. The result is a particular allocation of capital and labor resources to each industry. In other words, the output mix determines the input mix.

We can describe these mixtures of output and input monetarily. The demand for and supply of computers and wheat determine their relative prices, P_C/P_W. The derived demand for and supply of capital and labor determine the relative prices of capital and labor, r/w. It is important to note that these latter prices, r and w, also determine the incomes of capitalists and workers. We can define capitalists' income as rK where r is the price of capital and K is the amount of capital employed. And we can define workers' income as wL where w is the wage rate and L is the amount of labor employed. If labor and capital are the only resources, then the total income generated by social production is $rK + wL$.

As noted above, moving to free trade from autarky changes the composition of output and the allocation of resources. In autarky, residents can only consume what the economy produces, whereas with free trade, residents can consume more than what the domestic economy can produce; the extra consumption is imported. When free trade becomes possible, profit-seeking capitalists, observing that computer and wheat prices abroad differ from those at home, rearrange the composition of production, reallocating capital and labor in pursuit of profit opportunities.

Neoclassical assumptions

The Neoclassical trade model retains all the nine assumptions made in the previous chapter, but there are four further assumptions within the Neoclassical trade model:

1. *Residents in all nations have identical tastes and preferences.* Therefore, community indifference curves for A-Land and B-Land are identical. This means consumers in both nations would buy the same amount of computers and wheat if incomes and relative prices remain the same.
2. *Each nation possesses a fixed but different supply of two infinitely divisible factors of production, capital and labor.* We do not ask what determines these supplies or where they came from. In our illustration, we suppose that A-Land has relatively more capital and B-Land has relatively more labor. If $\overline{K^A}$ and $\overline{K^B}$ are the capital endowments and $\overline{L^A}$ and $\overline{L^B}$ the labor endowments for each nation, then $\overline{K^A/L^A} > \overline{K^B/L^B}$. Notice that A-Land can be capital abundant even if it has less capital than B-Land. We measure capital abundance (and scarcity) by the ratio of the two inputs, not their respective absolute amounts. Similarly, a

66 Neoclassical trade theory

nation is not necessarily labor abundant if it has a larger population of workers. Only the ratios matter.

3. *Producers in all nations have access to the same technology.* A technology is simply the set of all known ways of producing commodities. A production "technique" is one specific way of producing a particular commodity, and we describe this technique by the proportions in which firms combine capital and labor. Firms can produce commodities using many different techniques, and which technique they adopt depends on the market prices of capital and labor. For example, if capital (or labor) is relatively cheap, then production techniques will tend to be relatively capital (or labor) intensive. In both nations, we assume computer production is capital intensive and wheat production is labor intensive. Thus, $K_C/L_C > K_W/L_W$. Again, only the ratios in which capital and labor are used matter.

4. *Capitalists pay workers a uniform wage, w, and receive a uniform profit, r.* We express profit as a percentage of the capitalist's invested capital, K. The ratio w/r tells us if labor is relatively cheap or expensive in a nation. The supply and demand for labor and capital determine w and r, and, hence, w/r. This assumption is equivalent to assuming perfect competition everywhere.

We can make three observations using this information. First, if capital is relatively abundant in a nation (i.e., $\overline{K/L}$ is high), then profit rates will be relatively low and wages relatively high (i.e., w/r is high). Second, the ratio w/r influences capitalists' choice of production techniques. If labor is relatively expensive and capital relatively cheap, then capitalists will choose more capital-intensive techniques for the products they produce. Third, the aggregate income generated by production of computers and wheat can be written as $(w^A\overline{L^A} + r^A\overline{K^A})$ for A-Land and $(w^B\overline{L^B} + r^B\overline{K^B})$ for B-Land.

We note before proceeding further that it is conceptually difficult to measure the amount of capital K separately from the profit rate r without the labor theory of value. This is because K is valued as the present value of the estimated stream of future profits. A piece of equipment that contributes nothing to profits will have a value of zero and hence K will equal 0. Thus, we need to know the value of r in order to measure the value of K. Neoclassical economics has been unable to offer a satisfactory answer to this theoretical conundrum.

In summary, the Neoclassical theory of trade employs the following three key variables in its analysis:

1. Relative factor abundance for each nation, or $\overline{K/L}$
2. Relative factor intensity for each industry, or K/L.
3. Relative factor prices, or w/r.

The Neoclassical production possibilities frontier

The production possibilities frontier, or PPF, is a collection of all possible output combinations of two commodities that a nation can produce when firms fully

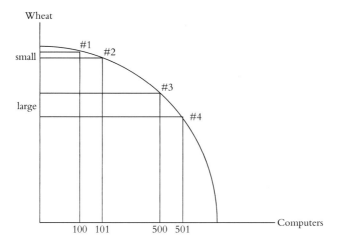

FIGURE 4.1 Production possibilities frontier

employ all available resources. In the Ricardian case, the PPF is linear because firms in all industries use capital and labor in the same proportions. Thus, the amount of capital and labor required to produce an additional unit of one commodity exactly equals the amount of capital and labor released when reducing the output of another commodity by the requisite amount. Therefore, the marginal cost of each commodity is constant over the entire range of possible production. This fixed capital–labor ratio allows us to focus only on labor as the critical input; the correct amount of capital will always be available.

Neoclassical economic theory builds on the assumption of variable input proportions, which means that firms can combine capital and labor in an infinite number of ways. This implies that the PPF is concave to the origin (bowed outward) and not linear. Concavity means that the production of additional computers requires the sacrifice of more and more wheat. Thus the marginal cost of each commodity increases.

Figure 4.1 shows the PPF for the computer–wheat model. Increasing production from 100 computers to 101 requires a relatively small sacrifice, as we must move from point #1 to #2 on the PPF. Increasing production from 500 computers to 501 requires a larger sacrifice, as we must now move from point #3 to #4. Moreover, as in the linear case, the slope of the Neoclassical PPF at any point is the marginal rate of transformation, MRT, which also equals the ratio of the marginal costs of computers and wheat: $MRT = MC_C/MC_W$.

What explains the concave shape of the Neoclassical PPF? Surprisingly, there are few satisfactory answers. Explanations either appeal to received wisdom ("most economists agree it is concave"), rely on circular reasoning ("it is concave because of increasing costs"), invoke an imaginary intuition ("it makes sense that it is concave"), tell fictitious stories about firms reallocating less and less adaptable or suitable resources to other industries,[2] or use casual empiricism by declaring that concavity "approximates reality."

68 Neoclassical trade theory

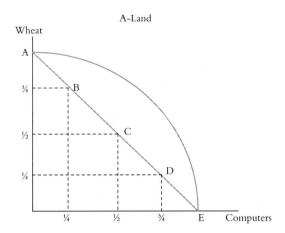

FIGURE 4.2 A-Land's production possibilities frontier

One often-used explanation builds on the fact that each industry employs capital and labor in different proportions. In Figure 4.2, suppose we allocate all of A-Land's capital and labor to the wheat industry. Production then occurs at point A, which is maximum wheat output. Similarly, if we allocate the entire endowment of capital and labor to the computer industry, production occurs at point E.

Suppose, now, that we give exactly ½ of the total capital endowment and ½ of the total labor endowment to each industry. Because there are no scale economies or diseconomies, each sector then would produce at point C, which is ½ their maximum outputs. If we then allocate ¾ of the total endowment to wheat and ¼ to computers, we get point B. Similarly, allocating ¼ to wheat and ¾ to computers yields point D. As we allocate varying fractions of the total endowment to each industry, we can generate the straight line AE.

This way of allocating resources does not take into consideration the fact that wheat production is labor intensive and computer production capital intensive. It would make more sense to give wheat producers a larger share of the labor endowment and computer producers a larger share of the capital endowment. This would result in a larger output of both wheat and computers. The output combination would therefore lie outside the line AB, which demonstrates that the PPF is concave PPF.

Neoclassical equilibrium: autarky to free trade

The question remains of what combination of computers and wheat will firms choose to produce in autarky. The answer depends on community preferences, the slopes of which we called the "marginal rate of substitution," or MRS. Figure 4.3 shows the same PPF for A-Land along with three representative CIC curves.[3] The highest attainable CIC is CIC-2 where firms produce combination A. Combinations B and C are also on the PPF but they lie on CIC-1 and are

Neoclassical trade theory 69

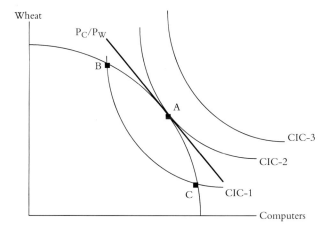

FIGURE 4.3 A-Land equilibrium

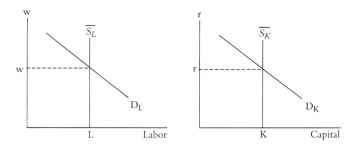

FIGURE 4.4 A-Land factor markets

therefore inferior to combination A. CIC-3 is unattainable given the technology and the resources available.

The equilibrium in this case is where feasible production maximizes community welfare. Given perfect competition, the slope of the heavily shaded line, drawn tangent to both the PPF and CIC-2 at A, shows the competitive equilibrium price ratio. At this point the following holds true:

$$MRT = MC_C/MC_W = P_C/P_W = MRS \qquad (5.1)$$

This is also the autarky solution for the nation: the rate at which consumers are willing to trade off computers for wheat exactly matches the rate at which producers can "transform" computers into wheat.

Finally, the output combination at point A implies a certain demand for capital and labor by each industry. In Figure 4.4, $\overline{S_K}$ and $\overline{S_L}$ represent the fixed endowments of capital and labor, and D_K and D_L represent the implied aggregate demand for each from the computer and wheat industries. Equilibrium in each market determines the uniform wage rate, w, and profit rate, r, and hence the relative factor price ratio r/w.

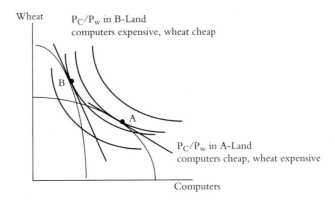

FIGURE 4.5 Autarky equilibrium

Autarky equilibrium in two nations

If Figure 4.4 shows the autarky situation in A-Land, then we can draw similar graphs for B-Land. Recall that we assume the CIC curves are identical for both nations. If A-Land and B-Land have the same capital and labor endowments as well, then their PPF curves also will be identical, as would all relative output and input prices. In other words, $P_C^A/P_W^A = P_C^B/P_W^B$ and $r^A/w^A = r^B/w^B$. In this case, there is no incentive to trade since prices everywhere are the same.

Now, what if A-Land has relatively more capital than B-Land, and B-Land has relatively more labor than A-Land? In other words, what if A-Land is relatively capital abundant and B-Land is relatively labor abundant? Clearly, A-Land's maximum computer output would be larger than B-Land's because computer production is relatively capital intensive and A-Land has relatively more capital. For similar reasons, B-Land's maximum wheat output would be larger than A-Land's because wheat production is relatively labor intensive and B-Land is relatively labor abundant. With identical CICs, relative computer and wheat prices now differ, leading to an incentive to trade. Figure 4.5 shows both PPF curves on the same axes, with A-Land's autarky equilibrium at point A and B-Land's at point B.

As the graph in Figure 4.5 makes clear, at point A computers in A-Land are cheap as compared to wheat, but only because A-Land is relatively capital abundant. This is why the heavily shaded price line is less steep than the price line in B-Land. Similarly, wheat is cheap in B-Land as compared to computers because labor is relatively abundant there. Thus, $P_C^A/P_W^A < P_C^B/P_W^B$. It follows that $r^A/w^A < r^B/w^B$ because $r^A < r^B$ due to A-Land's abundance of capital and $w^A > w^B$ due to B-Land's abundance of labor.

From autarky to free trade

As in the Ricardian case, capitalists in A-Land, seeing that computer prices are higher in B-Land, will produce more computers and export them to B-Land in

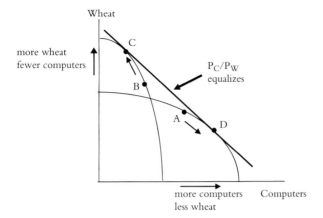

FIGURE 4.6 Final terms of trade

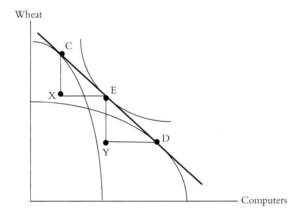

FIGURE 4.7 Free trade equilibrium

exchange for wheat where wheat prices are relatively low. A-Land floods B-Land with computers, bringing their computer prices down, and B-Land floods A-Land with wheat, bringing their wheat prices down. This causes P_C^A/P_W^A to rise because the denominator falls, and P_C^B/P_W^B to fall because the numerator falls. The final terms of trade are shown in Figure 4.6.

In A-Land, production shifts from point A to point D, meaning that they specialize in computer production, although they continue to produce some wheat. A-Landers then export some of their computer output to pay for wheat imports. Equivalently, in B-Land production shifts from point B to point C, meaning that B-Land's economy specializes in wheat, although they continue to produce some computers. B-Landers then export some of their wheat output to pay for computer imports. The final consumption equilibrium is at point E where we draw the terms of trade line tangent to the highest common CIC curve. This is shown in Figure 4.7.

72 Neoclassical trade theory

A-Land produces at D, then exports YD computers in exchange for YE units of wheat. B-Land produces at C, then exports XC units of wheat in exchange for XE computers. The rate of currency exchange will always guarantee that total exports equal total imports.

Five Neoclassical trade theorems

The foundation of Neoclassical trade theory consists of five theorems, each of which builds on the above analysis. These theorems are actually elaborations of a common theme. We summarize these theorems as follows, relying on intuition and omitting the mathematical proofs.

#1 Heckscher-Ohlin theorem: comparative advantage

The Swedish economist Eli Heckscher (1879–1952) first articulated this theorem in 1919 (Heckscher, 1919/1949). Bertil Ohlin (1899–1979), also a Swedish economist, independently stated the theorem in 1933 (Ohlin, 1933/1966). The theorem states that a nation will have a comparative advantage in the production of those commodities that use the abundant (i.e., cheap) factors intensively, and will export those commodities. In our illustration, this means that A-Land has a comparative advantage in computers because the production of computers is capital intensive and A-Land has a relative abundance of capital. A-Land will then specialize in and export computers. Similarly, B-Land has a comparative advantage in wheat because the production of wheat is labor intensive and B-Land has a relative abundance of labor. B-Land will then specialize in and export wheat.

#2 Stolper-Samuelson theorem: trade and income distribution

We ask the question, how do changes in relative output prices affect factor prices? A 1941 article by Wolfgang Stolper and Paul Samuelson answers this question using the familiar $2 \times 2 \times 2$ model (Stolper and Samuelson, 1941). The theorem states that a rise in the relative price of a good will cause a rise in the price of that factor of production used most intensively in the production of that good, and a fall in the other factor of production. In our illustration, if the relative price of computers goes up, then the profit rates will rise and wages will fall. This makes sense because capital is the main ingredient in computer production and hence capital owners will be the main beneficiaries.

Suppose instead that the relative price of wheat rises, say due to a tariff on wheat imports, the import-competing sector. What will the effect be in A-Land where the wheat industry has previously contracted to allow for the expansion of the computer industry? According to the Stolper-Samuelson theorem, wage earners will benefit because wheat production uses labor intensively in its production. Owners of capital will lose.

#3 Factor price equalization theorem: trade and world prices

Samuelson first developed this theorem in 1948 as an extension of the Heckscher-Ohlin (H-O) and Stolper-Samuelson (S-S) theorems (Samuelson, 1948). It states that free trade will eliminate differences in factor prices. Before trade, the price of the abundant factor is low while the price of the scarce factor is high. After trade, production shifts to the comparative advantage good, which intensively uses the abundant factor. The price of this abundant factor will rise and the scarce factor will fall. Factor prices in the other nation, the trading partner, will move in the opposite direction. Eventually, wage rates will be the same in both nations, as will be profit rates.

In our illustration, A-Land is capital abundant and labor scarce. Therefore, before trade, profit rates are low and wage rates high. Trade shifts production to computers, the capital-intensive sector. This reallocation favors capital; the demand for capital rises as do profit rates. The opposite happens for labor. In B-Land, capital is scarce and labor is abundant, so profit rates are initially high and wage rates low. Trade shifts production to wheat, the labor-intensive sector. This reallocation favors workers; the demand for labor rises as do wage rates. Profit rates fall. In conclusion, profit rates fall where they are initially high, and rise where they are initially low. Wage rates fall where they are initially high and rise where they are initially low. Eventually, all capitalists receive the same profit rate, and all workers receive the same wage rate.

#4 Rybczynski theorem: trade and economic growth

The author of this 1955 theorem is the Polish economist Tadeusz Rybczynski (1923–1998) (Rybczynski, 1955). Rybczynski set out to investigate how an increase in the endowment of a factor of production would affect production, consumption and the terms of trade. Building upon the H-O theorem, he showed that if the endowment of a particular factor of production increases, the commodity using that factor most intensively would experience a more than proportional increase in output. There would be a decrease in the output of the other industry. Additionally, when exports of the commodity intensively using the growing factor increase, its relative price falls, and the terms of trade deteriorate. However, if the factor growth benefits the imported commodity, the terms of trade will improve. In terms of our illustration, if the supply of capital in A-Land rises, then the output and export of computers will rise. Computers would become more readily available on the world market and so computer prices would drop. In other words, the terms of trade, P_C^A/P_W^A, fall because the numerator falls. On the other hand, if labor becomes more abundant in A-Land, then wheat production in A-Land would rise and the demand for foreign wheat would fall. The terms of trade, P_C^A/P_W^A, rise because the denominator falls.

74 Neoclassical trade theory

TABLE 4.1 The Leontief Paradox

	Exports	Imports
Capital (1947 dollars)	2,550,780	3,091,339
Labor (person–years)	182	170
Capital/labor	14,015	18,184

#5 Vanek-Leamer factor content theorem: multiple factors of production

In an article published in 1968, Czech-born economist Jaroslav Vanek extended the H-O model by shifting attention to the factor content of traded commodities (Vanek 1963 and 1968). The idea here is that trade in commodities implies trade in the factors of production embodied in those commodities.

To see how this works, refer once again to Figure 4.7. In A-Land, production occurs at point D while consumption occurs at point E. At D, aggregate output consists of mostly computers produced with capital-intensive production methods and relatively little wheat. Exports of YD computers will "embody" a disproportionately large share of capital with respect to labor. Imports of YE units of wheat will "embody" a disproportionately large share of labor with respect to capital. Exports have high capital content, and imports have high labor content. Therefore, the relative factor content of the commodities exported and imported reveals the relative factor abundance of the trading nations. This is the essence of Vanek's factor content theorem.

The Vanek theorem was important because it helped to resolve a nagging empirical problem, the so-called Leontief Paradox. In a 1953 article, Wassily Leontief used 1947 data to show that the US, a capital abundant economy, exported labor-intensive commodities and imported capital-intensive commodities, just the opposite of what the H-O theorem predicts (Leontief, 1953). Table 4.1 shows Leontief's calculations of the factor content of US exports and imports assuming that trading partners employed the same technologies as in the US.

As Table 4.1 shows, the capital content of US exports was lower than that of US imports. This curious result initiated 50 years' worth of literature trying to solve the puzzle. Some claimed 1947 was an atypical year because the Second World War had just ended. Others claimed that the results would be consistent with the H-O theorem if only Leontief had included natural resources or skilled and unskilled labor. Also, the US economy was not engaged in free trade, nor did it use the same technology as other nations.

A final reconciliation came from Edward Leamer who, building on Vanek's theorem, pointed out that Leontief's test was incorrect because he should have compared the factor content of production to the factor content of consumption (Leamer, 1980). Leontief falsely compared the factor content of exports and imports. In other words, we ought to compare the factor content at point D with that of point E.

Neoclassical trade theory **75**

Leamer's Theorem suggested, then, that if A-Land is capital abundant, then the capital–labor ratio embedded in the production of aggregate output (Point D) must exceed the capital–labor ratio of the combination of goods consumed (Point E). Entire careers have been devoted to confirming these and the other Neoclassical theorems.

Extensions of the Neoclassical trade model

By the late 1960s, economists had developed the basic elements of Neoclassical trade theory. Since then, many contributors have extended the theory either by dropping several of the Neoclassical assumptions or by applying it to special situations. The following are some of these extensions.

When identical nations have different tastes

The standard Neoclassical model assumes nations have different factor endowments and identical tastes. Here we reverse these assumptions: nations have identical factor endowments and heterogeneous tastes. Because endowments are identical, production possibilities frontiers are also identical. If trade occurs, then it will have nothing to do with comparative advantage. Despite this, differences in tastes will cause autarky prices to be different, and this can induce trade.

We base the analysis on Figure 4.8 which shows the production possibilities frontier and sample community indifference curves for the two nations. The indifference curves indicate that A-Landers are especially fond of computers but not wheat, and B-Landers are especially fond of wheat but not computers. In autarky, A-Land produces many computers to meet the high demand, and very little wheat. This corresponds to point A which is where A-Land reaches the highest community indifference curve. Computer prices are high relative to wheat prices because, at the margin, unit costs are rising as resources for computer production become increasingly scarce. At point A, the price line, which measures the relative price of computers, is therefore quite steep.[4] The opposite situation prevails in B-Land where production and consumption occur at point B. Wheat prices will be relatively high because of rising unit costs and computer prices will be relatively low. At the two autarky equilibrium points, A and B, we can say that $P_C^A/P_W^A < P_C^B/P_W^B$. For trade to occur, all we need is a difference in observed relative prices. Note that the difference emerges here from differences in tastes and preferences instead of in factor endowments. With free trade, B-Land computer producers will have an incentive to produce more computers and to sell them in A-Land where they can fetch a higher price, and A-Land wheat producers will have an incentive to produce more wheat and sell it in B-Land. The price difference will disappear as the prices converge to an international equilibrium terms of trade that is somewhere between the original autarky prices.

The point E in Figure 4.8 represents this new equilibrium point. A-Land moves along the PPF to E as does B-Land. Both nations attain a higher

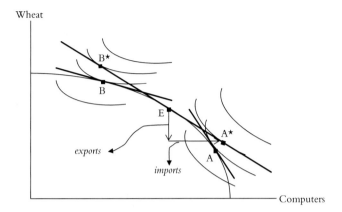

FIGURE 4.8 Taste bias model

community indifference curve while maintaining balanced trade. A-Land produces at E and consumes at A★ while B-Land also produces at E and consumes at B★. A-Land exports and imports the amounts indicated in the graph. Because B★ is on the same terms of trade line, B-Land's exports will equal A-Land's imports, and B-Land's imports will equal A-Land's exports. Trade is therefore balanced in equilibrium.

When factors of production are mobile across borders: the Mundell model

The standard Neoclassical model of free trade assumes factors of production are perfectly immobile between nations and that commodities are perfectly mobile. The model therefore deals with free trade in goods and autarky in trade in factors of production. It concludes that under these circumstances free trade, international commodity prices and factor prices will tend to equalize. But what if we permit labor and capital to migrate freely and costlessly across borders? How would this affect the results of the Neoclassical model?

Without question, migrations of labor and capital are significant aspects of the world economy and have large effects on both sending and receiving nations. The United States is famously a nation of immigrants and continues to host peoples from every continent. Europe too hosts immigrants, especially from the Mediterranean nations, Africa and Central and Eastern Europe. All migrants seek opportunities to earn higher incomes and better standards of living as well as political refuge. Capital migrates as well, most notably in the form of foreign direct investment and portfolio investment. The magnitude of international capital flows is huge with equally huge economic and political consequences.

In 1957, Robert Mundell addressed this question directly. "Commodity movements," said Mundell, "are at least to some extent a substitute for factor movements" (Mundell, 1957: 321). In other words, if we reverse the set of Neoclassical assumptions so that there is free trade in factors of production and autarky in commodities, we would arrive at the same result: commodity and factor prices would tend to equalize. Mundell further concluded that restricting commodity trade would stimulate trade in factors of production, and restricting factor mobility would stimulate commodity trade. Commodity mobility would substitute for factor mobility, and vice versa.

To Mundell, the real world lay somewhere between these two extremes. Some nations restrict capital flows and some nations restrict commodity flows. The extent to which factor mobility would substitute for commodity mobility depends on many factors such as the relative size of the trading nations, the technologies employed, tariffs and other barriers, restrictions (if any) on the repatriation of profits on capital, scale economics, market structures, and a multitude of other considerations. If we preserve all the restrictive assumptions made in the Neoclassical model, however, the conclusions about free trade remain unchanged.

This Neoclassical conclusion has serious policy implications. For example, it suggests that any kind of restriction on labor immigration, say to protect domestic workers from foreign competition, simply would be offset by an equivalent increase in imports of labor-intensive goods, exposing those domestic workers to even more foreign competition. So, if foreign labor cannot enter the country, commodities will. The reason is that a quota on labor immigration increases the relative labor abundance of the foreign country. That country becomes more labor abundant than it otherwise would be, and would produce even more labor-intensive goods for export.

In a similar vein, suppose a nation attempts to protect domestic labor by placing a tariff on some of its labor-intensive imports. Domestic prices of these importable commodities would rise, as would wages. This would then attract more foreign immigrants seeking to work at these higher wages, thereby undermining the attempt to protect domestic workers.

The Neoclassical message is plain: it is pointless to restrict the flows of commodities or factors of production; only free trade works. But, as Mundell readily admitted, his "analysis is remote from reality" and the preponderance of opinion about substitutability is ambiguous (Mundell, 1957: 335).

A recent application of Mundell's analysis is that of Kevin O'Rourke and Jeffrey Williamson (O'Rourke & Williamson, 1999). They address the possibility that trade in commodities and trade in factors of production may be complements and not substitutes. They ask, can rising commodity trade due to (say) trade liberalization policies actually induce more trade in factors of production? This is one way to look at globalization, namely, as a mutually reinforcing historical process in which trade in outputs and inputs both expand.

To answer this question, O'Rourke and Williamson look to 19th- and 20th-century Atlantic economic history. They find that the incidence of complementarity exceeds that of substitutability. They conclude: "In the four decades since [Mundell], the challenges to that conventional wisdom have been so many that nothing but theoretical ambiguity remains" (O'Rourke and Williamson, 1999: 267).

78 Neoclassical trade theory

When factors of production are immobile within a nation

The H-O model assumes that factors of production move costlessly and in differing proportions between industries in response to changes in factor prices. Factors of production cannot move across borders, however. In this view, capital and labor continuously adapt themselves to production activities by taking on different specific characteristics. Mechanical harvesters become trucks, and farmers become electricians, as the need arises.

Neoclassical theory treats capital and labor like putty, a malleable dough-like substance that firms can combine and recombine in an infinite number of combinations to produce any commodity.[5] Capital-labor ratios are therefore equally pliable. The Neoclassical model is therefore a "putty" model. This is what we mean when we say that factors of production are "homogenous:" their particular characteristics do not matter.

Treating capital as putty has always been problematic. Combining all the different kinds of capital into a single mass of capital called "K" conceals what ought to be explicit: capital is inherently heterogeneous, and we ought not to omit this feature. We can say the same thing about the inherent heterogeneity of labor, although it is easier to imagine farmers becoming electricians than it is to imagine mechanical harvesters becoming trucks.

If capital is heterogeneous, then it raises the question, what if one type of capital is "stuck" in a particular use. This is more like a "clay" situation than a "putty" situation. Clay is a metaphor for a hardened substance, the form of which a firm cannot easily alter. Moreover, if a particular sort of capital is stuck in a particular use, then firms are also stuck in using the same capital–labor ratio.

One attempt to deal with the heterogeneity of capital is the specific-factor model. Its roots go back to the 1930s and took formal shape in the 1970s. The specific-factor model assumes that capital is clay-like (i.e., heterogeneous) in one of the two industries and hence immobile across industries. Labor continues to be putty-like (i.e., homogenous). However, if capital is stuck in one industry, then there are really two kinds of capital. The second type of capital is stuck in the other industry. This makes the model $2 \times 2 \times 3$: two goods, two nations, three factors of production. The total endowments of labor and of the two types of capital in each sector are fixed and fully employed.

We can describe the results of this model intuitively. Because capital cannot move, it stands to reason that firms are unable to produce as efficiently as when all factors of production are perfectly mobile. There will be an "efficiency loss." What does this have to do with international trade?

Suppose trade between the two nations is liberalized, resulting in changes in output prices and the terms of trade. Imagine that in one nation export demand for computers rises while demand for import-competing wheat falls. In the computer industry, output prices rise, as would the demand for capital and labor, pushing up profits and wages. Because labor is homogeneous and mobile, wages would be higher and identical in both industries. And because capital is immobile, the

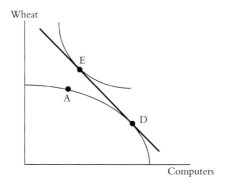

FIGURE 4.9 A-Land trade equilibrium

profit rate in the expanding export sector will be higher while the profit rate in the declining wheat sector will be lower (mainly because wages are everywhere higher).

The conclusion is that the profit rate in the computer sector will differ from the profit rate in the wheat sector. Competition will not equalize the two profit rates. Moreover, computer capitalists will become better off than wheat capitalists. What happens to workers depends on how much wheat and computers they consume. If workers consume lots of wheat and few computers they will be better off since relative wheat prices drop. Otherwise they will be worse off.

Is free trade really better?

The Neoclassical trade model insists that the move from autarky to free trade is "welfare enhancing." Is this true? We reproduce A-Land's autarky and free trade equilibria in Figure 4.9. The analysis that follows applies equally to B-Land. Point A represents autarky production and consumption; in free trade, production shifts to point D and consumption expands to point E. The question now is whether point E is better than point A.

Clearly, A-Landers consume more computers and wheat at E than at A, so they must be better off; they are on a higher indifference curve. Two considerations make this conclusion premature, however. Both have to do with the distribution of the trade benefits among owners of capital and among workers.

First, we need to examine what happens to the incomes of capitalists and workers when production shifts from autarky point A to free trade point D. Production of wheat contracts, which releases capital and labor. Since wheat is labor intensive, relatively more labor than capital becomes available. Since computers are capital intensive, that industry will want to hire more capital than labor as it expands. There arises an excess supply of labor and an excess demand for capital. The result is that wage rates fall and profit rates rise while total employment remains the same (by assumption). The increased consumption at E therefore benefits the capitalists whose income rises. Workers lose because they consume less as their incomes fall.

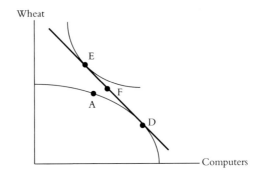

FIGURE 4.10 Is free trade better?

Because some benefit and others lose, can we still say that free trade benefits the people of A-Land?

Reluctant to concede that free trade may not be beneficial, Neoclassical economists came up with a positive response to this question. They adopted a method of analysis from the field of welfare economics called the "compensation principle." Developed by Nicholas Kaldor (1908–1986) and John Hicks (1904–1989), the compensation principle states that some new state of affairs is superior to an original state of affairs if those who benefit gain enough to compensate those who lose for their losses, leaving no one worse off and at least one person better off. As Hicks put it, "If A is made so much better off by the change that he could compensate B for his loss, and still have something left over, then the reorganization is an unequivocal improvement" (Hicks, 1941: 111). If the capitalists' gains are large enough to enable them to compensate the workers for their losses and still have something left over, then a move from autarky to free trade enhances welfare.

We can imagine various tax and subsidy programs that redistribute the gains from trade and put into practice the Kaldor-Hicks compensation principle. However, there is no perfect design of a system of taxation and subsidization upon which all can agree. Even if we can devise a perfect redistribution scheme, there remains another difficulty with the Kaldor-Hicks solution: there is no guarantee that the political system would adopt it. It depends entirely on the whims of political actors. Thus, the question is not whether winners *can* compensate losers but whether winners *will* compensate losers.

A second consideration makes the superiority of free trade doubtful. We show this in Figure 4.10. In this case, the final point of consumption, point E, lies to the left of point A. This means that A-Landers consume more wheat than they did before, but fewer computers.

Neoclassical economists can once again appeal to some redistribution scheme that would force the economy to move downward along the terms of trade line until it reaches a point such as F where more of both commodities is eventually consumed. The difficulty here is the same as before: it relies upon some unspecified redistribution scheme that political actors are unlikely to implement. In the end, free trade remains a matter of faith.

Conclusions

There is agreement among orthodox economists that the Neoclassical H-O model (1) logically demonstrates that free trade is an optimal policy and (2) empirically explains real-world trade patterns. Almost all contemporary economics textbooks make these claims.

In this concluding section we examine three aspects of the model that have drawn the attention of heterodox critics. These are: (1) the model's assumptions; (2) the way in which the model portrays capital and production; and (3) the model's empirical validity, both in terms of theory and policy.

Assumptions

There is no such thing as a correct or incorrect assumption. One can assume whatever one wishes. But there are consequences when making assumptions. This is because assumptions channel the reasoning process along certain paths. That is, they permit reasoning to proceed in certain directions and forbid it from proceeding in other directions. The conclusions reached at the end of the analysis therefore depend on the assumptions made in the beginning. Conversely, if we wish to arrive at certain conclusions, or if we wish to avoid certain conclusions, then all we need to do is to make the appropriate assumptions. For example, if we wish to conclude that free trade is ideal, then we can easily select assumptions that lead deductive reasoning to this conclusion. To see this, consider two of the thirteen H-O assumptions.

First, the H-O model assumes full employment always prevails, even as the economy adjusts to exogenous changes. Examples of an exogenous change are a regime shift from autarky to free trade and a change in factor endowments or technologies. In all such cases, the economy moves from one equilibrium position to another. A self-correcting, perfectly competitive economy always operates along its production possibilities curve. The economy is always technically efficient and fully employed. H-O theory therefore forbids the possibility that exogenous changes might throw people out of work and cause general unemployment.

Second, the H-O model assumes trade always remains balanced whenever any change in exports and imports occurs due to an exogenous shock. The freely fluctuating foreign exchange rate and the mobility of domestic resources preserves the balance between aggregate exports and imports. This assumption disallows the possibility that trade adjustments might create imbalances and balance of payments crises.

The assumptions made by the H-O model therefore lead us to conclude that free trade is harmonious and will not cause unemployment, class conflict, or balance of payments crises. Capitalism obviously is not that way; the model just assumes it is.

82 Neoclassical trade theory

Capital and production

In the 1950s, Cambridge University (UK) economists Joan Robinson and Piero Sraffa pointed out the ambiguous way in which Neoclassical production theory defines "capital." In the 1960s and 1970s, two more Cambridge economists, Pierangelo Garegnani and Luigi Pasinetti, joined Robinson and Sraffa in challenging Neoclassical capital theory. This led to a series of debates in the 1960s and 1970s with economists Paul Samuelson and Robert Solow at M.I.T. in Cambridge, Massachusetts, who defended Neoclassical theory. These "Cambridge Capital Controversies" lasted until the 1980s, at which time the new generation of Neoclassical economists had forgotten all about the debates.[6]

Simply put, the Cambridge critics claimed that you cannot measure the aggregate value of capital (K) in an economy. This is because K is an aggregate of heterogeneous capital goods that we cannot measure in physical units. You cannot add a computer and a truck. To add up the total value of K in the economy we must first know the profit rate, r. After all, the value of K is the present discounted value of future profit streams. If a machine tool, for example, lies idle in a factory, it will produce no profit for the firm and thus its value is zero. Therefore, r and K are interdependent. The demand for and supply of K cannot determine r because r must already be known in order to determine the value of K.

The implication of this interdependence of K and r is that it is not possible to describe production in the way H-O theory describes production. We cannot say that the K/L changes as r/w changes when an economy enters free trade from autarky, or when there are exogenous changes in factor endowments. This is because r and K are not separate and independent variables.

The mechanism by which comparative advantage dictates input and output combinations for trading nations is therefore faulty and based on circular reasoning. Despite this, economists today write as if this controversy had never occurred, and the Neoclassical method of defining K and K/L continues to prevail.

Empirical issues: H-O theory

Orthodox economists have written thousands of research articles trying to show empirically how differences in technologies, factor endowments and productivities, prices, and tastes and preferences determine comparative advantage, specialization and trade patterns. It is reasonable to suppose that these differences are important, but have these efforts succeeded in demonstrating that Neoclassical theory actually explains how these things are connected?

Econometric models are quite complex and go well beyond the $2 \times 2 \times 2$ case. They typically involve data for multiple nations, multiple factors and multiple goods. Among these models are Ricardian-inspired econometric tests that emphasize technological and productivity differences, and H-O inspired tests that emphasize differences in factor endowments. Some are only partial tests of particular relationships while some are much broader tests of equilibrium structures.

Empirical testing has proceeded incrementally, with each succeeding researcher recalculating variables with new data, defining new variables, using different techniques for measuring variables, and specifying different mathematical forms. Unfortunately, none of these efforts has brought us much closer to being able to verify H-O theory.

We have already seen in the previous chapter the failed efforts of MacDougall and others to verify that productivity differences predict trade patterns. In this chapter we introduced the Leontief Paradox which showed that US exports and imports fail to conform to the H-O predictions. Many empirical studies since MacDougall and Leontief indeed have found results consistent with H-O, but just as many others have failed to do so. And each time a researcher resolves one econometric problem, another econometric problem emerges.

Many empirical ambiguities remain, and evidence supporting the Neoclassical theory is scant. Yet faith in H-O continues unabated.

Empirical issues: free trade policy

Another lingering empirical question is whether free trade policies actually work. If this question asks if free trade is better than autarky, then there can be no answer because there are no examples of economies that have made such a transition. If the question asks if more free trade is better than less free trade (i.e., trade liberalization), then little support for this proposition exists either. What evidence does exist is anecdotal and so we cannot make general claims about the superiority of free trade.

Despite this, Neoclassical economists from rich nations have for decades advised poor developing nations to open their doors to free trade. They mostly have used Neoclassical trade theory to justify their advice. This is ironic since the richer nations had developed by following the opposite advice. Most nations have become rich by following some combination of interventionist trade and industrial policies.

One might reasonably argue that Smith got it right with his theory of absolute advantage, and that Ricardo's theory of comparative advantage led economists down the wrong path by limiting the scope of trade analysis. Consider the fact that world competition forces high-cost producers to lose out to low-cost producers. When a nation has high-cost firms, any exposure to international competition will create job losses and unemployment. Inability of uncompetitive firms to export may also lead to international debt and capital outflows, which the nation will pay by selling off current assets or by selling claims on future output and income. We cannot simply assume that resources will shift around automatically to preserve full employment and trade balance. Free trade, therefore, subjects weaker uncompetitive nations to stronger competitive nations, where "competitiveness" means absolute advantage.[7] While this was certainly not Smith's conclusion, it is a conclusion that follows from emphasizing absolute (or competitive) advantage.

Some economists have tried to resolve the weaknesses of Neoclassical trade theory by emphasizing market imperfections. These include the introduction of

84 Neoclassical trade theory

scale economies, externalities and imperfect competition. This has led to the development of yet another school of orthodox thought: New Trade Theory. We turn to this topic in the next chapter.

Notes

1 That is to say, a firm buys inputs from owners of inputs, then sells outputs to buyers. These are all market transactions and the firm is little more than an asocial black box in which the inputs are transformed into outputs according to abstract formulae (i.e., production functions).

2 This particular explanation dates back to the work of Gottfried Haberler in the 1930s. It claims that not all factors are equally productive in all possible uses. Thus, the first resources reallocated to an expanding industry from a declining industry are those that are most adaptable to the new uses. As the industry expands, however, and as we move downward along the PPF, released resources become less and less adaptable and per unit costs rise more and more. A variation of this theme is that resources are specialized in nature and more suitable in one industry than in another. As we move along the PPF, the resources transferred are less and less suitable to the expanding industry and per unit production costs begin to rise. Therefore, the PPF is concave: we must give up more and more of the other good to produce an additional unit of output in the expanding industry.

3 Recall that an infinite number of CIC curves pass through this space. The ones shown are only three of these.

4 We omit the autarky price lines for clarity.

5 Phelps (1963) coined the term "putty." See also Solow (1956 and 1962) and Johanson (1959).

6 See, e.g., Harcourt (1972) and Cohen and Harcourt (2003).

7 This point is made by Anwar Shaikh (2007).

References

Cohen, A. J., & Harcourt, G. C. (2003). "Retrospectives: Whatever Happened to the Cambridge Capital Theory Controversies?" *Journal of Economic Perspectives, 17*(1), 199–214.

Harcourt, G. C. (1972). *Some Cambridge Controversies in the Theory of Capital.* New York: Cambridge University Press.

Heckscher, E. (1919/1949). "The Effect of Foreign Trade on the Distribution of Income." In A. E. Association, *Readings in the Theory of International Trade* (pp. 272–300). Philadelphia: Blakiston.

Hicks, J. R. (1941). "The Rehabilitation of Consumers' Surplus." *Review of Economic Studies, 8*, 108–116.

Johanson, L. (1959). "Substitution Versus Fixed Production Coefficients in the Theory of Economic Growth: A Synthesis." *Econometrica, 27*(2), 157–176.

Leamer, E. (1980). "The Leontief Paradox, Reconsidered." *Journal of Political Economy, 88*, 495–503.

Leontief, W. W. (1953). "Domestic Production and Foreign Trade." *Proceedings of the American Philosophical Society, 97*, 332–347.

Mundell, R. A. (1957). "International Trade and Factor Mobility." *American Economic Review, 47*(3), 321–335.

Ohlin, B. (1933/1966). *Interregional and International Trade.* Cambridge, MA: Harvard University Press.

O'Rourke, K. H., & Williamson, J. G. (1999). *Globalization and History*. Cambridge, MA: MIT Press.

Phelps, E. S. (1963). "Substitution, Fixed Proportions, Growth and Distribution." *International Economic Review*, 4(3), 265–288.

Rybczynski, T. M. (1955). "Factor Endowment and Relative Commodity Prices." *Economica*, 22(88), 336–341.

Samuelson, P. (1948). "International Trade and the Equalisation of Factor Prices." *Economic Journal*, 58, 163–84.

Shaikh, A. (2007). "Globalization and the Myth of Free Trade." In A. Shaikh, *Globalization and the Myths of Free Trade: History, Theory and Empirical Evidence* (pp. 50–68). New York: Routledge.

Solow, R. M. (1956). "A Contribution to the Theory of Economic Growth." *Quarterly Journal of Economics*, 70(1), 65–94.

Solow, R. M. (1962). "Substitution and Fixed Proportions in the Theory of Capital." *Review of Economic Studies*, 29(3), 207–218.

Stolper, W., & Samuelson, P. A. (1941). "Protection and Real Wages." *Review of Economic Studies*, 9, 58–73.

Vanek, J. (1963). *The Natural Resource Content of United States Foreign Trade, 1870–1955*. Cambridge, MA: MIT Press.

Vanek, J. (1968). "Proportions Theory: The n-Factor Case." *Kyklos*, 4, 749–756.

5

THE NEW ORTHODOXY

Trade theory recast

Introduction

In explaining international trade, the Classical trade model emphasizes international differences in both labor productivity and technology while the Neoclassical model emphasizes international differences in factor endowments. In both cases, the *differences* that exist among nations determine comparative advantage and the pattern of trade. This has been the core of the orthodoxy.

However, we know that comparative advantage actually explains very little of world trade. In fact, a very large proportion of international trade takes place among nations that are similar in terms of labor productivity, technology and factor endowments. And a large proportion of world trade takes place among imperfectly competitive firms in the same industry (i.e., intra-industry trade).

To deal with these problems, orthodox trade theory has adapted by building trade models that presume to explain what comparative advantage cannot explain. The orthodoxy has been "recast," so to speak, into a more general theory which we now call the New Orthodoxy. In this New Orthodoxy, comparative advantage has lost its sacred place. This chapter surveys some of these newer models.

There are several things to look for as we work through these new models. First, all the newer models use the familiar Neoclassical tools of microeconomic analysis. One exception is the *game theory* model, which economists have already integrated into the body of orthodox economic theory. In strict Neoclassical theory, economic agents (consumers and firms) are autonomous. They make independent decisions based on concrete objectives, preferences and constraints. In game theory, however, agents are interdependent. One firm's decision directly affects another's. This is necessary to describe the interactions among real-world enterprises competing in global markets.

Second, in order to explain the real world of trade, the newer models relax

The New Orthodoxy: trade theory recast **87**

many of the highly restrictive assumptions of Classical and Neoclassical theory. However, added realism comes at a high price. Once we begin to drop assumptions and create more realistic models, things become more ambiguous and complex. In particular, it becomes impossible to make irrefutable statements about the positive effects of free trade. In fact, situations exist in which free trade is actually inferior to managed trade or even to autarky.

Third, we can no longer assert that competitive market forces determine which nations specialize in which industries. In fact, industries start up for a wide variety of reasons having little to do with market forces and a lot to do with historical "accident." Wars, mass worldwide migrations, expansive government policies, environmental and climatic factors, scientific discoveries and random forces all contribute to the establishment of industries within particular nations. The pattern of trade and the distribution of industries among nations are largely arbitrary.

Finally, despite the ambiguities, and notwithstanding the arguments favoring strategic government interventions in trade, the new orthodoxy continues to promote free trade as a practical, if not theoretically desirable policy stance. The utopian ideal of free trade thus continues to prevail despite arguments to the contrary. We will explain the reasoning in this chapter.

A note on scale economies

Before proceeding, it is useful to provide a brief definition of scale economies. This idea is central to many explanations of international trade. We begin by distinguishing between external and internal scale economies.

External economies of scale (EES) occur when per unit costs of production, or average total costs, decline as the volume of output of the *entire* industry expands. As more firms enter an industry, it becomes possible to support other businesses further down the supply chain that can supply cheaper inputs to the industry. A growing industry, especially when firms are located closely to one another, also can support large pools of skilled labor that give firms greater flexibility in hiring. As an industry expands in size it also becomes possible for the public sector to expand the provision of infrastructure such as education, transportation and systems of communications.

We must note that this idea says nothing about the size of the firms that constitute the industry. When external economies of scale exist, the industry might still have many small firms; in fact, we might still suppose that the industry is perfectly competitive, albeit expanding. As we shall see below, the existence of external scale economies has significant implications for international trade.

When external scale economies exist, decreasing average costs has little to do with anything an individual firm does; it has only to do with the fact that the firm happens to be located in an expanding market, and this alone provides the firm with advantages it otherwise would not have.

With *internal* scale economies (IES), decreasing average total costs are due to the choices that the *individual* firm makes. It has nothing to do with what happens industry-wide. Internal economies of scale occur mainly in larger firms with high fixed costs. These fixed costs spread themselves over larger quantities of output and offset the rising variable costs (e.g., labor and materials). Other factors that can reduce average total costs are quantity discounts, specialization within the firm, and adoption of expensive technologies possible only in larger firms. Automobile and aircraft companies are examples of firms that may experience internal scale economies.

External scale economies and trade

Trade among equals: the general equilibrium approach

Suppose that A-Land and B-Land are identical in every respect. That is, they share identical production possibilities frontiers as well as identical indifference curves. Both nations produce computers, the good with increasing returns to scale, and wheat, the good with constant returns to scale. We describe this situation in Figure 5.1. The heavily shaded convex curve is the PPF with maximum computer and wheat output shown as W_{MAX} and C_{MAX}. It is convex because every time we increase the output of computers, the amount of wheat that we must sacrifice diminishes rather than increases. This is a case of increasing returns to scale; it means that the marginal cost of computers falls as output expands, as does the average cost of computers. This is different from the standard case in which marginal costs and average costs rise with the expansion of output. The curves labeled u_1, u_2 and u_3 are three sample indifference curves. They too are convex because we still assume diminishing marginal utility for each good.

In autarky, neither A-Land nor B-Land can reach indifference curve u_3. Each nation maximizes its economic welfare at point E_1 where MRT = MRS, or more precisely from the previous chapter,

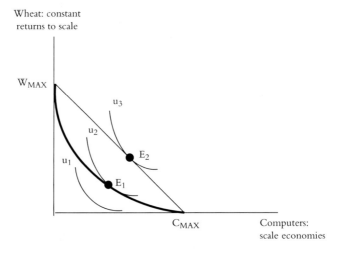

FIGURE 5.1 Constant and increasing returns to scale

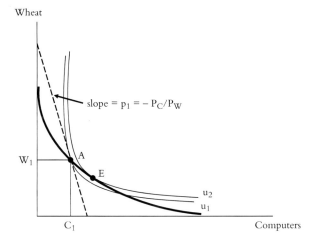

FIGURE 5.2 Adjustments toward optimality

$$MRT = MC_C/MC_W = P_C/P_W = MRS \qquad (5.1)$$

If A-Land chooses to specialize in computer production, it can produce C_{MAX}. If B-Land specializes in wheat, it can produce W_{MAX}. They can then trade along the straight line (the terms of trade line) connecting C_{MAX} and W_{MAX}, thereby maximizing their economic welfare at point E_2 on the higher indifference curve u_3.

Notice that we can reach the same result if A-Land specializes in wheat and B-Land specializes in computers. So, which nation should specialize in computers and which in wheat? The answer is that it does not matter; there is no answer! Either nation can specialize in either good.

If increasing returns to scale characterizes computer production, then the PPF is the heavily shaded curve in Figure 5.2. It is convex to the origin because increases in C production require smaller and smaller sacrifices of wheat production. We also show two possible indifference curves, u_1 and u_2. Remember that there are an infinite number of indifference curves passing through this space.

Suppose we begin at point A on indifference curve u_1. This point also lies on the PPF; it is therefore a feasible combination of output, C_1 and W_1. The dotted line drawn tangent to u_1 at point A has a slope of negative P_C/P_W. This slope represents the price of computers relative to the price of wheat when output is, C_1 and W_1. We call this particular price p_1. At this price, the market for C_1 and W_1 will clear. That is, supply will equal demand for both goods.

Note also that there is another point, point E, which is better than A. Point E is better because it lies on a higher indifference curve, u_2. This says that people in A-Land place a higher value on computers relative to wheat, and would prefer to transfer resources away from wheat and to computers. In fact, E is the optimal point since u_2 is the highest attainable indifference curve.

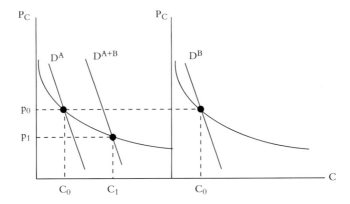

FIGURE 5.3 Cost and demand curves for computers

Moreover, the relative price of computers falls as computer production increases and as the economy moves toward E. We call the optimal price at this point P_E. To see this we must imagine the dashed price line becoming flatter as it reaches its tangency at E. We omit this new dashed line from the graph for clarity.

It is important to note that in the Neoclassical model presented in the previous chapter, the price of computers would rise, not fall, as computer output expands. This is because unit costs *rise* with rising output. Here we assume unit costs *fall* because of scale economies.

Trade among equals: the partial equilibrium approach

We can reach the same conclusion by separately studying the average cost curves for computers and wheat in A-Land and B-Land. We call this a partial equilibrium approach because we pay no attention to what happens in the wheat industries as changes occur in the computer industries.

As we noted above, the marginal and average costs fall with the expansion of output. We show the cost curves for computers only in Figure 5.3. The cost curves for wheat would rise as they normally do in the standard model.

We again assume the two nations are identical; the aggregate demand for computers in each nation (D^A and D^B) is the same, as are the downward-sloping cost curves. In autarky each nation produces C_0 units at a price of p_0. If we arbitrarily select A-Land to specialize in computers, then it could produce enough to meet the total demand for both nations, D^{A+B}, and, because of *external economies of scale*, the world price for computers would be lower at p_1. Both A-Land and B-Land would benefit from lower computer prices, and total computer output would be larger since $C_1 > 2C_0$.[1] Note that, just as in the above section, it does not matter which nation specializes. The results would be the same.

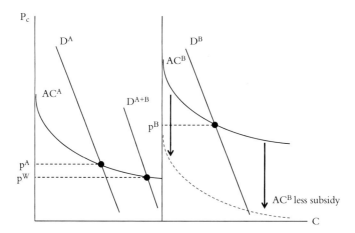

FIGURE 5.4 Trade among unequals

Trade among unequals: differences in scale economies

We now suppose external scale economies exist in both nations' computer industries, but in different degrees. Specifically, imagine that A-Land's and B-Land's cost curves look like those in Figure 5.4.

Demand is identical in both nations. In autarky, computer prices in A-Land are p^A, while computer prices in B-Land are higher at p^B. The average cost curves in both countries have a negative slope because of external scale economies. In this situation we would expect that, with free trade, A-Land would be the low-cost producer and would specialize in computer production. The computer industry in B-Land would likely shut down. Moreover, as the computer industry in A-Land expands output to supply the world market with computers, prices would fall below p^A to the world price p^W as producers there experience external economies of scale.

We might ask why A-Land winds up as the low-cost computer producer and not B-Land. We similarly might ask why London is Europe's financial services center or why the Silicon Valley is the world's high-technology center. One answer could be that A-Land is where there happens to exist the largest pool of engineering talent or where the government has invested the most in higher education. These are the typical explanations for the existence of external scale economies. But these beg further questions: why are these advantages more prevalent in A-Land than in B-Land? The answer typically boils down to serendipity, chance or historical contingency. In other words, there is no easy answer; this is just the way things have worked out.

Does trade always pay?

Suppose a third country, C-Land, now enters the picture. It too can produce computers with external economies of scale. We also assume C-Land is the low-cost

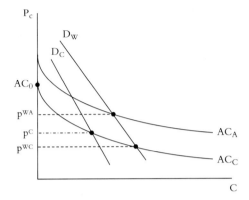

FIGURE 5.5 Three nation case

producer: it makes computers more cheaply than either A-Land or B-Land. We describe this situation in Figure 5.5. Recall that A-Land is already the world's dominant computer producer with average cost curve AC_A. World demand is D_W and the world price is p^{WA}.

Now, C-Land's average cost curve, AC_C, lies below that of A-Land. This is because we assume C-Land to be the world's low-cost producer. If C-Land had arrived on the scene first, it would have been the world's computer producer, and the world price would have been even lower, at p^{WC}.

However, A-Land got there first. Any firm in C-Land that now wishes to begin production would have to pay $\$AC_0$ per unit. This is higher than the ruling world price, p^{WC}. Thus, it would not be able to compete with the prevailing world price established by A-Land. This result is not an optimal use of the world's resources; C-Land ought to be the world's producer.

Another consideration is when C-Land blocks all computer imports in order to support its domestic computer industry. Suppose C-Land's demand curve is D_C in Figure 5.5. C-Land's autarky prices would be p^C. Notice that this price is *lower* than the free trade price of p^{WA} set by A-Land. Free trade does *not* pay!

Strategic government intervention in trade

In the above cases there exist incentives for governments to intervene in trade. When A-Land establishes itself as the "first mover," B-Land's government might respond by subsidizing its computer industry. Without such support, B-Land's computer industry would disappear. The effect of a subsidy could be to lower average costs as indicated in Figure 5.4. Such a policy could tilt the playing field in favor of B-Land so that its computer producers now dominate the world market. A similar result might occur in C-Land where free trade results in higher, not lower prices.

Scale economies: internal

With internal scale economies, cost advantages accrue to the individual firm because of the choices a firm makes. The choices that interest us here are those that determine (1) the volume of output; (2) the characteristics of the product; and (3) the price of the product. All three sets of choices are relevant to the Neoclassical theory of international trade.

The first choice—volume of output—reflects a new assumption, namely, that firms have high fixed costs. This assumption attempts to describe more accurately the nature of manufacturing firms engaged in international trade. Firms must pay these costs even before production operations begin, which is why some refer to these as "set-up costs." The point is that as the scale of operation expands, firms spread their fixed costs over larger amounts of output so that average fixed costs continuously fall. Furthermore, because fixed costs are large, the falling average fixed costs more than offset the increase in average variable costs (e.g., labor and materials). The result is a falling average total cost curve, just as in the case of external economies of scale.

The second choice—product characteristics—is important because firms in the same industry typically sell products with quite different characteristics. This too attempts to describe more accurately the nature of manufacturing firms engaged in international trade. In the automobile industry, for example, we can say that a car is a car, but we cannot say that a Mercedes is a Hyundai. Both cars deliver transportation services to owners, but under very different conditions (comfort, handling, prestige, etc.). We can say the same about Boeing and Airbus aircraft, LG and Sony television sets, and HP and Lenova computers. The key phrase here is *product diversity*, or *product differentiation*. Much if not most of international trade occurs in these kinds of industries, and many nations both import and export products in the same industry. Thus, Germany sells BMWs to Britain and Britain sells Land Rovers to Germany. We call this *intra-industry trade*.

The third choice—product price—reflects differing degrees of interdependence among firms in an industry. This means that all the decisions a firm makes take into account the expected responses of its rivals. This is especially true of price decisions. Thus, when Mercedes sets the price of its vehicles, it will take into account the price of a Lexus. It will likely pay less attention to the price of an entry-level Ford Focus.

All three of these attributes—large-scale production with internal scale economies, product diversity and price interdependence—apply to most international trade, especially trade among the more advanced developed economies. The New Orthodoxy considers these attributes to be a more accurate reflection of the real world of international trade.

This picture differs sharply from that of perfect competition assumed by the standard Neoclassical trade models. In perfect competition, there are a large number of small firms producing identical products at identical prices. Perfectly competitive firms pay no attention to decisions made by rivals, and take market

94 The New Orthodoxy: trade theory recast

prices as given. They are *price takers* while the firms we consider in this chapter are *price makers*. Moreover, the industries considered in the newer orthodox trade models are *imperfectly competitive* because they differ in these fundamental aspects. The implication, of course, is that the real world of international capitalism is "imperfect," but only to the extent that it departs from the ideals embedded in the Neoclassical imagination.

Monopolistic competition

Suppose there are many firms in a differentiated industry, each producing a good with a variety of diverse characteristics. An example is the mobile phone industry in which dozens of firms sell phones with countless features. Each firm has, so to speak, a monopoly in the particular good it produces, yet it competes with other firms producing the same category of good with very different characteristics. Competition is keen, and we assume there is free entry and exit into the industry. However, entry is not easy because fixed costs are relatively high. Neoclassical economics calls this *monopolistic competition* because each firm is a monopolist in its own particular market yet a competitor in the industry.

To simplify matters, assume an industry that produces and sells a constant output of s units. Further suppose there are n firms in this industry. A typical firm will sell $1/n^{th}$ of industry sales s if it charges the same price as everyone else. If the average industry price is $\overline{P}$, and if the firm's price is P, then when $P = \overline{P}$ the firm's market share is s/n. If it charges more than the industry average, its market share will fall, and if it charges less than the average its market share will rise. Because s is constant, if a particular firm in the industry sells more than its proportional share, $1/n$, then others in the industry will sell less. Increased sales can only come at the expense of the firm's competitors.

We can describe this relationship mathematically as

$$Q = s\left[\frac{1}{n} - b(P - \overline{P})\right] \qquad (5.2)$$

In this equation, Q is the quantity demanded of the individual firm's output. Note that when $P = \overline{P}$ then the equation reduces to $Q = s/n$, in which case the firm sells $1/n^{th}$ of industry sales, s. Figure 5.6 below describes these relationships graphically: When the firm raises its price above the average, its sales fall to Q_1 and when the firm reduces its price below the average its sales rise to Q_2. The slope parameter b measures the responsiveness of the firm's quantity demanded to changes in price.

If industry sales, s, expands, then the demand curve will shift to the right, to D', as shown in Figure 5.7. If all firms continue to charge the same price $(P = \overline{P})$, the quantity demanded $Q\star$ of the firm's output will rise to $Q\star\star$.

Similarly, if the number of firms in the industry (n) expands while s remains the same, the demand curve D will shift inward and the individual firm will sell proportionately less.

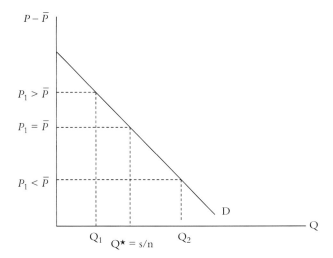

FIGURE 5.6 Firm demand curve

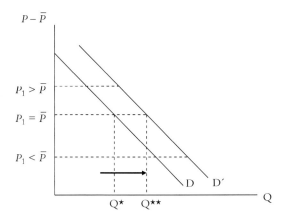

FIGURE 5.7 Shifting demand curve

The above analysis tries to explain the relationship between the firm and the industry of which it is part. The key variables are the number of firms in the industry, the output they produce and the prices they charge. What interests us here is how international trade affects the number of firms in the industry (and hence industry sales) and the average price charged. To answer these questions we construct another graph. This graph will identify the equilibrium number of firms and the equilibrium price. We will then be able to see how trade affects these variables.

First we show how average costs behave when the industry expands and contracts due to entry and exit. To do this we begin by assuming industry sales, s, to be constant. This means that when firms leave the industry, fewer firms share industry sales; each firm produces and sells more output and average costs fall because of scale economies. Therefore, a drop in the number of firms is associated with a

96 The New Orthodoxy: trade theory recast

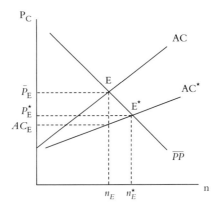

FIGURE 5.8 Average costs

drop in average costs. Similarly, entry of firms into the industry implies each firm receives a smaller share; firm output and sales fall and average costs rise. Therefore, a rise in the number of firms who share constant sales, s, implies a rise in average costs. *Average costs and the number of firms are positively related.* We show this positive relationship as AC in Figure 5.8.

Second, expansion and contraction of an industry affects the average industry price. The key measure here is the degree of competition in the market. As new firms enter the industry, there will be increased competition over the fixed industry sales, s, and vice versa. More competition means firms will lower prices in an attempt to preserve market share, while less competition will raise prices. *The average industry price and the number of firms are negatively related.* We show this relationship in Figure 5.8 as $\overline{PP}$.

The above analysis equips us to identify the market equilibrium. It is at point E where the AC curve intersects the $\overline{PP}$ curve. The equilibrium price is $\overline{P}_E$. If the average price rises above $\overline{P}_E$, there will be economic profits. This will attract new entrants into the industry; the price will fall back down toward the equilibrium price and average costs rise.

The final step shows how international trade affects the monopolistically competitive industry. The key assumption is that moving from autarky to free trade increases the size of the market; national borders no longer limit the size of the market. This means that the value of s in the above analysis increases and existing firms experience larger sales so that s/n rises. Because of scale economies, the higher output leads to lower average costs. This is shown as a shift of the AC curve to AC★ in Figure 5.8.

The market expansion has now increased economic profits. Firms still charge $\overline{P}_E$ but costs are still AC_E. The difference, $\overline{P}_E - AC_E$, is the economic profit. But this condition will not last because the economic profits will draw new firms into the industry. As the number of firms, n, increases, (1) market shares for each firm fall and average costs rise and (2) competition drives down prices, eating into profit margins. These adjustments continue until a new equilibrium is reached at E⋆ with a *lower* price P_E^* and n_E^*.

Once again, Neoclassical theory concludes that free trade, by expanding and integrating markets, increases the number of competing firms and hence the variety of goods produced and lowers prices. As we have already seen in previous sections of this chapter, free trade has little to do with comparative advantage but it is nonetheless good for everyone.

Oligopoly

While monopolistic competition assumes a market occupied by a large number of firms producing heterogeneous goods, oligopoly assumes only a few very large firms dominate the market. In *duopoly* there are two dominant firms, while in *monopoly* there is only one.

When internal scale economies exist, the firm that gets a head start or an early special advantage will profit handsomely, most likely at the expense of its competitors. This is because unit costs fall with rising output, and the firm with a head start can lower its unit costs as it increases its output. If the size of the whole market is limited so that only one firm out of all the oligopolistic firms can exist at a time, then the winner is the one who can capture the market first.

Comparative advantage has nothing to do with the outcome, and specialization—that is, which firm produces what good where—is arbitrary. This has been a recurring theme of this chapter. In addition, the success of a large oligopoly firm brings economic and political advantages to the local and regional communities in which it operates. For this reason there are usually substantial vested interests in the oligopolist's success. Consider, for example, how the fortunes of Boeing affect the fortunes of Seattle and the State of Washington.

We use game theory to model oligopoly. Game theory has proven popular in describing interactions between people and institutions. Its advantage is the ability to describe decision-making interdependencies among firms. By this we mean that the oligopolistic firm always takes into account its rivals' reactions to its business decisions. One such interdependency is the case when a firm decides whether to enter a certain market when it knows that its rivals are considering the same thing.

Consider the hypothetical case of a duopoly in the passenger aircraft manufacturing industry. Say that Boeing is located in A-Land and its rival, Airbus, is located in B-Land. Suppose further that neither Boeing nor Airbus sells its aircraft in its own country: both countries produce only for export to other countries. The decision each firm faces is whether it should produce a particular model of aircraft. The choice is "binary": either the firm produces (P) or it does not produce (NP). Producing yields profits if it is the only one to do so (i.e., the other firm chooses not to produce), while producing results in losses if both choose to produce.

We show in Table 5.1 a *payoff matrix* for this Boeing–Airbus game. The cells in the payoff matrix show the expected gains and losses from different choices.

98 The New Orthodoxy: trade theory recast

TABLE 5.1 Payoff matrix: Boeing and Airbus

		AIRBUS	
		Produce	Don't produce
BOEING	Produce	−5 / −5	0 / 100
	Don't produce	100 / 0	0 / 0

TABLE 5.2 New payoff matrix

		AIRBUS	
		Produce	Don't produce
BOEING	Produce	5 / −5	0 / 100
	Don't produce	110 / 0	0 / 0

If both Airbus and Boeing produce, then both lose $5 billion. We show this in the upper left cell. If Boeing chooses not to produce while Airbus does, then Airbus, as the sole producer, stands to gain $100 billion. Boeing neither gains nor loses. We show this in the lower left cell. Conversely, if Boeing chooses to produce while Airbus does not, then Boeing gains $100 while Airbus gains nothing. If neither produces, then neither gains anything.

There is no solution to this game. That is, none of these outcomes necessarily will occur. However, if we know for sure that one of the two companies will be the "first mover," then we can predict the outcome. If we know that Boeing will produce first, then we can predict that Airbus would choose not to produce since it would definitely lose $5 billion. The same would be true if Airbus produces first. Boeing would then certainly lose $5 billion, so it would stay out of the market.

What is distinctive about this game is that the government of either A-Land or B-Land can alter the outcome. For example, suppose the government of B-Land grants a subsidy of $10 billion to Airbus for each plane it produces, irrespective of what Boeing chooses to do. The new payoff matrix is shown in Table 5.2.

Instead of Airbus losing $5 billion when Boeing produces, it now gains $5 billion (− $5 + $10). And if Boeing chooses not to produce, then Airbus gains a whopping $110 ($100 + $10). Since the government pays the subsidy only if Airbus produces, then the right-hand column would remain the same as before.

What would Airbus and Boeing do in Table 5.2? Assuming both know what the payoff matrix looks like, Airbus would certainly produce since it cannot lose. Boeing, however, would choose to sit it out. If it knows Airbus will produce, then Boeing knows that it will lose $5 billion if it produces. This is a clear equilibrium solution to the game. The main message is that a government can tilt the playing field by altering the expected payoffs. A strategically placed subsidy can change the outcome of the game and bring the benefits of income and employment to the home country. This assumes, of course, that these benefits outweigh the costs of the subsidy and that supporting one industry does not take resources away from other industries.

The Baumol-Gomory Global Conflict Model

The Global Conflict Model demonstrates that trade, even free trade, is often mutually disadvantageous, especially when the trading partners are similar in terms of their economic development. The model is based on the work of Ralph E. Gomory and William J. Baumol (Gomory & Baumol, 2000 and 2009).

In theory, any industry in the world can be located in any nation in the world. It follows that, theoretically, we can distribute all existing industries among all nations in many different ways. Some distributions are better (i.e., more efficient) than others in terms of the world output and wealth they can produce. For example, if all industries are located in nations that provide easy access to the best resources and most advanced technologies, then world output and welfare would be high. On the other hand, if we locate industries in places where such access is limited or nonexistent, then world output and welfare would be low.

The existing real-world distribution of industries is just one of a very large number of possible industrial distributions. To appreciate how many possibilities there are, consider the simple case of ten industries and two nations, A-Land and B-Land. Further assume that each nation must have at least one of the ten industries and that both nations cannot host the same industry simultaneously. Given these assumptions, there would be over 1,023 possible distributions![2] Some of these would be very efficient while others would be very inefficient.

World income and national shares of world income

A given distribution of industries for A-Land and B-Land results in a given national income for each country, where national income is the total value of output (and hence income) produced by all the industries located in each nation. World national income is the sum of A-Land's and B-Land's national incomes. Suppose, for example, a given equilibrium results in A-Land producing a national income of $5 trillion and B-Land producing a national income of $15 trillion. Then world income is $20 trillion, of which A-Land gets 25% and B-Land gets 75%. Figure 5.9 shows this particular distribution and the national income it creates as point A.

The vertical axis measures world income and the horizontal axis measures the share of that total income going to A-Land. Note that we need only show A-Land's share of world income on the horizontal axis because B-Land's share is simply 100% minus A-Land's share, or 100% − 25% = 75%.

Figure 5.10 shows the location of all 1,023 hypothetical points, one of which is

100 The New Orthodoxy: trade theory recast

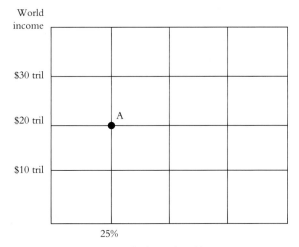

FIGURE 5.9 Output share graph for given distribution

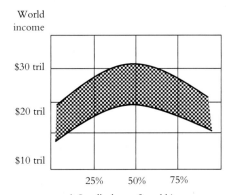

FIGURE 5.10 Output share graph for all possible distributions

Point A (not identified). Note there is an upper and lower bound between which all these points lie. What explains the shape of these boundaries?

The upper boundary represents the maximum world income attainable for each division of world income between A-Land and B-Land. World income reaches a peak, around $32 trillion, when A-Land's share is 45% of world income and B-land's share is 55%. At the endpoints, either A-Land or B-Land produces almost everything, and total world income is at its lowest level (around $20 trillion). In such an extreme case, the nation spreads its labor force over all its industries. Industries make very small quantities and many use resources ill-suited to production. There is very little opportunity for labor to specialize and to take advantage of economies of scale, and unit costs will be high. This situation characterizes many poor developing nations.

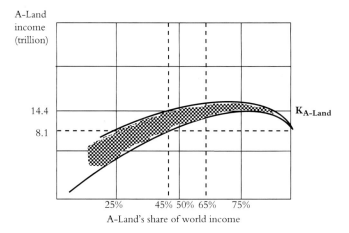

FIGURE 5.11 A-Land's share of world income

If we redistribute the 1,023 industries between A-Land and B-Land so that they produce where resources are better suited to particular activities and where industries can take advantage of unique national physical and human attributes, then efficiency would be greater and unit costs lower. Therefore, near the middle of the graph, world output and income reach a maximum. When A-Land's share is about 45% and B-Land's is about 55%, world output is $32 trillion. Here, A-Land and B-Land resemble developed nations, each with a large number of efficient industries.

Note, finally, that for any given world income share, some distributions are better than others. Thus, when A-Land produces and receives 45% of world income, it is possible that world income is only $18 trillion. This could occur when the assignment of industries to A-Land and B-Land is inappropriate to the resources available. A-Land still receives 45% of world income but that world income is substantially lower.

A-Land's income and its share of world income

Let us see how much national income A-Land produces when its share of world income varies between zero and 100%. We can derive the relationship from the data in Figure 5.10, and we show the result in Figure 5.11. The only difference between these two graphs is that the vertical axis in Figure 5.11 measures A-Land's income alone instead of world income. A-Land's income is simply total world income multiplied by A-Land's percentage share. What explains the shape of this curve?

When A-Land's share of world income is close to zero, it produces nearly nothing and so its income is very low. As its share rises above zero, so too does world output and the trend of all the 1,023 data points rises. This is because both nations start to benefit from specialization and scale economies. When A-Land gets

102 The New Orthodoxy: trade theory recast

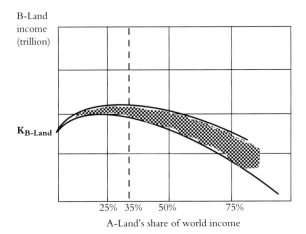

FIGURE 5.12 B-Land's share of world income

45% of world income, its own income lies between $14.4 trillion (45% of $32 trillion), the upper bound, and $8.1 trillion (45% of $18 trillion), the lower bound. When A-Land's share reaches 65% (and B-Land gets 35%), its maximum national income is the highest it can be. Then, as A-Land's share continues to rise beyond the peak of Figure 5.10, world output begins to fall as the distribution of industries becomes less and less efficient. A-Land then has too many industries and B-Land not enough. At the other extreme, when A-Land produces nearly everything, its income is nearly the same as world income (around $10 trillion). We indicate this point at $K_{A\text{-Land}}$. This is equivalent to the case of autarky since A-Land trades nothing and produces everything it consumes.

Figure 5.11 shows that many distributions of industries result in lower income levels than the autarky level of $K_{A\text{-Land}}$. Trade does not necessarily improve upon autarky at these lower points, and A-Land and B-Land would be worse off trading than if they had remained self-sufficient.

In Figure 5.12 we show the same information for B-Land. Because we continue to label the horizontal axis as A-Land's share, we must read the graph from right to left and the explanation for its shape is identical. It is, basically, a mirror image of Figure 5.11 except that B-Land's maximum national income occurs when its share of world income is 75%, or when A-Land gets 25%. In Figure 5.11, we saw that A-Land reaches maximum national income with a distribution of industries that gives it 65% of world income. A-Land's and B-Land's interests are quite different, and conflict can arise between the two nations.

Figure 5.13 combines the two perspectives.

We omit the 1,023 points for clarity and only include the upper and lower bounds for each nation. There we see that there are three zones. In Zone #1, A-Land's share rises from zero (autarky) and B-Land's share falls from 100%. National income increases for both nations in this zone as both gain from specialization and trade. In the middle zone, Zone #2, there is a conflict of interest.

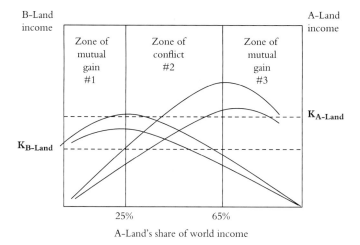

FIGURE 5.13 When conflict over trade exists

There, A-Land's share increases and so too does its national income. But it comes at the expense of B-Land. The latter's share falls and so too does its national income. What is good for one nation is bad for the other. Finally, in Zone #3, A-Land's rising share of world income brings with it declining national income for both nations.

In Zone #1, we could say that A-Land is a poor developing nation with very few industries and B-Land is a rich developing nation with most of the world's industries. Both nations can benefit if some of B-Land's industries relocate to A-Land because their national income would rise. The same interpretation could apply to Zone #3.

The middle zone is consistent with observed trade rivalries between developed nations, such as in the aircraft, automobile and television industries. One nation's ideal position is not the ideal position for other similarly developed nations. As Gomory and Baumol put it, it is not true that "maximizing world output automatically maximizes national prosperity" (Gomory and Baumol, 2000: 40).

Putting the pieces together

In Figure 5.14 we show the connection between the above graphs. It measures income along the vertical axis and A-Land's share along the horizontal axis. The figure only shows the maximum income lines for each nation as well as the world income line. We exclude the 1,023 points for clarity. The world income line is the vertical sum of the individual income lines.

$K_{A\text{-Land}}$ and $K_{B\text{-Land}}$ are the autarky points for each nation. A-Land's maximum income occurs when it gets 65% of total income and B-Land's maximum income occurs when it gets 75% of world income.

If we begin with A-Land producing nothing and B-Land producing everything,

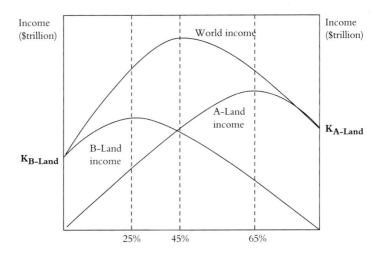

FIGURE 5.14 World income

we are at $K_{B\text{-Land}}$. As A-Land produces more, income for both nations rises, and so does world income. This is Zone #1. After this point, we enter Zone #2. A-Land's share continues to increase, and its income continues to rise. B-Land's income starts to fall, but less so than the increase in A-Land's income. As a result, world output continues to grow. This process continues until world income reaches its maximum. This is where A-Land receives 45% of world income and is the same as the data presented in Figure 5.10.

Policy implications

The invisible hand does not locate industries where they have comparative advantages. Instead, historical and random forces distribute industries, not natural market forces. If this is true, and if it is true that both developing and developed countries can benefit mutually from locating their industries differently, then how can this be done?

From the perspective of the poor developing country, it can try to marshal its economic and political resources to assist local entrepreneurs to enter industries that produce commodities it had formerly been importing. It can also try to obtain development assistance from richer developed countries. Alternatively, the country can try to attract foreign direct investment and technology. China has done this quite successfully. Based on this model, the richer developed countries would benefit from these strategies as well. In other words, they would all be operating in Zone #1.

Difficulties arise when one developed nation attempts to build new strengths in industries already located in another developed nation. This means operating in Zone #2, the zone of conflict. Any benefits derived from strategic economic policies to build up such industries would cause harm to the nation that already possesses that industry. An example is the competition between Boeing, an American company, and Airbus, owned by a consortium of European shareholders. Where should the aircraft industry be located, in Europe or in the United States? Anything the US does to enhance Boeing's market position, and therefore raise US income, comes at the expense of European income. Comparative advantage has nothing to do with the answer.

Conclusions

The harmonious world of Classical and Neoclassical trade theory does not fully describe the contemporary world of global capitalism. In this chapter we reviewed several contemporary models that describe the world as anything but harmonious. These models suggest the possibility that international trade may benefit one nation at the expense of another. They build on the real-world assumption that markets are imperfectly competitive and that much trade is intra-industry trade between nations that are similar.

These new trade theories make a positive contribution to understanding international economics by adding these real-world features to the arsenal of orthodox economic analysis. The orthodoxy thus has expanded to include new elements, which is why we refer to it as the "New" Orthodoxy. One part of the new orthodoxy is rooted in the old doctrine of perfect competition, comparative advantage and mutually beneficial trade, and another part is rooted in imperfect competition, mutually disadvantageous trade and arbitrary specialization.

There are two reasons for calling the new theories "orthodox" and for not considering them to be a heterodox challenge. The first is that these new theories are not that new. The second is that they continue to subscribe to the doctrine of free trade. We consider each of these in turn.

The newness of new trade theory

Mainstream economists often forget that the theory of imperfect competition goes back to the works of Edward Chamberlain and Joan Robinson in the 1930s (Chamberlin, 1933 and Robinson, 1933). This early work appears in almost all microeconomic theory textbooks as well as in the monopolistic competition trade models described above.

As for the reluctance among new trade theorists to accept comparative advantage and free trade as inviolable principles, Frank Graham already expressed this in 1923 when he wrote about the "lack of correspondence of the theory of international trade with the commercial policy of most nations" and about his hesitancy to accept the principle of comparative advantage as "an infallible criterion." Graham even stated that economists "have perhaps been too ready to attribute protection to sheer illusion" (Graham, 1923: 199). This is not to mention the Mercantilist and neo-Mercantilist writers discussed in Chapter 2.

We can also find a full development of the importance to trade of economies of scale in Alfred Marshall's *Pure Theory of Foreign Trade and Pure Theory of Domestic Values*, published in 1879 (Marshall, 1879/1935). There, Marshall showed that the existence of scale economies can lead to falling average cost curves, barriers to entry and multiple trade equilibria. A. C. Pigou said pretty much the same thing in his *Economics of Welfare* published in 1932 (Pigou, 1932).

Much of this older literature reappears again in the 1980s under the name of "new trade theory," albeit in a modern mathematical style.[3] The exception, of course, is game theory, which has been adapted to economic modeling in the 1960s, and the work of Gomory and Baumol. This suggests an historical continuity to orthodox economic theory. There is little to support the idea that the new theories are "counter-cultural" and break with the past in any significant way.[4]

The political economy of free trade

We have suggested in several places in this chapter that there exists in the new orthodoxy a rationale for government intervention in trade. This follows from the finding that free trade is not always optimal, and that governments are able to tilt the playing fields of trade and allow nations to realize economic benefits that might otherwise wind up someplace else. Many have called belief in the efficacy of such interventions the "new interventionism." Alternative names are "strategic trade policy" and "managed trade policy."

Support for government interventionism would truly be a revolutionary position for mainstream economists to take. The fact of the matter is that, with few exceptions, the economics profession does not accept this "new" position. The older Neoclassical orthodoxy greeted with disdain any suggestion that free trade is not ideal; it upheld comparative advantage as a sacred principle and had unshakable faith in the welfare benefits of free trade. While the new orthodoxy has removed the principle of comparative advantage from its pedestal, and introduced many important real world elements, faith in free trade remains unshakable. It is thus misleading to represent the new trade theories as some kind of radical break with the past. It is certainly an advance, and it is different. Yet it remains very much part of the core free trade paradigm.

Nobel laureate Paul Krugman took the job of reconciling theoretical appeal for government trade interventions with the need to remain true to free trade capitalist dogma. In his seminal 1987 article, "Is Free Trade Passé?" Krugman summarizes the main arguments *in favor* of trade intervention. This chapter has described many of these arguments. He then follows with five reasons *not* to follow the new interventionism (Krugman, 1987):

1. It is impossible for governments to know empirically how interventionist policies exactly affect firms' decisions. This is especially true in the game theoretic model: governments can never know the true payoff matrix, mainly because they cannot know the true costs of production. Reality

is far too complex, Krugman's argument goes, for any public agency to understand.

2. The benefits from government intervention may accrue to unintended parties, and may dissipate through the economy in unplanned and undesirable ways. For example, higher profits due to a subsidy might attract unwanted entry of competitors into the market. Alternatively, these added profits might go to foreign owners of the firm's assets.

3. We must assess interventions from a general equilibrium perspective. This means governments must evaluate the costs and benefits of policies not just in the industry directly affected but throughout the economy. The expansion of a subsidized industry might come at the expense of other industries by withdrawing resources. This would be especially troublesome if resources are fully employed. Such a broader macro-perspective once again requires governments to have more knowledge of the economy than it is reasonable to expect them to have.

4. One government's promotion of an industry might trigger a destructive retaliatory response. Governments may perceive interventions by trading partners as unfair and might be inclined to retaliate with offsetting interventions. One often sees just such an inclination in US–China trade relations.

5. Special interests and elites might capture the benefits of a trade intervention if they have special access to power or special knowledge of the policymaking machinery of government.

Krugman calls these arguments the "political economy case for free trade." He concludes that we must still accept free trade for practical reasons, even though the theory supporting it lacks the power to persuade. Says Krugman:

> The economic cautions about the difficulty of formulating useful interventions and the political economy concerns that interventions may go astray combine into a new case for free trade. This is not the old argument that free trade is optimal because markets are efficient. Instead, it is a sadder but wiser argument for free trade as a rule of thumb in a world whose politics are as imperfect as its markets.
>
> *(Krugman, 1987: 143)*

Notes

1 The reason for this is that the lower price causes an increase in the quantity demanded— and supplied—in both nations. If the price had remained the same, then the quantity demanded and supplied would simply be twice what it was before.

2 The calculation is $\sum_{i=110}^{10} C_i = 1023$. We assume each nation must have at least one industry because otherwise it cannot exist.

3 The basic literature on new trade includes: Dixit and Stiglitz (1977); Dixit and Norman (1980); Krugman (1979, 1980 and 1981); and Venables (1982 and 1984).

4 Krugman (2009) refers to those dissatisfied with the conventional trade theory as a counter-culture.

108 The New Orthodoxy: trade theory recast

References

Chamberlin, E. H. (1933). *The Theory of Monopoly Competition.* Cambridge: Harvard University Press.

Dixit, A. K., & Norman, V. (1980). *Theory of International Trade.* Cambridge, UK: Cambridge University Press.

Dixit, A. K., & Stiglitz, J. E. (1977). "Monopolistic Competition and Optimum Product Diversity." *American Economic Review, 67,* 297–308.

Gomory, R. E., & Baumol, W. J. (2000). *Global Trade and Conflicting National Interests.* Cambridge: MIT Press.

Gomory, R. E., & Baumol, W. J. (2009). "Globalization: Country and Company Interests in Conflict." *Journal of Policy Modeling, 31,* 540–555.

Graham, F. D. (1923). "Some Aspects of Protection Further Considered." *Quarterly Journal of Economics, 37,* 199–227.

Krugman, P. R. (1979). "Increasing Returns, Monopolistic Competition and International Trade." *Journal of International Economics, 9,* 469–479.

Krugman, P. R. (1980). "Scale Economies, Product Differentiation and the Pattern of Trade." *American Economic Review, 70,* 950–959.

Krugman, P. R. (1981). "Intra-industry Specialization and the Gains from Trade." *Journal of Political Economy, 89,* 959–973.

Krugman, P. R. (1987). "Is Free Trade Passe?" *Journal of Economic Perspectives, 1,* 131–144.

Krugman, P. R. (2009). "The Increasing Returns Revolution in Trade and Geography." *American Economic Review, 99,* 561–571.

Marshall, A. (1879/1935). *Pure Theory of Foreign Trade and Pure Theory of Domestic Values.* (London School of Economics Reprints of Scarce Works on Political Economy ed., Vol. 1). London: Lund Humphries.

Pigou, A. C. (1932). *Economics of Welfare* (4th ed.). London: Macmillan.

Robinson, J. (1933). *The Economics of Imperfect Competition.* London: Macmillan.

Venables, A. J. (1982). "Optimal Tariffs for Trade in Monopolistically Competitive Commodities." *Journal of International Economics, 12,* 225–241.

Venables, A. J. (1984). "Multiple Equilibria in the Theory of International Trade with Monopolistically Competitive Commodities." *Journal of International Economics, 16,* 103–121.

6

CLASSICAL AND KEYNESIAN INTERNATIONAL ECONOMICS

Introduction

For three quarters of a century, Classical and Keynesian macroeconomics have shared the stage in the mainstream orthodoxy. They have often traded places as the dominant player, usually in response to changes in the broader political and economic environment. Regardless of which school of thought is at the top, however, the heterodoxy has had little chance to participate in their debates.

Classical economics was the first to dominate the discipline until supplanted by the Keynesian Revolution in the 1930s. Keynesian economics then prevailed until the 1970s at which time it succumbed to a Classical counter-revolution. Today, the Classical and Keynesian schools continue to dominate the economics discipline, albeit in much-altered forms. For one thing, the mathematical sophistication of their modeling techniques has grown, so much so that few are able to penetrate their abstruse analyses. Once penetrated, however, one discovers a very simple and almost transcendental view of how the real world works. Additionally, the sharp differences that once existed between the two have now almost disappeared.

This chapter explores the development of each school of thought, with a special emphasis on international economic theory.

An overview of macroeconomics

Classical economists embrace the ideas of 18th- and 19th-century political economists such as Adam Smith, David Ricardo, Jean-Baptiste Say and Thomas Malthus. They believe in an idealized, prototypical capitalism in which full employment and economic stability are the natural state and in which the government plays a minimal and neutral role. Capitalism is self-healing. Left to its own, Classicals believe, capitalism always returns to this ideal state whenever it is disturbed by

110 Classical and Keynesian international economics

exogenous shocks. This is why Classical models assume full employment even though the real world is one of persistent unemployment.

Classical theory applies the same idealized view of capitalism to the world economy. It imagines a world of free markets, a world in which comparative advantage rules and in which governments permit free enterprise to flourish. Free international trade, like free domestic trade, supposedly maximizes the wellbeing of all who participate and allows capitalism everywhere to reach its ideal natural state. This was the mainstream orthodox opinion through the 1930s.

The rise of Keynesian economics

The publication, in 1936, of John Maynard Keynes's *The General Theory of Employment, Interest and Money* changed everything. The book arrived on the scene in the midst of the Great Depression and offered an alternative assessment of this economic catastrophe and of conventional economic theories that apparently had failed to cure it. The *General Theory* is indeed a milestone in the history of economic thought and stands with Adam Smith's *Wealth of Nations* and Karl Marx's *Capital* as one of the great achievements in economic theory.

Keynes's ideas were quite radical for his time. Some of his conservative adversaries even accused him of being a socialist, if not a communist, because he recommended government macroeconomic management of the economy. Keynes vehemently denied the charge. Compounding his critics' suspicions is the fact that the year of the *General Theory*'s publication coincided with the Moscow show trials and the rise of Stalinism. Also at this time many radical leftwing groups in the US and UK had been actively organizing and resisting capitalist institutions. The political and social environment in which Keynes's book arrived was thus highly contentious, to the say the least.

Like Marx, Keynes believed capitalism is inherently flawed. Without some sort of collective action the capitalist system will bring prolonged misery to large segments of the population. Unlike Marx, who believed a revolution is needed, Keynes believed we can design rational public policies to remedy capitalism's flaws.

As for international economics, Keynes had several gripes against Classical trade theory. The first was against the theory of comparative advantage and hence free trade policy. To Keynes, this mechanism works only if we assume full employment and perfect price flexibility. To Keynes, the theory breaks down if (1) unemployment exists; (2) if the economy is not perfectly competitive; or (3) if prices fail to adjust.

Keynes's second gripe was about Say's Law according to which supply creates its own demand. Applying Say's Law to international trade suggests that any increase in the supply of a nation's export good, say because of a technological advance that lowers production costs, also increases its demand while at the same time preserving trade balance. Demand increases because prices and exchange rates adjust. To Keynes this simple extension of Say's Law to international trade reflects wrongheaded supply-side thinking.

A third gripe of Keynes was that when a nation has a trade imbalance it is interest rates that change, not prices, wages and exchange rates. This is because the resulting capital flows either increase or decrease liquidity (i.e., bank reserves), which in turn affects interest rates, investment and employment. Current account imbalances go hand in hand with financial account imbalances.[1]

Keynes believed these Classical ideas fly in the face of reality. Chronic unemployment, excess capacity and persistent trade imbalances are built-in features of capitalism. Prices, wages and exchange rates do not automatically adjust to rebalance trade and guarantee full employment, and therefore tariff protection or some other trade restriction may be a reasonable policy response.

Within academia, *The General Theory* attracted the attention of the world's most famous British economists, including Roy Harrod, James Meade, Oskar Lange, Abba Lerner and J. R. Hicks. All attempted to explain what Keynes meant using geometry and mathematics. Keynes's influence spread even further after the Second World War due in part to Alvin Hansen—the "American Keynes"—who helped to popularize Keynesianism with his 1953 book, *A Guide to Keynes* (Hansen, 1953). In this book Hansen (separately with Hicks) gave Keynesianism its theoretical teeth with the now famous IS-LM model, an analytic framework still used today. Another scholar who popularized Keynes was Paul Samuelson, whose much-acclaimed 1948 textbook *Economics* was the first principles text to be written from a Keynesian viewpoint (Samuelson, 1948).

By the mid-1950s Keynesianism dominated academia and everyone was using the IS-LM model. Even Classical economists began using the model to demonstrate their ideas. Yet, the more attention *The General Theory* received, and the more it became part of the mainstream canon, the more it mutated into something else. As it did so, Keynesianism lost its revolutionary character.

One reason for this was that the political climate in the early 1950s was maliciously anti-communist and anti-left, making it dangerous for anyone to advocate government solutions to economic problems. So economists diluted Keynes's theory by grafting it onto the conventional—and politically more palatable—framework of Classical economics. What emerged was a synthesis of Keynes and the classics, a hybrid Keynesianism.[2] And the IS-LM model became its language. This synthesis was so pervasive that Paul Samuelson could remark, in 1955, that 90% of all economists were neither Keynesians nor Classicals but instead took a middle ground (Samuelson, 1955). Ten years later even Milton Friedman (1912–2006) quipped, "We are all Keynesians now."[3] But the old Keynesianism—the economics of Keynes—was no longer what Friedman had in mind. Joan Robinson (1903–1983) called it "bastard Keynesianism."[4] Paul Davidson calls it a "perversion" of Keynes.

Keynesianism as a special case: the Classical-Keynesian synthesis

Keynes built his theory around the observation that sustained periods of *involuntary* unemployment characterize capitalism. Often, millions are willing to work at

112 Classical and Keynesian international economics

existing wage rates but there are no jobs to hire them. Many Classicals claimed this was because wages were too high, creating an excess supply of labor. To them, the correct policy was to wait for wages to fall, as indeed they eventually must. Once wages fell the economy would correct itself. But waiting for wages to fall was cruel if not absurd given the hardships people were facing in the 1930s.

The hybridized version of Keynesianism explained involuntary unemployment by arguing that prices and wages are rigid or "sticky." Stickiness prevents the labor market from performing its magic. If wages did not fall, then involuntary unemployment would persist. If prices and wages were perfectly flexible, then the Classical conclusion would hold: wages would fall, the quantity of labor demanded would rise and full employment would occur. The original Keynesian theory, in contrast, argued involuntary unemployment could exist even if prices and wages were perfectly flexible.

Hybrid Keynesianism and the "Classical-Keynesian synthesis" refocused attention on market imperfections as the chief culprit. Monopoly and monopsony, government regulations, minimum wage laws, labor unions and trade barriers caused the Classical ideal world to "misbehave." If we remove these imperfections, then capitalism would behave according to Classical predictions. In this way Keynesianism became a special case of the more general Classical theory, rather than an alternative stand-alone vision of capitalism.

The Classical counter-revolution, or the "New Classical" economics

Classical economics experienced a revival in the 1960s and 1970s, spearheaded by Milton Friedman. Friedman's brand of macroeconomics—monetarism— successfully challenged Keynesianism and restored the reputation of the largely abandoned Classical laissez-faire ideology. Friedman galvanized scholarly and political opposition to activist government policymaking and gave new respect to conservative ideology.

The Classical counter-revolution coincided with the decline in enthusiasm for the Johnson-era Great Society programs, the quagmire of the Vietnam War and the rise of Ronald Reagan and Margaret Thatcher. It also coincided with the problems of unemployment and inflation that simultaneously afflicted the US economy in the 1970s. While external shocks, such as the 1973 Arab oil embargo, were largely to blame for these problems, Classical economists took this as an opportunity to blame Keynesianism for failing to explain economic events and even for creating the problems in the first place.

The Classical theory that became the new fashion—the "New Classical" macroeconomics—matured in the late 1980s. It asserts that microeconomics is all we need to understand macroeconomics, and that models of perfect markets and perfect competition are the best models to use. Keynesian theory lacks such a microeconomic foundation. New Classical theory rests on the idea of continuous market clearing, which means supply always equals demand and markets are perpetually in equilibrium. Businesses and individuals in the economy always optimize in the sense that they maximize their profits and utility subject to cost and budget constraints. This focus on the microeconomic foundations of macroeconomics has led to two important New Classical developments: rational expectations theory and real business cycle theory.

Rational expectations theory points to the impossibility of government policy to influence the long-term direction of the economy. This is because people presumably know, more or less, how the economy works and can forecast how government macroeconomic policies will affect them. They will therefore "rationally adapt" to and hence thwart those policies. Real business cycle theory similarly argues that economic fluctuations are merely rational and efficient responses to external shocks to the system. Short-term government macroeconomic policies such as those proposed by Keynesians only disturb the economy and prevent it from adjusting normally. Once again the message is the same: laissez-faire is the only reasonable policy.

And so the pendulum had shifted once again. As Alan Blinder observed, "By about 1980, it was hard to find an American academic macroeconomist under the age of 40 who professed to be a Keynesian. That was an astonishing intellectual turnabout in less than a decade—an intellectual revolution for sure" (Blinder, 1988: 278).

The Keynesian counter-counter revolution, or the "New Keynesian" economics

Mainstream Keynesianism rose to the challenge posed by New Classicals by accepting the latter's new microeconomic concerns. The mantra of both schools thus became "establish macroeconomic theory on microeconomic foundations." But whereas New Classicals continue to stress perfectly efficient markets in continuous full-employment equilibrium with rational optimizing agents, New Keynesians emphasize market failures: imperfect competition, imperfect capital markets and imperfect information. They no longer simply assert price and wage rigidity as causes of unemployment. Now, using microeconomic theory, they try to explain why these rigidities exist in the first place. These explanations, they argue, lie at the root of the unemployment problem.

Among these new microeconomic ideas is "efficiency wage theory." The general idea here is that risk-averse firms may rationally choose to keep wages fixed at above-equilibrium levels, believing this would encourage workers to be more productive. Wages therefore need not fall to market clearing levels, resulting in unemployment. The usual anecdotal argument that unions keep wages from falling thus becomes obsolete.

Another idea is that capital markets often fail to function efficiently because there are no futures markets for the goods that firms sell. Every production decision is risky and firms cannot shift those risks to others in a futures market as many farmers can do. Asymmetries in the information that capital market participants have of potential market risks reduce the efficiency of capital markets even further.

114 Classical and Keynesian international economics

These theoretical advances show that rational optimizing economic agents can make choices leading to the same phenomena—unemployment and price and wage rigidities—that Keynesians identified in their formal aggregate models. This in turn can lead to insufficient aggregate demand, a macroeconomic condition that government policies can correct with "Keynesian" macroeconomic policies.

Elements of Classical international macroeconomics

Classical theory centers on the decisions individuals make about savings and work. Increased thrift leads to more savings, lower interest rates, more investment and more output, income and employment. Increased willingness to work increases the supply of labor, reduces real wage rates and expands output, income and employment. It follows that extravagance and indolence lead to the opposite results. Technology and innovation are also central ingredients in determining economic activity, although without thrift and industriousness their effects would be minimal. In Classical economics these observations are universal and hence apply to all nations.

Pillars of the Classical open economy model

Classical international economic theory rests on the following theoretical pillars.

1. Species flow mechanism

This is the theory that trade imbalances trigger countervailing forces which then automatically eliminate the imbalances. These forces include changes in capital flows which affect the domestic money supply, price levels and exchange rates. For example, suppose a nation experiences a current account deficit such that imports exceed exports. This triggers a net outflow of bullion or species which reduces the domestic money supply, causing domestic prices to fall.[5] Lower prices, in turn, make domestic goods more attractive relative to foreign goods and export expenditures rise, returning the economy to its original balanced position. The opposite events occur if there is a currency account surplus. The balance of payments is therefore an automatic, self-adjusting mechanism.

This adjustment mechanism only works when the price elasticities of demand for traded goods take on certain values. It all depends on how foreigners respond to lower export prices. In the above example, Classical theory assumes that export revenues rise when export prices fall, reversing the trade imbalance. For this to happen exported goods must be relatively price elastic so that revenues from exports rise when export prices fall. Imported goods must also be relatively price elastic so that total import expenditures decrease when import prices rise. But this can only happen when the sum of the price elasticity of demand for imports and the price elasticity of demand for exports is greater than one. This is the so-called

Marshall-Lerner condition, the derivation of which we omit. It implies that the trade imbalance might actually worsen rather than improve.

2. Say's Law

Named after Jean-Baptiste Say, this law states that all income earned in production is spent. As the saying goes, "supply creates its own demand." Savings, which subtracts from aggregate spending, goes to investment, which adds to spending. Thus savings always equals investment and there can be no underproduction or overproduction.

Say's law applies globally as well. Suppose a nation experiences an increase in domestic supply. This will still create an equivalent increase in demand, but some of that demand may be for foreign goods (imports). This increased demand for foreign goods subtracts from aggregate domestic spending. However, it also raises the income of other nations, causing foreigners to spend more on domestically produced goods. This all works through the species-flow mechanism.

Thus, an increase in imports leads to an equivalent increase in exports and Say's Law is preserved. Because trade always balances, we can be certain that total domestic demand for foreign goods will equal total foreign demand for domestic goods— assuming perfectly flexible exchange rates and perfect capital mobility.[6]

3. Loanable funds theory

Savings is a supply of loanable funds and is a positive function of the real rate of interest, r; rising (falling) interest rates induce consumers to give up more (less) present consumption for the promise of more future consumption.[7] Investment is a demand for loanable funds and is a negative function of r; falling (rising) interest rates induce firms to borrow more (less). The real interest rate therefore equilibrates savings and investment by affecting the incentive to save and the inducement to invest. The loanable funds market ensures that savings will always equal investment.

Applying the Classical theory to international economics requires that we assume a global loanable funds market in which a nation's savings are part of a pool of global savings. Domestic investment, then, competes for funds in the global loanable funds market. This implies that if a nation is small relative to the rest of the world then there will be only one prevailing real interest rate—the global rate. Free and unrestricted loanable funds markets ensure that the domestic rate and the global rate will be the same, again assuming perfectly flexible exchange rates and perfect capital mobility.

4. Quantity theory of money

The quantity theory of money consists of four variables. The first is the money supply (M). Classical theory assumes M is exogenous, meaning that only the central bank determines its value. The second is the velocity of circulation of money,

116 Classical and Keynesian international economics

which we assume constant at V_0. It measures the rate at which people spend a unit of money on new domestically produced goods and services in a specific period. It reflects prevailing institutions and customs of payments which change only slowly over time.

The third variable is the domestic price level (P). This is the average price of all goods and services sold in markets. We define the inflation rate as the rate of change in P over some period. Finally, there is *real* aggregate output (Y). In the Classical model Y is the value of the output and income produced at full employment so that $Y = Y_{FE}$. We can now write the quantity theory of money as

$$MV_0 = PY_{FE} \qquad (6.1)$$

The quantity theory of money states that, with V constant, the money supply M only determines the aggregate price level P. It has no effect on real output Y_{FE} and employment, which are determined only by thrift, work and technology. The variable M therefore only determines the nominal value PY_{FE}. The idea that changes in the money supply have a neutral effect on real economic activity is called the *Classical dichotomy*.

International trade comes into play when we consider the terms of trade and the species–flow mechanism, described above. The terms of trade as measured by relative price levels across nations reflects global trade patterns as described by the comparative advantage principle. Suppose, for instance, that a nation's central bank causes inflation by expanding the money supply too rapidly. Higher prices make domestic goods relatively less attractive to foreigners, curtailing exports, expanding imports and causing a trade deficit.[8] However, this sets in motion countervailing forces. Specifically, there will now be a net outflow of bullion or species, reducing the domestic money supply and causing the price level to fall back to where it was before the central bank's inflationary monetary expansion. Lower prices then make domestic goods more attractive again relative to foreign goods and the economy returns to its original position. Exports rise, eliminating the trade deficit.

This analysis has strong implications for monetary policy and central bank control of the money supply. Clearly, trade flows affect the money supply; when there is disequilibrium in the balance of payments (e.g., a trade deficit or surplus) the automatic corrections either expand or contract a nation's money supply, which, according to the quantity theory equation, also affects domestic prices. Thus, monetary policy can have no long-lasting effects, a conclusion that contemporary Keynesian theory roundly rejects, as we shall see below.

5. The labor market and employment

Workers and businesses make employment decisions based on the real wage rate w where $w = W/P$. W is the money or nominal wage rate and P is the price level as determined by the money supply. The real wage rate equilibrates the supply and demand for labor, which by definition results in full employment (i.e., the absence of involuntary unemployment).

The supply of labor derives from workers' leisure–work decisions. We define the labor supply as NS = NS(W/P). The demand for labor depends on labor productivity. We define the demand for labor as ND = ND(W/P). Labor market equilibrium then is

$$NS(W/P) = ND(W/P) \tag{6.2}$$

Note that the nominal wage, W, fluctuates only in response to changes in labor supply and demand, not to changes in P. According to the quantity theory of money the price level P only changes when the money supply changes. Neither workers nor capitalists can influence P.

Things get a bit more complicated when we take into account global trade. The relevant price level in the labor market is not just P but also the prices of foreign goods. More precisely, it is the *terms of trade* that influences real wages and employment and hence output and income. Thus, both domestic and foreign prices enter into the calculations of workers and firms.

Prevailing real wages in other nations also affect employment decisions. As with the real global interest rate, where a single rate prevails, we might imagine that real wages around the world also equilibrate—if we assume labor is perfectly mobile across borders in search of higher wages.[9] Wage differentials would only reflect differences in skills. Accordingly, there emerges throughout the imaginary Classical world a uniform real rate of interest—because capital is perfectly mobile—and a uniform real wage rate—because labor is also perfectly mobile.[10] The money supply determines prices, but neither of these affects real income, output and employment.

6. The production function

The Classical model adopts a neo-Classical component: the production function. This function tells us that the level of employment N, as determined in the labor market, together with the existing stock of physical capital K_0, determines output and income. Formally, we say that, for a given level of technology,

$$Y = Y(K_0, N) \tag{6.3}$$

International trade affects the shape and position of the production function. Following the reasoning of Adam Smith, international trade expands the extent of a nation's market as well as the extent of the division of labor. Trade stimulates economic development, introduces new technologies and raises the skill levels of the nation's labor force. This effectively increases productivity and shifts the production function curve upward, resulting in a higher level of full employment output Y_{FE}.

7. Classical macroeconomic equilibrium

Aggregate output and income (Y) is the sum of domestic consumption (C), domestic savings (S) and imports (M) so that $Y = C + S + M$. The global real interest rate, r_g, determines how people divide their incomes between C and S so that $Y = C(r_g) + S(r_g) + IMP$.[11] For simplicity we provide no explanation here of what determines IMP. Aggregate spending is the sum of consumption spending (C), investment spending (I) and foreign spending or exports (EXP) so that $Y = C(r_g) + I(r_g) + EXP$. Here again we say nothing about what determines exports. The economy is in equilibrium when aggregate output and income equals aggregate spending. We describe this condition as

$$C(r) + S(r) + IMP = C(r) + I(r) + EXP \qquad (6.4)$$

or,

$$S(r) + IMP = I(r) + EXP \qquad (6.5)$$

Equation (6.5) implies that equilibrium between aggregate demand and aggregate supply does not strictly require domestic savings to equal domestic investment. This is because imports and exports automatically absorb any difference between the two. Appendix 6A shows the Classical macroeconomic model in its entirety.

The Keynesian open economy model

Mainstream Keynesian theory incorporates international trade by adding a foreign sector to the conventional "closed economy" IS-LM model. This new direction is due mainly to work by Robert Mundell and Marcus Fleming.[12]

The Mundell-Fleming open economy model consists of three sectors: (1) a domestic *production sector* where consumers and businesses buy consumer goods and capital goods; (2) a domestic *financial sector* where people use their savings to buy financial assets (including cash balances); and (3) an *external sector* where international transactions take place. Market forces generate equilibrium in all three sectors. If one or more sectors is not in equilibrium, then market adjustments occur that re-establish general equilibrium.

Two key endogenous variables link the three sectors: national income (Y) and the real interest rate (r). Both variables determine equilibrium in each sector and there will be only one set of values for Y and r that generates equilibrium in all three. We pay no attention to prices and wages because the model assumes they are rigid, or sticky. This is a major departure from the Classical model that assumes perfect price and wage flexibility.

The production sector

The production sector is in equilibrium when consumers, businesses, government and foreigners plan to purchase all the output produced in a specific period. We define planned aggregate demand as the sum of consumption, investment, government spending and net exports, or $(C + I + G + CA)$.[13] Since Y also represents output, we can write the equilibrium condition for the production sector as

$$Y = C(Y - T_0) + I(r) + G_0 + CA_0 \qquad (6.6)$$

where T_0, G_0 and CA_0 are constants representing tax revenues, government expenditures and exports, respectively. Note that in the Classical model $C = C(r)$ because $S = S(r)$. In the Keynesian model $C = C(Y)$ because $S = S(Y)$. Investment continues to be a function of the rate of interest so that $I = I(r)$.

Given a value for r, there is only one value for Y that can generate equilibrium. If people spend more or less than this amount then output Y adjusts up or down to restore equilibrium. Prices do not play this equilibrating role, because they are rigid. Moreover, a higher interest rate means less investment spending and so equilibrium Y must be lower. The Y–r relationship is negative, therefore, and we assume it is linear.

We name this Y–r relationship the IS curve and assume it is linear. It is a collection of all r–Y equilibrium-generating combinations. The name "IS" refers to the fact that, when aggregate demand equals aggregate output, savings leakages (savings and imports) and investment injections (investment and exports) are also equal.

We can write the following equation to describe the IS curve:

$$r = \alpha - \beta Y \qquad (6.7)$$

where α and β are exogenous parameters the values of which depend on many institutional and behavioral factors such as tax revenues, government expenditures and international trade. We will not specify them here. The parameter α is the vertical intercept of the IS curve and β is its slope, which is negative.

Note that the IS curve shifts right whenever one of the exogenous variables that constitute α and β changes in a way that causes the economy to expand. Examples are increases in government spending, tax reductions and increases in exports. The IS curve shifts left whenever one of these exogenous variables changes to cause a contraction, such as reductions in government spending, tax increases and increases in imports.

The financial sector

The financial sector is where people buy and sell financial assets. The logic of the financial market is as follows. Each person has a choice to make about how to hold income. To simplify, assume only two alternatives: money (defined

120 Classical and Keynesian international economics

narrowly as M1) and a generic non-money financial asset that we call a "bond." Money is riskless to hold yet earns no interest. Bonds earn interest yet are risky to hold.

The demand for money is the flip side of the demand for bonds. When people hold precisely the amount of money they wish, then they will also hold precisely the amount of bonds they wish. An excess supply of money means an excess demand for bonds, and vice versa. Thus, equilibrium between the supply and demand for money implies equilibrium between the supply and demand for bonds. We therefore need to pay attention to only one market. We arbitrarily choose the market for money.

We call the total demand for money L, for "liquidity." There are two parts to L: the *transactions* demand and the *speculative* demand. The former describes how much money people need to pay for day-to-day transactions. Income, Y, determines how large this demand will be. The speculative demand describes how people hold income after they have satisfied their transactions demand. This amount depends on the interest rate r. Higher rates of interest induce people to want to hold fewer cash balances and more interest-bearing bonds, and vice versa.

The other consideration is the real supply of money, M/P_0, where P_0 is the fixed price level. The monetary authorities determine M. This amount sets a limit on how much money people can actually hold. When people desire to hold *exactly* the amount of money the authorities make available, then there is equilibrium in the financial sector. If not, the interest rate changes, causing people to adjust their portfolios until the money supply equals the money demand, L.

For example, if the money supply exceeds the money demand—i.e., excess liquidity—then the interest is too high, or, equivalently, bond prices are too low. Low bond prices (high interest rates) induce people to use their excess cash balances to buy more bonds anticipating that bond prices will rise (interest rates will fall) in value in the future. The lower bond prices are, the greater this inducement. This reallocation of portfolios continues—money used to buy more bonds—until people willingly hold the existing money supply.

Only certain values of Y and r can generate equilibrium in the financial sector. Changes in income cause changes in the transactions demand for money; changes in interest rates cause changes in the speculative demand for money. Only one combination of Y and r brings the supply and demand for money into equilibrium. We can write the equilibrium condition as

$$L(Y, r) = M/P_0 \tag{6.8}$$

which we assume to be linear and positively sloped. We name this relationship between Y and r the LM curve (L for demand for money or liquidity, M for the money supply). It shows all the combinations of Y and r that generate equilibrium. The relationship is positive because a higher value of Y increases the transactions demand for money. With the money supply fixed, there must be a compensating decrease in the speculative demand for money if equilibrium is to be preserved.

This can only happen if people sell bonds, which lowers bond prices and pushes up interest rates. The relevant equation for the LM curve is

$$r = \gamma Y - \delta \qquad (6.9)$$

The parameters γ and δ are exogenous. Their values represent many different behavioral and institutional factors, the values of which we do not specify here. The parameter δ is the vertical intercept and γ is the slope parameter, which is positive.

As with the IS curve, the LM curve shifts to the right whenever one of the exogenous variables changes causing an economic expansion. Among the factors that can cause this to happen are increases in the nominal money supply or in people's willingness to bear risk.

Similarly, it will shift to the left whenever one of the exogenous variables changes, causing an economic contraction. An example is a contractionary monetary policy that decreases the money supply.

The external sector

The external sector shows the balance of payments, BOP, where BOP is the sum of the current account, CA, and the financial account, FA. Thus, BOP = CA + FA = 0. A perfectly flexible exchange rate and unrestricted international capital flows ensure that BOP = 0.

As in the two other sectors, r and Y are the two key endogenous variables. Their values determine the size of both CA and FA. However, only certain values of r and Y will result in BOP = 0. The relevant equation here is

$$r = \lambda Y + r_g + \sigma \qquad (6.10)$$

The exogenous parameter σ represents all those domestic and foreign influences on the balance of payments that we hold constant such as foreign incomes. The exogenous parameter r_g represents foreign interest rates.

Note the positive relationship between Y and r. To see why this is so, suppose domestic income rises. Imports then will increase, the current account balance will turn negative and indebtedness will rise. To make this new debt possible, a higher domestic interest rate is necessary to attract more capital to buy new debt instruments. Thus, a rising r accompanies a rising Y.

Two points require further explanation in this model. First, we assume a perfectly flexible foreign exchange rate. This means that a current account deficit would depress the value of the nation's currency as people sell off that currency to buy more foreign goods. It also means interest rates would rise, attracting foreign capital to buy the new debt instruments used to finance the current account deficit. This causes a surplus in the FA account, which offsets the CA deficit. Hence it is still true that BOP = 0.

Second, if we presume that all financial assets are identical in every respect, no matter the countries from which they originate, then there should be no difference between domestic and foreign interest rates. People would be indifferent between foreign and domestic bonds. If this is the case, then $r = r_g$ and

$$r - r_g = 0 = \lambda Y + \sigma \qquad (6.11)$$

Solving this equation for Y we get

$$Y = -\frac{\sigma}{\lambda} = \text{constant} \qquad (6.12)$$

Here the domestic interest rate coincides exactly with the global interest rate. Owners of wealth, all around the world, are indifferent between investing in their own domestic economies and investing elsewhere in the world. The capital inflows and outflows occurring in equilibrium serve to balance the current account.

The ease with which capital flows into and out of a country depends on currency restrictions and capital controls that many nations impose on foreign investment. If there is zero capital mobility between nations, then the interest differential $(r - r_g)$ does not matter. If there is "perfect" capital mobility, then an infinitesimal increase in r will cause the entire world's wealth to flow into that nation.

The model in its entirety

We now have three sectors and three equations that describe the entire open-economy:

Product sector equilibrium (IS curve) $r = \alpha - \beta Y$ (6.13)
Financial sector equilibrium (LM curve) $r = \gamma Y - \delta$ (6.14)
Balance of payments equilibrium (BOP curve) $r = \lambda Y + r_g + \sigma$ (6.15)

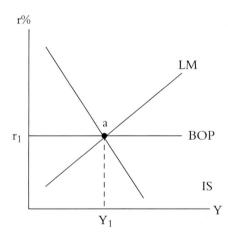

FIGURE 6.1 IS-LM-BOP equilibrium

This economic model has a single solution that consists of an interest rate, r_1, and a level of income and output Y_1. That solution is shown in Figure 6.1.

Internal and external balances: the Swan-Salter model

James Meade, in his seminal 1951 work *The Theory of International Economic Policy*, asked the following question (Meade, 1951). What is the interconnection between macroeconomic policy and internal and external balances? The internal balance is where aggregate demand equals aggregate supply. In Keynesian theory, this may or may not coincide with full employment. The external balance refers to the current account balance. What happens to the current account balance when the government, in an attempt to create full employment, applies an expansionary fiscal or monetary policy, thereby changing the internal balance?[14] Are the two accounts irreconcilable?

In 1955 the Australian economist Trevor Swan asked a similar question:

> Since Keynes published *The General Theory* in 1936, it has been widely accepted that the two fundamental propositions of a full employment policy are a) that incomes and employment depend on the level of spending; and b) that there is no automatic mechanism to keep spending near its full employment level without conscious action by economic and financial authorities. But the balance of payments equally depends on the level of spending. Must it be only a happy chance if the "internal balance" and "external balance" levels of spending coincide?
>
> *(Swan, 1968: 167)*

Swan's approach to this dilemma identifies two categories of government policies, *expenditure-changing* policies and *expenditure-switching* policies. An expenditure-changing policy is one that influences aggregate demand through either fiscal or monetary policy. An expansionary expenditure-changing policy increases income which, in turn, causes the current account to move toward deficit. The opposite holds true for a contractionary expenditure-changing policy. An expenditure-switching policy changes the nation's exchange rate. For example, depreciating a currency increases exports and decreases imports; it switches spending from foreign to domestic goods causing the current account to move toward surplus.

We can use this terminology to restate the above question: how can a nation use expenditure-changing and expenditure-switching policies to bring about simultaneously an internal and external balance? We refer to the Swan diagram in Figure 6.2.

The vertical axis measures the value of the dollar relative to the euro, while the horizontal axis measures aggregate expenditures.[15] The line labeled External Balance represents all points where the current account is balanced. Any point to the right of this line denotes a current account deficit. This is because, as we move to the right, expenditures increase, causing national income to increase as well, and

124 Classical and Keynesian international economics

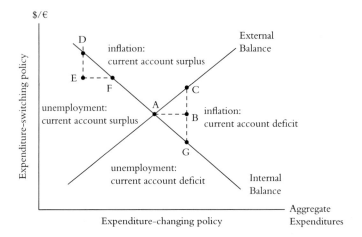

FIGURE 6.2 Swan diagram

with it imports (i.e., a current account deficit). For similar reasons any point to the left denotes a current account surplus.

The line labeled Internal Balance represents all points where aggregate expenditures equal output. By assumption, any point on this line also implies full employment. Any point to the right of this line denotes inflation. This is because the economy already is at full employment so that any increase in expenditures will cause inflation. Moreover, any point to the left of this line represents a decrease in expenditures and hence higher unemployment.

Based on this logic, the diagram has four discrete regions showing the four combinations of inflation, unemployment and current account surplus and deficit. These four regions are often called the "zones of unhappiness."

We start at point A. Here there is both internal and external balance as well as full employment. Suppose the government now initiates an expansionary expenditure-changing macroeconomic policy. Rising expenditures constitute a rightward movement from point A to point B. This will be inflationary since we are already at full employment. Also, at the existing exchange rate, incomes rise as do imports. This causes the current account to move to a deficit. To restore external balance the government would have to depreciate the currency; the value of the dollar must fall relative to the euro. This implies moving upward from B to C on the diagram.

If instead we start at point D and increase the value of the dollar, then exports will fall and imports will rise. Demand switches from domestic goods to foreign-made goods and unemployment will rise. We then will wind up at point E. In order to preserve full employment the government would then need to apply an expansionary expenditure-changing policy. This means moving from E to F.

An interesting case is point G in the diagram where we have a current account deficit and unemployment. What combination of policies will restore internal and external balance and full employment? To restore external balance requires a large

Classical and Keynesian international economics **125**

currency devaluation expanding exports and reducing imports. However, as this policy pushes point G toward B and C inflation sets in. This would require a *contractionary* policy to push the point leftward toward A. This is a rather counterintuitive result. Moreover, if the nation is committed to fixing or pegging its exchange rate then it may be impossible to have both internal and external balance. Additionally, a one-time currency devaluation might invite currency speculators to question the nation's credibility and initiate a speculative attack.

The effectiveness of monetary and fiscal policy: the Mundell-Fleming model

The Mundell-Fleming model is similar to the Swan model except that it only examines expenditure-changing macroeconomic policies. Specifically, Mundell-Fleming asks how different exchange rate regimes—flexible and fixed—influence the effectiveness of fiscal and monetary policy in a world of price rigidities. We begin with fiscal policy assuming all three sectors are in initially equilibrium at point *a* in Figure 6.3.

Fiscal policy entails changing the values of T_0 and G_0 in the IS curve. An expansionary fiscal policy consists of a decrease in T_0 and/or an increase in G_0, which generates more spending and saving. The IS curve shifts to the right and point *a* moves rightward as Y rises. What actually happens to the interest rate depends on how the LM and BOP curves react. This in turn depends on what kind of exchange rate regime we have. We explore this in the next two sections.

Monetary policy affects the LM curve. An expansionary monetary policy consists of an increase in the real money supply, which shifts the LM rightward. This also begins to move point *a* rightward. A falling price level (i.e., deflation) has the same effect because it expands the purchasing power of the money supply, which is the same as an increase in the nominal money supply. Once again the effect on interest rates depends on how the LM and BOP curves respond. Of course the IS and LM curves shift in the opposite direction when these policies are contractionary.

A floating exchange rate regime

In Figure 6.3 we begin at point *a*. First we apply an expansionary monetary policy which shifts the LM curve to LM'. We display the Keynesian narrative in this figure. The increased liquidity first lowers interest rates, inducing more investment. As a result, output and income also rise and the equilibrium point shifts to point *a'*. But this has a feedback effect on the IS curve because rising income expands imports, causing a CA deficit and a FA surplus. More capital begins to flow out of the country to pay for the CA deficit. Expanding imports of goods and expanding exports of financial assets depreciates the currency, making domestic products relatively cheaper for foreigners. This in turn expands exports. The IS curve now shifts rightward, to IS', moving the economy to a final equilibrium at *a''*. The result is that an expansionary monetary policy causes output and income Y to rise to

126 Classical and Keynesian international economics

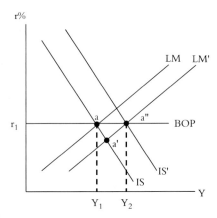

FIGURE 6.3 Expansionary monetary policy: floating rates

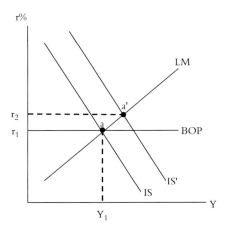

FIGURE 6.4 Expansionary fiscal policy: floating rates

Y_2 leaving interest rates unchanged while exchange rates rebalance the balance of payments.

Turning now to an expansionary fiscal policy, we begin again at r_1 and Y_1 or point a. The government now lowers taxes T_0 and/or increases spending G_0. This causes the IS curve to shift rightward from IS to IS' as in Figure 6.4.

At the original interest rate r_1, higher income means the demand for money rises, exceeding the supply of money. People respond by selling bonds which causes bond prices to fall and interest rates to rise to r_2. The new equilibrium point is a'. However, the adjustments continue as higher domestic interest rates attract more foreign capital. This inflow of capital increases the demand for the nation's currency causing its value to appreciate. This currency appreciation reduces the foreign demand for goods, causing exports to drop and shifting the IS' curve back to where it started at IS. Income remains at Y_1 and interest rates remain higher at

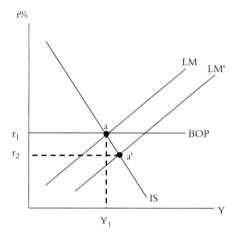

FIGURE 6.5 Expansionary monetary policy: fixed rates

r_2. Fiscal policy is ineffective because of the countervailing effects on capital flows and exchange rates.

The Keynesian conclusion is that when exchange rates are perfectly flexible monetary policy works and fiscal policy does not. Full employment may or may not exist at the general equilibrium points.

A fixed exchange rate regime

One can guess that the results here will be the opposite of those reached above. Indeed this is this case. Monetary policy now becomes ineffective while fiscal policy becomes effective.

In a fixed rate regime the monetary authorities engage in currency interventions in order to keep the exchange rate unchanged. They do this by buying and selling the nation's own currency in the world currency markets; they buy currency to push its value up and sell currency to push it down.

When the central bank pursues an expansionary policy it shifts the LM curve rightward to LM'. We show this shift in Figure 6.5. This policy expands income and lowers interest rates. Imports will rise because of the higher incomes and people will sell their currency to acquire foreign exchange. Also, the lower interest rate causes capital to flow out, seeking more attractive financial returns elsewhere in the world. The new equilibrium moves to point a'. Both of these events—expanded imports and capital outflows—depreciate the currency.

To preserve the value of its currency the central bank now must *buy* its currency on the world currency markets in order to offset the sell-off stemming from higher imports and capital outflows. This intervention effectively reduces the money supply which shifts the LM curve back to where it was originally. The result is that we wind up where we began, at point a: monetary policy is now ineffective. An expansion in the money supply is matched with a reduction in the money supply.

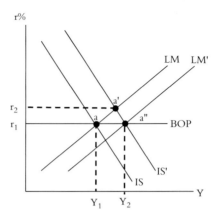

FIGURE 6.6 Expansionary fiscal policy: fixed rates

TABLE 6.1 Summary table: fixed and floating rates

	Fixed rate regime	Floating rate regime
Monetary policy	Does not work	Works
Fiscal policy	Works	Does not work

Turning to fiscal policy, assume the government lowers T_0 and/or increases G_0. In Figure 6.6 we see that this shifts the IS curve to IS', causing income to rise and interest rates to rise to r_2. The equilibrium point moves to a'.

The higher interest rates induce an inflow of capital. But foreigners must buy the nation's currency in order to buy domestic financial assets. This drives up the value of the currency. The central bank must now sell the nation's currency to neutralize the appreciated currency. This expands the money supply, causing LM to shift to LM' and the equilibrium to settle at a'' and income Y_2.

The final result is that the expansionary fiscal policy has raised incomes while leaving the interest rate—and the exchange rate—unchanged. Fiscal policy now works, aided by the necessity to keep exchange rates constant.

We show the results of our analysis in Table 6.1.

A nation that obligates itself to fix its exchange rate while permitting capital to freely flow in and out relinquishes control over its domestic monetary policy. Only if it also restricts capital flows can a nation continue to apply monetary policies directed at solving domestic economic problems. The literature coined the phrase "policy trilemma" to describe the choices a nation can make between monetary policy autonomy, exchange rate stability and unrestricted capital flows.

New open economy macroeconomics

Recent developments in New Classical and New Keynesian economics have led to complaints that the workhorse Mundell-Fleming model is too aggregative and

Classical and Keynesian international economics **129**

lacks suitable microeconomic foundations. How exactly, Classical critics ask, do decisions made by individual consumers and producers lead to the highly aggregative relationships shown in the IS-LM-BOP model? In 1995 Maurice Obstfeld and Kenneth Rogoff responded to this criticism with a much-cited article that triggered a new research program called the "New Open Economy Macroeconomics" (Obstfeld and Rogoff, 1995). The authors try to address the same general questions as the Mundell-Fleming model, namely, how domestic macroeconomic policies affect output, exchange rates and welfare in trading nations. But they do so using a Neoclassical microeconomic framework of analysis.

In many ways the Obstfeld-Rogoff approach is similar to the 2-nation, 2-good, 2-factor Neoclassical trade model examined in Chapter 5. There, each nation has a single aggregate community preference function that citizens collectively maximize subject to a cost constraint. That cost constraint is defined by each nation's production possibilities frontier and relative factor prices (i.e., wages and interest rates). Because that model assumes perfect competition, relative output prices are proportional to relative marginal costs (i.e., P = MC). The Neoclassical analysis leads to a balanced trade "solution" consisting of a certain quantity of imports and exports, terms of trade (i.e., import prices relative to export prices) and exchange rates. The general welfare conclusion of this model is that citizens in both nations consume more of each good when there is free trade than in autarky (in which case their consumption is limited to what they can produce by themselves).

Obstfeld and Rogoff, on the other hand, construct a 2-nation multi-good general equilibrium model of an economy without fixed capital and without trade barriers. They explicitly assume price rigidities and imperfect competition, which gives the model a distinct Keynesian character, although its analytical framework is still very Neoclassical.[16] The model requires advanced mathematical techniques, so we will only sketch its broad features here and enumerate some of the main conclusions.

The Obstfeld-Rogoff model is intertemporal, and hence dynamic. Agents make decisions over an infinite time horizon. The values of the system variables in each period determine their values in the next period. The older Neoclassical trade model, on the other hand, is static; everything happens in a single period and the solution is a single set of values for imports, exports, prices and exchange rates. In the Obstfeld-Rogoff model the solution is a *time path* of values that we call a "steady state" solution. A "steady-state solution" is one in which the values for variables grow over time at specific rates that maintain general equilibrium through time. Any deviation from this steady state equilibrium solution pushes the system off the rails, so to speak, causing disequilibrium and imbalances. Roughly speaking, we can say that the Obstfeld-Rogoff model shows how the old Neoclassical trade model moves through time, from one period to the next, into the infinite future.

In the Obstfeld-Rogoff model, each agent produces one good and consumes multiple goods. In every period agents must choose (1) how much to work and produce; (2) how much to consume; and (3) how to allocate savings between real money balances and bonds. Bonds trade internationally, are riskless and earn a real

130 Classical and Keynesian international economics

interest rate of r%. Agents make all these choices by maximizing their intertemporal utility subject to their intertemporal budget constraint. Three elements determine total utility: the amount consumed, real cash balances (M/P) and labor expended to produce output and income. The first two elements have a positive effect on utility while the third has a negative effect (disutility). Additionally, agents in both nations have identical preferences, making the analysis similar to the Neoclassical $2 \times 2 \times 2$ model that has only a single community preference function.

We write the utility function as

$$U_t^j = U_t^j\left(C, \frac{M}{P}, -ky\right) \tag{6.16}$$

where j is an index identifying each person in the population and t identifies a particular time period. C is total home consumption, M/P is real money balances, y is output/income and k is a constant that translates output into work effort (disutility). We can add the utility functions for each nation to derive the world utility function.

The budget constraint measures how much money is available to each agent. That amount equals: (1) the increase from the previous period in the value of money balances and bonds; (2) the current income generated from sale of output produced; (3) minus the amount consumed; and (4) minus taxes (T). We write the constraint as

$$P_t B_t^j + M_t^j = P_t B_{t-1}^j (1 + r_t) + M_{t-1}^j + p_t(j) y_t(j) - P_t C_t^j - P_t T \tag{6.17}$$

The left-hand side shows the size of a person j's wealth in period t. It consists of bonds valued at $P_t B_t^j$ and nominal money balances M_t^j. The right-hand side of the equation shows where this money comes from. It is the sum of (1) the value of bonds held in the previous period $P_t B_{t-1}^j$ multiplied by its growth at interest rate $(1 + r_t)$; (2) the unused money balances held over from the previous period; (3) the income earned from work in the current period (output y times price p); (4) total current consumption expenditures; and (5) total current lump sum taxes (government budgets always balance).

Prices are rigid because they are set in the previous period and taken as given in the current period. Also, because the model assumes imperfect competition, prices also exceed marginal costs. The exchange rate is simply the domestic price of the foreign currency. These considerations do not appear explicitly in the above equations. This is because we omit the more advanced mathematics.

Agents in the Obstfeld-Rogoff model are rational optimizers. They maximize utility over time subject to the budget constraint, which also changes over time. In each period there are equilibrium conditions that decisions must meet, namely: money supply must equal money demand; bond supply must equal bond demand; and total world production must equal total world consumption. The steady state solution is a time path of prices and output quantities, an interest rate and an exchange rate. Note, finally, that because there is imperfect competition, the output produced over time will always be less than what it would be in perfect competition. This is a well-known welfare result of microeconomics.

We now turn our attention to macroeconomic policy. The Obstfeld-Rogoff model introduces a monetary shock that takes the form of an unanticipated permanent rise in the money supply *in one of the nations*. The authors use their model to calculate the welfare effects of this policy in both nations. In other words, they ask how it affects intertemporal consumption, real money balances and work effort. These are the three items included in the utility functions. So we are really asking how it affects utility or wellbeing.

Avoiding the mathematical details, the model concludes that a monetary shock in the *home* nation increases *world* aggregate demand, mainly because the world interest rate falls. It also permanently increases consumption in *both* nations. Furthermore, the monetary shock depreciates the currency of the nation undertaking the monetary expansion, improves its terms of trade and causes its current account to move toward a surplus. This implies that demand shifts from the foreign nation to the home nation, causing home output to rise relative to the foreign nation.

Thus, both nations are better off. One reason for this has to do with the imperfect competition assumption. As we noted above, the level of output prior to the monetary shock was too low relative to perfect competition. A basic result of Neoclassical economics is that imperfect competition—monopolistic competition, oligopoly or monopoly—reduces output and transfers benefits from consumers to these imperfectly competitive businesses. This is a sub-optimal or inefficient result. This implies that an increase in world output due to a monetary shock moves both nations toward a more efficient position, thereby improving their welfare.

The positive effect on home and foreign output is asymmetric, however. It is also ambiguous for foreign output. This is because the lower interest induces more foreign output, yet, because of the depreciation of the home currency, foreign goods become more expensive. It is uncertain which force wins out. Nonetheless, both nations are better off—permanently.

Economists have paid less attention to the effects of a fiscal shock, although Obstfeld and Rogoff address this possibility in their first 1995 article. Assuming sticky prices and imperfect competition, they find that a permanent unilateral fiscal shock positively affects aggregate demand in both nations. Consumption increases everywhere. However, citizens of the home country alone shoulder the taxes that finance the fiscal shock, which causes home consumption to decrease *relative* to foreign consumption. Because of this, the home country's exchange rate devalues as the demand for its currency falls *relative* to the demand for the foreign currency. Home output increases as foreigners' demand for home-produced goods rises. The home country runs a surplus due to expenditure switching: more foreign demand, relatively less home demand. A permanent unanticipated fiscal policy thus "tilts" the time profile of spending.

All of these results derive from calculating analytical solutions to complex equations describing highly abstract and hypothetical situations. The Obstfeld-Rogoff model is important because it initiated a research program that incorporated "Keynesian" assumptions. The conclusions reached indicate that when trading economies are not perfectly competitive, and when prices are sticky, macroeconomic policies can have positive and permanent effects. This contradicts the conclusions of traditional Classical theory, which assumes perfect competition and perfect price flexibility. In the Classical world macroeconomics policies only affect nominal values and have no real effects at all. However, with imperfect competition and price rigidities macroeconomic policies can have real effects. They can also drive the economy closer toward the Classical optimal efficiency.

Global Classicism: Neoliberalism

The dispute between Classicals and Keynesians applies to many global policy issues. The issues that have attracted the most attention in recent years include transition policies for post-communist nations, Eurozone indebtedness, development strategies for poor nations, IMF and World Bank lending practices, currency crises and chronic trade imbalances. We cannot examine these issues here, although it ought to be rather easy by now to guess where Classicals and Keynesians stand. This section surveys the general approach each school takes in dealing with these issues.

Neoliberalism

Global Classicism, which we may also call *Neoliberalism*, is the application of Classical economics to global public policy. It seeks to reduce the role of government and to permit the market to make decisions normally left to non-market political and social institutions. It advocates free trade and the privatization of government assets. It renounces government management of the economy and government channeling of scarce resources to particular industries. It preaches fiscal discipline and fiscal austerity, reduced regulation and cutbacks in social programs. Neoliberals believe this is the only way to ensure growth and prosperity.

Neoliberalism rose to prominence in the 1980s during the Reagan and Thatcher administrations and coincided with the Classical counter-revolution. It quickly became the new conventional wisdom and dominated the policy agendas of most advanced capitalist nations and global institutions.

The term "liberalism" is potentially confusing and warrants clarification. Liberalism first appeared in the lexicon of political economy as a response to absolutism and feudal privilege. This was when capitalism was just beginning to take shape. Expressing the interests of the growing capitalist class against the entrenched interests of the aristocracy, monarchy and Church, liberalism provided the ideological foundation for a society increasingly dominated by commerce, production for profit and wage labor. When used in conjunction with the word "Classical," as in Classical Liberalism, it refers to the views of the 18th- and 19th-century Classical economists who promoted market capitalism and the freedom of individuals to pursue their self-interest. Adding the prefix "neo" to the word Liberalism signifies a set of economic policies founded on contemporary Classical economics.

The Washington Consensus

One often hears other terms describing global Classicism. For instance, some use the term *The American Model*, which suggests that these ideas originated in the US to promote American global interests and values. George Soros, the renowned financial entrepreneur and philanthropist, scornfully described global Classicism as *market fundamentalism*. The expression "fundamentalism" implies Neoliberals are misguided in their steadfast faith in market-based solutions to social and economic problems.

Yet another common term is *Washington Consensus*, a phrase John Williamson coined in 1989 to describe the Neoliberal policies recommended by so-called Beltway insiders. These were Washington economic advisors and consultants promoting the application of Classical ideology (Williamson, 1990). Many of these people are economists working for the president's administration, the Federal Reserve Bank, the US Treasury, the IMF, World Bank, World Trade Organization, United Nations and various Washington think tanks.

In his 1989 article Williamson offered a list of ten Neoliberal policy instruments to which, he believed, Washington insiders would readily consent. It is worth enumerating these policies here:

1. *Fiscal discipline.* This applies mainly to nations experiencing persistent budgetary and balance of payments deficits. It recommends making structural or administrative changes that allow governments to monitor and maintain vigilance in controlling spending. Failure to do this results in inflation, balance of payments deficits and capital flight. Fiscal discipline stops short of requiring balanced budgets, so long as the debt/GDP ratio does not deteriorate further.
2. *Reordering public expenditure priorities.* Governments must reallocate expenditures away from indiscriminate subsidies to particular sectors and special interest groups and to programs that the majority of people need such as health care and education as well as infrastructure investment.
3. *Tax reform.* The goal here is to raise tax revenues and to make taxation more efficient. One recommendation is to broaden the tax base and lower marginal tax rates to moderate levels.
4. *Interest rate liberalization.* The idea here is to ensure that interest rates are market determined and that real rates are positive in order to attract foreign capital.
5. *Competitive exchange rates.* A nation's exchange rate ought to be "appropriate" to (i.e., consistent with) the nation's macroeconomic policy objectives. Governments can accomplish this either by fixing the rate at the appropriate level or allowing the rate to float so that it seeks that level automatically.
6. *Trade liberalization.* This means eliminating quantitative import restrictions

134 Classical and Keynesian international economics

because these encourage corruption. Tariffs are preferred although the general view is that free trade is the best and protectionism is unacceptable.

7. *Unrestricted inward direct investment.* This entails elimination of controls over and channeling of inward direct investment.

8. *Privatization.* This entails selling off government-owned enterprises and assets to private investors. One advantage of such privatization is that a sell-off of government assets yields revenues that can help balance the government's budget. The underlying rationale is belief that private industry is more efficient than state-run industry.

9. *Deregulation.* This policy would do away with government regulations of market entry and exit for foreign corporations, terminating restrictions on competition and deregulating labor markets. A weakening of social and environmental protections often accompanies such deregulation.

10. *Property rights.* This is the widely accepted capitalist doctrine that nations must provide legal protection for all property owners.

Many Latin American nations made extensive use of Neoliberal policies in the 1980s and 1990s in response to growing levels of domestic and external debts. Influenced largely by international lending institutions such as the World Bank and the International Monetary Fund, these nations adopted many of the Neoliberal reforms itemized by Williamson. Similar polices were adopted in Asia after the East Asian financial crisis of 1997. Several Eurozone nations such as Portugal, Italy, Greece and Spain have been applying painful Neoliberal policies in the wake of the Eurozone sovereign debt crisis. Even nations with little or no debt problem have been sharply curtailing expenditures and raising taxes in fear of succumbing to "Greek-like" insolvency problems even if these policies promise to cause unemployment and slower growth.

Not surprisingly, Neoliberalism has encountered strong opposition, not only from grassroots organizations but also from prominent economists such as Nobel Prize winners Joseph Stiglitz and Amartya Sen. Common complaints include the charge that Neoliberalism erodes working conditions and the wellbeing of the working classes and the poor; that it transfers economic and political power away from local communities to property owners, large corporations and social elites; and that it exacerbates already intolerable inequalities in the distribution of income and wealth.

Global Keynesianism

Just as global Classicism (Neoliberalism) applies the ideology and theory of Classical economics, global Keynesianism applies the ideology and theory of orthodox Keynesian economics.

Global Keynesianism advocates government management of both domestic and international economic affairs, albeit within the context of the existing capitalist status quo. It promotes cooperation among nations in managing their financial

Classical and Keynesian international economics **135**

affairs and in addressing common economic problems. This requires nations to view themselves as belonging to an international community and to understand that income and employment in each nation depends on income and employment in other nations. The ultimate goal of global Keynesianism is to achieve and maintain high employment, rising standards of living and avoidance of global financial instability. Free markets, free trade, flexible exchange rates and perfect capital mobility are unlikely to accomplish these goals and may even undermine them.

The postwar Bretton Woods institutions—the International Monetary Fund, World Bank and the World Trade Organization—were designed to play a large role in reaching these goals.[17] Keynes, of course, was one of the architects of these institutions. The European Union and many other regional associations potentially serve these goals as well. But things have not quite worked out that way, especially after the Classical counter-revolution in the 1970s. Indeed, most global institutions began to espouse Neoliberal Classical policies that conflicted with Keynesianism and even imposed on member nations conditions requiring them to conform to the strict Classical teachings of the Washington Consensus. However, after several global financial crises, including the 2009 financial meltdown, there seems to have been a revival in Keynesian thinking and a retreat of Classical thinking.

Global capital flows

Cross-border capital flows make up a large part of the world economy. In 2007 such flows comprised about 20% of world GDP and were growing three times faster than world trade flows. Capital flows then contracted sharply during the 2009 global financial crisis and have slowly recovered.

There has been much debate about whether nations should liberalize or restrict capital flows. The Washington Consensus, of course, advises liberalization, believing that free and unfettered capital flows enhance global financial integration and supplement domestic savings and investment. Unrestricted access to foreign capital thus can be a powerful agent for economic development. The belief is that capital-rich nations have relatively few opportunities for investment while capital-poor nations have relatively many opportunities for investment. It would seem logical to facilitate the free flow of capital from the former to the latter. Yet, despite this logic, many nations restrict capital flows. This includes most Asian countries and many nations in Latin America and Africa.

There are two categories of capital flows: foreign direct investment and portfolio investment. Of the two, direct investment has been the preferred method. This is because it has a longer time horizon and is less susceptible to flee when things turn sour. Still, governments often channel and regulate foreign direct investment to ensure that it serves the nation's needs and that it goes to strategic sectors as determined by the host nation. The problem with unrestricted foreign direct investment is that it can make host nations vulnerable to the whims of foreign corporations and to financial speculation. A host nation might need hospitals but foreign capital might want shopping malls. There is therefore a conflict of interest between the

136 Classical and Keynesian international economics

needs of the host population and the profits of foreign capitalists and the domestic elites (who benefit from their presence). The latter often invite foreign corporations by loosening labor and environmental protections.

Portfolio investment, on the other hand, can be hazardous because foreign asset managers and speculators are able instantaneously to withdraw liquid capital from a nation, leaving much economic hardship in its wake. This is why many call portfolio capital "hot money" and the world of portfolio investment "casino capitalism." There have been many examples of financial crises triggered by hot money flows, such as the 1994 Mexican currency crisis and the 1997 East Asian crisis.

There has been a subtle shift in opinion in favor of regulating short-term portfolio investment. One prominent Yale economist, James Tobin, advised taxing short-term flows to discourage their sudden turn-on-a-dime exit and entry. Economists call it the "Tobin tax." In 2011, 257 economists, including Nobel laureate Joseph Stiglitz, signed a petition supporting just such a tax.

Research recently published by the National Bureau of Economic Research, the International Monetary Fund and elsewhere has found that limits on the inflow of short-term capital into developing nations can prevent dangerous asset bubbles and currency appreciations and can grant nations more autonomy in monetary policymaking.

Global Keynesianism generally agrees with government policies to channel direct investment to socially useful projects and to restrict portfolio capital flows by restricting currency convertibility or Tobin-like taxation to discourage instantaneous withdrawals of financial capital. Nonetheless, the range of opinion among Keynesians is wider than what this would suggest and it is an exaggeration to claim all Keynesians agree to these views. The point is that, to Keynesians, a Classical world of free capital mobility is an abstract illusion that creates more harm than benefit.

The East Asian Consensus

Just as a Washington Consensus developed around Classical economic theory, an East Asian Consensus developed around global Keynesian theory. From the mid-1960s through the 1990s East Asia—Hong Kong, Indonesia, Japan, Malaysia, South Korea, Singapore, Taiwan, China and Thailand—recorded remarkable rates of economic growth, faster than other developing economies. The World Bank (1993) dubbed this phenomenon the "East Asian Miracle."

Many economists have attempted to explain the East Asian Miracle, but one explanation stands out: selective government interventions. What emerged in East Asia is a consensus among East Asian economists and policymakers that the government must play a central role in directing and managing economic growth: the East Asian Consensus.

Robert Wade (1990) is frequently associated with this position, the fundamentals of which he outlined in his book, *Governing the Market: Economic Theory and the Role of Government in East Asia*. By governing the market Wade means that the government leads rather than follows the market. Leading the market means deciding which products, sectors and technologies to encourage and using the government's resources and political clout to achieve those ends. Following the market means accepting the initiatives of private enterprises, as Classical economics would propose.

A government can lead the market in many ways. These might include the following:

1. Encouraging private savings.
2. Establishing efficient financial markets.
3. Promoting domestic investment in selected sectors.
4. Channeling direct foreign investment to selected sectors.
5. Subsidizing and providing tax relief for selected industries.
6. Keeping borrowing rates low.
7. Supporting government banks.
8. Supporting import substitutes and promoting exports.

There are many ways for a government to lead an economy. In an East Asian context the "consensus" rests on cultural grounds and popular sentiments about the relationship between the individual, the community and the state in Asia.

Conclusions

The Classical and Keynesian schools of thought dominate orthodox international economics, to the exclusion of other heterodox paradigms. Indeed, it is rare to find heterodox traditions (Austrian, Institutionalist, Post Keynesian, Marxian or Feminist) taught in undergraduate and graduate economics programs. Neither does one see articles written from these traditions published in mainstream academic journals. We explore these heterodox traditions in the next chapters.

Both Classical and Keynesian schools have evolved over the years in ways that render them increasingly inaccessible to most audiences. This is due mainly to their advanced mathematical techniques and the narrow range of highly abstract questions they ask. It seems odd, for example, that, in a world in which large oligopolies and monopolies are so ubiquitous and wield such inordinate power in world markets, introducing imperfect competition and unemployment into an economic model should be such a big issue.

Neither of the Classical and Keynesian research agendas seems relevant to the struggles of daily life faced by the majority of the world's population. While questions about the efficacy of monetary and fiscal policy under alternative exchange rate regimes are important, there is certainly much more that afflicts the world economy and that deserves economists' attention. Unfortunately, economists relegate these issues to specialized sub-fields that function on the periphery of the discipline. Or else they leave it to the heterodoxy to deal with, which the orthodoxy then ignores.

138 Classical and Keynesian international economics

The difference between the two schools, put most simply, is that Classicals assume an idyllic full-employment world in which macroeconomic policies are ineffective if not harmful, while mainstream Keynesians take a hesitating step away from this ideal by allowing some imperfections to exist, thereby opening the door to limited government intervention.

Classical theory continues to appeal because it offers a rationale for those who wish the government to do nothing to resolve capitalism's fundamental issues. Keynesian theory also continues to appeal because it offers solace to those with more liberal inclinations. It does so without offending those who are wedded to free enterprise capitalism. Most mainstream Keynesians would agree that the world is flawed and messy and therefore not explainable by Classical theory, although this message has been mostly forgotten since the advent of the Hicks-Hanson IS-LM paradigm. Both Classical and Keynesian approaches have sunk into irrelevancy.

Notes

1 A current account deficit (imports of goods exceed exports) causes a financial account surplus (exports of financial debt instruments exceed imports) and a net capital inflow. The nation's indebtedness increases. The opposite is also true.
2 Paul Samuelson coined the term "neo-Classical synthesis" in his third edition of his popular textbook, *Economics*, to describe this combination of Keynes and the classics. This begs the question of what distinguishes Classical from Neoclassical when discussing Keynesianism. We do not pursue this here.
3 Although he also said, "nobody is any longer a Keynesian." The relevancy of this is explained below.
4 See for example Robinson (1976).
5 Recall that Classical theory relies on a quantity theory of money. Therefore prices move in proportion to movements on the money supply.
6 See the argument made by Harberger (1950).
7 The real rate is the nominal rate plus inflationary expectations, or $r = i + \pi_e$.
8 Presumably the economy would grow at some *natural* rate depending on thrift, work and technology. As the economy grows the money supply would also need to grow at the same rate in order to accommodate the expanding number of transactions. Money growth in excess of this natural rate would cause inflation.
9 This analysis is really an extension of the Factor-Price Equalization theorem of Chapter 5 which states that free trade eliminates differences in factor prices around the world.
10 As we have seen in an earlier chapter, the principle of comparative advantage continues to hold even if all resources are free to move around the world.
11 We read C(r) as an implicit mathematical function: "consumption C is a function of interest rate r." It does not mean C times r. The same is true for savings.
12 The history of open economy macroeconomics dates to the 1940s and we cannot include all its developments here. Useful reviews of the open economy macroeconomic literature include Fendel (2002), Lane (2001) and Obstfeld (2001).
13 We assume here that the current account CA is identical to *net* exports.
14 Meade (1964) defined internal balance to be an accepted combination of unemployment and inflation or price stability.
15 It makes much more sense to measure the value of the dollar as €/$. However, to be consistent with the relevant literature, we measure the value of the dollar as $/€. This means a vertical movement corresponds to a depreciating dollar.
16 The key literature includes Obstfeld (2001 and 2002) and Obstfeld and Rogoff (1995). The standard literature survey is Lane (2001).

17 Three global institutions emerged out of Bretton Woods: the International Monetary Fund (IMF), the World Bank and the International Trade Organization (ITO). The US failed to approve the ITO, and the General Agreement on Tariffs and Trade (GATT) was agreed to instead in 1947. The WTO replaced GATT in 1995.

References

Blinder, A. S. (1988). "The Rise and Fall of Keynesian Economies." *Economic Record, 64*, 278–294.

Fendel, R. (2002). "Open Economy Macroeconomics in the Post Mundell-Fleming Era." *Jahrbuch für Wirtschaftswissenschaften, 53*, 53–87.

Hansen, A. H. (1953). *A Guide to Keynes*. New York: McGraw-Hill.

Harberger, A. (1950). "Currency Depreciation, Income, and the Balance of Trade." *Journal of Political Economy, 58*, 47–60.

Lane, P. R. (2001). "The New Open Economy Macroeconomics: a Survey." *Journal of International Economics, 54*, 235–266.

Meade, J. E. (1951). *The Theory of International Economic Policy*. London: Oxford University Press.

Meade, J. E. (1964). *Trade and Welfare*. London: Oxford University Press.

Obstfeld, M. (2001). *International Macroeconomics: Beyond the Mundell-Fleming Model*. Center for International and Development Economics Research, Institute of Business and Economic Research. Berkeley, CA: University of California. Retrieved February 26 2013, from http://escholarship.org/uc/item/.

Obstfeld, M. (2002). *Exchange Rates and Adjustment: Perspectives from the New Open Economy Macroeconomics*. Center for International and Development Economics Research, Institute of Business and Economic Research, Economics. Berkeley: University of California. Retrieved January 23 2013, from http://escholarship.org/uc/item/5t38s42v.

Obstfeld, M., & Rogoff, K. (1995). "Exchange Rate Dynamics Redux." *Journal of Political Economy, 103*, 624–660.

Robinson, J. (1976). "The Age of Growth." *Challenge, 19*, 4–9.

Samuelson, P. A. (1948). *Economics*. New York: McGraw-Hill.

Samuelson, P. A. (1955). *Economics* (3rd ed.). New York: McGraw-Hill.

Swan, Trevor W. (1963). "Longer-Run Problems of the Balance of Payments." In H. W. Arndt and W. Max Corden (Eds.), *The Australian Economy*. Sydney: Cheshire, 384–395.

Wade, R. (1990). *Governing the Market: Economic Theory and the Role of Government in East Asia*. Princeton, NJ. Princeton University Press.

Williamson, J. (1990). "What Washington Means by Policy Reform." In *Latin American Adjustment: How Much Has Happened?* Washington, DC: Peterson Institute for International Economics. Retrieved March 8 2013, from http://www.iie.com/publications/papers/print.cfm?ResearchId=486&doc=pub.

World Bank. (1993). *The East Asian Miracle: Economic Growth and Public Policy*. New York: Oxford University Press.

Appendix 6A

Diagrammatic presentation of the Classical model

We display the Classical model in Figure 6.7. The labor market in panel C determines employment N_1, which, together with given capital K_0, determines full employment output Y_1 in the production function shown in panel A. Note the curvature of the production function. It derives from the assumption of diminishing marginal returns to labor.

Panel B shows the quantity theory of money. It determines the price level, P. We measure P on the horizontal axis and Y on the vertical axis. When the central bank fixes the money supply at M_1 the price level will be P_1 given V_0 and real output Y_1. Rearranging the quantity theory equation, $M_1 V_0 = P_1 Y_1$, we get

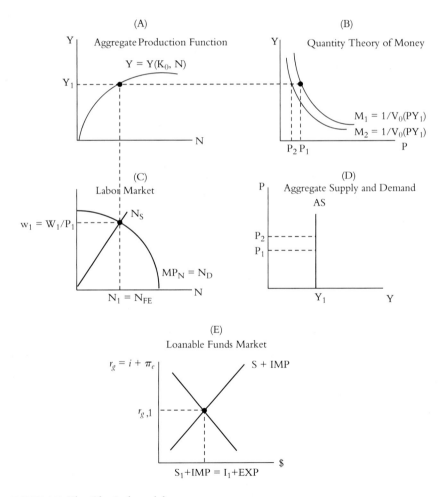

FIGURE 6.7 The Classical model

$Y_1 = \frac{1}{P_1}(M_1 V_0)$. The relationship between Y_1 and P_1 is inverse, as shown in Panel B. If the money supply falls to M_2 then the hyperbola in panel B shifts inward. Real output is unaffected at Y_1, since nothing "real" happens, and the price level falls to P_2. The two points $\{P_1, Y_1\}$ and $\{P_2, Y_1\}$ define the vertical aggregate supply curve in panel D.

Note that when the price level falls this causes the real wage rate to rise to $w_2 = W_1/P_2$, causing an excess labor supply and temporary involuntary unemployment. However, this unemployment causes the nominal wage rate to fall, which then brings the real wage back down to its original level.

The only remaining panel is panel E. This shows the loanable funds market. The interest rate that equilibrates leakages and injections is the global rate r_g which is the same as the domestic rate, r. This rate indicates how people distribute their income Y_1 to savings and how businesses choose to invest.

Appendix 6B

Diagrammatic presentation of the Keynesian model

Figure 6.8 shows the entire interactive system. The rest of the world, shown on the left side of the diagram, influences the domestic economy through global incomes Y_g, global interest rates r_g, and global prices P_g. We treat each of these as exogenous. We then divide the domestic economy into the three sectors; each shows the relevant equilibrium condition. The illustration also includes the labor market, which determines employment, and the bond market, which is in equilibrium (BS = BD) when the supply and demand for money are equal. To the right of the diagram is the foreign exchange market which interacts with all three sectors. The variable ϵ is the exchange rate, which can either be floating, managed or fixed.

Figure 6.9 shows the various possibilities for the BOP curve. Its shape depends on the assumptions we make about international capital mobility. We begin in Panel A where CA = FA = 0 at point a $\{Y_1, r_1\}$.

Now suppose Y rises from Y_1 to Y_2. This requires that r rise in order to preserve BOP = 0. By how much must r rise? If capital is relatively immobile then it would require a large increase in r to restore balance of payments equilibrium. Imagine that r must rise from r_1 to r_2. This puts us onto point b in the graph. If we connect points a and b we get the BOP_1 curve representing balance of payments equilibrium. All the necessary exchange rate adjustments take place behind the scenes, so to speak, to bring this about.

If capital is very mobile then we need a much smaller increase in r to induce the required capital inflows. If r must rise only to r_3 then we arrive at point c. Connecting the original point a with the new point c gives us a different BOP curve, BOP_2. The BOP curve is flatter. In the limit, as capital becomes perfectly mobile, the BOP curve becomes horizontal. Conversely, when capital is perfectly immobile the BOP curve becomes vertical. We show these two extreme cases in Panel B.

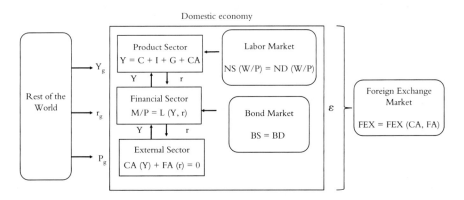

FIGURE 6.8 Mundell-Fleming model

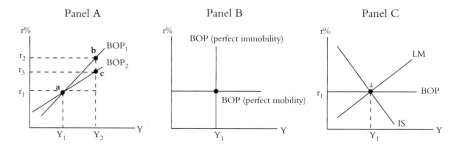

FIGURE 6.9 Balance of payments relationships

Panel C combines all three sectors, assuming perfect capital mobility and flexible exchange rates. Recall that each of the three curves shows all the combinations of Y and r that produce equilibrium in the relevant sector. A general equilibrium occurs at point a where all three curves intersect. Here, $Y = Y_1$ and $r = r_1$. Any other point would lie off one or more of the three curves and would generate counteracting forces, driving the economy back to the point. This is why the system is "stable." Note also that the economy need not be at full employment at Y_1.

In this Keynesian model, all we really see (i.e., what we can measure) is a prevailing interest rate r and output/income Y. Depending on what we assume about the relative size of the nation and about capital mobility and exchange rate flexibility, the interest rate, r, may be the same as the world rate, r_g.

7
AUSTRIAN INTERNATIONAL ECONOMICS

Introduction

Austrian economics emerged in Austria and Central Europe in the late 19th century at about the same time Institutionalism emerged in the United States. We will review Institutionalism in the next chapter. The Neoclassical orthodoxy also rose to dominance at about the same time.[1]

Austrian economics was originally a Viennese phenomenon. At the end of the 19th century Vienna was the intellectual and cultural center of Europe, the home of Mozart, Beethoven, Klimt, Freud and Wittgenstein. Dozens of Nobel laureates and scores of world famous scholars were among the faculty of the University of Vienna.

There have been three generations of Austrian economists. The first generation introduced marginal analysis and subjective value theory to economics. These ideas became fundamental principles of orthodox economics and represent a break from the Classical economics of Smith, Ricardo and Marx. The most famous of this first generation were Carl Menger (1840–1921), Friedrich Wieser (1851–1926) and Eugen Bohm-Bawerk (1851–1914). All three studied, taught and/or worked in Vienna.

The second generation continued the Vienna connection. The towering figures of this generation were Ludwig Von Mises (1881–1973), 1974 Nobel laureate Friedrich Hayek (1899–1992) and Joseph A. Schumpeter (1883–1950). Von Mises taught at the University of Vienna prior to emigrating to the US to escape Nazism. Hayek, a native Viennese, studied at the University of Vienna where the work of Wieser and Von Mises had strongly influenced his intellectual development. Hayek subsequently lectured at the London School of Economics and, after stints at the University of Chicago and the University of Freiburg in Germany, he returned to the University of Salzburg in Austria from where he retired. Schumpeter grew up in Vienna and studied law and economics at the University of Vienna. He then taught in the Ukraine, Austria and Germany before emigrating to the US in 1932 where he spent the remainder of his career at Harvard. The First World War and the rise of Nazism and Stalinism undoubtedly affected the economic and political views of all three scholars.

The reputation of Austrian economics, which was quite distinguished prior to the Second World War, languished after the war as the economics profession began to rely more and more on mathematical and statistical methods. Austrian economists have refused to go along with this new quantitative trend, for reasons we shall see in this chapter. However, Austrian economics has experienced a revival in the last three decades as a third generation has emerged, especially in the US. Prominent among this new third generation are Israel Kirzner (1930–), Ludwig Lachmann (1906–1990) and Murray Rothbard (1926–1995).

Today, Austrian economics is a mature school of thought with its own scholarly institutes and academic journals.[2] As with American Institutionalism, Austrian economics consists of several strains, or styles, each following one or another eminent Austrian economist from previous generations. Despite this diversity, it is still possible to outline the general themes of the Austrian school and to apply these to international economics.

The methodology of Austrian economics

Austrian economics employs a distinctive method of analysis. There are several parts to this method.

Methodological individualism

Methodological individualism is the mantra of Austrian economics. It is an uncomplicated idea which suggests that the individual must be the starting point of all economic analysis. The choices individuals make give rise to all social and economic phenomena. The social order, therefore, is simply the consequence of individual actions.

The individual is to Austrian economics as the gene is to biology and the atom is to physics. This is why economists sometimes use the term *atomism* to describe this idea. Groups of people, social classes (e.g., workers and capitalists), corporations, public and non-profit organizations are only collections of individuals. To understand the behaviors of groups of people we first must understand the behaviors of the individuals who comprise them.

Ludwig Von Mises is partly responsible for making methodological individualism a general principle. Comparing the individual to the collective, Von Mises stated,

> The hangman, not the state, executes a criminal . . . For a social collective has no existence and reality outside of the individual members' actions. The life

146 *Austrian international economics*

> of a collective is lived in the actions of the individuals constituting its body. . .
> Thus the way to a cognition of collective wholes is through an analysis of the
> individuals' actions.
>
> *(Von Mises, 1966: 42)*

Joseph A. Schumpeter, who actually coined the term "methodological individualism" in 1908, argued that economic theory cannot begin with the category "society." It must begin with the individual and then develop its arguments from there (Schumpeter, 1909: 216).

Yet Schumpeter also made it clear that methodological individualism is *not* a universal principle that governs *all* human behavior. It is merely one method of analysis, a tool used in doing "pure economic theory." There is much more to economic analysis than methodological individualism, said Schumpeter, and many other analytical methods are available to economists.

Even Hayek, a noted proponent of methodological individualism, saw that there is more to economic analysis than the individual actor. Like Schumpeter, Hayek observed,

> The overall order of actions in a group is in two respects more than the totality of regularities observable in the actions of the individuals and cannot be wholly reduced to them. It is so not only in the trivial sense in which the whole is more than the mere *sum* of its parts but presupposes also that these elements are related to each other in a particular manner.
>
> *(Hayek, 1967: 50–51)*

In other words, a complete theory of society must consist of a theory of individual behavior plus a theory of relations among individuals. Strict methodological individualism alone is insufficient. As Nobel laureate Kenneth Arrow said, "Individual behavior is always mediated by social relations" (Arrow, 1994: 4–5).

"Relations" among individuals refers to all those social structures and rules that make individual actions possible. It is the context in which individuals act. It includes property rights law, education, language, communications, etc. Just because we need to drill down to the level of the individual in order to know how society works does not mean we should not add anything else to the analysis.

This brings us very close to the American Institutionalist school, which we examine in Chapter 8. American Institutionalists pay attention to *relationships* between people in order to explain social phenomena, not just the actions taken by isolated, atomistic individual agents. Institutionalists argue that organizations have traits, routines and cultures that influence how individuals think and behave and that methodological individualism alone is inadequate to the task of explaining how this works.

Institutionalists would therefore modify Von Mises' statement about the hangman by saying a state's government apparatus, including its judicial system and its department of corrections, influences how individual executioners act; the state and the executioners are in an interactive social relationship, and without previously given laws and practices the hangman would never hang anyone. We can hardly imagine an ardent opponent of the death penalty working as a hangman.

The line dividing individualism and collectivism is murky. Austrians nonetheless position themselves firmly on the side of individualism, far from the murky dividing line.

Methodological subjectivism

Subjectivism complements methodological individualism. It first emerged in economics in the 19th century as an approach to the study of value and price. The question asked then was, what determines the value—and hence the market price—of a particular commodity?

Classical economists, including Smith, Ricardo and Marx, said the value of a commodity derives from "objective" concrete factors, outside the minds of individual economic actors. The foremost objective determinant of value—and hence of market price—is the amount of labor used to produce a commodity. This is alternatively called the labor theory, the cost of production theory or the objective theory of value.

For example, if it takes 10 hours of labor to produce commodity A and 20 hours of labor to produce commodity B, then the market price of B would be twice the price of A. In the long run, it does not matter how great the demand for each commodity is. In this theory demand has little to do with price. Only the cost of production—the labor cost of production—matters. Market competition always drives the market price down (or up) to match the cost of production. Thus, if demand drives up the market price so that it exceeds the cost of production, existing firms will make more profit and will then produce more output. New firms will also enter the market, supplementing the amount available for purchase. Market supply rises and the price falls back to its original cost of production level. So, over time, demand is irrelevant.

The subjective theory of value, on the other hand, says value is determined solely in the minds of consumers and producers. The value of Swiss cheese to me—its utility—may be high, and its value to you may be low. Therefore, I am willing to pay a higher price than you. The actual market price is simply the result of each one of us "voting" for—demanding—Swiss cheese in the market. Importantly, the value of a commodity is also determined in the minds of producers who must pay the costs of making and selling Swiss cheese. These costs are based on what sellers must sacrifice, or their opportunity costs. This is the "pain" of sacrifice when producers give up (i.e., abstain from) current consumption in order to purchase the inputs needed to produce Swiss cheese. The expected subjective "utility" of prospective buyers together with the expected subjective "pain" or sacrifice of sellers determines a commodity's value and hence its market price. This is why we call this a "subjective" theory of value.

The subjective theory of value is also the bread and butter of orthodox economics.

148 Austrian international economics

But Austrians have taken the idea further. To them, subjectivism explains the formation and dynamics of the entire social and economic order, not just the value of commodities. Subjective perceptions drive all human actions. To understand how this works we must understand how the minds of individuals work. This requires knowing how people attach meaning to the actions they take. Presumably, we do not need to know the details of anyone's inner thoughts; we need not be psychoanalysts. We need only to describe the logical thought processes people use to arrive at decisions to act.

Praxeology and the axioms of human action

Praxeology is the name Austrians give to the study of human action. As Von Mises put it, human action is

> will put into operation and transformed into an agency, is aiming at ends and goals, is the ego's meaningful response to stimuli and to the conditions of its environment, is a person's conscious adjustment to the state of the universe that determines his life.
>
> *(Von Mises, 1966: 11)*

Praxeology begins with a "fundamental axiom" that says all human action is purposeful and logical. Austrians believe the mind is a logical rational structure that willfully pursues concrete ends. Logical thought produces human action; all decisions filter through this logical mental structure. Moreover, people's minds are entrepreneurial. This means the mind constantly searches for alternatives and possibilities, takes risks and makes mistakes. It is never stationary or inert. As the British economist G. L. S. Shackle (1903–1992) put it: "[the mind is] always exploring, experimenting, guessing and gambling, and is constantly misled" (Shackle, 1972: 125). This suggests people have an entrepreneurial instinct, one that Israel Kirzner calls "entrepreneurial alertness"—the ability to discover opportunities that others overlook (Kirzner, 1979: 38–39).

We next introduce assumptions about the real environment in which human actions occur. After all, action is a "response to stimuli and to the conditions of its environment." These assumptions must correspond to and describe real-world experience. The analytic question now becomes how these assumed environmental conditions and stimuli affect the actions people take. If we specify the assumptions correctly then the theory ought to explain accurately why people take the actions they do. This is "logically correct praxeological reasoning."

Praxeological analysis breaks down the reasoning process as follows. When a person contemplates an action, such as purchasing a commodity or starting a business, it is because he or she experiences a feeling of uneasiness, an inner psychological sense that life could be improved somehow. No action will take place when a person is perfectly content with what he or she has. Action only takes place when a person has an inner urge to want more, to improve his or her well-being. Note that the impulse to act could be selfish or it could be altruistic; relieving one's unease might lead to improving someone else's well-being.

Austrian analysis claims to make no value judgment about a person's desires; nor does it inquire into the inner psychological forces that determine a person's desires. Lust, envy, mental depression, compassion and yearning are all possible psychological explanations of why a person might want more of something. But these inner motivations lie outside the scope of Austrian theories of human action. All we know is that people act by assessing the incremental costs and benefits in reaching a decision to act.

Feelings of unease are rank-ordered according to what Von Mises called a unique "scale of values." Some feelings of unease are more urgent to eliminate than others. We try to relieve higher order feelings before lower order feelings. A person's "ends" are simply to remove the felt "uneasiness."

The process of choosing an action involves attaining a certain end goal by selecting the appropriate means. Means are the methods people use to reach the ends. Means consist of acquiring goods, which are always scarce. Acquiring goods relieves the uneasiness. The goods might be food for the table or a fancy car. The goods have no intrinsic value; our actions bestow value on goods. A fancy car might have a great deal of value for one person and no value for another.

All actions entail exchange: people must incur costs in order to acquire the goods they believe will relieve their unease. They will acquire a good so long as the incremental value of the good acquired exceeds the incremental value of what must be given up to get it.

All human action is notional and undertaken in environments of uncertainty. We can never know for sure ahead of time what choices people will make or the exact outcomes of their actions. While we can explain the logic of choice and action, we cannot predict them.

Austrians claim their theory deals with real people—people as they are, not with idealized all-knowing, optimizing, lightening calculators of pleasure and pain. This, they say, is what separates Austrian from orthodox theory. Orthodox theory portrays people as robots obeying mathematically precise utility- and profit-maximizing rules. Austrians presumably show people as fallible and unpredictable, albeit logical.

In conclusion, praxeology is the name Austrians give to this general theory of human behavior. Presumably, Austrian praxeology applies regardless of the environmental circumstances in which people act. They can live in the US, China or Kenya. It is truly a global theory that transcends time and place. Praxeology then frames or contains specific theorems of Austrian economics.

The spontaneous order and anti-equilibrium

A key question for Austrians is how a social order is even possible. Societies require an extraordinary degree of coordination just to exist, and the question is how that coordination can take place if all individuals act independently. There is no grand

150 Austrian international economics

design or deliberate plan that causes the economy to function coherently and systematically. Yet somehow the economy continues to function.

Following the work of Hayek, Austrians believe the social order is the *spontaneous* and *unintended* result of individual actions. These spontaneous day-to-day results are rarely balanced and stable. In fact, the economy oscillates between unsustainable booms and economic collapse. These cyclical fluctuations trigger adjustments that individual actors make in response to the imbalances they experience in their lives. These adjustments eventually reverse the path of the economy, turning expansions into recessions and recessions into expansions.

Underlying these cycles is the fact that individual producers must make decisions today in anticipation of what consumers will do in the future. The problem is especially important for business investment. Investment requires present commitments in return for uncertain future rewards. Because there is no central coordination, decision makers frequently make mistakes in their calculations. Mistakes cumulate over time causing boom and bust cycles. The spontaneous economic order is never really balanced and economy-wide coordination failures always occur. Yet the economy muddles along, in a more or less orderly way.

These ideas make the orthodox notion of "equilibrium" irrelevant to Austrian economists.[3] Equilibrium describes a single unique position or state of affairs in which all economic plans have been reconciled with each other. Equilibrium describes the culmination of the market process, a process in which all excess supplies and demands have been eliminated; the economy is in balance. General equilibrium describes the economy at a particular moment of time. However, a cyclically fluctuating economy such as the one described by Austrians never arrives at any balanced and stable position. Each phase of the cycle has imbalances and engenders the next phase of the cycle with new imbalances; the economy is a cumulative process that never arrives at a unique position of balanced rest.

Voluntary free markets and economic power

Austrian economists believe free exchange is always beneficial to everyone involved. This is because voluntary action is the foundation of free exchange. No one coerces anyone else into exchanging in the marketplace. By extension, a free exchange economy "creates a delicate and even awe-inspiring mechanism of harmony, adjustment, and precision in allocating resources . . . gently but swiftly guiding the economic system toward the greatest possible satisfaction of the desires of all the consumers" (Rothbard, 1993: 880). Everyone remains free and uncoerced.

In such a world, economic power cannot exist. No one can coerce anyone else to behave or perform in a way they do not choose voluntarily. As Rothbard puts it, economics, through its value-free laws,

> informs us that the workings of the voluntary principle and of the free market
> lead inexorably to freedom, prosperity, harmony, efficiency, and order; while

coercion and government intervention lead inexorably to hegemony, conflict, exploitation of man by man, inefficiency, poverty, and chaos.

(Rothbard, 1993: 880–881)

Coercion, to Austrians, occurs only when someone forcibly intervenes in free markets. The chief culprit of such intervention is, of course, government. This is because governments possess the legal right to compel people to do things they would otherwise choose not to do. Taxation, military conscription and central bank control of the money supply are examples of the exercise of government coercion. Governments are also able to favor selected private groups by granting them special licenses or privileges.

In the absence of government, no one would be able to compel anyone else to behave and act against their own interests. The strong would be unable to impose their will upon the weak; the rich would have no power to coerce the poor.

Liberalism and state policy

The Austrian approach to economics denies that any nation can effectively coordinate or control its economy, even if it wanted to. Those who propose to change the historical path of capitalist development, and who believe they can do better than unfettered markets, are deluding themselves. They suffer from what Hayek termed a "fatal conceit."

Economic planning, in other words, is an impossible task. By economic planning we mean that a central government authority decides in advance how to allocate society's scarce resources. It would do so by first estimating people's preferences and then directing enterprises to always produce and deliver the "correct" amount of output to satisfy consumer wants. Alternatively, a government could calculate market-clearing prices ahead of time; these "correct prices" then would induce privately owned enterprises to make decisions voluntarily that abide by the plan. Either way, the government plan is a blueprint that compels or induces enterprises to produce the "correct" welfare-maximizing output.

The long-standing Austrian view, which dates back to Von Mises' seminal book, *Economic Calculation in the Socialist Commonwealth,* published in 1920, is that this kind of economic planning is impossible for any government to do (Von Mises, 1975). No government or central authority is capable of making the necessary calculations.

Hayek's famous 1945 article, "The Use of Knowledge in Society," added ammunition to this argument and became the standard Austrian explanation of this viewpoint (Hayek, 1945). In that article, Hayek stated that the data or knowledge which the government requires to construct a nation-wide economic plan never exists in one place. That knowledge exists "solely as dispersed bits of incomplete and frequently contradictory knowledge which all the separate individuals possess" (Hayek, 1945: 519). The economic problem is, as Hayek put it,

how to secure the best use of resources known to any of the members of society, for ends whose relative importance only these individuals know. Or, to put it briefly, it is a problem of the utilization of knowledge not given to anyone in its totality.

(Hayek, 1945: 520)

The conclusion reached is that only a policy of laissez-faire allows an economy to grow and prosper; the government logically and practically cannot improve on the outcome of the free market.

This Austrian argument originally intended to dispute socialist economic theories popular prior to the 1950s when Soviet-type economies indeed attempted to undertake national economic planning. This argument also rebuffs Keynesian policies that favor government macroeconomic management.

Austrian economists generally do not promote anarchy, the idea that society can do without any state authority. There are legitimate tasks for a government. One is to provide a general framework of laws that protect private property and enforce contracts. Another is to induce (through incentives, for example) the private sector to provide certain "public goods" that it would never find profitable enough to provide on its own. But a state ought not attempt to support or encourage any "higher aims" such as social justice or public welfare by using its powers of coercion. Seeking to achieve such higher aims will only undermine liberty, not advance it.

Implications for Austrian international economics

Austrians would apply the general theory of human action—praxeology—to people in all societies and cultures. As we stated above, Austrian praxeology transcends time and space; it applies to citizens of developing nations in Africa as well as developed nations in North America and Europe. It describes human behavior in the 18th as well as the 21st centuries.

The general Austrian praxeology frames the more specific theories of macroeconomics and international economics that we describe in the next sections of this chapter. In order to construct these specific theories we must add specific assumptions about the actual social and economic environments in which human action occurs. These environments differ, of course, from country to country and region to region.

A genuinely Austrian international economic theory would, therefore, account for the many varieties of institutions, customs and practices of the nations engaged in world trade and finance. For example, to understand fully US–China trade we would need to specify the cultural and economic institutions defining the US and China—while recognizing that all Americans and Chinese behave according to praxeological principles.

Austrian macroeconomics

Austrian macroeconomic is a rather messy set of propositions without precise and definite answers such as those given by orthodox macroeconomics. Despite this messiness, Austrians consistently argue against any kind of state economic intervention. They instead promote unfettered free markets.

Austrian macroeconomics begins with the behavior of individuals. It focuses on the *microfoundations* of human action under conditions of ignorance and uncertainty. Entrepreneurs base their decisions on what they actually know about current market conditions. But what they know is often in error. Some entrepreneurs will err in one direction while others will err in other directions.

These errors in judgment rarely balance out, however, especially during economic crises when there is an increasing preponderance of entrepreneurs who err in the same direction. That is to say, entrepreneurs increasingly make the same incorrect estimations of the future. These errors consist of expectations that cannot be fulfilled. The problem compounds as errors lead to more errors.

The most important mistakes occur in investment decisions. This is what economic crises are all about: a preponderance of people making similar mistakes about investment spending. To understand macroeconomic instability requires, therefore, that we examine the monetary conditions that foster these judgmental errors.

The state and the impossibility of expansionary monetary policy

Austrians argue macroeconomic stabilization policies destabilize the economy rather than stabilize it. In particular, expansionary policies designed to lift an economy out of recession actually cause unemployment after these policies end.

Austrians distrust the state and its ability to conduct discretionary policies; they believe narrow political interests cause the state to work against the public interest and to undermine whatever benefit discretionary macroeconomic policies had intended.

Austrians instead have complete faith in free markets, business entrepreneurship and competition to provide economic stability and growth. They are unconcerned that corporations would (or could) acquire economic power and exercise that power to serve their own narrow interests against those of the public. In other words, the state is the problem, pure and simple, not business enterprise.

The reasoning behind this assessment relies on the following argument. Monetary authorities are predisposed to undertake expansionary policies by lowering interest rates below what is necessary to equilibrate the savings and the supply and demand for credit. The reason for this may be political, to satisfy special economic interests. Or, it may be their belief in erroneous economic theories (e.g., Keynesian theories) that suggest recessions can be "cured" through expansionary monetary policies.

Expansionary monetary policy artificially lowers interest rates and encourages financial institutions to increase credit availability. This gives entrepreneurs the mistaken impression that the supply of household savings is increasing. In other words, entrepreneurs mistakenly believe low interest rates are a signal for them to step up investment.

The monetary authorities therefore send wrong signals to the financial markets; they distort capital markets and lead entrepreneurs to expect the artificially created

154 Austrian international economics

favorable conditions will continue. This causes them to shift resources away from the production of consumer goods and toward the production of capital goods. That is, it causes an *intertemporal misallocation of resources*.

These mistaken expectations eventually will curtail if not halt investment spending and cause unemployment to increase once again. This happens because the excessive investment demand will eventually push up input prices as businesses scramble to produce more and more capital goods. Higher input prices means rising costs which cuts into profit margins. In reaction, entrepreneurs begin to suspend capital projects and capital will begin to lie idle. The situation reverses. The central bank can now either continue its expansionary policy, further escalating the intertemporal misallocation of resources; or it can discontinue the expansionary policy, which would drive up interest rates and unemployment. To Austrians, such interventionist policies are senseless.

Austrian international monetary economics

International economics has never really played a central role in Austrian economics. They have given most of their attention to monetary theory and political economy.[4] An exception is the work of the Austrian economist Gottfried Haberler (1900–1995) who specialized in international trade theory and policy. A student of Friedrich Wieser and Ludwig Von Mises in Vienna, Haberler emigrated to the US in 1936 where he became Schumpeter's colleague at Harvard. We may consider Haberler the architect of contemporary orthodox Neoclassical trade theory. His seminal work, *The Theory of International Trade*, published in 1936, is virtually indistinguishable from current international trade textbooks (Haberler, 1936; see also Baldwin, 1982). In his work, Haberler uses the Austrian style of reasoning to argue in favor of unrestricted international trade.

To get a sense of how Austrians might approach international economics let us apply their methodology and economic theory to the world economy.

The seduction of cheap money

A central principle of Austrian economics is that government discretionary control of money and credit destabilizes economies. In particular, macroeconomic policies that intend to alleviate unemployment will ultimately fail, instead creating inflation and even more unemployment.

By extension, this same principle applies in the international arena: an international monetary authority (such as the European Central Bank) cannot do any better than a self-correcting global free market system. The reasoning is essentially political: economic authorities cannot resist the influence of special interests who appeal to "St. Maynard" (a sarcastic reference to John Maynard Keynes) to justify self-serving demands for economic interventions. The only way to defend against these special interests is a gold standard, balanced budgets and built-in limits to the creation of international liquidity.

As Hayek summarized the problem, "The pressure for more and cheaper money is an ever-present political force which monetary authorities have never been able to resist, unless they were in a position credibly to point to an absolute obstacle which made it impossible for them to meet such demands" (Hayek, 1976a: 15). Keynesian economics, Austrians allege, has removed these restraints by giving theoretical legitimacy to discretionary macroeconomic management of the economy.

An international gold standard

Austrians believe we need an international gold standard to guarantee economic stability. Such a standard would keep a tight rein on artificial monetary expansions that cause inflation. A gold standard ties the value of a nation's currency to the value of a natural mineral: gold. Silver has also been a popular alternative to gold.

A nation can adopt a gold standard by minting gold coins, with each coin containing the same amount of gold. Alternatively, a nation can use a paper currency pegged to a certain amount of gold. Anyone could exchange the paper currency for a specified amount of gold, or a certain amount of gold for a specified amount of currency. The government or central bank would fix the exchange rate between the paper currency and gold. Ultimately, the availability of gold in the world, as well as the costs of mining, minting and transporting, determines the value of gold and of currencies based on gold, not governments.

The point Austrians try to make is that nations ought to eliminate discretionary government control of the money supply and hence of exchange rates and international payments. If they do this, prices and exchange rates would be stable and international payments would always be in balance. The international system of trade and payments would automatically adjust to the world supply of gold.

Gold, in other words, is an anchor to which international prices and trade balances automatically adjust. To see why this is so, suppose a nation imports more than it exports; that is, it has a trade deficit. The nation now needs more foreign currency with which to buy foreign goods. To get this foreign currency people must sell more of its own domestic currency. The value of the domestic currency falls while the value of the foreign currency rises. This begins to make the nation's exports more attractive to foreigners. Also, gold begins to flows out of the country to pay for trade-related debts. The nation's money supply (i.e., gold) shrinks and prices will fall.[5] The money supply (i.e., gold) in other nations rises and their prices rise. These changing prices reverse trade activity: prices are now lower in the deficit nation and its exports begin to rise. At the same time, imports decrease because foreign prices are higher and less attractive. This automatic self-adjusting process restores balance and eliminates the trade deficit.

People have used gold as money for thousands of years. Many have also used silver, especially after Europeans discovered great quantities of it in Mexico and Bolivia in the 16th century. Between 1870 and 1914 most countries used a gold standard. This was also true between World War I and II. The Bretton Woods system, agreed to in 1944, put in place a hybrid gold standard that lasted until 1971.

156 Austrian international economics

There is not much agreement among economists on whether these gold standard systems were successful.

Free currency systems and free banking

In his *Denationalisation of Money*, Hayek proposed a radical alternative to an international gold standard: competitive currencies and free banking (Hayek, 1977). He opposed policy coordination among the monetary authorities of nations (e.g., the European Central Bank). His reason is that such coordinating authorities have a propensity to inflate their currencies in order to stimulate their economies in the short run. Here we see once again the Austrian fear that state authorities are always beholden to special interests and incapable of asserting independent policies that serve the public interest.

Hayek argued that people in all nations ought to have free choice in which currencies they choose to hold and use for transactions. Governments ought not to intervene in this choice: "There could be no more effective check against the abuse of money by the government than if people were free to refuse any money they distrusted and to prefer money in which they had confidence" (Hayek, 1976a: 18). We should rely not on the benevolence of governments but rather on the self-interest of those who issue currency.

In Hayek's scheme any institution in any country should be free to issue a currency and offer demand deposits. This means a private "bank" can manage the value of the currency it creates by either buying or selling its currency or by increasing or decreasing its loans. Issuers of money should be free to open branches anywhere in the world with no attention paid to national borders. The goal is to end the government's monopoly over the issuance of money. A "legal tender" is not necessary for a currency to be successful. Consumers and entrepreneurs would choose those currencies that best preserve its value, and would avoid using currencies that are either unstable or lose their value easily.

Issuers of currencies thus have an incentive to limit the quantity in order to preserve its value. Printing too much of a currency would depreciate its value. The best currency would naturally arise from free competition among different currencies. A currency based on the gold standard would be the most likely winner of such a competition among currencies.

Today, there are approximately 180 currencies in the world. Almost all of these circulate within the borders of the nations that issue them. Not all nations have their own currencies. The *euro*, the official common currency of "Eurozone" nations belonging to the European Union, floats freely relative to the US dollar. It is the second largest reserve currency and second most traded after the US dollar. A half-dozen Caribbean nations use the East Caribbean dollar, although they peg it to the US dollar. The US dollar, the pound sterling, the Japanese yen and the euro have in many ways won the global competition of currencies, despite the fact that all are issued by governments.

Many nations peg their currencies to the dollar, euro and yen because of the stability they provide. Some nations even adopt a foreign currency. El Salvador and Ecuador, for example, use the American dollar. This is called *dollarization*. The idea behind pegging and dollarization is to prevent the devaluation of a nation's currency and to avoid speculative attacks. This makes the local climate more attractive to foreign investors who otherwise might be scared away. They also prevent local monetary authorities from undertaking inflationary monetary policies; the quantity of money in the local economy is fixed by the amount of US dollars available. Some might consider this a disadvantage because it denies local authorities autonomy over their own affairs. In a way, the world's dominant currencies have won the currency competition, although this is still a far cry from Hayek's ideal.

Fixed vs. fluctuating exchange rates

Austrians have always opposed fixed or even managed exchange rates. Hayek, however, favored fixed exchange rates, but only so long as governments monopolized the issuance of currencies. Fixed exchange rates in contemporary circumstances would provide the necessary restraint and discipline on monetary policy. Hayek favored flexible exchange rates when world currencies freely compete and government monopolies over the issuance of currency no longer exist.

In today's international monetary system, monetary authorities manage exchange rates. When monetary authorities manage currencies they cause the relative prices of *all* tradable products to change. This inevitably results in recurring cycles of expansion and contraction. In Hayek's theoretical world, however, freely competing currencies, free banking and flexible exchange rates would preclude government interventions and promote international economic stability. In such a world there would be no balance of payments problems and freely adjusting exchange rates would automatically eliminate trade deficits and surpluses. Purely private economic relations would direct the flow of money between countries. No one would even pay attention to the balance of payments because it would be entirely self-correcting. This conclusion continues the counterintuitive Austrian theme that the more states try to stabilize their economies, the more instability they cause. Letting go of the state's reins on the economy is the best way to have economic stability.

Austrian international production theory

Austrian economics views production as consisting of chains of productive activities. Each link in a chain is an enterprise (or industry) that provides inputs for the next link in the chain.

The first link represents the enterprises producing a final consumer good. We call this final good a 1st order good. Enterprises in the second link supply inputs to the first link; we call this good a 2nd order good. The further away a link gets from the first link, the higher is its order. Low-order goods represent later stages of production (upstream), while higher order goods represent earlier stages of production (downstream). Capitalist production therefore comprises simultaneously functioning chains of production made up of thousands of individual activities or links resulting, over time, in finished consumer goods.

Goods produced in each link can have a wide range of applications across different chains of production. This means some intermediate goods may serve as inputs to many different chains of production while others are specific to a single chain. An example is stainless steel. It enters into the production of cookware, cutlery, surgical instruments, firearms and aircraft, just to name a few.

A central feature of capitalist production is that *time* elapses between links. It takes time to produce stainless steel before it is available to the producer of surgical instruments. The amount of time depends, among other things, on the complexity of the goods produced. Production, therefore, is *intertemporal*. And because production links spread out over the globe, they are *interspatial*.

What gives this view of production an Austrian flavor is the idea that individual entrepreneurs all over the world are the active agents in global chains. These entrepreneurs constantly scan, evaluate and act on opportunities in a global environment of uncertainty. The number and types of links in each chain constantly change as global entrepreneurs redesign their products, develop new products and improve production technologies.

In other words, human action in every part of the world makes the global economy work. Markets coordinate individual decisions and human actions, and, if left alone, will eliminate market imbalances and bottlenecks by adjusting the structures and patterns of production.

What is capital?

Given this Austrian perspective, what does the word "capital" mean? For one thing, capital is a produced input that either lasts for years (e.g., plant and equipment) or becomes part of another product (e.g., nuts and bolts). For another thing, capital is heterogeneous. Because of this, we can neither measure it nor add it up. How can we add one diesel engine, one warehouse and a thousand nuts and bolts? The only way to aggregate capital is first to assign a monetary value or price to each physical piece of capital. However, the quantities of physical capital supplied and demanded determine prices in the first place. So how can we use prices to determine the amount of capital? All we can say is that the prospective value to the consumer of final consumer goods determines the prices of lower-order goods.

The Austrian theory of production differs starkly from the formalistic orthodox (Neoclassical) theory. That theory simply defines capital as a homogeneous factor of production which enters into a production function equation such as $Q = f(L, K, N)$, where K stands for aggregate capital. We then determine "equilibrium" values for the magnitudes Q, K, L and N without referring to heterogeneity of capital and to how individual entrepreneurs scan, evaluate and act on uncertain market opportunities.

Looking at capital this way makes suspect the five Neoclassical trade theorems that rely on aggregate measures of K to analyze how factor and commodity prices adjust to changes in technology or in tastes. It also weakens orthodox conclusions about comparative advantage. This Austrian critique resembles the Cambridge criticisms we introduced in Chapter 4. We need to find another way to analyze and describe international economic relations if we are to avoid these pitfalls.

Roundaboutness

Roundaboutness describes the number of links in the production of a final consumer good. More links means greater roundaboutness. And greater roundaboutness means more specialized, differentiated inputs. It also means a greater division of labor. Think of what is involved in producing an automobile.

A standard description of roundaboutness divides all production processes into mining, refining, manufacturing, distribution and retailing. This traces the path of resources from their source in the natural environment to their final destination: store shelves.

Three factors influence the degree of roundaboutness. The first is *technology*. Technology can either increase or decrease roundaboutness. Casual observation suggests that technological development leads to increased specialization and division of labor as well as an increased variety of produced goods of all sorts.

The second factor is *monetary conditions*, especially interest rates. Interest rates determine the costs of tying up money in production. For example, when market interest rates are relatively high, say at 8%, it is relatively expensive to tie up money in time-consuming production processes. Moreover, if alternative financial instruments such as bonds pay rates of 8% then the rate of return on production must compete with this high rate. High interest rates mean high opportunity costs, which induce entrepreneurs to minimize the amount of time during which they tie up their money.

Alternatively, when interest rates are low, say at 2%, the opportunity costs of tying up money in production are also low. There is less pressure to lower the roundaboutness of production and the costs of experimentation and technological innovation are low as well.

The so-called Hayek Triangle in Figures 7.1 through 7.3 display the relationship between interest rates and the roundaboutness of production in a given production chain.

The vertical distance to the hypotenuse represents the total output of a particular stage of production. The maximum height shows the amount of final output of consumer goods. The horizontal distance represents the number of links or stages of production.[6] The longer this horizontal distance, the more time required to produce final output. Each stage of production in Figure 7.1 has a different shade, each representing a particular nation.

For example, consider the production chain leading to final production of stainless steel cutlery. South Africa is a major source of the mineral chromite. South Africa exports chromite ore to China, which refines it into ferrochrome, an important input into the production of stainless steel. Britain imports ferrochrome to

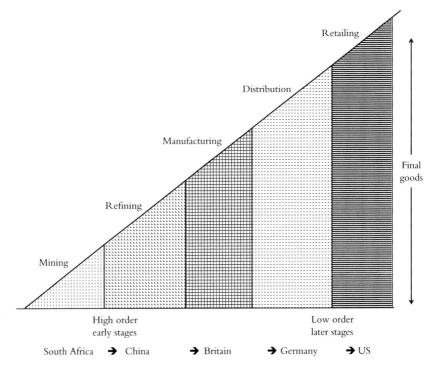

FIGURE 7.1 Time structure of production: A

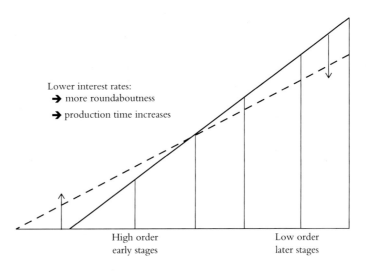

FIGURE 7.2 Time structure of production: B

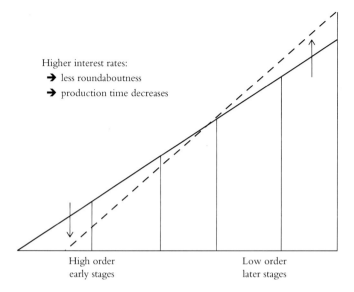

FIGURE 7.3 Time structure of production: C

make stainless steel, some of which is exported to Germany to make fine cutlery which is then distributed and sold in the United States. The links of the chain span the globe. In Austrian economics it is the actions taken by countless individual entrepreneurs, acting independently, each responding to market conditions, which determines roundaboutness.

A third factor determining roundaboutness is *relative international factor prices and exchange rates*. Low prices for mining and refining minerals in certain countries can increase the roundaboutness of production and at the same time relocate production stages from one part of the world to another. Depreciation of a nation's exchange rate cheapens the costs of production activities for export in certain stages and can shift the location of production.

Changing macroeconomic conditions in those countries can also induce entrepreneurs either to shorten or lengthen the roundaboutness of production. For example, rising labor costs or costs of extraction can induce innovations that discover substitute inputs that shorten or lengthen roundaboutness.

One important and much debated problem with the Austrian idea of roundaboutness is that the uniform inverse relationship between interest rates and roundaboutness (i.e., low interest rates, greater roundaboutness) is not logically valid. It is quite possible that, when interest rates are low, entrepreneurs will switch back to techniques that were once viable at high interest rates. In other words, one production technique can be profitable at a high rate of interest, then become unprofitable at a lower rate and then profitable once again at an even lower rate of interest. This phenomenon is called "reswitching." Economists have not established definitively whether reswitching is observable in the real world. The literature is very abstruse and we cannot pursue it here. (See, for example, Samuelson, 1966.)

162 Austrian international economics

Austrian theories of international entrepreneurship

Austrian economists make entrepreneurship a central driving force in the world economy. Who is this entrepreneur? What does this person do?

The entrepreneur is the primary agent of change, the main mover and shaker in the world economy. The world in which the entrepreneur works and competes is evolutionary, spontaneous and in a perpetual state of disequilibrium. Entrepreneurs in this world are rational strategists, but they do not "optimize." Uncertainty prevails, and knowledge and information are incomplete and scattered around the world.

The Austrian real-world economy seems somewhat out of focus and imprecise when compared to the mathematically precise and efficient world of orthodox economics. Despite this, a coherent economic order nonetheless arises, an order in which the self-interested actions of entrepreneurs eventually align with the social good.

Some classic theories of entrepreneurship

We cannot speak of entrepreneurship without first mentioning Joseph Schumpeter. To Schumpeter the entrepreneur is the personification of innovation.[7] He believed the capitalist economy was perpetually in motion, always adjusting, and never in equilibrium, at least not in the way orthodox economics defined it. In this way Schumpeter was a true Austrian economist. He did use the term equilibrium but only to explain how patterns of economic activity respond to the unsettling "disequilibrium" forces of innovation. These disequilibrium forces continuously revolutionize the economy from within, destroying old patterns and creating new ones. Schumpeter called this process *creative destruction*.[8]

In his famous book, *Theory of Economic Development*, Schumpeter identified five varieties of innovation (Schumpeter, 1934: 66):

1. Introducing a new good, or a good with new features.
2. Introducing a new method of production.
3. Opening of a new market.
4. Finding a new source of supply of raw materials or semi-manufactured goods.
5. Introducing a new business or industry organization.

Innovation and creative destruction are global phenomena that occur everywhere. The degree to which they occur and the effect they have on a nation's economy depend on the cultural and institutional environment. Governments can profoundly affect that environment by either encouraging or suppressing the forces of creativity. Additionally, the effects of entrepreneurship and innovation in one place spill over into other nations and regions.

More recently, William J. Baumol expanded the Schumpeterian idea of entrepreneurship to include rent-seeking activities (Baumol, 1990). These activities,

Austrian international economics **163**

such as bribery and influence peddling, seek only to manipulate the political and economic environment to redirect resources and profits. These activities do not contribute to economic growth; they only redistribute existing wealth. Rent seeking, of course, applies equally to the global economy.

Baumol distinguishes between productive and unproductive entrepreneurship. Says Baumol,

> while the total supply of entrepreneurs varies among societies, the productive contribution of the society's entrepreneurial activities varies much more because of their allocation between productive activities such as innovation and largely unproductive activities such as rent seeking or organized crime. This allocation is heavily influenced by the relative payoffs society offers to such activities.
>
> *(Baumol, 1990: 893)*

International criminal activities such as money laundering, illicit financial transactions, political corruption and tax evasion affect every country and region in the world. The collapse of the former Soviet Union and other communist nations in Central and Eastern Europe has opened the door to criminal entrepreneurs. China too has witnessed unprecedented levels of corruption. In addition, the economic liberalization of the past two or more decades, and the expansion of international trade, has given greater scope for unproductive entrepreneurship.

There are two implications of this. First, the reward structures and the rules of the game built into social institutions influence the choices made by entrepreneurs and hence the allocation of entrepreneurship between productive and unproductive activities. For example, limited legal protections, lack of transparency requirements, inadequate enforcement of national and international laws and overall weak governance allow unproductive entrepreneurship to flourish. Thus, we would expect to find high rates of illicit rent seeking in failed and critically weak states such as Somalia, Afghanistan and the Democratic Republic of Congo (Rice and Patrick, 2008).

Second, public policy influences the allocation of entrepreneurship. For example, securing property rights and an efficient judicial system, enforcing contracts, and limiting the coercive powers of government can raise the relative return to productive as opposed to unproductive entrepreneurship.

"Praxeological" international entrepreneurship

Contemporary Austrians use Von Mises' notion of praxeology to study international entrepreneurship. This means the so-called international entrepreneur scans the globe for economic opportunities, evaluates these opportunities and then acts to pursue one or more of them: scan, evaluate and act, all in an environment of uncertainty. The entrepreneur is "a decision-maker whose *entire*

164 Austrian international economics

role arises out of his alertness to hitherto unnoticed opportunities" (Kirzner, 1979: 38–39).

Everyone is an entrepreneur to some degree. Scanning, evaluating and acting on opportunities are things we all do in everyday life. Government bureaucrats can be entrepreneurs, as can students, taxi drivers and office workers. But the Austrian entrepreneur is not like everyone else.

Austrian entrepreneurs own factors of production, possess sufficient wealth to purchase or lease these factors, or can convince others who have wealth (e.g., venture capitalists) to provide them with the resources needed to pursue their ideas. The entrepreneur then puts the resources into action, and this is what makes the economy progress and prosper.

This all happens in an idealized institutional environment called a "pure market economy." The pure market economy exists within all capitalist economies, to greater or lesser degrees. Presumably, if we understand how this idealized pure market economy works we can also understand how real-world capitalism works.

Real economies differ from each other in terms of their cultural, political and natural environments as well as in the extent to which government restricts the actions of entrepreneurs. To Austrians, entrepreneurs are always in conflict with government agents no matter where in the world they operate. Both private entrepreneurs and governments are able to direct society's resources. Government agents do so by modifying or restricting property rights using institutionalized coercion. In international economics, governments intervene in trade and promote policies using such policies as tariffs and quotas which protect favored domestic industries. Private entrepreneurs, on the other hand, exercise no coercion and act voluntarily within the framework of existing national laws.

International entrepreneurship and the pure global market economy

A pure global market economy is an idealized picture of an international free market system in which trade freely occurs among nations that are also pure market economies. All nations use the same currency, although we might also assume the Hayekian idea of freely competing currencies. All have complete private property rights and unrestrained free enterprise. There are no barriers to trade and governments and central banks undertake no activist macroeconomic policies to alter the course of economic activity.

Entrepreneurs drive the world economy using their innate creativity and inventiveness; they scan, analyze and act on global opportunities. In this way, global entrepreneurs direct the world's resources to alternative uses. This global pure market economy embeds itself, to greater or lesser degrees, in the real global economy. Austrians believe that if we understand how this system works, we would also understand how the real world works.

The international entrepreneur is the primary catalyst for the special Austrian principle of comparative advantage. In fact, "[t]he principle of comparative advantage is a praxeological principle" (Gunning, 2006: 162). The entrepreneur is responsible for causing all the adjustments in exports, imports and world prices that we see in orthodox trade models. Unlike that model, however, the Austrian world economy never reaches equilibrium and all factors of production freely flow across all borders.

Nations whose governments restrict trade through use of tariffs and quotas will affect the economy in a predictable way: reduced efficiency, slower economic growth and diminished economic welfare. Once a government goes down the road of protection it encourages entrepreneurs to allocate resources to influencing politicians to adopt even more protective interventions. This is the kind of "rent seeking" described by Baumol. It is a slippery slope that undermines growth and development.

An empirical note: measuring global entrepreneurship

There has been much empirical research on international entrepreneurship (see Gunning, 2004; Jones, Wheeler and Dimitiratos, 2011). One such effort is the Global Entrepreneurship Monitor (GEM) project. The GEM is an annual assessment of entrepreneurial activity, aspirations and attitudes in over 100 countries. Table 7.1 shows the rate of entrepreneurship as a percentage of the population for selected countries. The table shows entrepreneurship to be most prevalent in China and Latin America. In many countries, however, a lack of employment opportunities drives entrepreneurship, not voluntary choice.

Remaining empirical questions about global entrepreneurship include whether such activity affects economic growth and if so by how much. It is also uncertain what determines a country's entrepreneurial activity. This is a fundamental sociological question.

Entrepreneurs or capitalists?

Orthodox economic theory has never really made clear who it is that directs economic activity. All we learn is that there are three factors of production—labor, land and capital—and that someone allocates these resources to their highest valued uses. Who the people are that play this role is unclear.

Austrian theory attaches great importance to the entrepreneur as the main driver of the domestic and global economy. Is this dynamic and productive Austrian entrepreneur the same person as the labor-exploiting "capitalist" we find in heterodox economic theories such as Marxian, Institutionalist and Post Keynesian economics? Indeed, the line between the entrepreneur and the "capitalist" is unclear. Both entrepreneur and capitalist employ labor in pursuit of economic opportunity. Both scan, evaluate and act on opportunities.

Most people cannot perform the entrepreneurial function because they either lack the wealth and or the access to wealth to do so. We are therefore necessarily describing a class system with a privileged few who engage in entrepreneurship, and a property-less majority who must work for the entrepreneurs. The penniless

166 Austrian international economics

TABLE 7.1 Entrepreneurship in selected countries

	Total early-stage ownership rate %	Necessity-driven entrepreneurial activity %
China	24.0	41.0
Chile	23.7	27.0
Peru	22.9	22.0
Colombia	21.4	25.0
Argentina	20.8	33.0
Panama	20.8	27.0
Thailand	19.5	19.0
Guatemala	19.3	33.0
United States	12.3	21.0
Turkey	11.9	32.0
Latvia	11.9	26.0
Lithuania	11.3	28.0
Australia	10.5	15.0
Mexico	9.6	19.0
Pakistan	9.1	47.0
South Africa	9.1	35.0
Poland	9.0	48.0
Taiwan	7.9	17.0
Korea (South)	7.8	41.0
United Kingdom	7.3	17.0
Hungary	6.3	31.0
France	5.7	15.0
Germany	5.6	19.0
Japan	5.2	25.0
Russia	4.6	27.0

Source: The Global Entrepreneurship Monitor, 2012.
Note: The "total early-stage ownership rate" is the percentage of the 18–64 population who are actively involved in setting up a business but have not yet done so, plus those who own and have been running a business for three months or less. The "necessity-driven entrepreneurial activity rate" is the percentage of those involved in early-stage ownership who do so because they have no other option for work.

individual who can convince venture capitalists to finance a brilliant idea is the exception not the rule. The only way around this problem is to presume that *anyone* with a good idea can get financial backing to start an enterprise and put resources to work.

This seems to be the Austrian approach. The entrepreneur and the capitalist are essentially the same people. They can function exactly the way the Austrian theory describes while still exploiting labor and the environment just as heterodox theories describe. Austrian economists, however, cast labor aside as the main actor on the economic stage and replace it with the fictional entrepreneur.

Austrians and global institutions

Austrians' distrust of government extends to regional and international organizations. The European Union as well as the three main Bretton Woods organizations—the World Trade Organization, the International Monetary Fund and the World Bank—fall into this category. Synchronization of national fiscal and monetary policies, coordination of currencies and harmonization of environmental and labor standards are targets of Austrian criticism. Put simply, Austrians believe these kinds of organizations and regulatory practices curtail economic growth, serve mainly special interests and threaten individual liberties.

But Austrians are not isolationists. In fact, they do support supra-national alliances. This might seem a contradiction. It is not contradictory if we consider that, to Austrians, the legitimate function of supra-national alliances is to protect private property, enforce contracts and promote free trade and free enterprise. They must also agree to remove all discretionary fiscal and monetary powers. Austrians imagine a world in which people everywhere freely interact in global markets so that no single nation is forcibly "isolated."

Such an arrangement is not likely to be very popular among international capitalists, as Hayek himself observed when he remarked that such libertarian policies "will set very definite limitations to the realization of widely cherished ambitions" (Hayek, 1948: 255). By this he meant capitalists will always use their "unproductive" entrepreneurial skills (viz., Baumol's rent seeking) to convince governments to protect their positions with trade restrictions and monopoly privileges. These are the so-called cherished ambitions that free trade regimes would frustrate.

Hayekian interstate federations

In his 1939 essay "The Economic Conditions of Interstate Federalism," Hayek proposed the creation of an "interstate federation." While he wrote this essay well before the European Union and other similar associations, Hayek's analysis has much to say about the contemporary world.

To Hayek, an interstate federation would combine economic and political functions. The economic function:

> would do away with the impediments as to the movement of men, goods, and capital between the states and . . . would render possible the creation of common rules of law, a uniform monetary system, and common control of communications.
>
> *(Hayek, 1948: 255)*

The political function of an interstate federation

> eliminates parochial and partisan frictions and establishes a system of dispute resolution. It pursues a common foreign policy and a common

168 Austrian international economics

> defense policy that eliminates external military threats by presenting a
> united front.
>
> *(Hayek, 1948: 255)*

To make all this work requires that nations subordinate themselves to the Federation; local and sectional interests must give way to the interest of the whole. In doing so, goods and resources can move freely across borders and it would be impossible for individual states to influence prices. Only differences in transportation costs would affect the prices in different places within the federation. Any change in the conditions of production of a particular commodity would, because of competition, equally affect its prices everywhere.

Furthermore, individual member nations would be unable to conduct protectionist and redistributive policies, and all forms of restraint on trade and monopolistic organizations (e.g., labor unions, cartels and professional associations) would cease to be tools of national governments.

Member nations would also be unable to conduct discretionary monetary and fiscal policies. All would accept a common monetary unit that no one could artificially influence. In fact, argues Hayek, independent national central banks would no longer exist. As for fiscal policy, a federation would restrict a nation's methods of raising tax revenues. Mobility of people and resources between the nations provide incentives to avoid any kind of tax that would drive capital or labor elsewhere.

Hayek's diversity thesis

Hayek's scheme is an attempt to generalize his opposition to all government power. He believed that if an international federation is large enough it could benefit from diversity among its members. By diversity he meant differences in members' economic conditions and levels of economic development.

A large federation is likely to have both declining industries and prospering industries. Hayek argued that any appeal by declining industries for special assistance or protection from the federation would confront opposite demands for freedom of trade and development from prospering nations. Said Hayek, "[it] will be much harder to retard progress in one part of the federation in order to maintain standards of life in another part than to do the same thing in a national state" (Hayek, 1948: 263).

In other words, it would be hard for people in declining sectors of a federation economy to impose protectionist policies that stifle the prosperity of progressive sectors in order to maintain the status quo. Diversity therefore discourages implementation of policies that protect special interests.

Finally, citizens in a member state would be reluctant to accept interference by the federation government in their local affairs when that federation government consists of people with different nationalities and cultures. Hayek concludes,

> There seems to be little possible doubt that the scope for the regulation
> of economic life will be much narrower for the central government of a

federation than for national states. And since, as we have seen, the power of the states which comprise the federation will be yet more limited, much of the interference with economic life to which we have become accustomed will be altogether impracticable under a federal organization.

(Hayek, 1948: 265)

Contemporary interstate federations

Hayek's ideas are germane to contemporary international federations. The European Union (EU), the International Monetary Fund and the World Bank are examples of federations that have drawn the attention of Austrian economists.

Fifty years in the making, European integration has achieved many of the goals advanced by Hayek and the Austrians. In particular, the EU, consisting of 27 nations, has established a single European market in which capital, goods and people freely circulate. The EU also has powerful institutions that maintain competition among European businesses.

One component of the EU is the Eurozone. The Eurozone consists of 17 of the 27 EU nations that have adopted a single currency—the euro. Another important component is the European Central Bank (ECB), which is responsible for conducting monetary policy within the zone. The ECB is similar to the Federal Reserve Bank in the United States. The central banks of the 17 Eurozone members own the capital of the ECB. The ECB's principal responsibility is maintaining price stability, which makes inflation its principal monetary policy target.

It is noteworthy that while the EU conducts a common monetary policy, there is no common fiscal governance. Monetary and fiscal policy coordination, or the lack of it, is a major issue in all advanced capitalist nations. Critics claim that lack of central control over the state budgets of Eurozone members has created a bias towards deficits. Indeed, since 2009 the national debt of many EU member nations has become unsustainably large, meaning they have had insufficient resources (e.g., tax revenues) to service their rapidly growing debt. This problem became especially severe (albeit for very different reasons) in Portugal, Italy, Greece and Spain where deficits became dangerously large and where recession and unemployment affect the lives of millions of people.

Austrians would praise the EU's free market environment and its protection of property rights and individual liberties. EU nations are also diverse in terms of culture and level of economic development. However, they would complain that ECB monetary policy destabilized rather than stabilized the EU economy. In particular, the willingness of the ECB to purchase the bonds issued by the debt-ridden Eurozone states simply sanctions wasteful spending and sustains big government. The ECB should instead avoid all discretionary policies and allow the euro to adjust automatically to changing circumstances.

Austrian economists also stress the need for fiscal austerity: large reductions in government spending combined with no tax increases. The point is to reduce the size of government everywhere—irrespective of the short-term pain that such a policy would inflict on populations already suffering economic hardship. As the saying goes, "No pain, no gain." Austrians have faith, however, that such policies would give greater scope to private enterprise and entrepreneurship in solving their economic problems and in enhancing the social and economic welfare of all.

It is unsurprising that Austrians are generally critical of both the International Monetary Fund (IMF) and the World Bank. The IMF lends short-term money to nations experiencing balance of payments and debt problems. The IMF generally imposes conditions on borrowing nations that require them to change their profligate ways. To Austrians, IMF lending is like giving drugs to drug addicts. Stated more elegantly, it creates a *moral hazard* by encouraging borrowing governments to continue their risky behavior because they know the IMF will bail them out again. The solution: either stop funding the IMF or abolish it.

The Austrian assessment of the World Bank is likewise harsh. The World Bank's mission is to lend long-term money to help nations develop. While its mission has changed significantly since its inception in 1944, Austrians point to extensive research showing that the World Bank has generally failed to meet its objectives and has likely had a negative effect on the growth and development of borrowing nations. The solution they offer is the same: either stop funding the World Bank or abolish it.

In conclusion, Austrians believe the causes of instability and economic crises are wrongheaded economic policies based on wrongheaded economic theories. The best thing to do is to remove the temptation to prolong the inevitable and to eliminate the ability of policymakers to undermine the natural workings of the free market.

The transformation from socialism to capitalism

For most of the 20th century, scholars have debated the transformation of capitalism to socialism. In many intellectual circles capitalism was an evil and exploitive system that people must replace with a more human system: socialism. The question is how to accomplish this transformation?

Beginning in 1989, history evolved in the opposite direction. The question became instead how to transform socialism into capitalism. The Soviet Union and the socialist countries of Central and Eastern Europe disintegrated, beginning a long and tortuous political and economic transformation into market-oriented capitalist economies. China and Vietnam also began similar transitions.

Austrians have hoped that these transitional nations would develop free market economies with free choice and voluntary exchange. They trusted that natural market forces would produce efficient, welfare-maximizing, capitalist market institutions. The question became how to accomplish this. Would appropriate institutions form spontaneously, or would central direction and coordination be necessary?

A new genre of economic literature emerged in the 1990s that addressed this question. Scholars tried to discover the optimal path of transition from centrally planned socialism to free market capitalism. Part of this discussion was whether a political transformation to democracy is also required to accompany and to enable the economic transition. They asked, what is the connection between political democracy and free market capitalism? While there has been no consensus, most Austrians lean toward answering in the affirmative, that democratic institutions must develop simultaneously with the development of free market capitalist institutions.

Conclusions

Austrian international economics is an extension of the ideology, vision, analytical methods and economic theories developed in the last century by prominent Austrian economists. Austrians imagine a world of free trade, free cross-border capital and labor flows, competitive global markets, competitive currencies (or, alternatively, a gold standard), free international banking, deregulation of business, privatization of government-owned enterprises, protection of private property rights and minimum government intervention. In this idealized world, entrepreneurship becomes the central economic driving force.

Austrians share with the Neoclassical orthodoxy faith in free trade and global capitalism. While they too believe in comparative advantage, Austrians reject equilibrium analysis and assume that all resources freely flow across national borders. They replace equilibrium with evolutionary dynamics, and abstract formal mathematical models with holistic "praxeological" models of human action. Austrians see lying beneath the forces of comparative advantage and international trade the actions of global entrepreneurs who constantly scan, evaluate and act on opportunities in a global environment of uncertainty. The decisions entrepreneurs make move resources and products from place to place around the world.

Austrians' unwavering faith in free markets and free enterprise is matched only by their distrust of collectivism and discretionary government intervention. This is possibly rooted in the personal experiences first-generation Austrians had with Nazism and Stalinism earlier in the 20th century. The free market system is a form of salvation from malevolent government bureaucrats seeking to protect special interests using the coercive tools of the state. This applies as well to the international arena. Trade regulations (e.g., tariffs, quotas and non-trade barriers) and transnational governmental organizations (e.g., European Union and Bretton Woods institutions) potentially undermine economic liberty and skew the benefits of international trade in favor of rent seekers and special interests.

Austrians assume economic competition prevents monopoly and economic despotism. But can we not also assume that free political competition, for votes, prevents rent seeking and tyranny in the public sector? Would not the values of the electorate determine political decisions and policy actions, and would not only those politicians survive who serve the public interest? If we profess faith in competition among entrepreneurs, can we not also profess faith in competition among politicians (e.g., democracy)? Political competition would then prevent the

172 Austrian international economics

emergence of a tyrannical state, just as economic competition would prevent the emergence of economic tyranny. Of course this conclusion becomes uncertain in a global context where democratic global institutions may be impractical.

Ultimately, the problem is not really the conflict between the state and the market. The problem lies instead in the fact that groups possessing enormous wealth (however acquired) are able to influence and manipulate *both* the government and the market, depriving the majority of the population of both economic security and liberty.

It is difficult to say if Austrian economists inherently distrust collectivism and discretionary government intervention as part of an implicit personal philosophy, or if they become distrustful because of empirical analysis. In other words, is their belief a built-in *a priori* bias that they bring to the study of international economics, or is it a scientific conclusion? We leave the answer to the reader.

Notes

1   We will occasionally refer to economists from this school of thought as "Austrians." This does not necessarily mean they are citizens of Austria. Indeed most Austrians today are Americans (see below).
2   Well-known Austrian institutes are the Cato Institute and the Ludwig Von Mises Institute. Austrian academic journals include the *Review of Austrian Economics* and its successor, the *Quarterly Journal of Austrian Economics* and the *Journal of Libertarian Studies*. The Cato Institute also publishes the *Cato Journal*.
3   Hayek introduced the word *catallaxy*, which he defined as "the order brought about by the mutual adjustment of many individual economies in a market" (Hayek, 1976: 269). He wanted to replace the word economics with the word catallactics.
4   For an extended discussion see Visser (1988).
5   This assumes a quantity theory of value according to which changes on the supply of money cause proportionate changes in price levels.
6   The hypotenuse does not need to be linear. It is possible, moreover, that increased roundaboutness might increase rather decrease consumer good output. This is an unsettled empirical issue (Young, 2005).
7   Schumpeter distinguishes invention from innovation. The former emphasizes new technical knowledge. The latter emphasizes new methods and products. We need not concern ourselves with this distinction here. In his later work Schumpeter identified innovation with large corporations that invest in research and development.
8   Schumpeter coined this term in his book *Capitalism, Socialism, and Democracy* (Schumpeter, 1942).

References

Arrow, K. (1994). "Methodological Individualism and Social Knowledge." *American Economic Review, 84*(2), 2–9.

Baldwin, R. E. (1982). "Gottfried Haberler's Contributions to International Trade Theory and Policy." *Quarterly Journal of Economics, 97*(1), 141–148.

Baumol, W. J. (1990). "Entrepreneurship: Productive, Unproductive, and Destructive." *Journal of Political Economy, 98*(5), 893–921.

Dana, L. P. (Ed.) (2004). *The Handbook of Research on International Entrepreneurship.* Northampton, MA: Edward Elgar Publishsers.

Global Entrepreneurship Monitor (2012, October 29). Retrieved September 21 2012, from http://www.gemconsortium.org/.

Gunning, J. P. (2006). "The Praxeological Concept of International Entrepreneurship." In L. P. Dana (Ed.), *Handbook of Research on International Entrepreneurship*. Brookfield, VT: Edward Elgar Publishing.

Haberler, G. (1936). *The Theory of International Trade, with Its Applications to Commercial Policy*. New York: Macmillan.

Hayek, F. A. (1945). "The Use of Knowledge in Society." *American Economic Review, 35*(4), 519–530.

Hayek, F. A. (1948). *Individualism and the Economic Order*. Chicago, IL: University of Chicago Press.

Hayek, F. A. (1967). *Studies in Philosophy, Politics and Economics*. Chicago, IL: University of Chicago Press.

Hayek, F. A. (1976a). *Choice in Currency: A Way to Stop Inflation*. London: Institute of Economic Affairs.

Hayek, F. A. (1976b). *Law, Legislation and Liberty*. London: Routledge.

Hayek, F. A. (1977). *Denationalisation of Money: An Analysis of the Theory and Practice of Concurrent Currencies*. London: Institute of Economic Afairs.

Jones, M. V., Wheeler, C., & Dimitiratos, P. (Eds.) (2011). *International Entrepreneurship in the Life Sciences*. Northampton, MA: Edward Elgar Publishers.

Kirzner, I. (1979). *Perception, Opportunity, and Profit*. Chicago, IL: University of Chicago Press.

Rice, S. E., & Patrick, S. (2008). *Index of State Weakness in the Developing World*. Washington, DC: Brookings Institute.

Rothbard, M. N. (1993). *Man, Economy, and State*. Auburn, AL: Ludwig Von Mises Institute.

Samuelson, P. A. (1966). "A Summing Up." *Quarterly Journal of Economics, 80*(4), 568–583.

Schumpeter, J. A. (1909). "On the Concept of Social Value." *Quarterly Journal of Economics, 23*(2), 213–232.

Schumpeter, J. A. (1934). *The Theory of Economic Development*. Cambridge, MA: Harvard University Press.

Schumpeter, J. A. (1942). *Capitalism, Socialism, and Democracy*. New York: Harper & Brothers.

Shackle, G. L. (1972). *Epistemics and Economics: A Critique of Economic Doctrines*. New York: Cambridge University Press.

Visser, H. (1988). "Austrian Thinking on International Economics." *Journal of Economic Studies, 15*(3 and 4), 106–122.

Von Mises, L. (1966 (1949)). *Human Action. A Treatise on Economics* (3rd revised ed.). Chicago, IL: Henery Regnery Company.

Von Mises, L. (1975). "Economic Calculation in the Socialist Commonwealth." In F. A. Hayek (Ed.), *Collectivist Economic Planning* (Reprint ed., pp. 87–130). Clifton, NJ: Augustus M. Kelley. Retrieved July 20 2012, from http://Von Mises.org/econcalc.asp.

Young, A. T. (2005). "Reallocating Labor to Initiate Changes in Capital Structures: Hayek Revisited." *Economic Letters, 89*(3), 275–282.

8

INSTITUTIONALIST INTERNATIONAL ECONOMICS

Introduction

Institutionalism is mostly an American academic tradition that began around the First World War. Prominent among early Institutional economists were Thorstein Veblen (1857–1929), John R. Commons (1862–1945), Wesley C. Mitchell (1874–1948) and Clarence Ayres (1891–1972). These were well-known scholars who commanded considerable respect from the economics profession. Their influence waned right after the Second World War, only to re-emerge once again in the turbulent 1970s. Since then, Institutional economics has become a vital *heterodox* approach to the study of economics with a devoted following and several professional organizations and academic journals.[1]

Institutionalists position themselves in opposition to the economic orthodoxy. Their main grievances with the orthodoxy are that its psychology of rational choice is too narrow and rigid; its assumptions are too unrealistic and its models too abstract; it has a dismissive attitude toward the other social sciences; it is unscientific, despite its claims otherwise; and it serves mainly as an apologetic for the capitalist system.

Institutional economics puts forward an alternative methodology that is evolutionary, holistic and interdisciplinary. It avoids the orthodox pretense of value-neutrality and explicitly builds social values into their analyses, including the values of the researcher-observer. Institutional economic theory widens the scope of the discipline beyond its narrow and obsessive concern with markets. It does this by analyzing non-market institutions and by paying close attention to the social and cultural context in which markets function. Finally, Institutionalist economic policies reject the idea that the state is by nature hostile to private interests and search for humane solutions to real-world problems. It eschews "faith in the market" as the only way to accomplish this.

During the 1960s and 1970s there was a growing drumbeat of criticism of orthodox economics. Critics argued that orthodox economic theory simply could not deal adequately with the issues of gender, race and class that plague contemporary capitalism. In failing to deal with these issues economics became, by default, the champion of everything the critics believed to be wrong with American society. This new critical environment fortified heterodox approaches to economics, including Institutionalism.

The assault on the orthodoxy in the 1960s and 1970s had an effect, albeit slight, on mainstream economists. In particular, it inspired the latter to shift their gaze away from the market toward non-market social institutions. This resulted in the so-called *New Institutional Economics* (NIE), not to be confused with American Institutionalism (Alchian, 1950), which is the subject of this chapter. Recent advances in NIE indeed have broadened the scope of economic analysis, taking it into previously neglected territory. We shall see examples of this later in this chapter.

Despite this apparent progress, NIE still has been unable to give up its market fetish. For all it has done is to apply the same individualistic, rationalistic and abstract methodology to non-market institutions as it does to market institutions. New Institutional Economics thus is not very Institutionalist at all; it simply reduces social phenomena to the Neoclassical calculus of rational choice.[2]

Before proceeding, we offer three cautionary notes about Institutional economics. First, it is diverse; there exists no single, universally accepted doctrine as in orthodox economics. There are instead lineages of thought, or "styles," that follow one or another prominent Institutional scholar. Despite this diversity, it is still possible to delineate a general Institutionalist approach to economics. Second, Institutionalists pay a great deal of attention to how they differ from orthodox economics. For this reason this chapter also pays a lot of attention to how Institutionalists differ from the orthodoxy. Third, Institutionalists have paid relatively little attention to international economics except for a handful of contributions that we will cite in this chapter.[3] All we can do in this chapter is to assemble these contributions into a narrative about the world economy that roots itself in the Institutionalist method.

Methodology of Institutional economics

We begin by defining the term "institution." Institutions are the basic building blocks of society. They frame and surround our lives. We live, work and play in institutions. Institutions are present everywhere and they make up the social structures in which all of us function daily.

An institution is a system of *rules*. A rule is simply a directive that says, "When circumstance X exists, do (or do not do) Y." No one actually barks commands or shouts directives at people. We all learn the rules and, for the most part, we abide by them.

Rules can be formal and codified into law. Civil and criminal law, workplace regulations, uniform weights and measures and corporate accounting practices are examples of formal rules. There are also informal rules such as social norms,

176 Institutionalist international economics

customs and practices. These are usually unwritten, yet everyone seems to understand what they are.

Often we are not even aware that we are following an institutional rule. We call this *habituation*, which is the subconscious tendency to conform to rule-based behavior. Obeying a social rule is, after all, nothing more than a *habit*, something we do automatically, usually without question or premeditation. Formal and informal *incentives* and *penalties* motivate people to abide by institutional rules, at least until behaviors become habitual, at which time incentives and penalties become unnecessary.

To round out our understanding of institutions we define two additional concepts. First, a *social convention* is a particular instance or application of a rule. Driving on the right side of the road is an American convention; driving on the left side of the road is a British convention. Paying taxes on April 15 is another social convention.

Second, a *social organization* is a special kind of institution with a particular set of rules. Organizations include families, corporations, churches, political parties, schools, unions, government entities and many more. Organizations employ particular institutional rules such as workplace rules and dress codes. Some organizations have rules that are unique and not shared by other organizations. The rules governing the division of labor in a family are different from the rules governing the division of labor in a corporation.

Organizations have special membership rules that establish the boundaries defining who belongs and who does not belong. They also have rules of hierarchy that delineate individual responsibilities and the distribution of power and authority. An organization can act as one; yet the individuals belonging to an organization can conflict. Organizations will therefore have special rules to reconcile and arbitrate differences among individual members.

Special characteristics of institutions

There are five important characteristics of institutions.

1. *Institutions are durable.* They replicate themselves over time and from generation to generation, albeit in altered form. This lends stability and predictability to social activity and human behavior. When you drive down the road you expect the oncoming traffic to remain on the other side. When you sell a product or provide a service, you expect payment. Institutions thus structure and channel human behavior. They constrain and enable human action and social interactions, thereby imposing stability and uniformity on society.
2. *People construct institutions.* Institutions are not natural or God given. People create institutions in certain historical circumstances and under certain conditions. People also modify them when they no longer work. Institutions are therefore flexible and continually evolve in response to changing internal and external conditions.

3. *Institutions influence people's tastes and preferences, beliefs, attitudes and values.* Members of the military will have different tastes and preferences than members of the priesthood. Yet people are not automatons; they also make independent choices that in turn influence the structure and function of institutions. Because there is interplay between individuals and institutions, we can say that institutions and human behavior are endogenous and interactive.

4. *Some institutions are necessary to make society function well, while others are anachronistic, archaic and wasteful.* Veblen called the former *instrumental* institutions and the latter *ceremonial* institutions. Instrumental institutions are institutions that make positive contributions to social well-being and are therefore valuable to society. Science and technology are examples of instrumental institutions. Ceremonial institutions play no positive role and may even be parasitical, retarding human progress. Examples are superstitions, sacred beliefs, privileges of status and other emotional attachments. Veblen's most noted example of a ceremonial institution is *conspicuous consumption*, which refers to unnecessary spending by the wealthy elite for the sole purpose of displaying and maintaining their superior social status. These two types of institutions—instrumental and ceremonial—are always in conflict. This conflict gives rise to social change as people discover ways to resolve their differences.

5. *Institutions differ among nations.* This is especially important in international economics. Global trade and investment crosses borders into societies with very different institutional rules. Therefore, for international economic interactions to take place, people must adapt to these differences. This results in *transactions costs*. International transactions require that people exchange currencies, translate documents into multiple languages, pay duties and taxes and conform to foreign customs and practices. These are not cheap.

Instincts: positive and negative

Following Veblen, Institutional economists argue that people have many types of inner impulses or *instincts* that govern their behavior. Some instincts are constructive and advance human progress, while others are destructive and prevent or even reverse human progress. The positive instincts are (1) the *instinct of workmanship*; (2) *idle curiosity*; and (3) the *parental tendency*. The main negative instinct is the *predatory instinct*.[4]

The instinct of workmanship is the unrelenting human inclination to find new and better ways of doing things. People are always innovating and experimenting, as if they have some inner restlessness. Some would say Steve Jobs of the Apple Inc. was endowed with the instinct of workmanship. The consequence of this creative instinct is economic progress. It is also the basis for technology because humans are always inventing new tools and new ways of using tools.

Idle curiosity means that people are intrinsically inquisitive and have an urge to want to know things, even if the knowledge acquired does not actually result in anything practical or usable. People will identify problems and come up with solutions even if there are no rewards for doing so. That's just the way we are.

178 Institutionalist international economics

The parental tendency is the general concern people have for others—family and children, one's ethnic group, the next generation or people in poor nations. It is similar to Adam Smith's notion of "fellow-feeling," which describes how we often imagine ourselves in someone else's shoes and feel pity when they are hurt and pleasure when they are happy.

In contrast, the predatory instinct is the nastier side of human behavior. It is the urge to control, compete, manipulate, subjugate and exploit. It is the exercise of power over others. By power we mean the ability to influence the ideas, actions, behaviors and well-being of people and institutions. Men subjugate and exercise power over women, capitalists over workers and the strong over the weak. In contemporary capitalism there is an ongoing pecuniary (i.e., monetary) struggle to accumulate wealth, to exhibit that wealth and to emulate the wealth of others. Being productive and *producing* wealth becomes less important than *acquiring* wealth and displaying wealth (see conspicuous consumption on p. 177).

To Veblen, the positive instincts are most prevalent among ordinary people, especially workers, entrepreneurs and engineers. These are the cooperative, creative and progressive people in economic society. Veblen used the term *industry* to describe what they do.

The predatory instinct, on the other hand, is the primary trait of businesspeople (Veblen, 1904). Veblen used the term *business* to describe the activities of profit-seeking financial engineering and the manipulation of markets for personal gain. Businesspeople include Wall Street bankers and financiers, advertisers, salespeople, absentee owners and the so-called "captains of industry." Predatory businesspeople benefit from obstructing or "sabotaging" production in order to increase the money value of their personal wealth. They are less interested in producing things of value for society than they are in getting their hands on the wealth produced by others.

In capitalism, industry struggles with business. Business enterprise tries to impose its will on the progressive members of society. When it succeeds, it creates economic instabilities, recessions and depressions and inequality. Business enterprise also exercises power by influencing government policy, the judicial system and legislative decision making.

Thus, workers and engineers are the progressive forces in society and businesspeople are the regressive forces (Veblen, 1934). Ultimately, economic progress relies on technology, and technology relies on science and industry. It requires that the positive instincts flourish and overpower the negative instincts.

Economic power

Unlike the orthodox emphasis on free will and rational choice, Institutionalism stresses economic power. By economic power we mean the ability of people or organizations to compel others to behave and act in ways that may be against their own interests. To put it bluntly, the strong impose their will upon the weak. How does this happen?

The explanation for this compliance with power is simply that weaker parties are either people who have no choice but to comply, perhaps because they risk losing their jobs, or those who simply do not understand what their interests are.

The rights of property ownership in capitalist society and the prevalence of managerial hierarchies in corporations clearly are tools for the exercise of power. Those who have economic power because of their wealth or position in corporate hierarchies can tell others what to do. When the boss tells an employee to do something, there is little choice but to comply.

How can those with power force others to act against their own interests? Here we invoke Veblen's theory about *enabling myths* (Dugger, 1992). Many of these myths involve beliefs about the distribution of income and wealth, beliefs about who deserves the largest pieces of the economic pie. Orthodox marginal productivity theory is one such myth: those with larger slices presumably contribute—and hence deserve—larger portions of the pie. A related myth is that the competitive market system dispenses social justice. Therefore, those who succeed in the marketplace deserve that success, and those who fail do not. Yet another myth is the natural inevitability of hierarchy: a small number of people will always be at the top who exercise authority over those positioned below them. Presumably, this is the natural order of things.

Global industry and global business

We can apply some of these ideas to international economics. The world economy consists of countless institutions and organizations. These include transnational corporations, small and mid-sized enterprises, national governments and global and regional organizations. Millions of transactions occur within and between these organizations.

Looking at the world economy from an Institutional perspective suggests that we separate those organizations that promote global economic stability, opportunity and well-being—*global industry*—from those that undermine economic stability, opportunity and well-being—*global business*.

Separating the malefactors from the virtuous is difficult and controversial. Among the malefactors would be the unscrupulous sub-prime mortgage lenders who enriched themselves by triggering the 2007 collapse in the housing industry in the US and Europe. Others would include hedge fund managers and currency speculators such as FX Concepts that allegedly contributed to the financial crises in the European Union. In 2011 Swedish Finance Minister Anders Borg said these businesses act "like a pack of wolves" (*Der Spiegel*, 2011). Controversy has also spread over the role the IMF played in 1997 in throwing people out of work when it imposed austerity conditions on developing Asian countries in return for help in stabilizing their currencies. Critics also have targeted scores of other global businesses from Monsanto to Wal-Mart for undermining social welfare and creating unemployment, especially in developing countries.

On the positive side of the ledger is global industry, those organizations that make positive contributions to global social welfare. These would be organizations governed by the instinct of workmanship, idle curiosity and the parental tendency. *Fortune Magazine* lists the top 10 most socially responsible companies, although some on the list are questionable. Google's 2004 SEC prospectus stated:

> Don't be evil. We believe strongly that in the long term, we will be better served—as shareholders and in all other ways—by a company that does good things for the world even if we forgo some short term gains. This is an important aspect of our culture and is broadly shared within the company.
>
> *(Securities and Exchange Commission, 2004)*

We might include on the positive side of the ledger corporations engaged in renewable alternative energy technologies, fair trade initiatives, microfinance, worker-owned cooperative enterprises, the Oslo Business for Peace Foundation and a multitude of non-government non-profit organizations.

Holism

In Institutional economics the economy is an integral part of the social, political and natural environment. This means that all economic, social, political and natural systems are interdependent and mutually reinforcing. Everything that happens in the economy immediately affects all other aspects of society as well as the physical environment. And everything that happens in society and the environment affects the economy. The term *holism* therefore means that we can only understand how a system works if we know how all the parts of the system are interconnected.

In Institutional economics, institutions always change. They are in a constant state of flux. Society is like a living organism that continuously transforms itself into other varieties in response to changes in its external and internal environment. The system is *evolutionary*.

Holism clearly requires that we take a multidisciplinary view of the relationships connecting people, organizations and institutions. Sociology, psychology and biology must combine with economics to yield explanations of social phenomena. This is especially important in international economics because economic relations between nations affect, and are affected by cultural, sociological and psychological factors.

Orthodox economics, in contrast, takes a different approach. We call this approach *atomism*. Atomism focuses on isolated, indivisible individual elements or "atoms" of society—individual consumers and firms. Their underlying characteristics—their gender, class, race and tastes and preferences—are given and beyond scrutiny. The individual is exogenous to the system. Atomism presumes that if we can understand how the individual elements of the system work we will automatically understand how the whole system works.

In Institutional economics, the *institution* is the basic unit of analysis, not the individual. There is no such thing as an isolated "individual." The individual is a product of society, a social phenomenon. The individual is endogenous to the system.

Formalism

Formalism is an approach that builds models of logical connections between autonomous *abstract* social categories. This approach is the foundation of orthodox economics.

The verb "to abstract" means to erase all specific empirical content from a category. What is left is a shell representing all varieties belonging to the category. Examples of abstract categories are "the individual consumer," "the perfectly competitive firm," "the nation" and the "market." Each category omits all details about particular attributes.

This is how Veblen described this abstract world:

> The conception of man is that of a lightening calculator of pleasures and pains, who oscillates like a homogeneous globule of desire and happiness under the impulse of stimuli that shift him about the area but leave him intact . . . Self imposed in elemental space, he spins symmetrically about his own spiritual axis until the parallelogram of forces bears down upon him, whereupon he follows the line of the resultant. When the force of the impact is spent, he comes to rest, a self-contained globule of desire as before.
>
> *(Veblen, 1898: 389–390)*

Formalism lends itself to the use of mathematics and to the derivation of axioms and truth-like principles and economic laws. Formal models do not describe the real world; instead, they describe an abstract world, a world entirely constructed by the economist. The assumption is that the principles underlying the abstract world also apply to the real world. Institutionalists are unwilling to make this leap of faith.

Instrumentalism and social values

Institutionalists believe formalism is a failed enterprise. They prefer to use an alternative methodology called *instrumentalism.*[5] According to instrumentalism, a good economic theory must have a purpose. It must achieve some end goal. Theory is the means, or the instrument, for achieving an end goal.

There are two kinds of instrumentalism in orthodox economics. One is *predictive instrumentalism*. This derives from the work of Nobel laureate Milton Friedman (1912–2006). Friedman placed primary emphasis on prediction rather than descriptive explanation. This implies that a theory's proper use is to generate propositions that economists can use to make predictions. If predictions turn out correctly, then the theory is a good one. It doesn't even matter if the theory accurately explains or describes the real world—so long as it can yield an equation that predicts well. So here the theory is the instrument, and the useful prediction is the end goal.

182 Institutionalist international economics

A second kind is *essentialist instrumentalism*. This approach assumes there are unseen forces that make the economy work. Economic theory permits us to uncover those "essential" forces that give order to an otherwise chaotic reality. These forces are what make things happen. We call these essential forces "principles" or "economic laws." Examples are the laws of supply and demand and the law of comparative advantage. We do not actually see the laws work; all we see are their effects. Here, theory is the instrument and unearthing a universally valid economic principle is the end goal.

Institutionalism takes another approach entirely. We call it *value instrumentalism*. Value instrumentalism says a theory is useful if it solves actual economic problems *and* improves the human condition at the same time. The theory is the instrumental *means* and improving human well-being is the *end*.

We call this "value" instrumentalism because *social values* are at the center of all economic analysis. It is impossible to be objective and value-free in developing the instrumental means to accomplish social ends. Values necessarily enter into the identification of economic facts, the development of economic theories and the formulation of solutions to problems (i.e., policies). Facts and values are inseparable.

People continually debate, negotiate and compromise over values in every decision they make and in every action they take. "Valuation" is an ongoing process that occurs side by side with all economic activity. In this process people attach worth, importance and meaning to their activities and to their property.

Social valuation occurs at every level of society, including the individual, family, church, school, corporation and nation. Each level values things in different ways using different criteria. Some organizations value things based on tradition. Americans like fried eggs for breakfast while Chinese like porridge and pickled vegetables. Others value things based on work effort, as when hand-made furniture is valued more highly than machine-made furniture. We miss a lot, therefore, when we assume that tastes and preferences are given.

To incorporate values into economic analysis we must consider (1) the values of the people and institutions whose activities we are studying; (2) the values of those affected by economic policies; and (3) the values of the economist doing the analysis. Values are always on the table, so to speak.

Finally, value instrumentalism is iterative. This means that economic analysis does not stop once we come up with and apply a new economic policy. The process starts all over again. New problems arise to which we must find new theories and new solutions. Old theories expire, and there are no everlasting, enduring economic truths or principles. Means lead to ends, which lead to new means, which lead to new ends, and so forth. This is a never-ending evolutionary process that Institutionalists call the *means–ends continuum*.

The means–ends dualism and social valuation

A commonly accepted philosophical idea is that we can divide existence into two realms: the physical world or *body* and the mental world or *mind*. We call this division of existence a *dualism*. Accordingly, the physical world is an empirical reality that exists independently of our minds. The realm of the mind, on the other hand, is where values, norms and beliefs reside. It is the realm of consciousness, passion and sense perceptions. Philosophers refer to this dualism as the *Cartesian dualism*, named after the French philosopher and mathematician René Descartes (1596–1650).

There are other kinds of dualisms similar to the body–mind dualism. Examples relevant to economics are objective–subjective, positive–normative, fact–value and means–ends.[6] The first word in each pair (objective, positive, fact and means) suggests a concrete and tangible reality that we can analyze without imposing our values and opinions. We can study world commodity markets, for instance, no matter if we are capitalists, communists, Christians or Muslims. This is the realm of knowledge and science. The second word in each pair (subjective, normative, value and ends) suggests opinion and bias. It is the world of the mind, the place where thinking and feeling occur. It is a place orthodox economists try to avoid.

The orthodox economic tradition employs this Cartesian dualism when it says that economists can be neutral and value-free when investigating economic problems. This is what economists call positive economics, the science of "what is." Positive economics identifies economic principles or laws (e.g., the laws of supply and demand, diminishing returns, etc.) that can guide economic policy mainly by spelling out the choices or policies available to decision makers and policymakers. The latter can then select those choices that help to achieve their subjective goals or ends. This is the realm of normative economics.

Another application of the Cartesian dualism in economics is the distinction between production possibilities based on facts and indifference curves based on values. In Chapters 3 and 4 we drew production possibilities curves showing how many computers and bushels of wheat two nations could produce with the capital and labor resources at their disposal. These curves represent hypothetical facts and industrial engineering data. The indifference curves, on the other hand, represent *given* personal tastes and preferences of the citizens of the nations. People then choose the production combinations that best suit their preferences. Because we wish to remain value free we avoid studying these preferences and how they are formed.

Institutional economists reject all these dualisms.[7] They argue that reality is a unified whole and cannot be partitioned into two static unchanging and independent categories. Instead of asserting an either–or world of fact–value or means–ends, Institutionalists see a world of *continua*. The idea is similar to the notions of "hot" and "cold." There are no absolute definitions of hot and cold; there is only a *continuum* along a temperature scale.

What this all implies is that it is unwise for economists to build abstract formal theories about rigidly defined categories while hiding behind a curtain of "scientific" value-neutrality. Economists can only succeed if they adopt a holistic, value-instrumental method of analysis in which values appear explicitly.

184 Institutionalist international economics

Overview of institutional-international economic theory

Institutional economics proposes no abstract and formal theory of the world economy. Neither does it propose any universal economic laws or principles. We will find in Institutionalism no use of the idea of equilibrium, no production possibilities curves, no indifference curves, and few supply and demand curves. Institutionalism uses a variety of other approaches to explain specific situations and issues and draws on the work of Veblen, Ayres and Commons among others.

Institutionalist theory divides economic exchange into two interactive spheres: the internal or domestic sphere and the external or international sphere. The institutions and values governing the external sphere differ from those governing the domestic sphere. This is because foreign nations have different social, cultural, economic and political norms, rules and practices (see Adams, 1987).

For trade to occur between two nations, either one nation must adopt the other's institutions or the two must negotiate and agree to some kind of bilateral compromise. This explains why we see so many bilateral and multilateral trade agreements and global organizations such as the United Nations, World Trade Organization, International Monetary Fund and World Bank, regional development banks and the like.

The international economic architecture arises from continual negotiations among nations. The outcome of these negotiations depends on the relative power of nations and the relative desire or need for the others' products, finances and technology. War and conquest are of course alternatives to negotiations and are prevalent throughout history.

Institutionalist theory focuses on how institutions differ among societies, how these differences are reconciled, and how they affect trade and investment among nations. The culture, history, economy, polity, technology and geography of every nation are unique and Institutionalists make global institutional heterogeneity and complexity the centerpieces of their analyses.

Network analysis

Institutional economists insist we describe in detail the transactions between economic agents and organizations. We can do this by mapping the layers of overlapping networks of business and social relationships that make the world economy function.

Some scholars, notably the sociologist Gary Gereffi, have developed a methodology for doing just that (Gereffi, 1994; Gereffi and Korzeniewicz, 1994). They call it *global commodity chain analysis* (GCC). Borrowing from anthropology, sociology, geography, urban studies and development economics, GCC analysis identifies (1) an input–output structure that shows how inputs combine to produce outputs and (2) a description of the geographical spread of those economic activities and transactions. The input–output structure of a commodity chain describes the prevailing technology and the inherent complexity of global production and distribution operations.

Commodity chain analysis builds on the idea of *world cities*. World cities are key nodes in commodity chains where firms provide the services needed to permit those chains to function. These services include marketing, legal, accountancy, real estate and financial services.

Two types of commodity chains

There are two types of commodity chains in GCC analysis: (1) *producer-driven* commodity chains and (2) *buyer-driven* commodity chains. Large integrated transnational industrial corporations dominate producer-driven chains. These chains include branches, subsidiaries and subcontractors. Typically, the headquarters of a transnational firm lies at the center of a commodity chain network and governs all upstream and downstream linkages. The last upstream link of the chain is the distribution network that sells finished commodities to consumer retail businesses.

Most producer-driven chains are mixtures of mega-firms and smaller specialized firms. For example, in 2010 the United States exported to China $11.2 billion of power generation equipment. This represents thousands of transactions between thousands of producers. The Association of Manufacturers of Power Generating Systems reports that more than 80 individual US corporations engage in this export business, from large transnational corporations such as General Electric to small specialist suppliers. These firms, in turn, engage in a complex web of interactions between US and Chinese factories, shipping companies, financial institutions, legal and accountancy firms, marketing and retailing businesses and government agencies. Once again, Institutional economists seek to analyze these layers of complex linkages.

The second type of chain is the buyer-driven chain. Transnational retail corporations dominate this kind of chain. Retailers such as Wal-Mart, Carrefour and Target are examples of buyer-driven chains. They link together producers of thousands of different types of products from automobile batteries to TVs.

Other buyer-driven chains specialize in niche brand name markets such as the garment and footwear industries. Examples are Nike and Liz Claiborne. Their activities revolve around innumerable research, design, marketing and financial services companies. These companies tend to be more labor intensive than the producer-driven chains and more decentralized.

Each commodity chain has its unique characteristics. It is the task of international economics to catalog these characteristics and to analyze their histories, cultures and values, and contributions to economic development and social well-being.

Network transactions diagrams

We define a vector V to be an arrow connecting two nodal points, N_1 and N_2. Nodal point N_1 represents an individual or business organization that transfers something of value—a commodity—to another individual or business organization represented by N_2. The vector symbolizes the direction of the physical transfer.

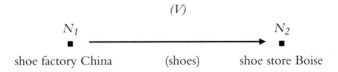

FIGURE 8.1 One link of an export chain

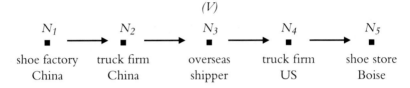

FIGURE 8.2 A chain of transfers for one transaction

We also assume for simplicity that the firms included in the commodity chains are independent. This means there are no subsidiaries, franchises, licensing agreements or long-term contracts. All firms are completely detached from one another and interact only as arm's-length buyers and sellers in the market. In a later section we drop this assumption.

An example of such a vector is the transfer of a container of sport shoes from N_1, the Ever Flying Shoe Company in Fujian Province, China, to N_2, a retail shoe store in Boise, Idaho. Figure 8.1 depicts this transfer.

The vector connecting the two nodes not only has a direction but also a magnitude. The vector represents not only where the shoes are going but also the value of the items transferred. The vector therefore represents a *transaction*.

In the real world, transactions are more complicated than this. The shoe factory will actually first transfer the container to a Chinese rail or trucking company that will in turn transfer it to an overseas shipping firm. Once the container arrives in the US port an agent will take the shipment through customs and deliver it to the shoe store in Boise. That store, in turn, will sell the shoes to final consumers. What we have is a chain of transfers that represents the entire transaction. We represent this transaction in Figure 8.2.

In this example, a set of four vectors comprises the entire *transaction*. We can write this set as $V = \{V_1, V_2, V_3, V_4\}$. The set of nodes N is written as $N = \{N_1, N_2, N_3, N_4, N_5\}$. Each of the Ns symbolizes an exchange of a commodity or service (overland transport, sea shipping, etc.). We could then add to the chain diagram the banking and insurance services required to make the chain work smoothly. This would make the diagram even more complex.[8]

Commodity chains are webs of economic activity. They are embedded in wider social structures that spread among many nations and regions, each having their own institutions. Institutional economic analysis acknowledges that *people* work and interact in each link of the chain. They all operate in particular institutional environments and bring with them particular cultural norms, values and practices.

Transactions analysis and the firm

Each link in a network adds value to a commodity as it moves along the chain. The aggregate value added to a commodity's original cost of production is the *transactions cost* of the whole chain. It is the real cost of getting the shoes from the factory in China to the local retail store in the US.

Transactions costs arise for geographical and social reasons. Changes in technology and in ideology influence how these costs evolve over time. The geographical separation of origins and destinations obviously adds transport costs to the general costs of production. The greater is the distance travelled, the greater are fuel and other shipping costs, the greater are the risks of damage or loss, and the higher are the costs of insurance, storage and warehousing along the way. Ever since the 1400s, advances in geographical knowledge and transportation and communication technology have lowered transactions costs and increased global trade and investment.

Social factors enter the picture because countries have different laws and regulations, currencies, languages and weights and measures. Changing attitudes toward global capitalism have influenced government trade and investment policies which in turn have altered transactions costs. For example, recent trends toward capitalist globalization and free market ideology have led many governments to liberalize trade by lowering or eliminating tariffs and non-tariff barriers.

Arm's-length market vs. intra-firm non-market transactions

We can represent each nodal point in a commodity chain as an enterprise located in a particular place in the world. The transactions relationship between enterprises in a chain can be (1) *arm's-length* or *market* or (2) *intra-firm* or *non-market*.

Arm's-length market relationships are between autonomous enterprises that exert no influence on the internal decisions and operations of the other enterprises with whom they trade. Their relations are strictly limited to market transactions. The agreed-upon price of the transaction is the *market price*. That price in turn depends on the intensity of supply and demand as well as on the structure of the market (e.g., degree of competition). These are the kind of relations described in orthodox trade theory. In Figure 8.1, N_1 and N_2 are autonomous arm's-length enterprises.

On the other hand, intra-firm transactions take place outside the marketplace. The relationship between enterprises can take many forms, the simplest of which is when two or more enterprises combine into a single firm. In Figure 8.1 this can happen if firm N_1 buys firm N_2 or vice versa; one then becomes a division or branch of the other. In this situation, N_1 does not sell commodities or services to N_2 at market prices. Instead, N_1 transfers commodities or services to N_2, in which case we call the prices *transfer prices*. Transfer prices are accounting prices; they only record magnitudes set by management for accounting or financial reasons, not by the market.

188 Institutionalist international economics

When two or more enterprises in different countries merge into one entity we call it a *transnational corporation* (TNC).[9] The creation of a TNC implies a foreign direct investment. If an American firm N_2 buys a Chinese firm N_1 then a direct investment occurs.

When a branch of a TNC transfers a product or service to another branch, the non-market transfer price likely will diverge from the arm's-length market price. TNCs can purposely raise or lower a transfer price in order to direct more or less cash from one branch to another. A reason for doing this might be to avoid paying taxes or to avoid restrictions on the repatriation of profits. Another reason might be to conceal an investment in a branch by accumulating cash reserves there.[10]

The importance of these distinctions for trade theory is that most international transactions are non-market. Institutionalists argue that this fact makes orthodox trade theory irrelevant because the latter focuses exclusively on market transactions.

Orthodox economics, New Institutionalism and the reason firms exist

Orthodox economists first believed transactions costs to be a residual, something left over after accounting for all the real costs of production. Transactions costs arise because of "institutional frictions" in an otherwise smoothly operating, self-regulating market system. These frictions result from market failure. Understanding transactions costs thus requires stepping outside the boundary of standard economic theory.[11]

The next step in the evolution of orthodox transactions cost theory was to analyze transactions costs not as a residual but as something central to all market and non-market transactions. The analysis begins with the question, why do firms exist at all? Why do people avoid using the market-price mechanism if that mechanism is so efficient?[12] The question is relevant not only to the domestic economy but also to the international economy: why do transnational firms exist if the global price mechanism is so efficient?

Three Nobel Prize winners—Ronald Coase, Douglas North and Oliver Williamson—provided an answer: firms exist in order to avoid transactions costs.[13] These costs include search and information costs, negotiating costs and monitoring costs to name just a few. The higher are these transactions costs, the more attractive it becomes to "internalize" or combine market activities into a single enterprise. Internalization—control through bureaucracy—substitutes reliance on markets with reliance on bureaucratic control.

Orthodox economists thus brought standard economic theory into the firm itself. The inner workings of the firm used to be a "black box." Now, they believe, economic theory can explain those inner workings. Accordingly, a firm will continue to expand its organization through internalization so long as the marginal benefits of internalization exceed the marginal costs of bureaucratic coordination.

Williamson invented the term New Institutional Economics (NIE) in 1975 to describe this "theory of institutions." NIE views institutions as aggregations of repetitious voluntary interactions between rational goal-seeking economic agents. And all this occurs inside the firm. Thus, relations between employees in firms are like relations between buyers and sellers in markets.

The NIE answer to the question of why firms exist seems odd. It is like asking, why does the government exist, or why do families exist? The NIE answer is that the costs of the alternatives (no family, no state) are too high. And we supposedly know the costs are too high because families and states exist. The reasoning is circular. We might just as well have begun by asking, why do markets exist? The answer would have been because intra-firm transactions are relatively too expensive.

Additionally, NIE developed as if the "true" or "original Institutional economics" never existed. Ignorant of the work of Veblen, Commons, Ayres and others, NIE economists believe they had discovered something new and profound. All they did, however, was to reduce the complex institution known as "the firm" to collections of voluntary markets.

Institutionalist economics and the nature of the firm

To Institutionalists, firms are not collections of markets. Instead, firms are places where some people exercise power and control over others. A capitalist firm is a place of conflict and struggle as well as of collaboration and teamwork. Firms have their own cultures with unique practices and corporate values. Some of these derive from the broader culture in which the firm exists; others originate from within the firm itself. Some firms impose their cultural values and practices upon employees; some negotiate and voluntarily agreed to them.

Moreover, Institutionalists do not always see the outcome of competition between firms in a favorable light. Competition between firms can be damaging. This explains why mergers take place, to protect against external threats of interference from rivals. The result of such mergers is often to create and to preserve monopolistic control of markets.

As Veblen put it, "transactions have a strategic purpose" whereby the "businessman aims to gain control" of certain assets "as a basis for further transactions out of which gain is expected" (Veblen, 1904: 30–31). The businessperson does not seek to minimize transactions costs but rather to control business activities with a view toward dominating a market for pecuniary gain. Efficiency is not the only aim. Their aim also is strategic maneuvering and putting their rivals at a disadvantage.

In conclusion, the question of why firms exist is, to Institutional economists, irrelevant and beside the point.

Transnational corporations

To understand the world economy we must begin with the transnational corporation. In 2010, the total value added by TNCs both in their domestic and international operations accounted for about 25% of the world's GDP. International production was about 40% of this amount (UNCTAD, 2011). In 1969 there were approximately 7,000 TNCs; in 2008 there were 82,000 TNCs with 810,000 subsidiaries. The number of TNCs continues to expand, as does the number of people employed by these firms and their share of world exports.

International production networks have been continually expanding. Their growth is partly due to the fact that domestic firms in many countries have been extending their reach beyond their own borders. One reason for this is that the global economic crisis of the late 2000s encouraged many domestic companies to their reduce costs. Many did this by moving abroad. Additionally, the growth of emerging and transitional (i.e., formerly socialist) economies since the 1990s has been accompanied by growth in TNCs headquartered in those countries. The same has been true of the so-called BRIC nations (Brazil, Russia, India and China).

The most common way of creating a TNC is through a merger or acquisition. This entails the exchange of equity through foreign direct investment. Another common mode of extending corporate governance and control is contract manufacturing. Here, a large TNC negotiates a contract with an independent firm to produce parts (or even whole products). An example of this is the Hon Hai Precision Industry Co. Ltd., also known as Foxconn. Foxconn is a Taiwanese electronics manufacturing company that produces electronic components (e.g., motherboards) for large TNCs such as Apple, Microsoft and Hewlett-Packard. Foxconn is itself a huge TNC and operates throughout the world, especially in China. Other non-equity modes of governance and control include strategic alliances, joint ventures, contract R&D, management contracts, after-sale services outsourcing, franchising and licensing.

Finally, many TNCs are state owned. This means national governments either have full control or at least substantial influence over TNCs. In 2010 there were 650 of such TNCs with 8,500 foreign affiliates. The German state of Lower Saxony, for instance, is the second largest shareholder of Volkswagen, owning a 20% stake of its outstanding shares. This is enough to exert substantial influence on corporate decisions. Forty-four percent of state-owned TNCs are majority-owned by governments, and 19 of them are among the 100 largest TNCs.

A main point that comes from this discussion is that it is irrelevant to view "the market" as an alternative to "the firm." Rather than being substitutes, firms—especially transnational firms—can support if not advance the prevalence of markets in the world economy. More TNCs, more markets.

The Institutionalist theory of transnational corporation

Stephen Hymer (1934–1974) broadened Coase's question when he asked, "Why do transnational firms exist?" Why globalize production? Why would a firm decide to do business in another country when the transactions costs are so high? Why direct foreign investment?

Hymer answered by pointing to the possibility of eliminating competition between firms in different countries and of reducing the power of labor by being footloose. He also pointed to the obvious advantages of scale economies and of being close to essential resources. Thus, when firms merge they choose to substitute internal coordination for international market coordination, thereby reducing the anarchy and uncertainty of global markets and increasing their economic power.

Hymer pursued a line of reasoning very much in the spirit of Veblen and the American Institutionalists. He described three sides of the TNC: international capital movements including foreign direct investment and other short-term capital flows; international production; and international governance. When a TNC invests in another country it sends out capital and management while at the same time it draws foreign capital and labor into an integrated world network. As Hymer put it in 1971: "When many firms from many countries do this together on an expanded scale, as has been true over the last decade and will be increasingly true in the next, they are forming a new world system" (Hymer, 1972: 92).

Hymer stressed the importance of this TNC global order of global corporate strategy, international oligopolistic collusion and the exploitation of monopoly power. He forged a theory that shows how TNCs are able to create a world order in their own image. In so doing, TNC global dominance erodes the traditional powers of national governments. To fill this void there emerge "supra-national" organizations such as the World Trade Organization, International Monetary Fund and World Bank.

TNCs build hierarchies of governance in which their main wealth and financial resources are concentrated in major headquarter cities (the "center"), mid- and lower-level layers of management locate in "sub-capitals" and branch plants locate in peripheral areas. The implications for economic development of this spatial distribution of assets are important. Hymer suggested that the global reach and spread of TNCs depends on the relative political might of the nations in which they desire to locate. Large TNCs are better able to throw their weight around and to get what they want, especially in poorer nations with powerful local elites that benefit financially from their presence and with little popular representation. The consequence is uneven economic development, with some nations benefitting and others suffering from TNC presence.

There is much more to Hymer's economics. We cannot do it justice here. It is sufficient to point out that international trade and investment occurs within a global corporate order made up of very large and very powerful corporations. International transactions and commodity networks are deeply embedded in these TNC structures. Their growth since the Second World War has created a supra-national institutional arrangement with enormous economic and political power which transcends even that of nation-states.

To Institutionalists, all of this makes even more obvious the inadequacy of orthodox theory: self-adjusting international markets and market prices should not be the starting point for economic analysis. Neither should the sovereign nation-state be the standard unit of economic theory. Trade in wheat and computers between A-Land and B-Land, described in previous chapters, is therefore quite beside the point and reveals little about the world economic system. And treating transactions costs as mere hindrances to otherwise free trade contributes little to our understanding.

Varieties of TNCs

There are many ways to organize our thoughts about the real world of cross-border transactions and transnational organizations. One approach is to envision the variety of corporate chains that can exist and the associated variety of ways commodities can flow across borders (Dicker, 1992).

For example, in the simplest case, a firm produces and sells a commodity in its own domestic market. Here, the commodity does not cross any borders, in which case the firm is not transnational. Another case is a single transnational firm that sells a finished commodity in one or more other national markets.

Another example is a producer-driven chain where one firm sells a semi-finished commodity to a firm in another nation where it undergoes further processing before it then proceeds to yet another firm, in another country, where it again undergoes further processing. This chain continues until the finished commodity is sold in a country at the end of the chain.

A final option is a buyer-driven chain where firms in several other countries each produce a finished good that is then sold to a single firm in one other country. An example of such an arrangement is Walmart which buys thousands of finished goods from firms all around the world.[14]

Of course there exist a great many variations of these models of cross-border trade. The possibilities can be very complex as we begin to include chains with separate headquarters, multiple production plants, regional sales and distribution offices, subsidiaries, licensing agreements, etc. By focusing on the differing transactional patterns and transnational corporate forms it is possible to make clear the distinctions between market trade and the more socially integrative forms of trade that predominate in the modern world economy.

Institutional economic policy

Orthodoxy, value relativism and economic policy

Orthodox trade theory makes economic efficiency (and hence social welfare) the irrefutable and unitary end of economic policy. Other ends such as global economic justice, income and wealth equity and environmental sustainability are not explicitly included as ends. Which means or policies best promote this end of economic efficiency? The usual answer is free trade, based on the logic of comparative advantage.

In this means–ends framework the individual is the ultimate source of social values, and free trade is the means that delivers the end of maximum efficiency and social welfare. Where individuals live, what social values they have and where these values come from does not matter because their preferences are already given. While this appears to be a positive, value-free approach, it is really a value-laden moral position that leads to the conclusion that governments must give free rein to individual and business decisions. Because individual values and preferences are strictly a private affair, we cannot judge them. I prefer fish, you prefer steak; I place a high value on outlawing child labor, you do not. I cannot judge your preferences and you cannot judge mine.[15] We call this *value-relativism*.

Orthodox economics often applies value-relativism to international economic policy. Suppose a poor developing nation that trades with the US has lax labor standards and allows workplace abuses outlawed in rich developed economies. Such abuses might include denial of the right to organize, unsafe and hazardous work conditions and child labor. Clearly, low labor standards could give a poor nation a comparative advantage in labor-intensive production by making labor costs relatively cheap.

Should the US and other developed economies with high labor standards require poorer developing nations to raise their labor standards as a precondition to trade? Put differently, should we *harmonize* trade by imposing higher labor standards on others? Would not trade be "fairer" if all partners adhered to common labor standards?

Orthodox theory suggests that lower labor standards merely reflect the preferences of citizens of that nation. Therefore we ought not to pass judgments upon them. Nor should we require them to change their ways. This kind of value relativism means we should not require trading partners to adopt different standards since this would force upon them American values. Moreover, doing so introduces distortions into the international market economy. Specifically, it would alter comparative advantage calculations and divert resources away from the production of comparative-advantage goods. The world supply of such goods would decrease and their price increase, altering the terms of trade. We can make similar arguments about health, climate and environment, food safety, pharmaceutical testing and product labeling.

Pure value-relativism is admittedly an extreme orthodox position and most would take a more nuanced approach. In fact, ethical concerns about human rights often override value-relativism. In the US this has resulted in passage of many laws protecting workers. Examples go back to 1890 with passage of the McKinley Act prohibiting the import of goods made by convict labor. Another example is the 1986 Anti-Apartheid Act requiring US firms operating in South Africa to conform to US labor standards. Both the United Nations Declaration of Human Rights and the International Labor Organization's Declaration of Fundamental Principles also affirm core labor standards, including prohibition of forced labor, freedom of association, the right to organize and bargain collectively, elimination of child labor, and non-discrimination in employment.

In addition to human rights concerns, some argue that a country with low labor standards gains an unfair advantage and forces all countries to lower their standards as well. This is the so-called "race to the bottom" argument supporting harmonization and the creation of a "level playing field."

Opposing harmonization are those who benefit from low standards. This includes domestic producers who fear it would increase their own labor costs and undermine their comparative advantage. It also includes TNCs who benefit from

194 Institutionalist international economics

locating production facilities in nations with low labor standards and low wages. Some oppose harmonization because expanded trade and economic development eventually would lead to elevated standards anyway.

Many regional and bilateral trade agreements include harmonization clauses. However, enforcement and compliance have been minimal if not nonexistent. Neither the World Trade Organization (WTO) nor the North American Free Trade Agreement (NAFTA) has adopted explicit labor standards, and the subject remains controversial.

In conclusion, value-relativism is the default position of orthodox international economic theory. In practice, however, ethical concerns challenge this position, especially by trade unions and progressive governments and by self-interested businesses that benefit from rising labor standards and labor costs in nations with whom they compete.

Institutional economics and trade policy

As we have shown above, Institutionalists take a different approach to social valuation and hence to economic policy. Unlike their orthodox brethren, Institutionalists would not hesitate to address value differences across cultures. In fact, to an Institutional economist, *failure* to harmonize standards distorts trade by building socially unjust standards into the global market system.

In this section we identify five key tenets of Institutionalist economic policymaking.[16]

1. *Ends-in-view.* Institutionalists say we should not pay much attention to high-flown, grandiose ends such as "maximum global economic efficiency" and "maximum social welfare." While these may sound good, we cannot link these to any concrete economic problems. Simply to suggest that free trade maximizes world social welfare is insufficient. Instead, we ought to identify what the American philosopher John Dewey (1859–1952) called "ends-in-view." Ends-in-view are narrowly defined, attainable and measurable real-world ends that can guide economic policy. Ends-in-view are concrete targets which, when reached, solve readily identifiable economic problems.

    Economic problems take the form of discrepancies between "what is" and "what ought to be." What ought to be is necessarily based on social values and should not be masked by value-neutrality and scientific objectivity. Institutionalists would state their values up front when itemizing ends-in-view. They would analyze and debate values openly.
2. *Fact-based process orientation.* The ends-in-view approach requires that we identify the most pressing economic problems and the social values that make these problems important. Ends-in-view might include trade imbalances in specific industries, unemployment problems in export sectors and assistance for workers who lose jobs due to imports. We can then devise the best tools and instruments for solving these problems. How can we do this?

We must begin by establishing the facts and then by separating these facts from myths. Next, we find out who exercises control over a situation and where the locus of economic power lies. What are the costs and benefits, successes and failures of various policy tools? How are these costs and benefits distributed among various classes of citizens? The process continues by adjusting the ends-in-view and, if necessary, the social values (i.e., re-evaluation). The process then repeats itself. This approach to policymaking is what instrumentalism is all about. It involves a great deal of measurement, diagnosis, experimentation, pragmatism and re-evaluation.

3. *Evolutionary holism.* Society is like a living organism that continuously transforms itself into other varieties in response to changes in the external and internal environments. Sound policymaking requires that governments actively guide this change so that the path followed takes us toward the ends-in-view. And this means taking a multidisciplinary and holistic view of the relationships connecting people, organizations and institutions.

4. *Government activism.* The government must take an active role in guiding the economy. Laissez-faire and free trade are not policy orientations to which Institutionalists would agree. In fact, there is a long tradition in Institutionalism of government social management and economic planning. This does not mean they would avoid using market-based policy tools. Institutionalists refrain from any dogmatic adherence to universal policy prescriptions such as free trade or immutable economic laws such as comparative advantage.

5. *Democratic decision-making.* If there is one over-arching value judgment that most Institutional economists accept, it is that democracy—particularly participatory democracy—is the best possible social decision-making arrangement. This is because democracy permits the broadest expression and the fairest adjudication of divergent social values. This is especially true in our expanding interdependent world economy, an economy in which diverse cultural norms and values come into frequent and sometimes intense contact. The economic policies undertaken by competing nations, especially those involving trade restrictions and exchange rate and capital flow regulations, often conflict and work in opposite directions. To lessen tensions, democracy is essential to coordinate both national and international economic affairs.

These are five lofty aims, and Institutionalists argue constantly over their proper interpretation and implementation.

Institutionalism and free trade policy

As we know by now, arguments favoring free trade policy usually rely on the theory of comparative advantage. Accordingly, differing production conditions among nations give rise to differing patterns of specialization and trade. Krugman offered another defense of free trade policy by contending this is still the best

196 Institutionalist international economics

practical policy even though comparative advantage may be irrelevant; any attempt to manage trade would only make things worse.

Maintaining a global free trade regime is no easy task given the enormous complexity of the world economy. Free trade requires diplomacy, negotiations and cooperation as well as the international organizations that can implement and supervise free trade agreements.

That said, Institutionalism argues that nations *ought* to have the freedom to determine their own trade regimes, whatever these may be. Some nations might choose to open their economies and minimize restrictions on trade and investment while others might choose to regulate trade and finance. Tensions will certainly arise between those wanting free access and those wanting restrictions, and only cooperation and negotiation can reduce these tensions and establish working trade rules. The merits of any given trade regime can be judged only by examining the specifics of each case. Faith and ideology only obstruct such efforts.

Institutionalism subscribes not to the ideologically loaded idea of free trade but rather to freedom of nations to choose their trade regimes. This philosophy rejects absolute truth. As economist John Adams put it,

> Freedom of inter-social exchange ought not only to embrace the freedom to allocate re-sources to gain private profits but must encompass the liberation of people and ideas from the binding powers of nation states and big businesses. Reconstituting international institutions on the basis of globally shared values in order to attain greater freedom of inter-social exchanges will be the principal task of the human race in the twenty-first century.
>
> *(Adams, 1987: 1860)*

Conclusions

Institutionalism is a heterodox school of thought. By "heterodox" we mean that it separates itself from the standard, mainstream orthodoxy. It does so in many ways. It rejects the orthodox methodology of individualism and focuses instead on collective behaviors and cultures. It replaces equilibrium with evolutionary dynamics, and abstract formal models with holistic models. Institutionalists do not regard the market as the centerpiece of economic analysis; indeed much of what happens occurs outside the domain of markets. Also, Institutionalism endeavors to put values back into economic analysis as an explicit subject. Finally, it seeks to improve the human condition in a pragmatic way that does not fear use of government institutions.

Institutional economists have not progressed very far in developing a full-blown general theory of international economics. This is of no surprise since Institutional economists shy away from building general universally valid models. Neither have there been many applications of Institutional methods to the study of the world economy. Exceptions are studies of transitional and developing economies.

Nonetheless, we have introduced several approaches to international economics that conform to Institutionalist methodology. These include network chain analysis, transactions analysis and a theory of transnational corporations.

When it comes to international economics, the problem that Institutional economics addresses is the opacity and the complexity of the world economy. Most prices are transfer prices, not market prices, and most business decisions concerning the allocation of the world's resources are not transparent market decisions. Scholars today do not have free access to the inner workings of TNCs and their boardrooms, and the mechanisms of international economic power and exploitation are not obvious. Substituting the opacity and complexity of the real-world economy with the orthodox imagination of global markets based on individual rational choice and comparative advantage simply will not do.

In conclusion, Institutional international economics is not for those who demand clear-cut models that produce simple explanations and predictions and universal truths. Ambiguity, uncertainty and complexity are the preferred modes of Institutional analysis.

Notes

1 These include the Association for Institutional Thought, Association for Evolutionary Economics, European Association for Evolutionary Political Economy, Japan Association for Evolutionary Economics and the Society for the Advancement of Socio-Economics. Among the scholarly journals are the *Journal of Economic Issues*, the *Journal of Institutional Economics* and the *Review of Social Economy*.
2 The interested reader can consult the following literature on New Institutionalism: (1) evolutionary theory, Alchian (1950) and Nelson and Winter (1982); (2) Austrian process-oriented theory, Hayek (1948); (3) property rights theory, Coase (1937); (4) transactions cost theory, Williamson (1979); (5) contract and organization theories, Alchian and Demsetz (1972), Adams and Scaperlanda (1996), Van den Berg (2012) and Cheung (1983); and (6) economic theory of social institutions, North (1990). See also Hodgson (2007).
3 This includes one collection of scholarly papers and one international economics textbook: Adams and Scaperlanda (1996) and Van den Berg (2012).
4 Thorstein Veblen coined these terms (Veblen, 1899 and 1904).
5 This approach derives from the American philosopher John Dewey (1859–1952).
6 The word "means" refers to the strategies, techniques and choices available to people. These can be identified in a value-free way. The "ends" are the goals that these means are intended to achieve. The ends directly depend on personal or social values. For example, if being rich is the end, then working and robbing banks are two means.
7 Much of what follows borrows from Waller (1989).
8 We can make this analysis far more complex by introducing more and more elements of the real world. We can add more nodes and vectors representing insurance, shipping inspection services, banking and currency exchange services and the like. We can also link the analysis to national income and product accounting. See Mirowski (1991).
9 There is an extensive literature on TNCs. See for example Hymer (1979) and Markusen (2004). The United Nations Conference on Trade and Development also publishes a journal, *Transnational Corporations*.
10 There are often strict regulations governing transfer prices, which require that they approximate fair market values. The idea is to prevent artificial shifting of profits out of taxing jurisdictions and to facilitate foreign direct investment and cross-border

trade. Both the United Nations and the Organization for Economic Co-operation and Development have guidelines for transfer pricing. The International Monetary Fund's *Balance of Payments Manual* instructs compilers of international economic data to make adjustments in the Balance of Payments when significant distortions in transfer prices occur.

11 For a history of transaction cost theory see Klaes (2000).

12 To understand the meaning of this question, suppose a firm separates its accounting, marketing and production departments into individual enterprises that then sell their services in the market to the original parent company as well as to other firms. Would this be more economically efficient than the original situation in which all three departments combined to one enterprise?

13 The key literature includes: Coase (1937); North (1990); and Williamson (1979 and 1985).

14 A variation of this model is where firms in several other nations each produce a component that is then shipped to a firm in yet another country, which then produces and/or assembles the final product.

15 DeMartino (2000) makes this case.

16 This section is based on Gordon (1990), Petr (1984) and Tool (1979).

References

Adams, J. (1987). "Trade and Payments as Instituted Process: the Institutional Theory of the External Sector." *Journal of Economic Issues, 21*(4), 1839–1860.

Adams, J., & Scaperlanda, A. (Eds.) (1996). *The Institutional Economics of the International Economy*. Boston, MA: Kluwer Academic Publishers.

Alchian, A. A. (1950). "Uncertainty, Evolution and Economic Theory." *Journal of Political Economy, 56*(3), 211–222.

Alchian, A. A., & Demsetz, H. (1972). "Production, Information Costs, and Economic Organization." *American Economic Review, 62*(5), 777–795.

Cheung, S. N. (1983). "The Contractual Nature of the Firm." *Journal of Law and Economics, 26*(1), 1–21.

Coase, R. (1937). "The Nature of the Firm." *Economica, 4*(16), 386–405.

DeMartino, G. F. (2000). *Global Economy, Global Justice*. New York: Routledge.

Der Spiegel (2011, August 22). "Out of Control: The Destructive Power of the Financial Markets." Retrieved August 23 2011, from http://www.spiegel.de/international/business/0,1518,781590,00.html.

Dicker, P. (1992). *Global Shift: the Internationalization of the Economy* (2nd ed.). New York: The Guilford Press.

Dugger, W. M. (1992). *Underground Economics: Decade of Institutionalist Dissent*. Armonk, NY: M. E. Sharpe.

Gereffi, G. (1994). "The Global Economy: Organization, Governance, and Development." In N. J. Smelser, & R. Swedberg (Eds.), *The Handbook of Economic Sociology* (pp. 160–182). Princeton, NJ: Princeton University Press.

Gereffi, G., & Korzeniewicz, M. (1994). *Commodity Chains and Global Capitalism*. Westport, CT: Praeger.

Gordon, W. (1990). "The Role of Tool's Social Value Principle." *Journal of Economic Issues, 24*(3), 879–886.

Hayek, F. A. (1948). *Individualism and the Economic Order*. Chicago, IL: University of Chicago Press.

Hodgson, G. M. (2007). "The Revival of Veblenian Institutional Economics." *Journal of Economic Issues, 41*(2), 325–340.

Hymer, S. (1972). "The Internationalization of Capital." *Journal of Economic Issues, 6*(1), 91–111.

Hymer, S. H. (1979). *The Multinational Corporation: A Radical Approach: Papers by Stephen Herbert Hymer* (R. B. Cohen, N. Felton, M. Nkosi, & J. van Liere, Eds.). New York: Cambridge University Press.

Klaes, M. (2000). "The History of the Concept of Transaction Costs: Neglected Aspects." *Journal of the History of Economic Thought, 22*(2), 191–216.

Markusen, J. R. (2004). *Multinational Firms and the Theory of International Trade*. Cambridge, MA: MIT Press.

Mirowski, P. (1991). "Postmodernism and the Social Theory of Value." *Journal of Post Keynesian Economics, 13*(4), 564–582.

Nelson, R. R., & Winter, S. G. (1982). *An Evolutionary Theory of Economic Change*. Cambridge, MA: Harvard University Press.

North, D. C. (1990). *Institutions, Institutional Change and Economic Performance*. New York: Cambridge University Press.

Petr, J. L. (1984). "Fundamentals of an Institutional Perspective on Economic Policy." *Journal of Economic Issues, 18*(1), 1–17.

Security and Exchange Commission (2004, July 26). *Amendment No. 4 to Form S-1 Registration Statement*. Retrieved April 17 2012, from Securities and Exchange Commission: http://sec.gov/Archives/edgar/data/1288776/000119312504124025/ds1a.htm.

Tool, M. R. (1979). *The Discretionary Economy: a Normative Theory of Political Economy*. Santa Monica, CA: Goodyear.

UNCTAD (2011). *World Investment Report 2011*. New York: United Nations Conference on Trade and Development.

Van den Berg, H. (2012). *International Economics: A Heterodox Approach*. Armonk, NY: M. E. Sharpe.

Veblen, T. (1898). "Why is Economics Not an Evolutionary Science?" *Quarterly Journal of Economics, 12*(4), 373–397.

Veblen, T. (1899). *The Theory of the Leisure Class*. New York: Macmillan.

Veblen, T. (1904). *The Theory of Business Enterprise*. New York: Charles Scribner's Sons.

Veblen, T. (1934). *The Engineers and the Price System*. New York: Viking Press.

Waller, Jr., W. T. (1989). "Criticism of Institutionalism, Methodolgy, and Value Theory." *Journal of Economic Issues, 23*(3), 873–879.

Williamson, O. E. (1979). "Transaction-Cost Economics: The Governance of Contractual Relations." *Journal of Law and Economics, 22*(2), 233–261.

Williamson, O. E. (1985). "Reflections on the New Institutional Economics." *Journal of Institutional and Theoretical Economics, 141*, 187–195.

9
POST KEYNESIAN INTERNATIONAL ECONOMICS

Introduction

A year prior to the 1936 publication of *The General Theory of Employment, Interest and Money*, Keynes wrote in a letter, "To understand my state of mind . . . you have to know that I believe myself to be writing a book on economic theory which will largely revolutionize . . . the way the world thinks about economic problems" (Aslanbeigui and Oakes, 2002: 5). In the decade following publication, the economics profession indeed viewed Keynes's book as a major break with the past, but it then proceeded to dilute its revolutionary content by blending it with orthodox theory. The result was the Classical-Keynesian synthesis examined in Chapter 6.

While Keynes was working on his book he also exchanged ideas with several younger Cambridge (UK) economists—the so-called Cambridge Circus—that included Richard Kahn (1905–1989), James Meade (1907–1995), Joan Robinson (1903–1983) and Austin Robinson (1897–1993). Two outsiders also joined the group, Piero Sraffa (1898–1983) from Italy and Michał Kalecki (1899–1970) from Poland. Keynes's interactions with this group of younger scholars helped him to develop his own ideas. And indeed Keynes's influence on this group was incalculable.

After publication of *The General Theory*, members of the Cambridge Circus kept Keynes's revolutionary theory alive well into the 1970s and 1980s. Subsequent generations of scholars continued to build on Keynes's ideas, many combining them with elements of Marxism and Institutionalism. The result of these efforts is contemporary Post Keynesianism.

An overview of Post Keynesian economics

There are several strands of Post Keynesianism. Each strand follows in the footsteps of a noted member of the Cambridge Circus.

The Keynesian strand

Post Keynesians build on several key elements of Keynes's work. The first is an emphasis on the short run. In the short run the stock of capital is fixed and determined by past investment decisions. Current investment decisions determine current national income and employment. In the short run, a capitalist economy does not generate full employment. Neither should we expect full employment in the long run. The existence of a central tendency toward full employment equilibrium is a mystical orthodox idea.

A second element is that uncertainty is ubiquitous in capitalism and essential to understand how businesses make investment decisions. In the current period, businesses commit capital resources (i.e., current investment) which then produce a stream of output into the distant future. Businesses expect from this commitment a stream of returns, a prospective yield over the life of the project. But, because the future is always unknown, one never knows if there will be a demand for the output which those capital resources will produce. The yield on investment is therefore uncertain, and often disappointed. As Keynes points out in Chapter 12 of the *General Theory*,

> The outstanding fact is the extreme precariousness of the basis of knowledge on which our estimates of prospective yield have to be made. Our knowledge of the factors which will govern the yield of an investment some years hence is usually very slight and often negligible. If we speak frankly, we have to admit that our basis of knowledge for estimating the yield ten years hence of a railway, a copper mine, a textile factory, the goodwill of a patent medicine, an Atlantic liner, a building in the City of London amounts to little and sometimes to nothing; or even five years hence. In fact, those who seriously attempt to make any such estimate are often so much in the minority that their behaviour does not govern the market.
>
> *(Keynes, 1936: 149)*

This is not just a matter of "risk," where agents estimate a probability distribution of all known future outcomes of a decision. Uncertainty means we cannot even identify what those outcomes are.

It is a basic tenet of orthodox theory that agents make prudent investment decisions based on rationally formed expectations using all available information. Keynesian uncertainty, however, removes rational calculation from the analysis of investment and replaces it with the psychology of "herd like" behavior or what Keynes called "animal spirits." Individual agents can act rationally in choosing to go along with the herd, even if the herd irrationally runs off a cliff. Instinct, rather than logic, is at work when it comes to group behavior and business investment works in the same way. As Keynes put it,

> Our decisions to do something positive can only be taken as the result of animal spirits—a spontaneous urge to action rather than inaction, and not

202 Post Keynesian international economics

as the outcome of a weighted average of quantitative benefits multiplied by quantitative probabilities.

(Keynes, 1936: 162)

This leads to the third element of Post Keynesian economics: the inherent instability of capitalism. This instability is due to the pervasiveness of uncertainty and the capriciousness of speculation. Post Keynesians such as Hyman Minksy (1919–1996) and Paul Davidson (1930–) build on these ideas, as we shall see later in this chapter. They emphasize the fragility of financial markets and argue that financial instability is endogenous to market capitalism.

The Joan Robinson strand

Joan Robinson was a Keynesian devotee, yet her postwar contributions were eclectic and spanned a multitude of subjects. Her writing style was analytical and expository and she used little mathematics (which she normally confined to footnotes). After the Second World War, Robinson became increasingly radical, at least politically, and by the 1960s and 1970s many radical economists adopted her as an icon of cultural iconoclasm. She took a sober and non-ideological view of Marx, yet she was not a Marxist. Her approach to economic theory, while certainly in the Keynesian vein, was not especially radical. This is how she described her orientation: "I am the archetypal left-wing Keynesian. I was drawing pinkish rather than bluish conclusions from the *General Theory* long before it was published" (Robinson, 1953: 19).

Robinson was a severe critic of orthodox economic theory, finding it misleading and wrongheaded. Her main gripes were its belief in class harmony, its routine assumption of full employment equilibria and balanced trade, and its reductionist and mechanical representation of the real world. She accepted the world as it is, with all its messy imperfections. After all, she first came onto the scene in the 1930s when capitalism was experiencing a catastrophic meltdown. Robinson believed economic theory ought to base itself on these imperfections and not on idealized models of perfect competition, efficiency and harmony.[1]

International economics did not have a central place in Robinson's life work, although she did offer many important insights which we review below. When it came to international trade theory she asserted, "There is no branch of economics in which there is a wider gap between orthodox doctrine and actual problems than in the theory of international trade" (Robinson, 1978: 213).

The Kaleckian strand

Michał Kalecki had an enormous impact on the development of Post Keynesianism. In 1933 he had already arrived at many of the same conclusions that Keynes had reached in the *General Theory*. In fact, Joan Robinson said, "Michał Kalecki's claim to priority of publication is indisputable" (Robinson, 1966a: 337).

Kalecki melded aggregative macroeconomics with a Marxian class analysis in which capitalists and workers struggle over income shares. This idea is in the Classical-Marxian tradition and contradicts the Neoclassical theory that incomes are based on marginal contributions to output.

In Kaleckian economics, capitalists' income consists of property income (profit, interest and rent) and derives from ownership of assets, while workers' income consists of wages and derives from labor. The share each class receives of national income depends on their respective economic, social and political power. If workers become more powerful, then they win higher wages and the share of capitalist income falls. The sum of class incomes, however divided, is national income.

In Kaleckian economics the spending behavior of each class differs. Workers spend all their income on consumption so that their marginal propensity to consumption is unitary. Capitalists, however, spend only a small part of their income on consumption. They save and invest the rest. The amount workers spend on consumption and the amount capitalists save and invest determines national income. This is similar to Keynes, without the class distinctions.

Another of Kalecki's innovations replaces market pricing with administered pricing. To Kalecki, large oligopolistic corporations dominate the capitalist economy. Microeconomic models of competitive supply and demand are therefore inappropriate. Instead, Kalecki introduces a theory of "mark-up pricing" in which firms arrive at prices by marking up their costs (including labor costs) by a certain margin. This mark-up is the source of profit income, and its size depends on the degree of monopoly. More competition implies smaller mark-ups, and more monopoly implies larger mark-ups.

Finally, Kalecki had a keen political sense and recognized that a capitalist government would never adopt a "Keynesian" policy of maintaining full employment, especially if based on deficit spending. Capitalists will always oppose such policies because they represent the intrusion of the state into spheres of private activity normally reserved for them. To Kalecki, a policy of maintaining full employment requires entirely new social and political institutions, and this can only happen if the working class wins more economic power and influence.

The Sraffian strand

In 1927, Keynes nominated Piero Sraffa for a position at Cambridge University. Sraffa accepted the job offer that same year (Marcuzzo, 2005). He published little but still strongly influenced the development of Post Keynesianism.

Sraffa saw in capitalism certain underlying hidden forces which move capital from industry to industry in search of maximum profit (Sraffa, 1960). In the long run, profits equalize across all industrial sectors and a uniform rate of profit prevails. However, the magnitude of aggregate profits depends on the uniform wage rate paid in all industries. Aggregate profits and wages constitute aggregate national income.

Like Kalecki, Sraffa argued that the distribution of income between profit and

204 Post Keynesian international economics

wages is not a market phenomenon. It has nothing to do with marginal productivity. Rather, class struggle determines income distribution, and this distribution reflects the relative economic, social and political power of capital and labor. If labor wins higher wages then the uniform profit rate will fall, and vice versa. The interests of the two classes are antagonistic.

The amount of capital and labor ultimately employed in each industry, together with the established profit and wage rates, determines the prices of produced commodities. These prices have nothing to do with market supply and demand. This is difficult to understand for those reared in orthodox Neoclassical microeconomics. We explain this further in the next chapter.

Sraffa's work is highly abstract and mathematically rigorous. It has roots in Classical and Marxian theory. Sraffa emphasizes the logical *structure* of a capitalist economy and de-emphasizes the psychological behaviors and motivations of economic agents. This structure includes legal and financial institutions, the degree of competition of industries, technology, the composition of social classes and political institutions. Sraffa takes a long-run view in which these economic structures serve as the background against which capital and labor circulate throughout the economy resulting in the creation and distribution of profit and wage income.

Sraffa's perspective lies very close to the Marxian tradition. For this reason we defer development of his approach to the next chapter. Despite his affinity to Marxism, most still regard Sraffa as a variety of Post Keynesianism.

Robinson's critique of Neoclassical trade theory

The standard Neoclassical explanation of trade and finance is that automatic adjustments in exchange rates always bring the current account into balance (i.e., exports equal imports) and that the domestic economy always tends toward full employment (i.e., the economy is always on the production possibilities frontier). Financial account transactions only pay for international trade and speculative capital flows have little to do with trade. This leaves only one role for the currency market to play: to establish the *nominal* value of trade by determining the value of a nation's currency. The quantity of money in circulation among trading nations has no effect on *real* international transactions. It is as if all trade is barter trade.

It follows from this Neoclassical analysis that governments can do nothing to improve a nation's income and employment, nor can they improve the efficiency with which the economy employs resources and produces output. This is, once again, the basic argument for free trade that we encountered in earlier chapters. Government policies to expand exports by devaluing currencies and reducing domestic wages are pointless because they trigger automatic adjustments that annul or reverse any improvements that might initially result.

Robinson took strong exception to this narrow and idealistic line of reasoning. Unemployment, she believed, is the normal state of the economy, not full employment. She reminisced,

> I was a student at a time when vulgar [Neoclassical] economics was in a particularly vulgar state. There was Great Britain with never less than a million workers unemployed, and there was I with my supervisor teaching me that it is logically impossible to have unemployment because of Say's Law.[2]
>
> *(Robinson, 1953: 19)*

By asserting full employment and balanced trade, orthodox economists simply ignore all those real-world problems that give rise to protectionism in the first place. For instance, it ignores the powerful and independent role played by speculation, uncertainty and panics in global financial markets. To Robinson, money is not neutral, as Neoclassical theory claimed, and the financial accounts in the balance of payments do much more than merely accommodate current account transactions. In the real world, there exists no adjustment mechanism that automatically balances trade.

To Robinson, "The [neo]Classical theory of international trade is very remote from the problems which perplex us at the present day" (Robinson, 1946–1947: 98). She declared, "It seems . . . that as soon as the assumption of full employment is removed, the [neo] Classical model for the analysis of international trade is reduced to wreckage" (Robinson, 1946–1947: 112). Robinson saw instead that the real world was a far more complex place. Global financial crises, chronically deficient aggregate demand and unemployment, international imperfect competition, income inequality and class struggle, financial speculation and uncertainty, currency market imbalances and disequilibria are all interrelated real-world phenomena that we must comprehend together, in one analytical framework. For this reason, Robinson turned away from orthodoxy and toward Keynes.

Foreign exchange markets and trade policy

Robinson's 1937 article, "The Foreign Exchanges," was an early attempt to apply Keynes's ideas to international economics (Robinson, 1937). Among the topics she investigated was the relationship between the current account (labelled CA), the financial account (labelled FA) and the macro economy.

To follow her reasoning, we start with the elementary accounting identity $S + M = I + X$. The left-hand side denotes domestic spending leakages (savings, S, and imports, M) while the right-hand side denotes domestic spending injections (investment, I, and exports, X). We can rewrite this identity in two ways: (1) $S = I + CA$ or (2) $I = S - CA$ where CA is the trade (current account) balance, $(X - M)$.

The first equation says home savings (S) go to finance home investment (I) and net foreign lending (CA). If CA is positive (i.e., exports exceed imports) then the home nation is a net lender of the money foreigners require to pay for their excess imports of home-made goods.[3] Equivalently, if CA is negative then the home country is a net foreign borrower of the money needed to pay for its excess imports of foreign-made goods. The second equation, which is algebraically identical to

206 Post Keynesian international economics

the first, states there are two sources of investment funds: domestic savings and net borrowing from foreigners (which can be either positive or negative).

The point, however, is to go beyond identities. We are interested in causality. To Robinson, a host of complicated factors determines the actual trade balance, CA. Among these are global tastes, techniques of production, the distribution of class incomes and aggregate demand. Similarly, a host of complicated factors determines the financial account balance FA which records exports and imports of all financial assets. These include global interest rates and "all those considerations which may be lumped together under the heading of 'the state of confidence'" (Robinson, 1937: 137). Robinson explains that changes can occur independently on any of these fronts, causing adjustments and corrections in the CA and FA balances and hence in exchange rates. It would be a remarkable coincidence if all these balanced out.

Using Keynesian reasoning, Robinson goes on to explain that any increase in CA will have a positive multiplied effect on national income and expand employment (and reduce unemployment). The increase in CA can arise independently from any of the above named factors. It can also arise from conscious economic policies including currency devaluations and import restrictions.

To see how this works, suppose there is a currency devaluation. A cheaper currency affects the relative prices of traded goods. Goods exported from the country now become cheaper while imported goods become more expensive. This expands revenues from trade and production in export sectors, whose prices now become more competitive. It also shrinks imports, whose prices become less competitive. The more favorable trade balance then expands GDP and employment. This is because the trade balance is a component of aggregate demand: C + I + G + CA.

However, according to Robinson, devaluation may not actually improve a nation's trade balance. It all depends on how people respond to the changes in export and import prices. For example, higher import prices reduce the quantity of imported goods demanded, but if this demand is price inelastic then total spending on imports may actually rise, not fall. Similarly, lower export prices may reduce export revenues, not raise them. It all depends on the price elasticities of exported and imported goods. In "The Foreign Exchanges" Robinson provides the first full-fledged theoretical analysis of how these elasticities affect the economy's response to changing currency values and trade balances. Called the "Elasticity Approach," it is a forerunner of the Marshall-Lerner conditions discussed in Chapter 6.

Exchange rates and economic fundamentals

The above analysis is not particularly heterodox. It is simply an early attempt to demonstrate, using a very conventional Keynesian framework, how expanding exports can have a multiplied effect on income and employment—assuming the appropriate elasticity values hold. But Robinson reveals her heterodox outlook in her analysis of how domestic macroeconomic conditions correspond to exchange rates and her rejection of equilibrium thinking.

Neoclassical economic theory explains that exchange rates reflect current macroeconomic conditions. Measures of current macroeconomic conditions include output, income, employment, wages, inflation, interest rates and trade. We call these items "economic fundamentals." The central orthodox idea is that there exists a unique set of equilibrium values for these fundamentals and that this equilibrium set determines a unique equilibrium set of exchange rates.

Robinson was suspicious of this tight correspondence between economic fundamentals and exchange rates. She observed, already in 1937, that

> It is now obvious that there is no one rate of exchange which is the equilibrium rate corresponding to a given state of world demands and techniques. . .
> The notion of *the* equilibrium exchange rate is a chimera. The rate of exchange, the rate of interest, the level of effective demand and the level of money wages react upon each other like the balls in Marshall's bowl, and no one is determined unless all the rest are given.
>
> *(Robinson, 1937: 154)*

In other words, no unique exchange rate equilibrium exists that is determined by economic fundamentals. Supporting Robinson's finding, the modern empirical literature also has been unable to establish a connection between economic fundamentals and exchange rates. In fact, a classic 1983 study by Richard A. Meese and Kenneth Rogoff, still cited 30 years later, demonstrates that a random walk model outperforms any model based on economic fundamentals. This means that random variations come closer to explaining exchange rate variations than systematic variations in macroeconomic fundamentals (Meese and Rogoff, 1983; see also Lyons, 2001). To Robinson, this result is not at all surprising and shows that the mainstream orthodox international theory lacks explanatory power.

Real-world trade policy

The upshot of Robinson's critique of orthodox trade theory is that currency devaluations and other trade promotion policies (wage reductions, export subsidies, import protection) can indeed increase domestic employment opportunities and reduce unemployment.

However, Robinson reaches this heterodox conclusion with a touch of cynicism. She points out that an increase in a nation's trade balance has the same expansionary effect on income and employment as an increase in domestic investment. There is one major difference, however. An increase in home investment also has a net positive effect on the world economy. All trading partners benefit when one nation's investment increases and its economic growth subsequently expands. An expansionary trade policy, on the other hand, while benefitting the home country, has no real effect on the income and employment of the rest of the world. After all, the aggregate world trade balance is always zero, so that if one nation devalues its currency to expand its exports, other countries will pay for this with increased imports. Therefore, national policies that increase trade balances

208 Post Keynesian international economics

come at the expense of other nations. Robinson calls these policies "beggar-my-neighbor" policies.

Robinson was a realist: the world is not perfectly competitive, and all nations pursue protectionism in one form or another. So long as there is no consensus among nations to coordinate policies to maintain full employment everywhere, the temporary effects of an expansionary trade policy in one or more nations will be greeted with retaliation from other nations. In fact it pays each nation to retaliate so long as unemployment exists. As Robinson pointed out, however, this is a self-destructive environment:

> In times of general unemployment a game of beggar-my-neighbor is played between nations, each one endeavoring to throw a larger share of the burden upon others. As soon as one succeeds in increasing its trade balance at the expense of the rest, others retaliate, and the total volume of international trade sinks continuously, relatively to the total volume of world activity. Political, strategic and sentimental considerations add fuel to the fire, and the flames of economic nationalism blaze ever higher and higher.
> *(Robinson, 1947: 156–157)*

A nation that refuses to play this game, say in the name of free trade, will only suffer the consequences of worsening unemployment. Ideological free-trade purity can only be achieved at the expense of domestic employment. Moreover, there are no natural full employment equilibria that nations can hope to attain by refusing to engage in strategic trade policies. Nations suffering from unemployment crises thus have little choice but to engage in beggar-my-neighbor policies: "In short, the notion of a unique natural position of equilibrium is a mirage, and for better or worse, international trade must be directed by conscious policy" (Robinson, 1946–1947: 112).

Robinson's conclusion anticipates Krugman's strategic trade policy and New Trade Theory. According to this theory, free trade is not always optimal and governments are able to tilt the playing fields of trade to their advantage. In such a beggar-my-neighbor world, "[t]here are circumstances in which a limited indulgence in [such policies] cannot be regarded as a crime" (Robinson, 1947: 157). One justification for strategic trade policy is self-defense. Another is to prevent other nations from benefiting from domestic economic stimuli and thereby keeping its employment gains at home. This causes "a larger share of the reward of virtue [i.e., domestic investment] to fall to the virtuous nation" (Robinson, 1947: 157).

The New Mercantilism

In her article, "The New Mercantilism," Robinson expressed the belief that postwar capitalism had changed fundamentally in that there is now a chronic inability of firms to sell all that they can produce (Robinson, 1966b). In other words, the powers of production exceed the powers of consumption. This means global markets have not grown fast enough to make room for all firms. Governments therefore must commit themselves to increasing their nation's share of global markets for the benefit of its own citizens, even if this comes at the expense of other nations and peoples—the beggar-my-neighbor approach. The global economy is therefore a zero-sum game. If all nations were to experience full employment simultaneously then these mercantilist policies would be unnecessary.

Protectionism has become as strong as ever, observed Robinson, although the policy tools used are no longer the usual tariffs and quotas. Because these violate global trade liberalization agreements, governments more often use subsidies for selected export industries, currency devaluations, tax and credit preferences, low-wage policies, etc. Nations that pursue free trade most vigorously are those that can gain an advantage over others, Robinson argued. Free trade economics is "just a more subtle form of mercantilism. It is believed only by those who gain an advantage from it" (Robinson, 1966b: 24). She criticized the hypocrisy of advanced nations that preach free trade on one hand, but on the other hand restrict imports from poorer developing nations when these imports jeopardize the well-being of established domestic corporations. Robinson was also critical of a world financial system that favored rich nations and discriminated against poor nations. She was clearly ahead of her time.

Michał Kalecki: income distribution and macroeconomics

A central theme in Kalecki's economics is the struggle between capitalists and workers over income shares, or the profit–wage distribution of income. The outcome of this struggle, determined by the relative bargaining strength of corporations and labor, influences aggregate output, income and employment.[4] Moreover, given the interconnectedness of global business and government, the profit–wage distribution in one nation affects the profit–wage distribution in other nations. International class relations and the macroeconomic behavior of economies around the world are interactive. The channels through which these interactions occur are international trade, finance and currency exchange markets.

Degree of monopoly, mark-up pricing and profit share

As we noted above, the source of business profits is the "mark-up" over unit costs. The size of this mark-up depends on the "degree of monopoly" which reflects the power firms have in the market to set prices.[5]

One factor affecting the degree of monopoly is the countervailing power of organized labor. When the labor force is unionized, workers can demand a larger share of firms' profits, thereby reducing mark-ups. This depends, of course, on the state of the economy. Another factor is politics, since the capital–labor struggle affects the activities of the state and its economic policies.

The profit–wage distribution directly relates to international economics. For example, recent efforts to liberalize world trade have exposed firms to more

210 Post Keynesian international economics

global competition. This has had a negative influence on industrial concentration, mark-ups and profits. Similarly, advances in foreign labor productivity and reductions in transportation and communication costs also reduce the domestic degree of monopoly by making foreign firms more competitive with domestic firms.

Everything else remaining the same, higher mark-ups increase the profit share and reduce the wage share, and vice versa. It all depends on the relative economic power of each class. Moreover, the size of these shares determines aggregate spending, national income and employment. This is how class conflict enters Kalecki's macroeconomic analysis.

To see the connection between income shares and mark-ups, define β as the average economy-wide mark-up. Ignoring the costs of overhead and raw materials, there are two kinds of costs: labor (wages) and capital (profits). Let p be the average price of a single unit of output, w the nominal wage rate and a the amount of labor needed to produce one unit of output,[6] then

$$p = wa + \beta wa \tag{9.1}$$

The term wa represents total wages (i.e., the wage per worker times the number of workers) per unit of output and βwa represents the mark-up per unit of output. The latter is simply a multiple, β, of wa. Total wages are $W = waY$ and total profits are $R = \beta waY$ where Y is aggregate output. The profit share of total income is π, which we can define as

$$\pi = \frac{\beta wa}{\beta wa + wa} = \frac{p - wa}{p} = \frac{\beta}{\beta + 1} \tag{9.2}$$

Equation (9.2) shows the relationship between the profit share π and the average mark-up rate β. This relationship is positive: the higher the mark-up, the higher the profit share (although the relationship is nonlinear).[7]

Capitalists get what they spend

Capitalists and workers have different spending habits. This is why the profit–wage distribution is so important to macroeconomics. In a Kaleckian world, workers spend all their wage income on consumption while capitalists spend only part of their profit income on consumption; the rest they spend on investment.

We begin with the conventional Keynesian equilibrium condition in which aggregate spending on consumer goods (C) and capital goods (I) equals aggregate output/income (Y):

$$Y = C + I \tag{9.3}$$

Now, disaggregate Y into its two components, capitalists' profits, R, and workers' wages, W. Accordingly, we can write

$$Y = R + W = C + I \tag{9.4}$$

We also disaggregate consumption into capitalists' consumption, C_k, and workers' consumption, C_w so that $C = C_k + C_w$. The new equilibrium condition becomes

$$R + W = C_k + C_w + I \tag{9.5}$$

Kalecki assumes workers spend all their income, so that $W = C_w$. We can thus subtract W and C_w from both sides of Equation (9.5), resulting in

$$R = C_k + I \tag{9.6}$$

We now use the standard linear consumption function to describe capitalists' consumption:

$$C_k = A + c_k R \tag{9.7}$$

where A is the vertical intercept of the consumption function and c_r is the capitalists' marginal propensity to consume out of profit income R. We assume A and c_r are constants. Placing Equation (9.7) into Equation (9.6) yields

$$R = A + c_k R + I \tag{9.8}$$

We can now calculate equilibrium profit income R_e by solving Equation (9.8) for R:

$$R_e = \frac{1}{(1 - c_r)}(A + I) \tag{9.9}$$

The expression $1/(1 - c_r)$ is the capitalists' spending multiplier. It shows how equilibrium profits change when capitalists spend more or less on consumption and/or investment. This equation is important because it shows that capitalists' spending on C and I determines their own profits! As Kalecki's aphorism goes, "workers spend what they get and capitalists get what they spend."

Kaleckian open economy model

In 1934, two years prior to the *General Theory*, Kalecki showed that an increase in net exports—i.e., an increase in the trade surplus—will have a multiplied positive effect on national income (Kalecki, 1971). It expands capitalists' profits, stimulates investment spending and initiates an economic expansion. However, as income expands, imports also expand, but by less than the expansion in exports (because the marginal propensity to import is less than unitary). A growing fiscal deficit works the same way.[8] This is similar to the conclusion Robinson reached.

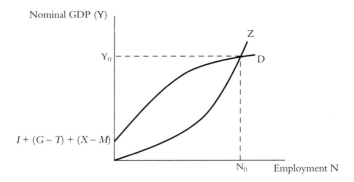

FIGURE 9.1 Aggregate supply and demand

This section introduces a model that analyzes these interactions.[9] It is similar to the IS-LM approach of orthodox Neoclassical-Keynesian macroeconomics, with some major exceptions. One exception is that it relies on Keynes's theory of effective demand, which, as we shall see, is not the same as the theory of aggregate demand used in Classical-Keynesian models. Another exception is that it makes no assumptions about full employment and balanced trade. A final exception is that it incorporates changes in the profit–wage distribution in trading partners.

Effective demand

We add four additional exogenous variables to the model in the previous section: gross tax revenues, T; government expenditures on goods and services, G; exports, X; and imports, M. National income (Y) flows entirely to R, W and T; therefore R and W measure *after-tax* incomes.

Keynes defines *effective demand* in Chapter 3 of *The General Theory*. Two factors determine the size of effective demand.

1. Aggregate demand (D-curve)

The first factor is the sales revenues (or "proceeds") capitalists *expect* to receive when they sell the output produced with a given amount of employment. When capitalists increase employment, output and expected sales revenues rise, and vice versa. Keynes called this the *aggregate demand function*. It consists of the four elements defined above: consumption (C), investment (I), net government spending (G − T) and net export spending (X − M). With D representing aggregate demand and N total employment, $D = D(N)$. We show the D function in Figure 9.1.

The vertical axis is nominal GDP, or Y, where $Y = C + I + G + (X - M)$. Non-consumption spending, which is the sum $I + (G - T) + (X - M)$, is exogenous and determines the vertical intercept. We must add expected sales from consumption to this amount to arrive at D. However, as employment increases consumption spending also increases but at a decreasing rate. This is because of the marginal propensity to consume, which is less than unitary. Investment spending, I, depends on domestic interest rates, r, and *expected* future profits π_{exp} so that $I = I(r, \pi_{exp})$. The domestic interest rate is important because it influences the cost of borrowing.

The shape and position of the D-curve changes whenever there are changes in the exogenous variables. The shape and position also change when the distribution of income changes. For example, if workers get a relatively larger share of income, then a given level of employment generates more wage income. Since workers have a higher marginal propensity to consume than capitalists, consumption spending rises, shifting the D-curve upward. Of course this might also cause capitalists to lower their future profit expectations, thereby reducing investment spending, I.

2. Aggregate Supply Price (Z-curve)

Capitalists require a minimum amount of sales revenues to make production worthwhile. These revenues cover all costs and pay capitalists a minimum profit. We show this as the Z-curve in Figure 9.1. The revenues capitalists require, Z, may be more or less than the amount they expect to receive as shown by D. If D exceeds Z then expected sales revenues exceed what is minimally required and employment and production increases. The opposite holds true when Z exceeds D.

The Z-curve rises at an increasing rate because, as employment rises, output rises at a slower rate due to diminishing returns. We define this relationship as $Z = Z(N)$. Actual employment, N_0, occurs in Figure 9.1 where the aggregate demand curve intersects the aggregate supply curve, or where $Z = D$. This is what Keynes called *effective demand*. This level of employment may or may not correspond to full employment. The associated nominal GDP is Y_0.

Income distribution and macroeconomics

The Keynesian equilibrium condition for effective demand in Figure 9.1 is:

$$Y_0 = R + W + T = C_k + C_w + I + G + (X - M) \tag{9.10}$$

The terms W and C_w cancel out because $W = C_w$ (i.e., workers do not save). The equation then reduces to

$$R = A + c_k R + I + (G - T) + (X - M) \tag{9.11}$$

where R is profit.

Assume for the time being that both the government's budget $(G - T)$ and the nation's trade balance $(X - M)$ are exogenous. Solving for R gives us a new equilibrium expressed in terms of profit income R_0:

214 Post Keynesian international economics

$$R_0 = \frac{1}{(1 - c_r)}[A + I + (G - T) + (X - M)] \qquad (9.12)$$

As before, this equation shows that the capitalists' own spending and investment decisions determines their own profit income. But it also shows that the government's budget and the trade balance *positively* affect capitalists' profits. Increases in budget deficits (i.e., G > T) and increases in trade surpluses (i.e., X > M) are good for domestic profits, given the strict assumptions of the model.

The last step is to assume the shares of national income going to profits and wages are fixed. As we have seen above, these shares are normally determined by the relative bargaining power of capitalists and workers and by the general social and political environment. Let the parameter π represent the profit share and $(1 - \pi)$ the wage share. In this case $R = \pi Y$ and $W = (1 - \pi)Y$. Using these expressions we can once again find equilibrium Y_0 from R_0 by replacing R with πY:

$$R_0 = \pi Y_0 = \frac{1}{(1 - c_r)}[A + I + (G - T) + (X - M)] \qquad (9.13)$$

We can now solve for Y_0 by dividing both sides of the equation by π:

$$Y_0 = \frac{1}{\pi(1 - c_r)}[A + I + (G - T) + (X - M)] \qquad (9.14)$$

Note that the profit share variable π appears in the denominator of the multiplier expression. This means equilibrium national income depends *negatively* on the profit share of national income. If the share going to profits rises, then everyone's income falls; if the share going to workers rises, then π decreases and everyone's income rises. Given the assumptions we have made, this makes sense: workers spend a much larger portion of their incomes on consumption than capitalists. Redistribution of income from capitalists to workers is therefore expansionary, and both capitalists and workers receive more income since the entire economy expands. In terms of the theory of effective demand, a redistribution of income from profits to wages would shift the D-curve upward to D'. This in turn raises both employment and nominal income/GDP. We show this in Figure 9.2. Employment rises to N_1 and aggregate income rises to Y_1.

Trade balance

The channel through which economic changes in one nation affect economic conditions in the other is trade and exchange rates. Economic conditions existing in each nation determine exports and imports as well as the supply and demand for the other's currency.

Suppose there are only two identical capitalist nations, a home nation and a foreign nation. Home nation uses the dollar ($) and foreign nation uses the euro (€).

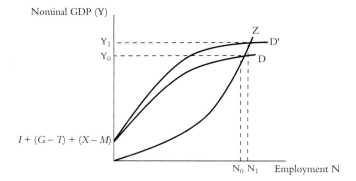

FIGURE 9.2 Income redistribution

Foreign goods sold to the home nation are valued in euros when they leave the foreign port but are then valued in dollars when they arrive at the home port. To use the import variable M in the home nation model we must first convert it into home currency using the *real* exchange rate, e, where $e = Ep^*/p$ where the asterisk represents foreign variables. The *nominal* exchange rate, E, is simply the price of dollars in terms of euros, or \$/€. The variable p is home country's average price per unit of output and p^* is foreign country's average price per unit of output.

Home country's exports (X) are identical to foreign country's imports, M★, where an asterisk identifies foreign variables. It follows that X = M★. We use a linear equation to describe each nation's imports:

$$\text{Home: } M = \alpha e + mY \text{ or } M = \alpha e + m\frac{R}{\pi} \qquad (9.15)$$

$$\text{Foreign: } M^* = \alpha^* e + m^* Y^* \text{ or } M^* = \alpha^* e + m^* \frac{R^*}{\pi^*} \qquad (9.16)$$

Two variables determine imports: the real exchange rate, e, and national income, Y. The coefficients α and m are slope parameters that measure the responsiveness of imports to changes in e and Y. The coefficient α is negative: for given world prices, if a euro can buy more dollars (i.e., \$/€ rises), then imports fall and exports rise.[10] The coefficient m is the familiar *marginal propensity to import* and its value is positive: an increase in home income generates more imports. Also, we introduce the profit–wage distribution directly into the import function by replacing Y with R/π (since $R = \pi Y$).

Figure 9.3 displays the trade (current account) balance for the home nation. The vertical axis still measures nominal GDP while the horizontal axis measures the real exchange rate, e, or Ep^*/p where E = \$/€. The straight line represents all those combinations of e and Y that generate balanced trade. Everywhere along this line exports equal imports (X = M). Any point off the line represents either a trade surplus or trade deficit. Unlike orthodox theory, there is no presumption that trade will balance and that the economy would be on the TB line.

Consider point A. There the exchange rate e_0 and national income Y_0 generate

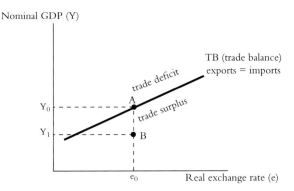

FIGURE 9.3 Trade balance

a trade balance. However, if national income falls to Y_1 and the exchange rate remains where it is at e_0 then we would be at point B. At B, the drop in income decreases imports so that, with given exports and with world prices and exchange rates remaining the same, the trade balance becomes a surplus. Generalizing, any point to the right of the TB line generates a trade surplus and any point to the left of TB generates a trade deficit.

The foreign exchange market

The market for foreign exchange determines the real exchange rate, $e = Ep^*/p$ where e is measured as \$/€. Four international flows determine the value of e: (1) home exports; (2) home imports; (3) inflows of foreign financial assets; and (4) outflows of home financial assets. Relative home–foreign income levels determine trade flows while relative home–foreign interest rates r/r^* determine financial asset flows. We assume p^*/p is constant.

Increased exports (i.e., a rising domestic trade surplus) drive e down because foreigners have to sell off euros to acquire the dollars they need to pay for the exports. Similarly, increased foreign purchases of home financial assets drive down e because foreigners must sell euros to get the dollars they need to purchase these assets. The opposite reasoning applies to imports and the inflow of foreign financial assets.

In our case, if home interest rates are higher than foreign interest rates then home financial assets become relatively more attractive. This leads to increased foreign purchases of home financial assets, driving down the value of e.

According to Post Keynesians, global financial asset flows are more important than trade flows in determining exchange rates. For this reason we focus on the relationship between relative interest rates and exchange rates. We do this in Figure 9.4.

Starting at point A, the real exchange rate is e_0 and the interest rate is r_0. Now, if the interest rises to r_1 foreigners buy more home financial assets. This pushes down the exchange rate to e_1. The new combination— r_1 and e_1—describes point B. All

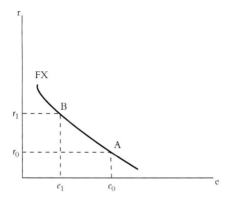

FIGURE 9.4 Interest rates and exchange rates

other things remaining the same, higher home interest rates are associated with lower real exchange rates.

Money and liquidity preference

The curve LM in Figure 9.5 shows all combinations of home employment and home interest rates that generate equivalence between the supply and demand for money. To see how this works, suppose we start at point A. There, employment is N_0, which implies a certain level of production. Also at point A the supply of money equals the demand for money and the corresponding rate of interest is r_0. All firms have enough cash on hand to finance their ongoing operations and the transactions and speculative demands for money are satisfied.

Now suppose employment rises to N_1 because production rises. This increased production requires more credit and bank loans to finance the additional outlays on inputs. Resource owners deposit their new income into banks, which increases bank reserves. The supply of money begins to rise. The transactions demand for money, which is a function of income, rises at the same time. Thus, both the supply and demand for money increase.

If the increased money supply entirely satisfies the increased supply for money, then interest rates would remain unchanged. However, this may not be the case. In Figure 9.5 we presume that money demand rises a bit faster, which pushes up market interest rates to r_1. We are now at point B.

This analysis is significant because it shows that the money supply is mostly endogenous. We say "mostly" because the central bank also exercises considerable influence over bank reserves and credit availability. The partial endogeneity of the money supply is a uniquely Post Keynesian idea.[11]

218 Post Keynesian international economics

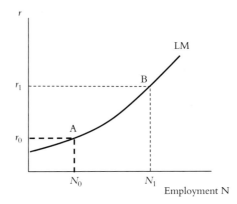

FIGURE 9.5 LM curve

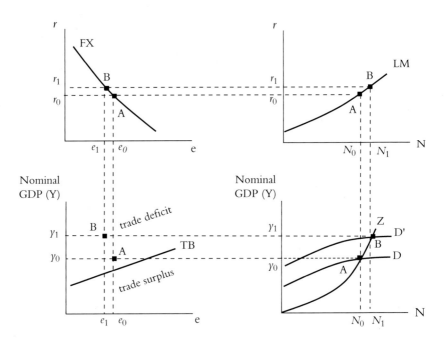

FIGURE 9.6 General open economy model

A Post Keynesian open economy model

In Figure 9.6 we piece together all the components of the Post Keynesian open economy model. Each of the four panels contains a point labeled A and a point labeled B. The As represent our initial position and the Bs represent the final position after we have made some changes to be discussed below. The narrative goes as follows.

Effective demand in the home economy is at A where the D-curve and Z-curve intersect. This is the lower right panel. When employment is N_0 and nominal income/GDP is Y_0, then expected sales revenue equals required sales revenue. The value of N may or may not be at full employment. The production activity implied by N_0 results in a home interest rate of r_0. This is point A in the top right panel. Here, the demand for money equals the supply of money. Next, when the interest rate is r_0 the exchange rate is e_0, assuming foreign interest rates remain unchanged. This is point A in the top left panel. Finally, the combination of Y_0 and e_0 results in a trade deficit. This trade deficit corresponds to point A in the lower left panel. Note that there exists no mechanism that automatically restores trade balance.

There are many scenarios that we can study using this model. For example, suppose the D-curve shifts upward to D'. Expected sales revenues from employment of N_1 workers will rise, producing the new effective demand point B. With nominal GDP and income now at Y_1 the demand for money increases, pushing interest rates up to r_1 at point B in the top right panel. Banks meet part of this increased demand for money by increasing credit availability and hence the money supply. The interest rate therefore does not rise as much as it would have had the money supply remained constant. Next, the higher interest rate attracts foreign capital which lowers the value of the euro to e_1, shown at point B in the top right panel. The higher income and the lower exchange rate produce an even higher trade deficit shown as point B in the lower left panel. We could examine many more scenarios, but we leave these as an exercise for consideration elsewhere.

Class struggle across borders: trade and competitiveness

We can use the above Kaleckian model to examine how fluctuations in one nation's economy affect another nation's economy. What distinguishes this macro model from orthodox models is (1) its division of society into a capitalist class and a working class and its focus on the distribution of class income and (2) its analysis of mark-ups over costs as the source of profit income. When we extend these considerations to international economics it follows that class struggles over income shares in one nation affect international trade and class relations in other nations.

We retain the assumptions made in the above section about class income shares and consumption, namely, that workers spend all their wage income, capitalists spend a portion of their profit income on consumption and save (i.e., invest) the rest, and wage and profit shares are constant. Thus, $W = C_w$ where $W = (1 - \pi)Y$ and $C_k = A + c_r R$ where $R = \pi Y$. To simplify things even further, we make these additional assumptions about home and foreign variables:

1. $p = p^\star$
2. $\pi = \pi^\star$
3. $\alpha = \alpha^\star$ and $m = m^\star$
4. I, G and T are everywhere exogenous $(G - T) = (G^* - T^*) = 0$.

220 Post Keynesian international economics

These assumptions assure that both countries are indeed identical. Assumption #3 implies that the import equations (9.15) and (9.16) are identical.

We now describe macroeconomic equilibrium in both nations using Equation (9.12):

$$R_0 = \frac{1}{(1 - c_r)}[A + I + (G - T) + (M^* - eM)] \tag{9.17}$$

The last term uses Equations (9.15) and (9.16) and reflects the fact that $X = M^\star$. The foreign country has an identical equation, which we need not repeat here. All we need to do now is to insert the import functions into this equation:

$$R_0 = \frac{1}{(1 - c_r)}\left[A + I + (G - T) + \left(\alpha^* e + m^*\frac{R^*}{\pi^*} - e\alpha e - em\frac{R}{\pi}\right)\right] \tag{9.18}$$

Notice that R also appears on the right hand side of the equation. This is because the home country's import function is itself a function of Y, or R/π. Solving this equation for R, and skipping several tedious algebraic steps, we obtain:

$$R_0 = \frac{\left[A + I + (G - T) + \alpha^* e - e\alpha e + \dfrac{m^* R^*}{\pi^*}\right]\pi}{\pi(1 - c_r) + me} \tag{9.19}$$

We can use this equation to identify the economic forces that push home country national income up and down. One set of forces originates in the currency market where the real exchange rate, e, is determined. Recall that $e = Ep^\star/p$. The market nominal exchange rate, E, depends on the elasticities of supply and demand for these currencies (as Robinson pointed out) as well as on the price elasticities of exports and imports. It also depends on what happens to prices in each nation or $p^\star/p$. We assumed $p = p^\star$, but this need not be the case. If the change in e is matched by an opposite and equal increase in $p^\star/p$ then the real exchange rate, e, remains unchanged. We call this particular result "purchasing power parity" because the purchasing power of the dollar in the home country and of the euro in the foreign country remains unaltered. If purchasing power parity prevails, then the e in Equation (9.17) is a constant. This is unlikely to be the case, however.

Many events can push profits R_0 in one direction or another. For example, there can be changes in the marginal propensities to consume (c_r) and import (m), which affect the spending multipliers. These two parameters play key roles in Equation (9.17). Also, there can be feedback effects onto investment, a variable we assumed exogenous. But investment is actually endogenous because income (both actual and expected) strongly influences I. As R adjusts to other changes in the economy, changes in investment can either magnify or dampen these adjustments.

As R moves toward R_0, changes in the competitiveness of one nation or the other might occur. These can cause mark-ups and relative prices ($p^\star/p$) to change

Post Keynesian international economics **221**

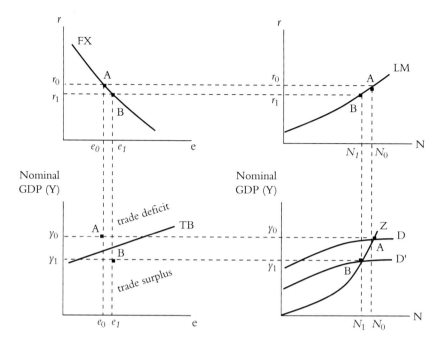

FIGURE 9.7 Change in foreign profit share

and so too real exchange rates. Also, each nation might react to changing economic circumstances by engaging in expansionary fiscal policies, which means that G is no longer equal to T. In this way either nation can influence the outcome.

All these considerations are straightforward, albeit difficult to deal with algebraically. They fit solidly into orthodox Keynesian macroeconomic theory. However, the way in which income distribution affects macroeconomic outcomes, and the way in which firms set prices on the basis of mark-ups, are what make the analysis Kaleckian.

For example, if the profit share of foreign capitalists, $\pi^\star$, rises, then, according to Equation (9.17), home country profit income, R_0 would fall.[12] Any attempt by *foreign* capitalists to grab a larger share of their own nation's income reduces profits for *home* country capitalists. This dampens home investment spending and triggers an economic downturn. This is equivalent to a downward shift of the D-curve to D' in Figure 9.7. As before, the original points are labeled A. The new D'-curve results in less employment at N_1 and less GDP/income at Y_1. This reduces money demand, causing interest to fall to r_1 and with it a rise in the real exchange rate to e_1. All of these new points are labeled B. The trade balance, which once was in deficit, is now in surplus.

Conversely, redistribution of income from foreign profits to foreign wages, say because of the growing power and influence of labor, increases home country profits and wages since this stimulates home country exports. The logic behind this analysis lies in the fact that workers spend a larger portion of their income than capitalists, so any redistribution that favors workers is expansionary in both economies.[13] All of these results depend, of course, on the slopes and positions (i.e., the elasticities) of the curves in each of the panels. This is largely an empirical matter.

Finally, it is essential to point out the role played by the psychology of expectations in this Post Keynesian interpretation. Each panel in Figures 9.6 and 9.7 rests on a set of beliefs about what will happen in the near future, and these beliefs strongly influence the decisions people make in the present. Expectations are also fickle. This is because they are interdependent; they rely on opinions about other people's opinions. Keynes spoke of "herd-like instincts," a form of crowd or mob behavior that is the root cause of periodic bubbles and panics. This gives market capitalism a speculative character, as if people make economic decisions in a Las Vegas casino.

The influence of expectations on economic performance becomes even more complex when considered in a global perspective. International relative prices, interest rates, incomes and profit–wage distributions change constantly and thereby expose the world economy to volatility and speculation.

We turn now to the work of Hyman Minsky, best known for his theories of economic instability.

Hyman P. Minsky and global financial instability

The centerpiece of Minsky's economics is his theory of financial instability. To Minsky, instability is an endogenous feature of capitalism. To use a worn-out cliché, "it is baked into the cake." Instability originates in the financial sector, which, since the 1950s, has grown enormously in relative importance. Orthodox economics, on the other hand, claims capitalism is inherently stable and that instabilities arise because of exogenous disturbances and market imperfections.

Minsky's main concern was with the US economy. Nevertheless, his ideas offer much to our understanding of international economics. This is because the causes of instability that Minsky identified are global in nature. National economies are highly integrated so that internal domestic sources of instability trigger booms and busts, and panics and contagions that spread across borders like wildfire.

Uncertainty, investment and cash flow

To produce output, firms purchase productive assets—capital goods—that are by nature long lasting and hence illiquid. When firms borrow to finance these purchases they commit to making regular principal and interest payments over the life of the loan. The economic conditions that will exist during the life of the loan are unknown. This is where uncertainty, risk-taking and speculation enter the analysis.

From a microeconomic perspective, the ability of a firm to service its debt depends on the adequacy of its cash flows. Cash flow is a term that describes the present and expected future streams of revenues and expenses that a firm realizes.

To make production possible and profitable, expected revenue streams must exceed expected expense streams by an adequate margin. When this condition is fulfilled, the illiquid capital assets that businesses own will preserve their value and there will be enough cash to service their debts and pay out profits.

Cash flows, then, depend on macroeconomic performance. To sustain "normal" operations, aggregate effective demand and national income must generate sufficient sales revenues to cover the expected costs of production. This will depend on aggregate investment, which, in Post Keynesian theory, is what determines the size of current profits: "workers spend what they get and capitalists get what they spend," as Kalecki put it. It will also depend on the national profit–wage distribution of income, which, as we have seen above, affects the macro economy of trading partners.

Thus, macroeconomic conditions determine microeconomic conditions. Post Keynesians call this the "macroeconomic foundations of microeconomics," a reversal of the popular Neoclassical catchphrase. Any deterioration in macroeconomic conditions discourages investment, reduces employment and compels investors to switch to more liquid assets such as short-term government bonds or cash. Agents "run to liquidity," causing a liquidity crisis. This negatively affects cash flows and firms find it hard to meet their debt obligations. A recession then sets in. An opposite set of events can also occur.

Subjective opinions—expectations—about the future influence all economic decisions. These expectations are fickle and subject to sudden changes in direction, ranging from buoyant enthusiasm to panic. In such an uncertain environment domestic and international investment is necessarily erratic, causing large cyclical variations in output, income and employment. As these variations take place, the values of existing capital assets change as well.

Output prices and asset prices

There are two price systems in Minsky's theory. One is the system of current output prices. These are the prices of currently produced consumption, investment, government and export goods. As with Kalecki, firms determine these prices by adding a mark-up to labor costs.

The second price system is asset prices. Assets are produced capital goods whose prices depend on their costs of production and on the prices capitalists are willing to pay to acquire them. This is where uncertainty and expectations enter: firms will be willing to pay higher prices for capital assets if they expect that their use will generate more profits in the future, and vice versa.

Current investment requires that current output prices remain higher than asset prices. The greater this gap, the higher the expected profits, the greater the incentive to invest. When this gap shrinks, or if asset prices exceed output prices, then investment naturally shrinks. In other words, prices must be high enough to guarantee that business cash flows are sufficient to pay for the costs of production, to service debts and to provide sufficient profit income for capitalists. As Minsky put

224 Post Keynesian international economics

it, "Business cycles result from the dance of these two price levels" (Minsky, 2008: 160).

Minsky's business cycle theory

In Minsky's instability thesis, a business cycle begins with the economy performing satisfactorily. This is the first or initial stage in the business cycle. Economic growth is high enough to maintain full employment. Moderation and risk-aversion prevail among creditors and debtors and expectations of future profits and cash flows are cautious. Borrowers are able to make all their principal and interest payments from existing cash flows. Minsky described financial decisions in this environment as "hedge finance." Hedge borrowers seek to reduce risk by making simultaneous investments in other financial instruments that are likely to move in the opposite direction. In this way they can avoid unanticipated losses and gains.

The second stage in the cycle occurs when this state of normal expectations gives rise to growing positive expectations about future profits and cash flows. Agents become less conservative and investment spending increases, driving up asset prices. A boom sets in as agents borrow more to finance their increasing investment. Speculators now enter the game, betting that the upward trend will continue. They drive asset prices up even further. Lenders, now more optimistic about the future, are more than happy to satisfy the increasing demand for loans. Liquidity decreases, credit availability rises and so too does the supply of money. Minsky described financial decisions in this environment as "speculative finance." Speculative borrowers purposively seek to take on risk. They can make interest payments from cash flows but must regularly refinance (or rollover) the maturing debt principal.

In the third stage positivism gradually turns into euphoria. Asset prices climb further and risk-taking becomes reckless. This is the classic bubble economy. According to Minsky, this is when "Ponzi finance" infects decision making: outstanding debt becomes so large that firms' cash flows can meet neither their interest obligations nor their principal obligations.[14] Ponzi borrowers use loans to purchase an asset but expect to be able to service the debt only if the asset appreciates more than the debt liability. In other words, only if the asset rises in value will the borrower be able to pay off the principal and accumulated interest. Ponzi finance takes place only when agents have euphoric expectations of the future. When the euphoria becomes disappointed, existing investment projects become unviable and businesses have to sell off assets to service their debt. Bankruptcies increase, the euphoria turns into panic and the bubble bursts. Asset prices plummet, investment collapses, unemployment rises as the economy falls into recession.[15]

Global instability and financialization

In the late 2000s, when the US and European economies began their freefall into the Great Recession, international investors shifted large amounts of money into the emerging BRIC economies: Brazil, Russia, India and China. Discouraged by low rates of return in the US and Europe, equity and debt investment exploded in BRIC countries, where growth rates were higher. Between 2008 and 2011, investment in the BRIC countries rose by 177%, 142%, 88% and 77% respectively. BRIC exchange rates rose concomitantly as investors and speculators scrambled to buy the currencies they needed to finance their asset purchases. A bubble was in the making. Then, in 2013, the herd-like behavior abruptly ended as investors took their capital elsewhere. The BRIC bubble was now bursting.

This had become a common Minsky-like global pattern. The narrative usually goes like this: investors, responding to changes in relative global profit rates, discover and then become enthralled with profit opportunities in one or more foreign countries. Speculative exuberance follows, causing asset values in those countries to inflate. The result is a bubble. Then, usually with the restoration of profitability at home or elsewhere, investors begin to lose confidence in their current investments. They reverse course and move elsewhere. The bubble bursts and asset values deflate, creating widespread financial turmoil and unemployment in the ill-fated country.

We saw this pattern in the commercial real estate bubble in the late 1980s, the European Monetary System crises of 1992–1993, the Mexican peso crisis of 1994, the Asian financial crisis in 1997, the dot-com bubble in 1997–2000, the residential real estate and the derivative bubble in the 2000s. The precise causes of these crises vary but their patterns are similar. This global phenomenon is quite new, however, especially common since the 1980s. In the 1950s, 1960s and 1970s the world economy was not so susceptible to such bubbles and panics. What has changed?

Money manager capitalism and financialization

Minsky and Post Keynesians say that the main thing that has changed is global financialization brought about by financial liberalization. Financial liberalization means the removal of controls on the international flow of international capital. Finance capital has become "liberated," so to speak, and speculative "hot money" now freely circulates among national economies. This causes bubbles when capital enters and economic chaos and hardship when it leaves.

Minsky believed that capitalism had gone through a major transformation in the 1970s, from "paternalistic capitalism" to "money manager capitalism." In paternalistic capitalism a large interventionist state conducts counter-cyclical macroeconomic policy. It also has a powerful central bank that serves as a lender of last resort, and the chief source of corporate investment finance is internally generated profits.

In money manager capitalism the chief source of investment finance is external debt from banks and financial markets. External debt is often cheaper than shareholder equity because the lender is first in line to receive payments from cash flow. Dividend payments to shareholders are residuals, paid out after servicing external debt. Also, lenders are more risk averse than equity owners since their returns are limited by the loan contracts.

226 Post Keynesian international economics

One result of these changes in financing practices is that the time horizon for decision making has shifted from the long run to the short term. This introduces more volatility into the economy. Moreover, mutual funds and pension funds own a large portion of marketable financial assets. Lightning-fast programmed trading, in which computer programs decide when to buy and sell based on mathematical algorithms, highlight international financial markets.

Adding to global financial instability has been the deregulation of financial markets in the 1990s and 2000s. In 1999 the US Congress repealed the 1933 Glass-Steagall Act, which restricted commercial bank securities activities. This, plus failure to regulate derivatives markets, has encouraged financial speculation and added to the volatility of global financial markets.

Increasing the uncertainty surrounding global investment is the fact that the assets and liabilities of creditors and debtors across the globe are denominated in many different currencies. So long as currency markets adjust quickly and all governments pursue sound fiscal and monetary policies the associated risks of contagious speculative panics are controllable. This is rarely the case, however.

Post Keynesians use the term "financialization" to describe the growing importance of world financial markets. Today, at least a third of the capital raised by corporations is through the issuance of financial assets in foreign financial markets. Cross-border capital flows are enormous. Foreign portfolio holdings of US securities doubled in size between 2005 and 2012, from $6.9 trillion to $13.3 trillion. US portfolio holdings of foreign securities also doubled in the same period, from $10 trillion to $19.3 trillion (Department of the Treasury, 2013).

As economist Gerald Epstein observed,

> sometime in the mid- to late 1970s or early 1980s, structural shifts of dramatic proportions took place in a number of countries that led to significant increases in financial transactions, real interest rates, the profitability of financial firms, and the shares of national income accruing to the holders of financial assets.
>
> *(Epstein, 2006: 4)*

Financialization has increased the economic and social importance of the international financial capitalist class as it continues to accumulate political and economic influence in the US and abroad. The immense political power of the financial industry in most advanced capitalist nations has prevented any real reforms from taking place. A reduction in labor union power and an increase in the profit share of national incomes has accompanied the rise of the financial capitalist class.

To Post Keynesians and the followers of Minsky, financialization has contributed to the global financial instabilities experienced since the 1980s. Stock market crashes, bursting real estate bubbles, currency collapses and capital flight have become regular features of global capitalism. Small economic shocks can reverse the general state of expectations, causing wide-ranging financial and macroeconomic crises and contagions. Nations face capital flight risk, risks of contagion and sovereign debt risk that fetter the autonomy of governments. Speculative profit expectations during booms lead capitalists to take on more and more debt until they can no longer pay off that debt with cash flows. This makes economies increasingly unstable and subject to cycles of debt-financed euphoric booms followed by panicky busts and depressions.

Minsky's financial instability hypothesis is thus a truly global phenomenon. Global capitalism has become a speculation-driven, casino-like system that can hardly bring about an efficient allocation of the world's resources, as idealized by orthodox economists. As Keynes once remarked, "When the capital development of a country becomes a by-product of the activities of a casino, the job is likely to be ill-done" (Keynes, 1936: 159).

Post Keynesian views on the international monetary system

Post Keynesian policy analyses address three problems. One is capital flight, hot money and speculative international portfolio investment. A second is global stagnation and unemployment as central tendencies of floating exchange rate regimes. A third is the use of the US currency as an international reserve currency. We investigate each in turn.

Controlling capital flows

Foreign capital enters and leaves nations under varying constraints and conditions. All nations have rules prescribing what foreign investors and corporations can and cannot do. These rules determine who benefits from and who pays for the presence of foreign capital.

Foreign capital can aid substantially a nation's economic growth and development by supplementing domestic savings and increasing investment. However, while there are benefits to hosting foreign capital, there are also risks. These risks include capital flight, speculative attacks on currencies, panics, contagions and sovereign debt crises. To minimize these risks, nations often consider regulating inward and outward capital flows. These apply to both long-term foreign direct investment (FDI) and short-term portfolio investment.

FDI is not as problematical in terms of capital flight because it entails illiquid long-term "brick and mortar" projects. Once built, they do not move. But FDI can be problematical in other ways. For example, FDI can be harmful if its sources are large multinational corporations from rich powerful nations and the hosts are poorer developing nations. In such cases foreign capital can extract from weaker hosts concessions that work against local interests. For example, FDI can impede the development of local enterprises, lower environmental protections and reduce social protections. It can also tilt the host country's distribution of income and wealth by favoring the local comprador classes.[16]

In order to preserve sovereignty over its economy a host nation can restrict inward-bound FDI to sectors and projects that it chooses. It can require foreign

228 Post Keynesian international economics

companies to share technologies, locate in certain places and employ local citizens. It can restrict how much profit foreign firms can take out of the country. Finally, a nation can regulate outward-bound direct investment by host nation firms in order to keep scarce capital at home.

Most agree that short-term portfolio investment poses a far greater risk than FDI. Much of such investment is speculative and subject to the whims and impulses of foreign portfolio managers. This is where capital flight can be destabilizing.

One way of preventing capital flight is to place restrictions on the purchase and sale of the host country's currency. If a foreign investor cannot buy local currency, then it cannot purchase local financial assets. Another method is to control the amount of foreign currency-denominated debt domestic firms can take on. This limits the ability of foreigners to lend to local firms without prior government approval. A nation can also regulate, if not prohibit, foreign ownership of host country stocks and bonds. Lastly, a nation can levy a tax on short-term investment.

Since the 1980s, China has adopted most of these capital control strategies. It has channeled FDI into desired sectors, regulated currency exchange and sharply limited foreign ownership of domestic financial assets. China did this quite effectively, to the consternation of impatient foreign investors. China recently has loosened many of these restrictions as it integrated with the world trading and investment system.

Unsurprisingly, the economic orthodoxy rejects capital controls, and most economists regard them as a form of protectionism. Only by liberalizing capital flows, they believe, can nations reduce the risks of capital flight and the spread of financial crises. This orthodox position hardened with the new wave of trade and finance liberalization (i.e., Neoliberalism) that commenced in the 1990s. Even the IMF changed its articles of agreement in the late 1990s, forbidding capital controls. However, in 2009, after a series of destructive global financial crises, the IMF has to some degree reversed course. It now recommends that emerging market economies use capital controls to deal with capital flight.

Post Keynesians believe the financial crises that have afflicted the world economy in the past two decades arise in the first place because of unfettered global capital markets and the free mobility of capital, especially short-term capital. They take their inspiration from Keynes, who also believed that capital controls are a necessary tool for managing a nation's macro economy and for maintaining financial stability. Keynes believed nations ought to channel foreign investment toward projects that generate the most employment and that stimulate growth. He advanced these ideas at the 1944 Bretton Woods Conference where he declared,

> It is widely held that control of capital movements, both inward and outward, should be a permanent feature of the post-war system—at least so far as we are concerned. If control is to be effective, it probably involves the *machinery* of exchange control for *all* transactions. . . . But such control will be more difficult to work . . .by unilateral action than if movements of capital can be controlled *at both ends*.

> *(quoted in Obstfeld and Taylor, 2004: 149)*

As this quote indicates, Keynes strongly believed that the 44 Allied nations should construct an international currency union that would adopt capital controls. But they had to do this in concert; no one nation can do it alone. Today, many Post Keynesians believe the same thing. They recommend the creation of an international system of governance that would supervise and regulate global capital flows. They argue that such a system would work well and in support they point to empirical studies by the IMF and the National Bureau of Economic Research (Ostry, et al., 2010: 5).[17]

We can take the Post Keynesian position a Kaleckian step further by viewing the debate over capital controls as a manifestation of the global struggle between capital and labor. Capital desires freedom of mobility to pursue profit anywhere in the world. The economic orthodoxy defends capital's position. Labor, on the other hand, desires security of employment, a living wage and global financial stability. Post Keynesians defend labor's position. They view capital controls as weapons in labor's struggle against the political and economic power of global corporations.

Finally, Post Keynesians believe that, with capital controls, nations would be free from foreign influence and thus be better able to manage their economies with macroeconomic policy. In a world of unfettered capital mobility, there would be a world equilibrium rate of interest to which any nation's domestic interest rates would be bound. Any change in domestic rates would create bubbles or panics as capital rushes in or flees. This reduces a nation's ability to use monetary policy to regulate its domestic interest rates.

Paul Davidson and stagnation bias

Paul Davidson has been one of the strongest advocates of Keynes's radical agenda. Co-founder with Sidney Weintraub (1914–1983) of the *Journal of Post Keynesian Economics*, Davidson has focused mainly on monetary theory. But he also made important contributions to international monetary policy. One such contribution is the thesis that the existing system of international trade and finance has a built-in stagnation bias. The international monetary system, argues Davidson, has a tendency to generate worldwide unemployment. The reason for this, Davidson explains, is that the burden of adjusting to trade imbalances falls on deficit countries and these adjustments increase unemployment in all countries, debtors and creditors alike.

Trade-deficit (debtor) countries must engage in austerity to balance trade—or else pay escalating international debts, which poorer nations can ill afford. Balancing trade means reducing imports or expanding exports using either contractionary fiscal policies or currency devaluation. The effect is to increase unemployment. As Davidson points out, this also hurts trade-surplus nations (creditors) because demand for their products shrinks. Unemployment rises in these nations as well.

Another consequence is that currency speculators see falling exchange rates in deficit countries and come to expect these rates to fall even further, causing

230 Post Keynesian international economics

currency crises. The power of speculation thwarts attempts by any single nation's central bank to prevent such crises, unless of course all central banks act in concert.

Trade-surplus nations can make the situation worse because they have an incentive to continue to grow their trade surpluses and to accumulate foreign exchange reserves. This builds domestic liquidity and reduces uncertainty. China has been an example of this as they have accumulated huge balances of US dollar reserves.

To resolve the stagnation–unemployment bias problem, Davidson proposes fixed exchange rates coupled with an international monetary system that issues an international reserve currency to replace the US dollar. This so-called Davidson Plan is a modern version of the plan Keynes introduced at Bretton Woods (Davidson, 2009). We explore Keynes's plan next.

The Keynes Solution: a world reserve currency

For most of the last century the US dollar has served as the world's reserve currency. The importance of the dollar to the rest of the world dates back to the postwar Bretton Woods agreement which formally made the dollar the world's currency of choice. The agreement created an international monetary system with the US at the center. Each nation agreed to peg its currency to the US dollar. The US, in turn, agreed to convert dollars into gold at a constant $35 per ounce. The idea was that this arrangement would provide international financial stability and assist in the postwar reconstruction of Europe.

However, by the late 1960s the system became untenable. This was because the US, without the cooperation of its trading partners, was unable to maintain the quantity of gold reserves needed to make the system work. It was possible during the Cold War years, but as time went by the other nations became less willing to cooperate in this multilateral scheme. Then, in 1971, Nixon unilaterally discontinued the US obligation to convert dollars into gold. Since then the global currency system has become a floating exchange rate system.

However, the US dollar continues to serve as the world's reserve currency. Foreign governments, central banks and private investors prefer to hold their liquid assets in the form of dollars—or US Treasury bonds denominated in dollars—instead of other currencies or assets. The dollar thus remains the world's "safe haven."

One problem with this arrangement is that the value of the dollar hinges on the volatile opinions of global bankers and investors. National treasuries and central banks possess an enormous volume of dollars and any slight variation in the dollar's value can cause large losses for these institutions. So far, the US's dominant position in the world has given the dollar much prestige and stability, ensuring that its value will not change too much.

However, there is always fear that the dollar's value might collapse. Any change in the willingness of nations and central banks to hold dollars can cause havoc, especially if nations threaten to switch to another reserve currency. For example, China's willingness to buy dollar-denominated Treasury bonds with its dollar reserves has kept the prices of these bonds high and interest rates low. This has made it possible for the US government to borrow at low interest rates. It has also fueled (albeit slowly) a recovery from the Great Recession. Any change in China's willingness to hold in reserve dollar-denominated assets could cause turmoil in the US.

Keynes had a solution to the problem of using as a reserve asset the currency of only one dominant nation. He suggested the introduction of an artificial international reserve currency called the *bancor* to which each nation would peg its currency. It would be a type of fixed-rate system. Each nation starts out with a fund of *bancors*, the size of which depends on the size of the nation's trade balance. Trade surpluses add to this fund while trade deficits reduce it. The system then penalizes nations for building up credit and debit balances. Deficit nations have to agree to depreciate their currencies relative to the *bancor* while surplus countries have to agree to appreciate their currencies. The idea is to remove a single nation's currency, such as the US dollar, from international reserve currency status. It would discourage hoarding or manipulating foreign reserves, as China has done, and induce surplus countries to use their accumulated credits to buy goods from other countries or else risk losing their credit balances.

This "Keynes Solution" resurfaced again after the 2009 global financial crisis. China became alarmed by instabilities in the value of the dollar and hence in the value of the billions of dollar-denominated US Treasury bonds held by the People's Bank of China. The Keynes Solution attracted the attention of the governor of the People's Bank of China, Zhou Xiaochuan, who stated,

> The desirable goal of reforming the international monetary system, therefore, is to create an international reserve currency that is disconnected from individual nations and is able to remain stable in the long run, thus removing the inherent deficiencies caused by using credit-based national currencies.
>
> *(Zhou, 2009)*

Even the IMF recommended such a solution in a 2010 report (International Monetary Fund, 2010). The Keynes Solution would mean a sweeping change in the international monetary system and, given the political realities of the day, has been unable to attract much support.

Conclusions

Post Keynesian economics continues Keynes's heterodox ideas about the flaws of capitalism and about how to fix it. Post Keynesians believe capitalism has three fundamental flaws. One is that it generates insufficient effective demand to create full employment. A second is that it is inherently unstable because of pervasive uncertainty and speculation. A third is that it perpetuates and widens class inequality which further dampens effective demand. Post Keynesians find the solution to these problems in an activist, interventionist government that (1) regulates

232 Post Keynesian international economics

the "spirits and speculative urges" of capitalists; (2) protects the working class; (3) manages the economy with the usual toolbox of rational macroeconomic policies; and (4) seeks to create a more humane society.

Post Keynesian ideas apply equally well to the world economy. First, neither free currency markets nor international financial markets automatically correct trade imbalances. Second, debtor and creditor nations, operating in their self-interest, undertake trade adjustment policies that worsen unemployment opportunities for everyone. Third, class struggles over profits and wages within nations affect class relations and macroeconomic performance in their trading partners. Fourth, the financial instabilities that afflict capitalist nations internally rapidly spread across borders as alternating states of euphoria and panic lead global portfolio managers to invest and then withdraw their capital. Finally, Post Keynesians are critical of the international monetary system and the use of the US dollar as the reserve currency of choice.

Post Keynesian solutions to these international problems would have nations rely on capital and currency controls to reduce global speculation and unfettered portfolio capital flows. They also recommend something like the Davidson Plan that would create an artificial multinational reserve currency to replace the dollar and that would encourage trade-surplus nations to spend their surpluses and thus generate more employment everywhere.

Saving capitalism from itself

In the 1930s, scholars and intellectuals of all ideological persuasions lived in fear that fascism, communism or economic depression would annihilate capitalism. Nazism was sweeping through Germany, the Great Terror and the Moscow trials in Stalinist Russia threatened Europe with a dangerous menace, and the Great Depression had ruined the lives of millions.

Some, like the Austrians, looked to the philosophy of free markets and laissez-faire as the most powerful antidote against these threats. Keynes and his mainstream followers believed society required progressive-minded collective action to better the human condition and to protect it from these dangers. They believed governments around the world, acting together, can improve the well-being of their populations by erecting multinational institutions to control and regulate trade and finance—while preserving the main elements of capitalism.

Marxists in the US, especially those associated with the Monthly Review School, agreed with the Post Keynesians that capitalism tended to stagnate and to favor the capitalist class.[18] However, they rejected the possibility of saving capitalism through Keynesian state interventions because, they argued, the state itself had been "captured" by capitalist vested interests. The state, therefore, would never adopt progressive policies that promoted the interests of labor over capital. To the US Marxists, the Post Keynesian recommendation that we create a supra-national state organization to manage currency and financial markets is a fantasy. The capitalist classes of the world would "capture" such a global organization just as it had captured national governments. This would make world unemployment and inequality even worse.

Most contemporary schools of international economics have their roots in this highly charged and politicized environment of the 1930s. There is little evidence, however, that the threats affecting the world in the 1930s had much influence on the development of orthodox international economics. Since the 1930s, Post Keynesianism has skirted along the edges between Keynes and Marx. Some position themselves slightly on the side of Keynes (e.g., Minksy and Davidson) while other position themselves slightly on the side of Marx (e.g., Kalecki and Sraffa).

Notes

1 For an overview of Robinson's work see Gibson (2005).
2 Recall that according to Say's Law supply always creates sufficient demand to buy up everything produced. Therefore unemployment is not possible.
3 If CA is positive (trade surplus), then CA is negative (trade deficit) for the nation's trading partners. The latter import more than they export to the trade surplus nation, which then must finance their excess imports.
4 The effect of changes in income distribution on aggregate spending is actually more complicated. This is because profits consist of *rentier* income (interest and dividend income), which has a small effect on investment spending, and *non-rentier* income (corporate profits), which has a large effect on investment spending. Moreover, the wealth of capitalists and workers also affects spending. We cannot examine these complications in this chapter. See Onaran, Stockhammer and Grafl (2010).
5 For a thorough Post Keynesian explanation see Eichner (1976).
6 This is the inverse of labor productivity, which we define as output per worker.
7 As the value of β rises from zero to infinity, the value of π rises from zero to 1.
8 Kalecki viewed the fiscal deficit as a kind of private sector trade surplus with the government: the government buys more goods and services from the private sector than the private sector buys from the government in the form of taxes (which we can interpret as purchases of government services). Kalecki called this "domestic exports."
9 The model presented in this section borrows from Harvey (2010).
10 Readers should always be aware of how a text defines the exchange rate. Sometimes texts use the ratio of the domestic currency to the foreign currency, and sometimes it is the other way around.
11 The Post Keynesian analysis of money and credit is not homogenous as there are many competing views. On this topic see Lavoie (2011).
12 If the value of π^+ increases in Equation (9.17), then, everything else remaining unchanged, the value of the entire numerator decreases, as does the value of R_0.
13 If we were to take all of these considerations into account the resulting mathematical model would be far too cumbersome to develop here. One such attempt by Robert Blecker (1999) confirms the above analysis, namely, that an improvement in one country's competitiveness redistributes profits away from its trading partner: "[a]ny improvement in one country's competitive position takes profit income as well as market shares and employment opportunities away from the other . . ."
14 Ponzi takes its name from Charles Ponzi who, in the 1920s, promised investors high returns but could only pay these returns with money obtained from new investors.
15 This analysis lends itself to dynamic mathematical modeling, which we avoid here. See Steve Keen (1995 and 2013); Department of the Treasury, Federal Reserve Bank of New York, & Federal Reserve Bank Board of Governors (2013).
16 The comprador class consists of local managers who are subordinate to foreign managers

234 Post Keynesian international economics

but who nonetheless benefit materially from their employment. The term is usually applied to developing nations.

17 See also Magud and Reinhart (2006).

18 The Monthly Review School includes mostly US Marxists writing in the *Monthly Review*, a monthly socialist magazine published since 1949. Prominent contributors included Paul Baran (1910–1964), Harry Braverman (1920–1976), Leo Huberman (1903–1968), Harry Magdoff (1913–2006) and Paul Sweezy (1910–2004).

References

Aslanbeigui, N., & Oakse, G. (2002). "The Theory Arsenal: the Cambridge Circus and the Origins of the Keynesian Revolution." *Journal of the History of Economic Thought, 24*(1), 5–37.

Blecker, R. (1999). "Open Economy Macroeconomics." In J. Deprez, & J. T. Harvey (Eds.), *Foundations of International Economics: Post Keynesian Perspectives* (pp. 116–149). New York: Routledge.

Davidson, P. (2009). *The Keynes Solution: The Path to Global Economic Prosperity*. New York: Palgrave Macmillan.

Department of the Treasury, Federal Reserve Bank of New York, & Federal Reserve Bank Board of Governors. (2013). *Foreign Portfolio Holdings of US Securities*. Washington, DC: U. S. Department of the Treasury.

Eichner, A. S. (1976). *The Megacorp and Oligopoly: Micro Foundations of Macro Dynamics*. New York: Cambridge University Press.

Epstein, G. A. (2006). "Introduction: Financialization and the World Economy." In G. A. Epstein (Ed.), *Financialization and the World Economy* (pp. 3–17). New York: Edward Elgar.

Gibson, B. (Ed.). (2005). *Joan Robinson's Economics: A Centennial Celebration*. Northampton, MA: Edward Elgar.

Harvey, J. T. (2010). *Currencies, Capital Flows and Crises: a Post Keynesian Analysis of Exchange Rate Determination*. New York: Routledge.

International Monetary Fund. (2010). *Reserve Accumulation and International Monetary Stability*. International Monetary Fund, Strategy, Policy and Review Department. Retrieved March 19, 2013, from http://www.imf.org/external/np/pp/eng/2010/041310.pdf.

Kalecki, M. (1971). "On Foreign Trade and 'Domestic Exports'." In M. Kalecki, *Selected Essays on the Dynamics of the Capitalist Economy. 1933–1970* (pp. 15–25). New York: Cambridge University Press.

Keen, S. (1995). "Finance and Economic Breakdown: Modeling Minsky's 'Financial Instability Hypothesis'." *Journal of Post Keynesian Economics, 17*(4), 607–635.

Keen, S. (2013). "A Monetary Minsky Model of the Great Moderation and the Great Recession." *Journal of Economic Behavior & Organization, 86*, 221–235.

Keynes, J. M. (1936). *The General Theory of Employment, Interest and Money*. London: Macmillan.

Lavoie, M. (2011). "Money, Credit and Central Banks in Post-Keynesian Economics." In E. Hein, & E. Stockhammer (Eds.), *A Modern Guide to Keynesian Macroeconomics and Economic Policies* (pp. 34–60). Northampton, MA: Edward Elgar.

Lyons, R. K. (2001). *The Microstructure Approach to Exchange Rate*. Cambridge, MA: MIT Press.

Magud, N., & Reinhart, C. M. (2006). *Capital Controls: an Evaluation*. Working Paper 11973, National Bureau of Economic Research. Retrieved August 28, 2013, from http://www.nber.org/papers/w11973.

Marcuzzo, M. C. (2005). "Piero Sraffa at the University of Cambridge." *European Journal of the History of Economic Thought, 12*(3), 425–452.

Meese, R., & Rogoff, K. (1983). "Empirical Exchange Rate Models of the Seventies: Do They Fit Out of Sample?" *Journal of International Economics, 14*(1 and 2), 3–24.

Minsky, H. (2008). *Stabilizng an Unstable Economy.* New York: McGraw-Hill.

Obstfeld, M., & Taylor, A. M. (2004). *Global Capital Markets: Integration, Crisis and Growth.* New York: Cambridge University Press.

Onaran, Ö., Stockhammer, E., & Grafl, L. (2010). *Financialization, Income Distribution, and Aggregate Demand in the USA.* Discussion Paper No 136, Middlesex University Business School, Department of Economics and Statistics, London.

Ostry, J., Ghosh, A., Habermeier, K., Chamon, M., Qureshi, M. S., & Reinhardt, D. B. (2010). "Capital Inflows; The Role of Controls." *IMF Staff Position Notes, 4.* Retrieved July 8, 2013, from http://EconPapers.repec.org/RePEc:imf:imfspn:2010/04.

Robinson, J. (1937). "The Foreign Exchanges." In J. Robinson, *Essays in the Theory of Employment* (2nd ed., pp. 134–155). Oxford: Basil Blackwell & Mott.

Robinson, J. (1946–1947). "The Pure Theory of International Trade." *Review of Economic Stdies, 14*(2), 98–112.

Robinson, J. (1947). "Beggar-My-Neighbor Remedies for Unemployment." In J. Robinson, *Essays in the Theory of Employment* (2nd ed., pp. 156–172). Oxford: Basil Blackwell & Mott.

Robinson, J. (1953). "An Open Letter from a Keynesian to a Marxist." In J. Robinson, *On Re-Reading Marx* (pp. 19–23). Cambridge, UK: Students' Bookshop Ltd. Retrieved July 2, 2013, from http://collections.mun.ca/PDFs/radical/OnReReadingMarx.pdf.

Robinson, J. (1966a). "Kalecki and Keynes." In *Problems of Economic Dynamics and Planning: Essays in Honour of Michał Kalecki* (pp. 335–343). Warsaw: PWN-Polish Scientific Publishers.

Robinson, J. (1966b). *The New Mercantilism: An Inaugural Lecture By Joan Robinson.* Cambridge, UK: Cambridge University Press.

Robinson, J. (1978). "A Need for a Reconsideration of the Theory of International Trade." In J. Robinson, *Contributions to Modern Economics* (pp. 213–222). San Diego, CA: Academic Press.

Sraffa, P. (1960). *Production of Commodities by Means of Commodities: Prelude to a Critique of Economic Theory.* New York: Cambridge University Press.

Zhou, X. (2009, April 2). *Reform the International Monetary System.* Retrieved September 3, 2013, from Bank for International Settlements, Press & Speeches: http://www.bis.org/review/r090402c.pdf.

10

MARXIAN THEORIES OF IMPERIALISM AND CAPITALIST DEVELOPMENT

Introduction

Karl Marx (1818–1883) was the consummate social scientist of the 19th century. He was a philosopher, economist, sociologist, political theorist, historian, journalist and revolutionary. His influence has endured to this day, and his vision of a future humane and egalitarian society has inspired revolutionary movements on every continent.

Marxian economics is the starting point for any serious critique of global capitalism. Indeed, Marx has inspired many generations of scholars in many academic disciplines from all over the world. These are scholars who reject the prevailing economic orthodoxies and the supremacy of global capitalism.

A central component of Marxian economic theory is the class structure of capitalism, the principal feature of which is the division of society into a capitalist class that owns the means of production and a working class that owns nothing. The working class is therefore "enslaved" by the capitalist class although, paradoxically, workers are perfectly free to choose which capitalist to work for. This social pattern is replicated in virtually all societies that capitalism has touched. As capitalism expands around the world it dominates and rearranges local social institutions, eventually eliminating traditional forms of subsistence production and replacing them with capitalist forms of production.

That capitalism is a class-divided system is nothing new in the history of economic thought. Most Classical, Institutionalist and Post Keynesian economists share this idea. Neither is it new that class conflict determines income and wealth distribution. However, Marx took this a step further by identifying how this exploitation occurs. To use a popular expression, class exploitation is baked into the capitalist cake.

Because Marx viewed capitalism as a world phenomenon, he naturally believed that economic relations between advanced capitalist nations and struggling developing nations are also exploitive. In fact, prosperity in the rich nations causes poverty in poor nations. Likewise, poverty in poor nations produces wealth in rich countries. Moreover, the global expansion of free trade is nothing more than the global expansion of imperialism and exploitation. Explaining why this is so is the Marxian problematic.

The claim that capitalist relations are intrinsically exploitive, domestically as well as internationally, is anathema to Neoclassical economics. The latter argues that exploitation, to the extent that it exists at all, is the consequence of imperfections in the marketplace: imperfect competition, imperfect information and government failure. In a perfect world, all trade is always mutually advantageous and we would never observe symptoms of imperialism and exploitation.

The path we follow in this chapter is as follows. We start out with an examination of one of Marx's early statements on the question of free trade. We will explain why Marx favored free trade over protectionism despite his allegation that free trade expands the capitalists' exploitation of workers on a global scale. This sets the stage for the next two sections, each of which analyzes imperialism, one from a Leninist perspective and the other from a Neo-Marxian perspective.

As a counterpoint to Marxian theories of imperialism we offer the reader an alternative, anti-Marxian theory developed by the Austrian economist Joseph A. Schumpeter. We complete the chapter with a comparison of the terms imperialism and globalism.

Marxian theories of international economics have also followed another route. This is called *unequal exchange*. Unequal exchange attempts to explain the market mechanisms that permit exploitation to exist in a world of free trade. The coexistence of exploitation and free trade appears ironic. Just as capitalists in Marxian theory exploit workers despite the fact that each party voluntarily enters into employment contracts, so too do rich countries exploit poor countries despite the fact that they trade freely with each other. We will pursue this particular theme in the next chapter.

Marx on free trade

In 1815, the British Parliament imposed an import tax on grain. Known as the Corn Laws, this tax protected British landowners from imports of cheap foreign-grown grains. With support from the rising industrial capitalist class, Parliament repealed the law in 1846. Trade in grain had now become free.

Why did the industrial class support the repeal? The reason is best explained by Ricardo's theory of comparative advantage. With free trade, Britain would specialize in manufactured goods and other countries (e.g., Portugal) would specialize in agricultural goods. Free trade in grain, said Ricardo, would lower the cost of food. Because wages were supposedly based on subsistence, lower food prices would also reduce wages. And as wages fell, profits would rise. As did most Classical economists, Ricardo thought wages and profits moved in opposite directions. According

238 Marxian theories of imperialism

to Ricardo's logic, increased profits would encourage industrial growth and make British manufactured goods more competitive on world markets. Ultimately, this would increase the demand for labor and increase wages. The Ricardian lesson was that whatever is good for capitalists is also good for workers.

In an 1848 speech, Marx strongly attacked free trade and the Ricardian logic upon which it was based (Marx, 1976: 450). Marx claimed British workers understood well enough the conflict raging at the time between industrial and agricultural interests. They also understood that, despite Ricardian theory, repeal of the Corn Laws really was intended only to lower wages and to redistribute wealth from farmers to manufacturers. Both food prices and wages would indeed drop, although it was unlikely that the workers' status would change much at the end. They would continue to be poor as they had always been. Comparative advantage and free trade were, to Marx, little more than capitalist rhetoric.

Marx alleged that Ricardo's analysis did not go far enough. Indeed, there would be further economic development accompanying industrial growth. Moreover, growth results in the use of more and more capital (machinery and raw materials) in proportion to labor. The total amount of this capital which the capitalist class owns expands. Marx called this the *centralization of capital*. Likewise, capital comes to be controlled by fewer and fewer capitalists; Marx called this the *concentration of capital*. Smaller, less successful capitalists then fall into the ranks of the working class.

What, then, is Marx's bottom line with respect to free trade? He summarized his position like this:

> To sum up, what is free trade, what is free trade under the present condition of society? It is freedom of capital. When you have overthrown the few national barriers which still restrict the progress of capital, you will merely have given it complete freedom of action. So long as you let the relation of wage labor to capital exist, it does not matter how favorable the conditions under which the exchange of commodities takes place, there will always be a class which will exploit and a class which will be exploited. It is really difficult to understand the claim of the free-traders who imagine that the more advantageous application of capital will abolish the antagonism between industrial capitalists and wage workers. On the contrary, the only result will be that the antagonism of these two classes will stand out still more clearly.
>
> *(Marx, 1976: 450)*

Despite this very negative assessment of free trade, Marx still supported it! Why? The reason is that free trade increases the antagonism between capitalists and workers. It intensifies "class struggle." Free trade pushes that antagonism to the breaking point and hastens the coming social revolution. Said Marx, "It is in this revolutionary sense alone, gentlemen, that I vote in favor of free trade" (Marx, 1976: 465).

Economic imperialism: Marxism and Leninism

Marx believed that the development of capitalism is revolutionary. As he described it in *The Communist Manifesto*:

> The bourgeoisie cannot exist without constantly revolutionizing the instruments of production, and thereby the relations of production, and with them the whole relations of society. . . . The bourgeoisie, during its rule of scarce one hundred years has created more massive and more colossal productive forces than have all preceding generations together.
>
> *(Marx, 1848: Chapter 1)*

To Marx, capitalism spreads outward, inexorably, from Britain and Europe where capitalism was most advanced, to the rest of the world where capitalism had not yet taken root. The following passage aptly summarizes Marx's view:

> The need of a constantly expanding market for its products chases the bourgeoisie over the entire surface of the globe. It must nestle everywhere, settle everywhere, establish connexions everywhere. The bourgeoisie . . . draws all, even the most barbarian, nations into civilisation. It compels all nations, on pain of extinction, to adopt the bourgeois mode of production; it compels them to introduce what it calls civilisation into their midst, i.e., to become bourgeois themselves. In one word, it creates a world after its own image.
>
> *(Marx, 1848: Chapter 1)*

This is the heart of Marx's perspective on the world economy. Regrettably, he never completed a full-blown theoretical explanation of global capitalism. This was left to his successors.

Imperialism: a progressive or destructive force

Before proceeding it is useful to distinguish between imperialism and colonialism. Imperialism usually involves a single nation or kingdom that dominates other nations or territories. The imperial power exercises its sovereignty through a variety of cultural, social, political and economic methods. Imperialism is thus a system of "hegemony." Colonialism is a special case of imperialism. It is a system in which one nation—the colonizer—has formal control over, and ownership of, another nation or territory—the colony. The colonized country "belongs" to the colonizer and becomes part of its global empire.

Colonialism was practiced for about 500 years until it ended in the 1950s and 1960s. When it ended, other non-colonial forms of imperialism took its place. These have functioned without the need for direct control over and possession of a colony. These forms of imperialism achieve the same economic results as colonialism but use other mechanisms of domination such as foreign trade and investment.

240 Marxian theories of imperialism

Many scholars use the term "neo-colonialism" and "post-colonialism" to describe these postwar forms of imperialism.

Oddly, it is impossible to find the words "colonialism" and "imperialism" in any of Marx's writings. Perhaps he assumed all his readers understood perfectly well that imperialism and colonialism were universal and thus required no further explanation. Nonetheless, it is clear from his writings that Marx believed capitalism is an exploitive global phenomenon. Capitalism and imperialism went hand in hand.

A question asked by successive generations of Marxian scholars is whether imperialism is a progressive force or a destructive force. Those who believe it is a progressive force believe it is necessary for a society to pass through a capitalist stage, however unpleasant, before reaching socialism and then communism. As capitalism develops so too do the contradictions that will ultimately trigger a socialist revolution. Among these contradictions is class struggle.

Imperialism introduces the capitalist mode of production to "backward" nations. These nations will then progress along the same lines as did the European capitalist nations. Imperialism makes a socialist revolution possible by introducing and then promoting capitalist production and capitalist social relations. Capitalist development therefore prepares the ground for the eventual arrival of a more humane, post-capitalist society. It is a form of salvation through suffering. As Marx saw it, "[i]n broad outline, the Asian, ancient, feudal and modern bourgeois [capitalist] modes of production may be designated as progressive epochs of the socioeconomic order" (Marx, 1859).

But there are those Marxists who say imperialism is a destructive force. They argue it permanently cripples less developed societies by keeping them in a perpetual state of dependency, poverty and exploitation, precluding any possibility of a socialist revolution. Imperialism therefore is indicative of a fundamental *failure* of capitalism and offers little hope to poor nations for progressing to a more humane, socialist future. Rather, imperialism obstructs progressive change, and therefore resistance to the intrusion of capitalism is necessary. Proponents imply that there is thus no need to pass through a capitalist stage in order to establish a socialist society, especially in rural societies. This is the position of later Neo-Marxists and dependency theorists, which we review below.

Imperialism after Marx

After Marx died a new generation of intellectuals addressed the question of imperialism. Prominent among them were Rosa Luxemburg (1871–1919), John A. Hobson (1858–1904), Rudolf Hilferding (1877–1941) and Nikolai Bukharin (1888–1938). All sought to elaborate on Marx's theory that capitalism is by nature a system that expands on a world scale and spreads its influence to non-capitalist regions of the world, transforming the latter's economies and social institutions.

Hilferding and Bukharin wrote that financial capital played a paramount role in perpetuating imperialism. This was a fairly new approach. The previous emphasis had been on industrial capital. They argued that both industrial and financial corporations, operating through large interlocking groups, dominate foreign investment.

Hobson and Luxemburg added a twist to the explanation of imperialism, namely, that firms were finding it more and more difficult to sell their commodities in domestic markets and therefore had to seek foreign markets to sell what they could not sell domestically. This idea, that consumption demand at home is insufficient, is called the *under-consumption thesis*.

Hobson also advanced the idea, pursued later by Karl Kautsky (1854–1938) in 1914, that imperialism would become a benign and peaceful force. The various European nations, Kautsky argued, would combine into cartels and peacefully administer the colonial empires under their control. They would then abandon the use of military power and limit international competition in order to preserve their global economic interests. Kautsky called this *ultra-imperialism*.

Lenin on imperialism, the highest stage of capitalism

In 1916, on the eve of the Russian Revolution, Vladimir Ilyich Lenin (1870–1924) published *Imperialism: The Highest Stage of Capitalism*. Strongly influenced by these other writers, Lenin argued that "imperialism is the monopoly stage of capitalism" (Lenin, 1917). By this he meant that imperialism had become a core attribute of capitalism and that the home market (i.e., Europe) had become inexorably bound up with foreign markets.

By 1916, said Lenin, European capitalism had advanced to the monopoly stage, the highest and final stage of development. In this stage, "[m]onopolist capitalist associations, cartels, syndicates and trusts . . . divided the home market among themselves and obtained more or less complete possession of the industry of their own country" (Lenin, 1917: Chapter 5).

Lenin claimed that the monopoly stage has four attributes. The first is the centralization and concentration of capital. The second is the dominance of financial capital; finance capital had "spread its net over all countries of the world" (Lenin, 1917: Chapter 4).

The third attribute is the export of capital. This had become even more important than the export of commodities. As Lenin described it, "The export of capital is made possible by a number of backward countries having already been drawn into world capitalist intercourse. . . . The need to export capital arises from the fact that in a few countries capitalism has become 'overripe' and (owing to the backward state of agriculture and the poverty of the masses) capital cannot find a field for 'profitable' investment" (Lenin, 1917: Chapter 4; Baran & Sweezy, 1966).

The final attribute is the formation of a financial-industrial oligarchy that partitions the territories of the world among the advanced European capitalist nations.

Lenin's thesis supposedly explained what was going on in the world at the time. It explained why a proletarian revolution had not yet taken place, as Marx had anticipated. Capitalism must first go through all its stages of development before the conditions would be ripe for a revolution. It explained colonialism, the division of

242 Marxian theories of imperialism

Africa among the major European nations and the struggle for influence in China. And it explained the deadly struggles between rival monopolies and the colonial wars between the colonizing nations. Indeed, the First World War was just such a war. Out of its soil a world proletarian revolution would eventually grow.

Future Marxian scholars built on Lenin's idea that there could be multiple stages of capitalist development and that economic relations between advanced and less developed nations depend on what stage capitalism is in.

Economic imperialism: Neo-Marxism

After the Second World War a new wave of Marxian scholarship appeared on the scene. While most wrote in the Marxian tradition, many rejected Classical Marxism in favor of theories that better reflected the realities of postwar capitalism.

Baran and Sweezy: monopoly capitalism, imperialism and surplus absorption

Fifty years after Lenin, Paul A. Baran (1909–1964) and Paul M. Sweezy (1910–2004) published their landmark book, *Monopoly Capital* (Baran and Sweezy, 1966). In it they argued that the main feature of postwar monopoly capitalism is the domination of giant multinational corporations. The function of the state in monopoly capitalism is to assist these corporations in exploiting the resources and markets of less developed economies.

Marx's economic theory does not deal directly with monopoly capitalism. It deals instead with the preceding stage: competitive laissez-faire capitalism. In that theory Marx uses a labor theory of value to explain where profits came from and how market prices are established. Put simply, the labor theory argues that the amount of labor used to produce commodities determines their prices. In capitalism, labor too is a commodity, so the labor theory applies to it as well: the amount of labor used to produce the labor commodity (i.e., subsistence goods) determines wages. Profit, said Marx, is the new value that labor produces in excess of labor costs. Profit is a *surplus value* that the capitalist appropriates because he or she owns the means of production. Finally, in Marx's theory competition among capitalists equalizes the rate of profit among all industries as capital flows from low profit industries to high profit industries. This movement of capital among industries means that prices will not be exactly proportional to the amount or labor used in production. We will see why in the next chapter.

When applying this theory to international economics Marx assumed, as a first approximation, that we must "treat the whole world of trade as one nation, and assume that capitalist production is established everywhere and has taken possession of every branch of industry" (Marx, 1936: 636). The capitalist class appropriates the surplus value produced by labor—no matter where production takes place in the world. The same conditions of production, and the same technologies, apply everywhere.

The problem with this reasoning is that the whole world is not at the same stage of development. World markets are not perfectly competitive, countries are at different stages of technological development and labor productivity varies enormously. Because of this economic diversity, the profit equalization mechanism fails to work and Marx's labor theory of value cannot explain the formation of world prices, wages and profits. This means we can no longer measure economic variables in terms of hours of labor. We can only measure them in dollars, without linking them directly to labor values.

In the Neo-Marxist approach of Baran and Sweezy and others, the economic surplus is redefined simply as national output minus (1) the output minimally necessary to provide for the maintenance of the existing capital stock and (2) the subsistence output needed by the population, all measured in dollars. The labor theory explanation is set aside. Imperialism is thus a system in which capitalists in advanced nations appropriate the surplus produced by workers in poorer developing nations.

There is another theme in Baran and Sweezy's Neo-Marxian theory: monopoly capitalism suffers from a chronic deficiency of aggregate demand. Their reasoning goes like this. Giant corporations suppress price competition in favor of non-price competition. Prices are "sticky," to use Keynesian terminology. In order to increase their profits, firms cut costs by continually introducing new technologies. The result is that the gap between prices and costs widens: prices remain relatively stable while costs decrease. The difference is the economic surplus, which continuously rises. The problem, now, is how to absorb this growing surplus? There are several options.

One option is to raise wages. This would allow workers to buy more. But this is unlikely to happen because it would cut into profits, at least in the short run. Another is for capitalists to spend more themselves on consumption. But even they have an upper limit on how much they can consume. A third option is for capitalists to spend the surplus on new business investment. But this would expand the surplus even further, making the problem even worse.

A last option is foreign investment. However, Baran and Sweezy pointed out that, historically, the inward flow of profits generated by foreign investment is actually greater than the outward flow of investment. Foreign investment is "a method of pumping surplus out of underdeveloped areas" (Baran and Sweezy, 1966: 105; Magdoff, 1969). Foreign investment thus worsens the surplus absorption problem.

Monopoly capitalism thus suffers from chronic under-consumption and stagnation. Its powers of production exceed its powers of consumption. The only way out of this irrational situation is for capitalists to "waste" the surplus by spending it on advertising, unnecessary product differentiation and other unproductive activities. Military spending, argue Baran and Sweezy, has been another very useful way to absorb the surplus. The dangers of this for global stability were obvious in the Cold War era.

Magdoff on the new imperialism

Shortly after Baran and Sweezy's published *Monopoly Capital*, Harry Magdoff (1913–2006) gave the Marxian theory of imperialism a makeover in his popular

244 Marxian theories of imperialism

1969 book, *The Age of Imperialism* (Magdoff, 1969; see also 1978). The Vietnam War was then raging and antiwar scholars and activists were demanding an explanation for American military interventions in Southeast Asia. There was renewed interest in Marxism at the time and Magdoff's analysis, strongly influenced by Lenin, gave these scholars and activists what they wanted—a Marxian political-economic explanation of US global hegemony. He called it the "new imperialism."

Magdoff suggested that the new imperialism was the latest of five stages in global capitalist development that spanned 500 years. The previous four stages included (1) robbery, looting, plunder, and piracy; (2) global domination of commercial capital; (3) global inter-capitalist rivalry; and (4) global domination of industrial capital, and finally (5) the new imperialism.

This new imperialism is similar to European imperialism during the era of colonialism. The main difference is that the US no longer needs to possess and govern formal colonies in order to get what it wants. According to Magdoff, the Vietnam War was the product of a concerted effort by the US government to create and maintain a global empire in which the US capitalist class could prosper. The US maintained this empire through the exercise of military power, foreign aid, strategic alliances and political influence over the domestic affairs of foreign nations. The Cold War simply provided legitimacy for this hegemonic foreign policy.

What was new about Magdoff's new imperialism? Theoretically, not much was new. The global "world-historical" struggle to compete, dominate, and profit from less advanced parts of the world yet untouched by capitalism continued to be the primary force that we call imperialism. Marx and Lenin had already explained all that. Empirically, however, Magdoff contributed greatly to the Marxian analysis of imperialism by updating the theory using contemporary data and real-world events.

Late capitalism: a third stage of capitalism

In 1975, Ernest Mandel (1923–1995) reasoned in his book *Late Capitalism* that there is a third stage in capitalist development that follows monopoly capitalism (Mandel, 1975). He called this *late capitalism*. Mandel claimed late capitalism began after the Second World War, when the world economy was on a long-term cyclical upswing, or "long wave." There had already been a large literature about business cycles lasting 50 years or more, a literature popularized by the Russian economist Nikolai Kondratiev (1892–1938). To Mandel, one such long wave reached a peak in the mid-1970s and then started a downward swing with increasing economic crises and slower growth rates. This was an attractive thesis because capitalist economies at the time were in fact experiencing serious economic difficulties.

Mandel's three stages of capitalist development correspond to three global economic regimes: colonialism (in the competitive stage), imperialism (the monopoly stage) and multinational capital and globalized markets (the late capitalist stage). Here it is assumed that colonialism and imperialism are different global systems. We had argued earlier that colonialism is a form of imperialism.

In late capitalism, the world economy is partitioned into two integrated spheres:

Marxian theories of imperialism **245**

developed countries and underdeveloped countries. In this stage "development and underdevelopment reciprocally determine each other. Without underdeveloped regions there can be no transfer of surplus to industrialized regions and hence no accumulation of capital" (Mandel, 1975: 102). The developed economies thus feed on the resources of the underdeveloped economics.

Mandel observes that capital in this third stage expands into areas previously impervious to its economic logic. It eradicates all vestiges of pre-capitalist forms of society as multinational corporations conquer the entire world system. Late capitalism thus represents "generalized universal industrialization and commodification" (Mandel, 1975: 387). Capitalist industrial production becomes standard practice everywhere as all products and services are made only for sale on markets. In this sense, argues Mandel, Marx's theory of capitalism applies in its "purest" form; it becomes universal: "the capitalist world system is to a significant degree precisely a function of the universal validity of the law of unequal and combined development" (Mandel, 1975: 23). Marx's theory of value and price has finally become relevant, once again.

Post Modernism, post-Fordism and Empire

Post Modernism is a philosophy which holds that contemporary capitalism represents a radical break with all previous stages of capitalism. It proclaims that all the "grand" theories of Western thought have become outmoded and irrelevant in our radically changed world. These grand theories include Enlightenment philosophies such as liberalism, rationalism and scientific thought as well as Christianity, Freudianism and Marxism. What these grand theories have in common is the presumption that there are knowable, comprehensive and universal explanations for all historical events and human actions. To postmodernists, these are not explanations but rather narratives, tales and stories told by storytellers passing themselves off as scholars (see, for example, Jameson, 1991).

As far as the world economy is concerned, postmodernists claim that we have entered a new period of global domination in which the usual categories and theories of Classical Marxism and Neo-Marxism no longer work. A new kind of transnational-techno capitalism has restructured the world, making it more fragmented, heterogeneous and diverse. Some economists, following the work of David Harvey (1935–), have applied the term *post-Fordism* to describe this new world economy (Harvey, 1990).

Fordism describes the system of standardized and regimented mass production and consumption which existed prior to the 1970s. Named after Henry Ford, the core sectors of a Fordist economy are large-scale heavy industry. Labor unions strongly influence labor-management relations and collective bargaining delivers members livable wages and benefits to a large segment of the workforce while permitting acceptable profit rates.

The core sectors of the post-Fordist economy are information, communications, computing and white-collar services. Labor union membership, along with

246 Marxian theories of imperialism

collective bargaining, dwindles to insignificance as firms increasingly rely on contingent and temporary labor. There is a decline in traditional blue-collar working-class identity. The post-Fordist economy is also based on flexible globalized production. Sweatshops and subcontracting become prevalent, especially in less developed countries. Capital zips into and out of countries; in many respects the world economy begins to resemble a fast-food restaurant.[1]

A most recent variation of this theme of radical change is Michael Hardt and Antonio Negri's *Empire* (Hardt and Negri, 2000). They also maintain that capitalism has reached yet another stage, the stage of "empire." In this stage the very idea of a nation state loses relevance. Transnational corporations, political and economic elites and global economic institutions replace states as key players in the global economy. As Hardt and Negri describe it,

> the spatial divisions of the three worlds (First, Second and Third) have been scrambled so that we continuously find the First World in the Third, the Third in the First, and the Second almost nowhere at all. Capital seems to be faced with a smooth world. . . defined by new and complex regimes of differentiation, deterritorialization and reterrotorialization. . . . Our basic hypothesis, however, [is] that a new imperial form of sovereignty has emerged. . . . Imperialism is over. No nation will be world leader in the way modern European nations were. . . .The concept of Empire is characterized fundamentally by a lack of boundaries: Empire's rule has no boundaries.
>
> *(Hardt and Negri, 2000: xiii–iv)*

Dependency and world systems theory

The long-held view that rich industrially advanced countries exploit poor underdeveloped countries continues today with two related perspectives: dependency theory and world systems theory. Each bears a strong Latin American imprint.[2]

Rich nations, proponents of both views say, acquire the natural and human resources of poor nations at low prices and sell them outdated technologies and manufactured commodities at high prices. This results in net flows of profits from poor nations to rich countries. Moreover, the class structure of poor nations reflects their economic subservience. Local industrial, financial and merchant interests align themselves with the interests of foreign capital. These groups have a powerful influence over the economic policies of their nations and in this way perpetuate their dependence on the core capitalist nations. Finally, governments, independent global institutions such as the IMF and World Bank and multinational corporations keep poor nations in this position of dependency using a variety of economic, political, military and cultural means.

How nations integrate into the world economy determines their prospects for development. Yet, the normal working of this bipolar capitalist global system only widens the gap between the rich and poor. The latter therefore have little hope of breaking away from the influence of external powers or of building autonomy over their own economic affairs.

Dependency and world system theory are reactions to orthodox international economics and Western-sponsored modernization strategies. The orthodox modernization perspective put its faith in the ability of advanced Western nations to help poor nations overcome their "backwardness" and to put them on the road to economic progress. They believed that by mimicking the paths taken by advanced nations, and by adopting the same economic, social and political institutions, they would be able to surmount all obstacles to growth and development. This did not happen.

The relationship of dependency and world system theory to Marxian theories of imperialism bears further comment. First, these theories are not necessarily Marxian, although they have a very close affinity to Marxism. Second, imperialism focuses on how capitalism expands its global influence, while dependency and world system theory focus on how nations remain mired in a state of underdevelopment.

Austrian counterpoint: Joseph Schumpeter on imperialism

The Austrian economist Joseph A. Schumpeter (1883–1950) was an influential opponent of Marxism. In his essay, "The Sociology of Imperialisms," published in 1919 at about the same time as Lenin's pamphlet, Schumpeter offers a provocative alternative explanation of imperialism (Schumpeter, 1955). It is as far from Marxian theory as one can possibly get and is worth considering as a counterpoint.

In his essay Schumpeter starts out by observing that imperialism is ultimately an aggressive act. He says that the aggressive attitudes of societies (nation states, empires, kingdoms, tribes, etc.) derive from the "real and concrete interests of the people." An example would be a landlocked state wishing to get access to the sea or a tribe wishing to gain access to hunting grounds. These concrete interests can be transparent or opaque and need not be economic. Nor need they be the interests of the entire population; they could be those of special interest groups.

But Schumpeter now takes his argument to another dimension. He argues that imperialism cannot be explained by concrete interests alone. Concrete interests are necessary but not sufficient to explain imperialism. Imperialism is actually an aggressive act that states pursue *for its own sake*: "expansion for the sake of expanding, war for the sake of fighting, victory for the sake of winning, dominion for the sake of ruling" (Schumpeter, 1955: 143). The object of imperialism "has no adequate object beyond itself" (ibid.). It is as if people have an innate and instinctive propensity to belligerently expand the range of their power and influence, no matter what the reasons they offer to justify it.

To Schumpeter, imperialism has been cast into the human psyche. For reasons that go back thousands of years, a warrior-like disposition has become part of the human character and social structures have reflected this disposition. While at one time there undoubtedly had been life-preserving reasons for this kind of behavior, these reasons no longer exist in the modern world. Yet humans continue to bear

248 Marxian theories of imperialism

the imprint of aggression, even when there is no longer any life-preserving need for it. As Schumpeter put it, "[i]mperialism thus is atavistic in character. . . . It is an atavism in the social structure, in individual, psychological habits of emotional reaction"[3] (ibid.: 188).

Despite this, Schumpeter is optimistic about the future. He argues that this atavistic trait eventually will disappear. Social and economic development will make imperialism impracticable and will eliminate all social structures and institutions that support it. Imperialism will disappear, Schumpeter predicts, as a "habitual emotional reaction" when society and economy have become rationalized: "A purely capitalist world therefore can offer no fertile soil to imperialist impulses. . . its people are likely to be essentially of an unwarlike disposition" (ibid.: 66; Kerr and Harcourt, 2002). Capitalism, then, will save the day. It will relegate imperialism to the scrap-heap of history.

The only qualification is that this can happen only in a world of free trade. Free trade is the essential antidote to the self-serving desires of the bourgeoisie to protect themselves from foreign competition. When free trade prevails there will no longer be any motive for aggressive global expansion. Will this happen?

Schumpeter justifies his beliefs by maintaining that acts of imperialism (e.g., wars and invasions) are costly and the capitalist class will eventually refuse to bear the expense. The capitalists will then, of their own accord, usher in an era of global free trade. Once this is achieved, imperialism vanishes. Capitalism and free trade therefore make imperialism impossible.

Schumpeter's perspective is avowedly anti-Marxist and he denies the Marxian thesis that imperialism is a necessary outgrowth of capitalism. Schumpeter thought this idea to be nonsensical. He surveyed history from ancient to modern times to prove his point. Yet, despite this negative assessment, Schumpeter was strongly influenced by Marx. Indeed, Schumpeter was one of the few critics who genuinely understood Marx and they had much in common. For example, they both saw capitalism as an organic and transitory system that was born, then flourished, and will eventually die. And both had a keen understanding and appreciation of history and the role it plays in economic analysis.

Globalism or imperialism?

The term imperialism carries a negative connotation. We never hear the term used in orthodox international economics. This is not surprising as the orthodoxy denies, as did Schumpeter, that the expansion of capitalism around the world is a bad thing. To the contrary, global capitalist expansion is a good thing, unless of course it is marred by imperfect competition, trade restrictions, imperfect information or misguided governments. But to avoid any negative connotation, and to uphold the belief that capitalist expansion is good, orthodox economists (and many others) have used the word globalism.

Everyone would agree, orthodox and heterodox economists alike, that the influence of capitalism has expanded globally. Capitalist production, distribution and finance relations have spread to previously untouched regions and countries of the world. The world economy also has become more integrated and this integration extends to the social, cultural and political spheres as well.

These international forces have existed before. The spread of Greek culture thousands of years ago and the European colonization of the world hundreds of years ago were precursors of what is now occurring. Writers today, however, generally argue that something is different about what is happening today. The common explanation for this is the role played by information and communications technologies. This is why many call capitalism *techno-capitalism*. It is what lies behind restructuring and reorganization of the world economy, polity and culture.

But globalism suggests that this enlargement of capitalist influence leads to prosperity and peace for all; it empowers and enhances the well-being of all people. Imperialism suggests this leads to exploitation, the destruction of local cultures and continuous economic crises. Viewed in this way, the words globalism and imperialism are ideological constructs. Globalism is closely associated with neo–liberalism while imperialism is closely associated with Marxism. Neither is a neutral term. To resolve this we will use the word *world integration*.

One often debated issue is the belief that the world is becoming more uniform or homogenous as it is becoming integrated. The people of the world are becoming more alike in the way they lead their lives; they are merging into a single world society. Urban environments on every continent are becoming similar in terms of types of businesses, popular culture and the uses of urban space. One often hears pejorative phrases such as "McDonaldization" and "Walmartization" to describe this.

Others say the opposite, that the world is becoming more diverse and heterogeneous. Nation states are losing their importance in favor of local communities and local organizations. Some scholars have introduced the term *hybridization* to describe the way in which local social forms have detached themselves from existing dominant patterns of living and recombined themselves with new styles and ways of life.

A related issue is the belief that the integration of the world has meant the spread of Western culture. Once again, to the extent that Westernization has occurred, some think this is a good thing because it means modernization and democratization. Others believe it is a bad thing because it forces upon non-Western societies a particular way of life that dissolves local customs and traditions. Many call this phenomenon cultural imperialism.

Conclusions

We began this chapter with Marx's theory of capitalism as a world phenomenon. Capitalism to Marx contains an inner drive to expand to every corner of the world, bringing along with it its particular logic. World trade is a system in which capitalists in advanced nations extract surplus from less developed states and regions. In so doing the world's population is transformed into a working-class proletariat.

250 Marxian theories of imperialism

Capitalist development also results in the exploitation and alienation of the world proletariat, which in turn creates the conditions for a socialist revolution.

We then explored various Marxian and Neo-Marxian theories of imperialism. We saw that the way in which Marxian scholars analyze imperialism depends on how they interpret the historical development of capitalism. We then considered Schumpeter's anti-Marxist theory of imperialism, finishing the chapter with a comparison of the terms globalism and imperialism.

Generally speaking, there are three ways of thinking about imperialism and the international economy from a Marxian perspective. One is the view that imperialism is a necessary outgrowth of capitalism and free trade. Its worldwide expansion worsens the contradictions of global capitalism (e.g., economic crises, alienation and exploitation) and hastens its demise. It then ushers in a new age of socialism. A second view is that imperialism is a necessary outgrowth of capitalism but fails to lead to socialism. Instead it obstructs progress toward a more humane global economic system. Finally, the development of capitalism will make imperialism disappear. These are, respectively, the Marxian, Neo-Marxian and Schumpeterian views.

How the global economy really works is clearly up for grabs. It depends on the analyst's ideological predispositions. If one is inclined toward a Marxian interpretation then it is likely that he or she will be unconvinced by contrary evidence. Similarly, if one is inclined to an orthodox or Austrian interpretation then it is likely that evidence favoring a Marxian approach will be unconvincing. As Joan Robinson once quipped, "He who is convinced against his will, is of the same opinion still," by which she meant the "stubborn persistence in an error after it has been exposed" (quoted in Kerr and Harcourt, 2002: 27).

Notes

1   George Ritzer called this the "McDonaldization of society" (Ritzer 1993).
2   The chief contributors to dependency theory include Hans Singer (1910–2006), Raul Prebisch (1901–1986), Andre Gunder Frank (1929–2005), Theotonio Dos Santos (1936–), Fernando Henrique Cardoso and Samir Amin (1931–). World systems theory originates with Immanuel Wallerstein (1930–).
3   Ibid., p. 65. Webster's dictionary defines atavism as "recurrence of or reversion to a past style, manner, outlook, approach, or activity."

References

Baran, P. A., & Sweezy, P. M. (1966). *Monopoly Capitalism*. New York: Monthly Review Press.

Hardt, M., & Negri, A. (2000). *Empire*. Cambridge, MA: Harvard University Press.

Harvey, D. (1990). *The Conditions of Postmodernity*. Cambridge, MA: Blackwell Publishers.

Jameson, F. (1991). *Post Modernism, or, The Cultural Logic of Late Capitalism*. Durham, NC: Duke University Press.

Kerr, P., & Harcourt, G. C. (Eds.) (2002). *Joan Robinson: Critical Assessments of Leading Economists*. London: Routledge.

Lenin, V. (1917). *Imperialism, the Highest Stage of Capitalism.* Retrieved January 1, 2014, from www.Marxians.org/archive/lenin/works/1916/imp-hsc/.

Magdoff, H. (1969). *The Age of Imperialism.* New York: Monthly Review Press.

Magdoff, H. (1978). *Imperialism: From the Colonial Age to the Present.* New York: Monthly Review Press.

Mandel, E. (1975). *Late Capitalism.* London: Humanities Press.

Marx, K. (1848). *The Communist Manifesto.* Retrieved 26 December 2013, from https://www.marxists.org/archive/marx/works/1848/communist-manifesto/ch01.htm.

Marx, K. (1859). *Preface of a Contribution to the Critique of Political Economy.* Retrieved December 3, 2013, from https://www.marxists.org/archive/marx/works/1859/critique-pol-economy/preface-abs.htm.

Marx, Karl (1936). *Capital: A Critique of Political Economy, Volume I.* (S. Moore and E. Aveling, trans.) New York: The Modern Library.

Marx, K. (1976). "Speech on the Question of Free Trade Delivered to the Democratic Association of Brussels at its Public Meeting on January 9, 1848." In K. Marx, & F. Engels, *Marx Engels Collected Works* (Reprint ed., Vol. 6, pp. 450–465). Moscow: Progress Publishers. Retrieved December 8, 2013, from https://www.marxists.org/archive/marx/works/1888/free-trade/.

Ritzer, G. (1993). *The McDonaldization of Society.* Thousands Oaks, CA: Pine Forge Press.

Schumpeter, J. A. (1955). "The Sociology of Imperialism." In J. A. Schumpeter, *Imperialism and Social Classes* (H. Norden, Trans., pp. 2–98). Cleveland, OH: The World Publishing Company.

11

MARXIAN AND SRAFFIAN THEORIES OF UNEQUAL EXCHANGE

Introduction

There are two strands of Marxian international economics. One strand deals with imperialism. The emphasis there is on the motivations for capitalist expansion overseas and how that expansion is related to particular stages of capitalist development. We explored this topic in the previous chapter. A second strand is unequal exchange, which describes how international trade transfers economic surplus from less developed to developed capitalist nations. This transfer of surplus is a net transfer of real resources or financial claims on real resources and is a form of exploitation. Ironically, free trade is the mechanism through which this transfer takes place. This second strand is the topic for this chapter.

To explain how unequal exchange works we use Marx's labor theory of value and price to analyze international differences in the conditions of production and how these differences affect global profit rates and world prices. For readers not familiar with Marx's price theory we offer a brief summary in Appendix 11A.

Unfortunately, Marx died before he could finish his analysis. However, three 20th-century scholars continued where Marx left off. These include Henryk Grossman (1881–1950), Arghiri Emmanuel (1911–2001) and Piero Sraffa (1898–1983). Grossman and Emmanuel continued to use a labor theory of value to analyze unequal exchange. Sraffa, however, did not use the labor theory so his approach is a bit different. Once again, for readers not familiar with the basic Sraffa model we provide a summary in Appendix 11B.

International value theory: prelude to unequal exchange theory

Some of Marx's adversaries claimed that profit rates in England were higher than in backward nations. In Volume III of *Capital*, Marx used the logic of his labor

Marxian and Sraffian theories of unequal exchange **253**

TABLE 11.1 Marxian value ratios example #1

	Rate of exploitation $\alpha = S/V$	Organic composition $\beta = C/V$	Rate of profit $\pi = S/(C + V)$
Europe	100%	5.25	16%
Asia	25%	0.19	21%

value theory to dispute these claims. He contended that the opposite was true, that advanced nations had lower profit rates than "backward" nations and that this differential explained how the former exploited the latter. Much of his argument was devoid of empirical content, however, as he possessed neither the data nor the econometric techniques to test his contention.

Marx offered three illustrations to make his point. In his first illustration, which appears in Chapter 8 of Volume III, Marx compares Europe with Asia. He believed Asian economies were backward and therefore used little fixed capital and few raw materials per worker. Europe had more advanced economies and hence used more fixed capital and raw materials per worker. This implies that the organic composition of capital is higher in Europe than in Asia. Marx used the following numerical example:

$$\text{Europe} \quad 84C + 16V + 16S = 116 \tag{11.1}$$

$$\text{Asia} \quad 16C + 84V + 21S = 121 \tag{11.2}$$

Using these numbers we summarize the relevant Marxian ratios in Table 11.1.[1] In Europe, workers labor half of the workday to replace the value of their subsistence ($17/(17 + 17)$) and the other half of the workday for the capitalist employer. This translates into a 100% rate of exploitation. In Asia, workers labor 4/5 of the workday replacing the value of their subsistence ($84/(84 + 21)$) and 1/5 for the capitalist employer. The rate of exploitation in Asia is only 25%.[2] Because the organic composition of capital is much higher in Europe than in Asia (5.25 vs. 0.19), the European rate of profit is lower—despite the fact that the rate of surplus value is four times higher!

In Chapter 13 of Volume III Marx introduces a second illustration, in which he compares a single nation at two different stages of development. The relevant equations now are:

$$\text{Undeveloped economy} \quad 50C + 100V + 100S = 250 \tag{11.3}$$

$$\text{Higher stage of development} \quad 400C + 100V + 100S = 600 \tag{11.4}$$

Using this hypothetical data Marx shows that the rising organic composition of capital lowers profit rates *even if the rate of exploitation is identical* in both places. We can see this in Table 11.2.

254 Marxian and Sraffian theories of unequal exchange

TABLE 11.2 Marxian value ratios example #2

	Rate of exploitation $\alpha = S/V$	Organic composition $\beta = C/V$	Rate of profit $\pi = S/(C + V)$
Undeveloped	100%	0.50	$66^2/_3\%$
Higher stage of development	100%	4.0	20%

Economic progress, from a lower to a higher stage of development, increases the organic composition of capital from 0.5 to 4.0 and lowers the profit rate from $66^2/_3\%$ to 20%. Marx notes that this also applies to two coexisting countries, one with a lower and the other with a higher stage of development.

Marx then asks whether these differences in rates of profit would reverse or even disappear if labor were less productive in the less developed country. Wouldn't lower labor productivity result in lower profits? In Marx's schema, labor productivity is measured by how much time workers must spend each day reproducing the value equivalent of their means of subsistence, or necessary labor time. This is the value of their daily wage rate and is reflected in variable capital. If labor productivity declines then necessary labor time would rise, leaving less labor time to produce surplus value (and hence profit). It would seem that the profit rate would decline.

Changing the hypothetical data for the less developed economy, and leaving the advanced economy unchanged, the new equations become:

$$\text{Undeveloped economy} \qquad 50C + 113^1/_3V + 66^2/_3S = 230 \qquad (11.5)$$

$$\text{Higher stage of development} \qquad 400C + 100V + 100S = 600 \qquad (11.6)$$

Instead of working 100 hours to produce their means of subsistence, we assume they work $113^1/_3$ hours, and instead of working 100 hours producing surplus value they work only $66^2/_3$ hours. The value of total output shrinks from 250 to 230. The new Marxian value ratios are shown in Table 11.3. Indeed, the profit rate falls, yet there is still a substantial profit differential that benefits the advanced nation.

In Volume III Marx explored a number of other variations on this theme. It is sufficient to point out that, to Marx, capitalists are compelled to invest their capital in poor undeveloped nations because the rates of profit there are so much

TABLE 11.3 Marxian value ratios example #3

	Rate of exploitation $\alpha = S/V$	Organic composition $\beta = C/V$	Rate of profit $\pi = S/(C + V)$
Undeveloped	59%	0.44	41%
Higher stage of development	100%	4.0	20%

higher. As the capitalists see it, they look to backward economies because they have primary resources otherwise not available domestically. They also have cheap labor, markets for their commodities and other financial opportunities. Further, technological innovation increases the organic composition of capital, causing a downward secular pull on profit rates which expands even further the incentive to move capital to less developed regions. This will continue until poor nations catch up with rich nations and global profit rates equalize.

This, in a nutshell, is the essence of Marxian "economic imperialism." Marx viewed capitalism as a global phenomenon. Unfortunately, however, he never fully developed the international dimensions of his theory of value and price. As we have seen, much of what he did say appeared in Volume III, well after he died.

Unequal international exchange theory I: Henryk Grossman

Much of Marx's writings on international commodity exchange appears in Volume III of *Capital*. Marx died before he could publish the entirety of *Capital*, so much of his analysis is incomplete and has been left to his successors. His colleague and friend, Friedrich Engels, assembled the notes he left behind and published the second and third volumes of *Capital* posthumously.

One of Marx's successors was Henryk Grossman (1881–1950), who, in his *The Law of Accumulation and Breakdown of the Capitalist System*, elaborated on Marx's models in Volume III (Grossman, 1929/1992: Chapter 3). This was an early version of the theory of unequal exchange that had become a central feature of Marxian international economics after the Second World War.

Grossman pointed out that, in international trade, prices do not exchange at their values. Some prices will exceed values while some values will exceed prices. We saw this already in our summary of Marx's theory of value and price. Prices of production deviate from direct prices because rates of profit equalize among industries with differing organic compositions of capital. Increments of surplus value need to flow away from industries where profit rates lie above the national average and to industries where profit rates lie below the national average. The pricing system enables these readjustments.

Grossman expands on Marx's first illustration above by dropping the assumption that prices equal values. He allows prices to deviate from values. We reproduce Marx's first illustration below:

$$\text{Europe} \quad 84C + 16V + 16S = 116 \tag{11.7}$$

$$\text{Asia} \quad 16C + 84V + 21S = 121 \tag{11.8}$$

Suppose, now, that competition equalizes the European and Asian rates of profit. What will that profit rate be? Grossman calculates the solution as follows. Notice that the aggregate global capital advanced is 200, the sum of C and V in each region. The aggregate surplus value produced is 37 or 16S + 21S. The global average rate

256 Marxian and Sraffian theories of unequal exchange

of surplus value or profit is 18.5%. In order for the profit rate to change, one nation will have to realize less surplus value, and the other nation would have to realize more surplus value. Prices would have to change to bring this about. What will the new prices be?

The new equations are:

$$\text{Europe} \quad 84C + 16V + 18.5S = 118.5 \tag{11.9}$$

$$\text{Asia} \quad 16C + 84V + 18.5S = 118.5 \tag{11.10}$$

The new prices will be 118.5. It is the sum of the values in Europe and Asia: C + V + S. The only difference is that the surplus value *realized* due to profit equalization differs from the surplus value actually produced. We can confirm that the profit rates in Europe and Asia are identical, or 18.5% (= S/(C + V) = 18.5/100). Each of the two commodities will sell at 118.5. European commodities with the higher organic composition sell at prices higher than value; those of the backward country sell at prices lower than value. Note also that aggregate world capital advanced is 200 (=84C + 16C + 16V + 84V) and aggregate world surplus value is 37 (= 18.5S + 18.5S). The world rate of surplus value is 37/200 or 18.5%.

The lesson of this story is that, because of market competition, Europe ends up with an additional 2.5 units of surplus value (18.5 rather than 16) while Asia ends up with 2.5 units fewer (18.5 rather than 21). Exchange is unequal; free trade simply transfers surplus value from Asia to Europe. This transfer accelerates accumulation and growth in advanced economies and retards accumulation and growth in developing economies.

Unequal international exchange theory II: Arghiri Emmanuel

In the early 1960s Arghiri Emmanuel, a Greek economist, argued that unequal exchange occurred not because the organic composition of capitals diverged among rich and poor nations, but because of growing wage differentials between them (Emmanuel, 1972). International capital flows will equalize rates of profit because capital is internationally mobile. However, wage rates will remain unequal, with workers in poor nations receiving low wages and workers in rich nations receiving high wages. International trade will not equalize wages, because labor is immobile.[3]

Emmanuel argued along with Marx that sociological and historical factors determine wages, not just biological subsistence factors. In particular, trade unions are the key to understanding why wages are higher in advanced nations since unions there are more active and powerful. As a result, said Emmanuel, poor nations will always exchange a larger amount of their labor value for a smaller amount of the rich nation's labor value. The product of a developing nation's labor force will never have the same value internationally as the product of the same amount of labor expended in a developed country.

Marxian and Sraffian theories of unequal exchange **257**

TABLE 11.4 Emmanuel model

	Rate of exploitation $\alpha = S/V$	Organic composition $\beta = C/V$	Rate of profit $\pi = S/(C+V)$
Rich nation A	100%	4.0	20%
Poor nation B	300%	4.0	60%

Emmanuel, in his 1972 book *Unequal Exchange*, reformulated Marx's formulas for the transformation of value into prices of production in order to explain why the terms of trade for developing countries are unfavorable. Emmanuel assumed that the poor nation produces and trades tea, a commodity specific to poor nations. The rich nation produces automobiles, a technologically complex commodity specific to rich nations. In his illustration, Emmanuel assumes rich nation A produces 30 automobiles with an aggregate labor value of 720 hours, and poor nation B produces 30 tons of tea with an aggregate value of 480 hours. We suppose that each nation's output is homogenous (i.e., there is only one kind of car and one kind of tea).

Using the following hypothetical data we can calculate the total labor value per automobile and ton of tea as:

$$\text{Rich nation A} \quad 480C + 120V + 120S = 720 \quad 720/30 = 24 \quad (11.11)$$

$$\text{Poor nation B} \quad 240C + 60V + 180S = 480 \quad 480/30 = 16 \quad (11.12)$$

Automobiles made in the rich nation have a labor value of 24 each, while tea made in the poor nation has a labor value of 16 per ton. The rate of exploitation, organic composition of capital and rate of profit are shown in Table 11.4. Wages in the poor nation are half the wages paid in the rich nation (60V vs. 120V). The organic composition of capital is identical (4.0), which distinguishes this model from Marx, who assumed they differed. The rate of exploitation in the poor nation is three times as great, as is the profit rate.

Because labor is immobile, we keep the wage differential constant. However, international capital flows would equalize the profit rates. The total surplus value produced in both nations is $(120 + 180) = 300$ hours. The total capital employed in both nations is $(480 + 120) + (240 + 60) = 900$ hours. The average rate of profit is, therefore, $300/900 = 33^1/_3\%$. If the profit rate equalizes at $33^1/_3\%$ then the following data apply:

$$\text{Rich nation A} \quad (480C + 120V)(1.33) = 800 \quad 800/30 = 26.67 \quad (11.13)$$

$$\text{Poor nation B} \quad (240C + 60V)(1.33) = 400 \quad 400/30 = 13.33 \quad (11.14)$$

Before profit rates equalize, the prices of production for automobiles and tea were 24 and 16, respectively. The price of an automobile was 1.5 times the price of 30 tons of tea. Now, after profit rates equalize at $33^1/_3\%$, the price of an automobile is 2 times the price of tea (= 26.67/13.33).

To see what this means, suppose rich nation A imports 6 tons of tea at a price of 13.33. Nation A's expenditure will be 6 ×13.33 = 80 hours. Nation B can use these 80 units of value to buy 3 automobiles at a price of 26.67 each. Thus, 6 tons of tea exchange for 3 automobiles and trade remains balanced because exports equal imports.

But the analysis does not stop here. Assume A and B continue to exchange 3 automobiles for 6 tons of tea. At the old prices, A's imports were worth 6 × 16 = 96 hours and its exports were worth 3 × 24 = 72 hours. This resulted in a net transfer of 24 hours of value from A to B. Now, at the new prices, there is no longer a net transfer to the poor nation. A's imports are now worth 6 × 13.33 = 80 hours while its exports also are worth 3 × 26.67 = 80 hours. Eighty hours exchange for 80 hours. Looking at it from B's viewpoint, at the old price B's imports were worth 3 × 24 = 72 hours and its exports were worth 6 × 16 = 96 hours. Nation B earned a net 24 hours in the exchange. Now it exports 80 hours of value and imports 80 hours of value, earning nothing extra. The equalization of profit rates causes prices of production to change and, as a result, the rich nation receives an additional 24 hours of value from the poor nation.

Foreign trade is therefore unequal, as the poor nation continues to transfer value to the rich nation. This transfer allows the rich nation to develop and prosper at the expense of the poor nation. The poor nation receives no such benefit from trade and will languish at its lower stage of development. Moreover, because of this unequal exchange, wages in the rich nation will rise as well. Workers in the rich nation thus benefit directly from the exploitation of workers in the poor nation. And, to make matters worse, the growing wage differential exacerbates the unequal exchange and the rich grow richer while the poor grow relatively poorer.

Emmanuel concluded that Marx's battle cry, "workers of the world unite," is utopian, as little or no class solidarity exists among workers in rich and poor nations. International trade, therefore, is the foundation of imperialism and not the export of capital and global finance as argued by Lenin and his contemporaries. As Emmanuel observed, "all imperialisms are, in the last resort, mercantile in character" (Emmanuel, 1972: 187).

Samir Amin's 1976 book *Unequal Development* extended Emmanuel's model to include commodities produced in both rich and poor nations. These are so-called non-specific commodities because their production is not restricted specifically to the poor nation. He also included non-capitalist nations in his analysis.

Criticism of Emmanuel and Amin came from several places.[4] Charles Bettelheim charged that the problem with poor nations is the low development of the forces of production (Bettleheim, 1972). Wage differentials were the result and not the cause of underdevelopment. De Janvery and Kramer argued that you cannot assume wage differentials will persist, because labor is internationally immobile (De Janvery and Kramer, 1979). Wages will eventually equalize for specific and non-specific goods because low wages in the poor nation will attract investment, causing job growth; relative wages will rise in the long run. Similarly, the outward flow of capital from rich to poor nations causes disinvestment and a relative decline in wages in the rich nations. Therefore, wages will eventually equalize. The Emmanuel and Amin conclusions do not apply, say De Janvery and Kramer, to the case of non-specific commodities, although they might apply to specific commodities.

Unequal international exchange theory III: Piero Sraffa

Piero Sraffa was an Italian economist whose Marxian pedigree has always been in doubt. Some claim he belonged in the Marxian camp, while others believed he was in the Ricardian camp. We will avoid these entanglements and other related arcane issues, however, and focus only on how Sraffa's model can be used to illuminate the process of unequal exchange.

Like Marx, Kalecki and Robinson, Sraffa argued that class struggle determines income shares. Profit and wage income, therefore, have nothing at all to do with marginal productivity as proposed by the Neoclassical orthodoxy. The income shares each group ultimately receives depend on the economic and political power they possess.

Sraffa's model, which he presented in his unusually terse book, *Production of Commodities by Means of Commodities: Prelude to a Critique of Economic Theory*, shows how the distribution of wage and profit income affects the pricing of commodities (Sraffa, 1960). This model is quite similar to Marx's schema. Like other Marxists, Sraffa presumes two classes: a capitalist class that owns the means of production and a working class that owns nothing. However, unlike Marx, Sraffa scraps the labor theory of value. This means Sraffa's model contains no theory of income distribution. Profits and wages come from an economic surplus that is produced annually. This economic surplus is simply the excess output over the amount minimally necessary to reproduce the system. The division of this surplus into profits and wages is open ended. It does not rely on a theory of subsistence or necessary labor time as it did for Ricardo and Marx. Instead, unspecified social forces determine the profit wage distribution. Distribution is what it is.

Sraffa also organized production differently than Marx, dividing the economy into two sectors: a basic sector and a non-basic sector. The basic sector includes all industries that produce outputs used in *all* other industries. Marx, on the other hand, divided the economy into "Departments" that produce capital goods (constant capital) and subsistence goods (variable capital).

Sraffa gave little attention to international economics. Nevertheless, we can adopt his general approach to the study of international exchange. In this section we develop a Sraffa-like model that suggests that free international trade is exploitive and not mutually advantageous. Specifically, it shows that advanced nations extract a surplus from poor developing nations. This constitutes a transfer of wealth which perpetuates the pauperization of peripheral nations. Free exchange is,

260 Marxian and Sraffian theories of unequal exchange

therefore, *unequal* and simply perpetuates existing global inequalities. This conclusion is similar to the unequal exchange arguments put forward by Marx, Grossman and Emmanuel.

We now construct a Sraffian-type model. Suppose rich nation R specializes in iron production and poor nation P specializes in grain production. Iron production in R requires grain imports from P (to feed iron workers), and grain production in P requires iron imports (tools for growing grain) from R. We do not presume that comparative advantage has anything at all to do with why these nations specialize in iron and grain, although geographical advantages and history can certainly play a role. It is more likely that grain farming occurs in poor nation P because it was once a colony and that people had little choice over what to produce. And it is likely that iron making occurs in rich nation R because industrialization there necessitated the creation of an iron industry. Specialization in this model is thus a consequence of historical, social, political and economic factors.

We assume capital is perfectly mobile between R and P so that the profit rate r is identical in both countries as well as in both industries. However, labor is immobile. This means that there will be two wages rates, w_R in the rich country and w_P in the poor country. The first equation represents the production of iron in the rich country alone, and the second equation represents the production of grain in the poor country alone.

$$\text{Rich nation } (13P_i + 2P_g)(1 + r) + 10w_R = 27P_i \qquad (11.15)$$

$$\text{Poor nation } (10P_i + 4P_g)(1 + r) + 10w_P = 12P_g \qquad (11.16)$$

Capitalists in the rich nation advance capital worth $(13P_i + 2P_g)$ and capitalists in the poor nation advance $(10P_i + 4P_g)$. The equalized rate of profit is r and the two wage rates are w_R and w_P. The rich nation's physical economic surplus is 4 tons of iron, which equals total output of 27 tons minus the 23 tons used (13 + 10). The poor nation's economic surplus is 6 tons of grain, which equals total output of 12 tons minus 6 tons used in production (2 + 4). The values of the economic surplus for the rich and poor nation are, respectively, $[(13P_i + 2P_g)r + 10w_r]$ and $[(10P_i + 4P_g)r + 10w_p]$.

The two equations in (11.15) and (11.16) contain five unknowns: the two prices, the two different wage rates and the uniform rate of profit. However, if we set $P_i = 1$, the number of unknowns is reduced to four. The price of iron is the so-called *numeraire*. We can solve for the four remaining unknowns by choosing an arbitrary value for r and then varying the corresponding value of w_R. In effect, we assume values for three of the variables (P_i, r and w_R) and then find the solution values of the two remaining unknown variables (P_g and w_P). In Table 11.5, we arbitrarily choose $r = 10\%$ and $r = 20\%$ and vary the value of w_R from 0.05 to 0.95:

TABLE 11.5 Profits, wages and prices for rich and poor nation

	r = 10%				r = 20%	
w_R	w_P	P_g	P_i	w_R	w_P	P_g
0.05	3.11	5.55	1	2.07	4.54	2.07
0.25	2.42	4.64	1	1.47	3.71	1.47
0.35	2.08	4.18	1	0.87	2.88	0.87
0.5	1.56	3.5	1	0.72	2.67	0.72
0.7	0.87	2.59	1	0.57	2.46	0.57
0.74	0.74	2.42	1	0.56	2.44	0.56
0.8	0.52	2.14	1	0.42	2.25	0.42
0.95	0.01	1.45	1	0.12	1.83	0.12

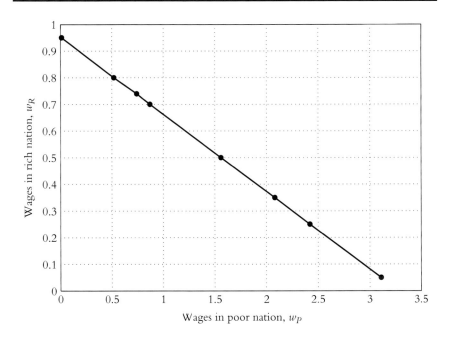

FIGURE 11.1 Wages in rich and poor nation when $r = 10\%$

Wage rates in rich and poor nations

Table 11.5 shows that when the wage rate in the rich nation rises, the wage rate in the poor nation falls, as does the price of the poor nation's grain exports. It does not matter what the profit rate happens to be. This inverse wage relationship is described in Figure 11.1 for $r = 10\%$.

We divide the aggregate economic surplus of both nations among three groups: the workers in the poor nation, the workers in the rich nation and the capitalists in both places. The capitalists receive the same uniform rate of return because capital is mobile. If workers in the rich nation get a larger piece of the rich nation's pie then workers in the poor nation will receive a smaller piece of the poor nation's pie, so

262 Marxian and Sraffian theories of unequal exchange

TABLE 11.6 Distribution of global surplus

1	2	3	4	5	6	7	8
Wage rate in R	*Wage rate in P*	*Price of grain*	*Value of global surplus*	*Rich capitalists' share of global surplus (%)*	*Poor capitalists' share of global surplus (%)*	*Rich-nation workers' share of global surplus*	*Poor-nation workers' share of global surplus*
w_R	w_P	P_g	$(4P_i + 6P_g)$				
0.05	3.11	5.545	37.270	6.46	8.63	1.34	83.56
0.25	2.42	4.636	31.820	7.00	8.97	7.86	76.17
0.35	2.08	4.182	29.090	7.34	9.19	12.03	71.44
0.50	1.56	3.500	25.000	8.00	9.60	20.00	62.40
0.70	0.87	2.591	19.550	9.30	10.42	35.81	44.47
0.74	0.74	2.418	18.510	9.64	10.63	39.87	39.87
0.80	0.52	2.136	17.820	10.27	11.03	47.57	31.13
0.95	0.01	1.450	12.700	12.52	12.44	74.80	0.43

long as the capitalists continue to receive the same profit rate. Put differently, when the wage rate in the rich nation rises relative to the poor nation, the terms of trade between iron and grain changes to benefit rich-nation workers at the expense of poor-nation workers. This price change is the mechanism used to transfer more economic surplus from poor workers to rich workers. The rich-nation workers thus participate in the exploitation of poor-nation workers.

Another way to understand the relationships described in this model is to focus on the *absolute amount* of surplus received by each group rather than wage *rates* and profit *rates*. Table 11.6 shows how the global surplus is distributed among the workers and the capitalists in both places when r = 10%. When workers in rich and poor nations get the same wage (0.74 per worker), they also get the same percentage share of the world surplus (39.87%). The 10% return that the capitalists in the poor nation receive gives them a slightly higher share of the world surplus than does the 10% return to the rich nation capitalists. This is because, at a grain price of P_g = 2.418, the value of the capital which poor-nation capitalists have invested is slightly larger than the value of the capital that is invested in the rich nation. In other words, the iron industry uses relatively little grain input as compared to iron input (2 tons of grain to 13 tons of iron) while the grain industry uses relatively more grain input as compared to iron input (4 tons of grain to 10 tons of iron). When the wage rate rises from 0.74 to 0.80 in the rich nation (and r remains at 10%), the wage rate in the poor nation falls from 0.74 to 0.52 and the latter's share of the surplus shrinks from 39.87% of the whole world's surplus to 31.13%.

But there is also another peculiar result when this happens: capitalists in both nations benefit! The amount of surplus released in the poor nation when their wages fall to 0.52 is more than enough to pay workers in the rich nation a wage rate of 0.80;

the capitalists get the rest, which is added to their profit income. This is due to the fact that labor and capital are combined in different proportions: there is relatively more labor used compared to capital in the poor nation, so a lowering of wages there will release lots of surplus, enough to pay rich workers and all capitalists more.

The Sraffian theory of unequal exchange developed here is only an introduction to a wider literature that studies global capitalism from a Marxian viewpoint. The analysis shows that prosperity in rich hegemonic nations can cause poverty in poor peripheral nations. Changes in world commodity prices reflect class relationships between workers in each nation and the global capitalist class. This is what the term "unequal exchange" implies. Global trade relations simply mirror unequal global class relations. Free trade is not mutually advantageous. Free trade simply permits these relations to persist, a viewpoint first articulated by Marx in 1848.

Empirical evidence of Marxian theory

There are three main questions that economists have asked about the empirical validity of Marx's key propositions. The first is whether we can actually observe a secular decline in profit rates. If we can, then this might explain the capitalists' drive for profits abroad, a motive lying at the root of imperialism.

A second question is whether there is an observable relationship between (1) *market prices*; (2) *prices of production*; and (3) *direct prices* (or labor values). Marxian theory requires that a relationship exist between all three; Sraffian theory requires only a relationship between production prices and market prices.[5] An affirmative answer is necessary to validate theories of unequal exchange. If no relationship can be found to exist, then we would need to find some other theory to explain unequal exchange.

The third question is whether we can actually observe unequal exchange, never mind what theory we use to explain it. What does "unequal" exchange mean and how can we measure it?

Do rules of profit fall?

According to Marx, capital accumulation leads to an increase in the organic composition of capital (constant capital divided variable capital, or C/V), which leads to a lower value rate of profit—all other things remaining constant. But all other things do not remain constant.

For one thing, increased capital expenditure could increase the productivity of the means of production more than it increases the productivity of the means of subsistence. This would reduce C more than it would reduce V, causing the organic composition, C/V, to actually fall. The value rate of profit would then rise, the opposite of what Marx predicted. Additionally, the rate of exploitation, S/V, which Marx assumed constant, could increase for political or sociological reasons, causing the value rate of profit to rise, not fall.

These are all "counteracting tendencies" that would make it impossible to actually observe falling profit rates. So, if we observe profit rates rising instead of falling, does this mean Marx was wrong? Not really. It's just that the counteracting tendencies have kicked in. Empirically this means that we need to measure three variables: the value rate of profit, the organic composition of capital and the rate of exploitation. This is not an easy task, one reason being data for these variables are not measured in terms of labor value.

Joseph M. Gillman made one of the first major postwar studies of these issues in his 1959 book *The Falling Rate of Profit: Marx's Law and its Significance to Twentieth-century Capitalism*. Gillman measured aggregate surplus value as net national profit income. Using this data he found that profit rates fell prior to 1919 but rose from 1919 to 1939. The year 1919 roughly divided the competitive laissez-faire era from the monopoly capital era. However, by excluding the wages of "unproductive" labor (labor employed in non-production activities such as adverting and administration), profits indeed had fallen throughout both periods. Gillman observed that the rising organic composition of capital explained profit rates before 1919 and that secular increases in unproductive labor explained falling profits after 1919.

In the 1970s there was a flurry of renewed interest in this subject. This was due to a growing interest in Marxism and radical economics generally. One landmark study by Andrew Glyn and Bob Sutcliffe showed that the rate of profit in Britain had indeed been falling (Glyn and Sutcliffe, 1972). However, they argued that this was not because the organic composition of capital was rising. Instead, it was because the rate of exploitation (S/V) was falling due to the rising political influence of labor. The result was a squeeze on profits and, hence, falling profit rates.

The debates about the validity of Marxian economics even drew mainstream economists into the fray. Not surprisingly, they all found evidence contradicting Marx's law of falling profits. Among those were Edward Wolff (1979), Martin Feldstein, Lawrence Summers and Michael Wachtel (1977) and William Nordhaus (1974).

Interest in the subject waned until the 1990s and 2000s when researchers writing in the Marxian tradition found new evidence of falling rates of surplus value and profits. Basu and Manolakos (2013), for example, found that the US profit rate had declined, at about 0.3% per year, from 1948 to 2007. Others such as Dumenil and Levy (2002) and Fred Moseley (1991) found similar evidence (Shaikh, "The Transformation from Marx to Sraffa," 1984).

Mainstream opponents of Marxian economics seem to have lost interest in the subject and have remained silent, possibly because they no longer feel as threatened by the challenge of radical economics as they once did.

The connection between market prices, prices of production and labor values

A second line of empirical inquiry estimates the relationship between market prices, prices of production and direct prices (i.e., labor values). These are the main variables of the Marxian and Sraffian reproduction equations.

It is important to know if the deviations between these types of prices are large or small. If the deviations are very small, then it would not matter which prices we used in our studies. For example, if we find evidence of unequal exchange or of falling profits when these are measured in terms of (say) market prices, then we would discover the same evidence if we had used either production or direct prices. The Marxian and Sraffian equations then would be meaningful representations of global economic relations.

There were several leading studies of price deviations in the 1980s. Two seminal studies were by Anwar Shaikh (Shaikh, 1984 and 1998). In his 1984 study Shaikh used input–output data for the US and Italy and found that prices of production deviated from direct prices by about 19% in 1959 and 17% in 1967. He also found that the average deviation of market prices from direct prices was ± 20–25%. In his expanded 1998 study, Shaikh found that market prices deviate from labor values by about 9.2% and from prices of production by only 8.2%.

Shaikh concluded from all this that the labor theory of value is a good predictor of prices of production and market prices: "On the whole these results seem to provide powerful support for the Classical and Marxian emphasis on the structural determinants of relative prices in the modern world" (Shaikh, 1998: 245).

Later, in the 1990s and 2000s, Petrovic (1987), Ochoa (1989), Cockshott, Cottrell and Michaelson (1995) and Tsoulfidis and Maniatis (2002) corroborated Shaikh's findings for Yugoslavia, the US, the UK and Greece, respectively. In these years there were also many disputes about the empirical techniques used to analyze the correlations between prices and values.[6] But the general opinion seems to be that there is a reliable correlation between market, production and direct prices and that deviations between them are relatively small. As Cockshott, Cottrell and Michaelson summarized it,

> Our most general conclusion, in line with the other recent work cited in the Introduction, is that Marxian economics has nothing to fear, and a good deal to gain, from a confrontation with the data-record for actual capitalist economies.
>
> *(Cockshott, Cottrell and Michaelson, 1995: 123)*

Does unequal exchange exist?

What evidence is there that unequal exchange exists? Unfortunately most of the work done in this area has been theoretical, not empirical. The first to find empirical support for unequal exchange were the Prebisch-Singer studies. These studies measured unequal exchange using terms of trade data. The research showed that the terms of trade for developing countries in the periphery had deteriorated with respect to advanced economies. The Prebisch-Singer thesis explained that primary goods markets are income inelastic, so that as world incomes rise the demand for these commodities would not rise by as much. Poorer developing nations are

266 Marxian and Sraffian theories of unequal exchange

therefore unable to earn more export earnings to pay for increasingly expensive manufactured goods. The Prebisch-Singer thesis suggested that this phenomenon is built in to the capitalist world trading system; it is the very structure of world trade that causes unequal exchange (Prebisch, 1950; Singer, 1950).

Equal exchange means that commodities trade at prices proportional to the amount of labor time used to produce them (direct prices). Because the organic composition of capital differs among sectors, so too do value rates of profit. Profit equalization requires that surplus value be redistributed from sectors with above-average profit rates to sectors with below-average profit rates. This entails a transfer of real resources, which is the basis of unequal exchange. The consequence of these transfers is that direct prices "transform" into prices of production and then to market prices. Prices then deviate from values. These price–value deviations offer one measure of equal—or unequal—exchange.

International trade between societies at different stages of development makes the price–value transformations much more complicated. For one thing, the rates of surplus value (or, the rate of exploitation), which equalize within a national economy, differ among trading nations. There are a multitude of social and political reasons that could explain this. For another thing, the technical and organic compositions of capital used in similar industries also differ among nations. Finally, labor productivity, and hence wages, would differ among nations at different stages of development, which is an important factor lying behind the differences in surplus value.

The problem of finding empirical evidence for unequal exchange is how to unravel all these complex interrelated factors. When we add to this the difficulties of measuring labor values and prices of production, which we discussed above, empirical evidence of unequal exchange becomes difficult to find.

A 1980 study by Gibson (1980) showed that Peru lost the equivalent of 38% of its exports to the US in 1969 (Gibson, 1980; see also Raffer, 1987). Another attempt to find evidence for unequal exchange is a 1991 study by Gheverghese and Tomlinson (1991). They used input–output data from the 1970s for Australia and Papua New Guinea. They estimated the hours of labor embodied in the exports of each nation to the other and compared the dollar value of exports to the labor hours exported. Joseph and Tomlinson calculated that if the hours exported from Papua New Guinea had been paid at Australian rates, their export revenues would have been 75% higher. This would seem to support the existence of unequal exchange between the center and peripheral nations.

Using a similar methodology, Nakajima and Izumi (1995) confirm the existence of unequal exchange between the US, Japan and South Korea. But not so according to Subasat (2013) and Houston and Paus (1987). Amin (1976) estimated aggregate losses due to unequal exchange between developed and developing countries in 1966 as $22 billion. In the late 1990s, Gernot Köhler, using balance of payments data, estimated aggregate global unequal exchange in 1965 as $19 billion between OECD and non-OECD countries.

Köhler (1998 and 2014) also found that these estimates increased very dramatically in 1995. He found that the three countries that lost the most through unequal exchange were China, Indonesia and Mexico, while the three that gained the most were Japan, the US and Germany. In another study Köhler identified a bundle of traded commodities and compared their prices with purchasing power parity to ascertain if these commodities were under- or overvalued. Köhler found that for low-income countries the values were systematically undervalued, indicating unequal exchange. Said Köhler, "I conclude that the currency value of low-income countries tends to be undervalued. The effect is exploitive. The core countries appear to extract a large amount of value from the periphery countries through the clever monetary device called exchange rate system" (Köhler, 1998: 12). Surplus value is thus also extracted through the financial and exchange rate system.

This is a sample of the empirical work on this topic. Orthodox international trade theorists, of course, deny that unequal exchange exists, mainly on theoretical grounds, and promote the idea that free trade actually has the opposite effect, of decreasing global income inequality.

Conclusions

The main idea behind Marxian international economics is that capitalism is everywhere a system of exploitation, and exploitation is necessary for the accumulation of capital. As Marx put it in *Capital*, "Accumulate, accumulate! That is Moses and the prophets!" (Marx, 1936: 653). It applies domestically as well as internationally. This implies that the growth and development of economically advanced nations (the center) derives from the expropriation of economic surplus from poorer less developed nations (the periphery). Colonialism, imperialism and globalism are various "isms" that have been applied to describe the forms of economic exploitation that have existed since the dawn of capitalism. How this global capitalist system exactly works, how best to deal with it, and where it will lead in the future are questions that have divided economists for a century or more.

In Marxian international economics trade and foreign investment are the primary conduits through which economic surplus flows, in the form of goods and money, from the periphery to the center. These conduits are reinforced, maintained and protected by nation states and global institutions.

Trade between center and periphery is similar to trade between capitalists and workers. At least in the post-colonial era (after the Second World War), each party freely enters into international market transactions. However, neither party has much choice but to do so. The worker is free to choose which capitalist to work for, but has no choice but to work for one capitalist or another. The same holds true for nations in the periphery. They are free to choose what to import and export and to whom, but they have little choice but to continue importing from and exporting to someone. Neither workers nor nations are free to function "off the capitalist grid," so to speak. Trade thus occurs among unequal partners, and this inequality is self-perpetuating. Unequal exchange theory tries to show how this works.

Foreign investment functions on parallel tracks with commodity trade. In the post-colonial era it also functions to create and transfer economic surplus from periphery to center. It involves the purchase of productive assets in peripheral nations by multinational corporations domiciled in the center. In this way the corporations can influence directly the allocation of resources and the distribution of income and wealth in the periphery.

All in all, Marxian international economics continues to lie on the fringes of the mainstream discipline. This is not because Marxism is flawed or irrelevant. Indeed, there is considerable empirical support for many of the Marxian hypotheses, which, not surprisingly, orthodox economists dismiss out of hand. Part of the reason for this marginalization is the overpowering domination of economic orthodoxy. Why this is so is the subject of another book.

Notes

1   We can say that each equation represents aggregate output GDP, measured in labor value; the price therefore is a general price index.
2   Note that this does not say Asia workers are better off or happier than European workers.
3   Ricardo's theory assumed the immobility of capital and the equalization of wages at subsistence in a full employment economy.
4   For an overview of criticisms of Emmanuel see Howard and King (1992: Chapter 10).
5   Recall that Sraffa models do not use Marx's labor theory of value and so do not consider direct prices.
6   For a review of these issues see Baeza (1994).

References

Amin, S. (1976). *Unequal Development.* New York: Monthly Review Press.
Baeza, A. V. (1994). "Correspondence Between Labour Values and Prices: a New Approach." *Review of Radical Political Economics, 26*(2), 57–66.
Basu, D., & Manolakos, P. T. (2013). "Is There a Tendency for the Rate of Profit to Fall? Econometric Evidence for the U.S. Ecomomy, 1948–2007." *Review of Radical Politic al Economy, 45*(1), 76–95.
Bettleheim, C. (1972). "Theoretical Comments." In A. Emmanuel, *Unequal Exchange: a Study of the Imperialism of Trade* (pp. 301–303). New York: Monthly Review Press.
Cockshott, P., Cottrell, A., & Michaelson, G. (1995). "Testing Marx: Some New Results From UK Data." *Capital and Class, 15*(55), 103–130.
De Janvery, A., & Kramer, F. (1979). "The Limits of Unequal Exchange." *Review of Radical Political Economy, 11*(4), 3–15.
Dumenil, G., & Levy, D. (2002). "The Profit Rate: Where and How Much Did It Fall? Did It Recover? (USA 1948–2000)." *Review of Radical Political Economics, 34*(4), 437–461.
Emmanuel, A. (1972). *Unequal Exchange: A Study of the Imperialism of Trade.* New York: Monthly Review Press.
Feldstein, M., Summers, L., & Wachter, M. (1977). "Is the Rate of Profit Falling?" *Brookings Papers on Economic Activity, 1977*(1), 211–228.
Gheverghese, G. J., & Tomlinson, M. (1991). "Testing the Existence and Measuring the Magnitude of Unequal Exchange Resulting from International Trade: A Marxian Approach." *Indian Economic Review, 26*(2), 123–148.
Gibson, B. (1980). "Unequal Exchange: Theoretical Issues and Empirical Findings." *Review of Radical Political Economics, 12*(3), 15–35.

Gillman, J. M. (1959). *The Falling Rate of Profit: Marx's Law and its Significance to Twentieth-century Capitalism.* London: Dennis Dobson.

Glyn, A., & Sutcliffe, B. (1972). *British Capitalism, Workers and the Profit Squeeze.* Harmondsworth, UK: Penguin.

Grossman, H. (1929/1992). *The Law of Accumulation and Breakdown of the Capitalist System: Being Also a Theory of Crisis.* London: Pluto Press. Retrieved February 2, 2014, from http://www.Marxians.org/archive/grossman/1929/breakdown/ch03.htm.

Houston, D., & Paus, E. (1987). "The Theory of Unequal Exchange: An Indictment." *Review of Radical Political Economics, 19*(1), 90–97.

Howard, M., & King, J. E. (1992). *A History of Marxian Economics: Volume II, 1929 – 1990.* London: Macmillan.

Köhler, G. (1998). "The Structure of Global Money and World Tables of Unequal Exchange." *Journal of World-Systems Research, 4*(2), 145–178.

Köhler, G. (2014, January 27). *Unequal Exchange: 1965–1995: World Trend and World Tables.* Retrieved from http://wsarch.ucr.edu/archive/papers/kohler/kohler3.htm.

Moseley, F. (1991). *The Falling Rate of Profit in the Postwar United States Economy.* London: Macmillan.

Nakajima, A., & Izumi, H. (1995). "Economic Development and Unequal Exchange Among Nations: Analysis of the U.S., Japan and South Korea." *Review of Radical Political Economics, 27*(3), 86–94.

Nordhaus, W. D. (1974). "The Falling Share of Profits." *Brookings Papers on Economic Activity, 1974*(1), 179–217.

Ochoa, E. M. (1989). "Values, Prices, and Wage-profit Curves in the US Economy." *Cambridge Journal of Economic, 13*(3), 413–429.

Petrovic, P. (1987). "The Deviation of Production Prices from Labor Values: Some Methodological and Empirical Issues." *Cambridge Journal of Economics, 11*(3), 197–210.

Prebisch, R. (1950). *The Economic Development of Latin America and Its Principal Problems.* UN document no. E/CN. 12/89/Rev. 1. Lake Success, NY: United Nations.

Raffer, K. (1987). *Unequal Exchange and the Evolution of the World System.* London: Macmillan.

Shaikh, A. (1984). "The Transformation from Marx to Sraffa." In A. Freeman, & E. Mandel (Eds.), *Ricardo, Marx and Sraffa* (pp. 43–84). London: Verso.

Shaikh, A. (1998). "The Empirical Strength of the Labor Theory of Value." In R. Bellofiore (Ed.), *Conference Proceedings of Marxian Economics: A Centenary Appraisal* (pp. 225–251). London: Macmillan.

Singer, H. W. (1950). "The Distribution of Gains Between Investing and Borrowing Countries." *American Economic Review, 40*(2), 473–485.

Sraffa, P. (1960). *Production of Commodities by Means of Commodities: Prelude to a Critique of Economic Theory.* New York: Cambridge University Press.

Subusat, T. (2013). "Can Differences in International Prices Measure Unequal Exchange in International Trade?" *Competition and Change, 17*(4), 372–379.

Tsoulfidid, L., & Maniatis, T. (2002). "Values, Prices of Production and Market Prices: Some More Evidence from the Greek Economy." *Cambridge Journal of Economics, 26*(3), 359–369.

Wolff, E. N. (1979). "The Rate of Surplus Value, the Organic Composition and the General Rate of Profit in the U.S. Economy, 1947–1967." *American Economic Review, 69*(3), 329–341.

270 Marxian and Sraffian theories of unequal exchange

Appendix 11A

An overview of Marx's theory of value and price

Marx defined a commodity as anything produced for the sole purpose of selling it on a market. Commodities are not produced for personal consumption. It is crucial to point out that labor is also a commodity because it too is bought and sold on markets. Selling at a profit is, of course, the primary motivation.

Marx's Capital

In the first volume of *Capital*, Marx claims that a commodity's *value* is directly proportional to the total amount of labor embodied in its production. We can measure this value with units of currency, in which case the result is the *direct price* of the commodity. Direct prices will always be proportional to labor value.

In the third volume, Marx allows capital to flow between sectors of the economy in pursuit of the highest rate of return. After all, there is no reason to expect rates of profit to be equal everywhere. The free flow of capital between sectors will then equalize profit rates. However, as capital circulates around the economy in search of the highest return, prices will begin to deviate from direct prices. Some prices will fall below their value or direct price while others will rise above. This is because the proportions in which capital and labor are used vary from industry to industry.

As profit *rates* equalize throughout the economy, profit will need to be redistributed from higher-than-average-profit industries to lower-than-average-profit industries. We will explain this further below. Once the profit rate equalizes throughout the economy, capital will stop moving around, and prices will stop adjusting. We call the new set of equilibrium prices, *prices of production*.

Finally, if there is perfect competition then prices of production will be actual *market prices*. If there is imperfect competition then some market prices may deviate from their prices of production.

Notice that we are defining three kinds of prices: direct prices, prices of production and market prices. Market prices track production prices and production prices gravitate around direct prices.

Value

Calculating value is more complicated than simply adding up hours of labor. First, when we add up quantities of labor to determine a commodity's value, we only count the amount *socially necessary* for production—socially necessary in terms of accepted production norms and practices. For sure, some inefficient firms use more labor than is necessary while others use much less. We cannot say that a commodity produced by an inefficient enterprise has more value just because the enterprise does not manage its resources efficiently. We thus count only the average amount of labor—the socially necessary amount—in calculating a commodity's value.

Second, when adding up the quantity of socially necessary labor we disregard all distinctions between the various kinds of labor employed. We thus ignore all differences between (say) carpenters, bookkeepers and unskilled labor; we only consider labor "in general." Marx called this *abstract labor*. He used the term *concrete labor* to describe the specific characteristics of labor, but this is not part of the value calculation.[1] In any case, once a firm sends a commodity to the market for sale, no one pays attention any longer to the different forms of labor used to make it. How often do we think of the various types of labor used to grow, pick and transport onions when we are in the supermarket?

To summarize, the value of a commodity is the total amount of *socially necessary abstract labor* used to produce a commodity. The value of a commodity then becomes the basis for determining its price.

The value of labor power

Perhaps Marx's most important idea was that a worker's capacity to work—his or her *labor power*—becomes a commodity like all other commodities. We must therefore calculate the value of this peculiar commodity in the same way as we determine the value of any other commodity: by the amount of socially necessary abstract labor required to produce it.

What goes into the production of labor power? The answer is food, clothing, shelter and whatever else workers need to survive at the existing standard of living. These items are also commodities produced by labor; we name these the *means of subsistence*. The amount of labor necessary to produce the commodity "labor power" is simply the amount of labor required to produce the means of subsistence needed to support one worker. This, then, is the value of the labor commodity, and the amount a capitalist "invests" at the start of the production period to buy labor is called *variable capital*. We will use the letter V to represent this magnitude.

As an illustration, suppose it takes four hours of labor to produce one day's subsistence goods for one worker. If we assume the monetary system consists of one-dollar gold coins, each of which requires one hour of labor to produce, then one hour of labor sells for $1. The dollar value of the price of labor power—the day's wage rate—is then $4.[2] Because labor sells freely on the labor market, we can say that this wage is a "fair day's" wage.

Surplus value

Once the capitalist has purchased a certain amount of labor, he or she can then make workers create more value than what they cost in wages. They do this by extending the length of the workday beyond the four hours necessary to produce an equivalent of the workers' means of subsistence. Capitalists thus receive (i.e., expropriate) more value from "their" workers than what they cost. They can get away with this because they own the means of production.

If, for example, the customary workday is eight hours, then each worker spends four hours producing the equivalent of his or her means of subsistence and an additional four hours producing surplus value for the capitalist. The eight-hour day is the customary "fair day's work." We can say therefore that each worker receives a "fair day's wage for a fair day's work."

The value that workers produce in excess of what is required to replace their means of subsistence Marx called *surplus value*. Surplus value is newly created value and is the source of the capitalist's profit. In other words, workers produce profit for capitalists. This profit then circulates among them in the form of interest and rent payments. Profit cannot come from buying low and selling high.

The value of the means of production

The *means of production*, like labor power, are also commodities sold on markets. These include inputs such as machinery, facilities and raw materials. The value of these inputs, as with all commodities, depends on the amount of socially necessary abstract labor used to produce them.

The value of the means of production is "transferred" to the final commodity. For example, when a carpenter drives a screw that requires one hour of labor to produce into a new bookcase, the value of that bookcase increases by one hour. If a power screwdriver is used, then only a small fraction (i.e., the depreciated portion) of the value of that machine tool transfers to the bookcase.

Marx called the total value of the means of production transferred to the production of a commodity *constant capital*. We use the letter C to represent this magnitude. This value is constant because the total amount of value represented by the means of production remains constant during the production process; the value just "transfers" to the final product and does not expand. Labor power, on the other hand, is variable capital because the total amount of value represented by that labor power produces an equivalent amount of value *plus* a surplus value. The amount of surplus value produced depends on the customary length of the workday as well as on a variety of political and social considerations that regularly change over time.

Marxian value equations

We can now use the above ideas to describe capitalist commodity production. For any firm, the total value of all the commodities produced in a given period, measured in labor hours, is C + V + S. Of this amount the capitalist invests a total of (C + V) and receives a total profit of S. Letting W represent the aggregate value produced in one period, we can write

$$W = C + V + S \tag{11.17}$$

From this we can calculate the value of each unit produced. If we let n be total units of output then the unit labor value is simply W/n. Note that we can only make this calculation if all n units are homogenous.

We next define the *value rate of profit*, π, as the ratio of surplus value S to the labor value of the capital advanced $(C + V)$:

$$\pi = \frac{S}{(C + V)} \tag{11.18}$$

We call this the *value rate of profit*.

Marx claimed that capitalists exploit workers by forcing them to work an entire workday. For part of that day workers produce an amount of value equal to their means of subsistence (V) and the rest of the day they produce a surplus value (S). Marx called the proportion of the day devoted to producing S and V the *rate of exploitation*, or equivalently, the *rate of surplus value*, as:

$$\alpha = \frac{S}{V} \tag{11.19}$$

We would expect the rate of exploitation to be roughly the same throughout society.

Finally, Marx defines the *organic composition of capital* β as the ratio of constant capital to variable capital:

$$\beta = \frac{C}{V} \tag{11.20}$$

The organic composition of capital is a ratio of *values* not a ratio of physical quantities. Marx called the latter the *technical composition of capital*, which is similar to the capital–labor ratio in mainstream economics. The organic composition is "organic" in the sense that it grows out of the technical and social conditions of production and varies over time and from industry to industry. Further, we would expect that the organic composition and the technical composition are correlated. Let us assume that this correlation is perfect, although it need not be.

We can see the connection between these equations if we divide both the numerator and denominator in Equation (11.18) by V:

$$\pi = \frac{S/V}{C/V + 1} \tag{11.21}$$

This is equivalent to

$$\text{value rate of profit} = \frac{\text{rate of exploitation}}{\text{organic composition} + 1} \tag{11.22}$$

Equation (11.22) says that the rate of profit is a direct function of the rate of exploitation and an inverse function of the organic composition of capital. This

274 Marxian and Sraffian theories of unequal exchange

means, first, that if the rate of worker exploitation increases, say due to an increase in the length of the workday, then workers produce more surplus value, and S rises. With V remaining unchanged, the numerator S/V increases and so too does the profit rate: more exploitation, more surplus value, more profit. Second, if the organic composition of capital in the denominator rises, then the profit rate will fall. This is because a rise in the organic composition implies using relatively more means of production (C) compared to means of subsistence (V). The capitalist can only exploit current labor in order to produce profit.[3] So it stands to reason that if proportionately more C is used, and proportionately less V, then profits must fall.

The most important lesson to come out of this Marxian analysis is that labor produces profit for the capitalists.[4] Profit does not arise from risk taking as argued by orthodox economics. Risk taking is only an argument that justifies the capitalist's expropriation of profit, a profit that only labor can produce. This idea will figure into the analysis of global trade in which capitalist economies interact to produce and distribute surplus value.

The law of the tendency of profits to fall

Marx used Equation (11.22) to reach a quite remarkable conclusion. He believed that capitalist economic development in the long run tends to increase the proportion of constant to variable capital used in production. This is because of the capitalists' compulsion to innovate and reduce costs, especially labor costs. Reducing reliance on unreliable and unpredictable human beings—labor—and replacing them with superior technologies—capital—promises to raise profits. However, the lure of higher profits from new labor-saving techniques entices other capitalists to do the same. Profits may rise in the short run for those adopting these new techniques. However, competition eventually eliminates those higher profits as everyone adopts the new technologies. Once profits fall back to competitive levels, new rounds of innovation and investment begin all over again: profits rise, competitors imitate the innovations, and profit rates fall again to new competitive levels.

During this process, each commodity produced embodies relatively more "dead" labor in the constant capital it uses, and relatively less current or variable capital. The proportion of constant capital C to variable capital V rises continuously. In terms of Equation (11.22), if the numerator S/V remains constant, the denominator C/V increases and the whole fraction—the value rate of profit, π—decreases.

Marx pointed out that this is only a *tendency*, a secular trend. There also exist "counteracting factors" that work against this tendency. These include increases in the rate of exploitation, the numerator in Equation (11.22), and reductions in wages below their subsistence value, which reduces V and expands S. As we will see below, foreign trade and investment are important devices that might offset the tendency of the profit rate to fall.

From value to prices of production

We now divide the economy into two sectors. Firms in Sector I produce only means of production while firms in Sector II produce only means of subsistence (i.e., wage goods).

We use the letter W to represent the total mass of value produced in each sector. Output in each sector is not homogenous; indeed, firms in each sector produce many kinds of commodities. This implies that we can no longer divide the total mass of value produced W by n to calculate per unit value.

Using Equation (11.17), we write

$$\text{Sector I} \qquad C_I + V_I + S_I = W_I \tag{11.23}$$

$$\text{Sector II} \qquad C_{II} + V_{II} + S_{II} = W_{II}$$

Because $\pi = S/(C + V)$, we can rewrite these equations as

$$\text{Sector I} \qquad (C_I + V_I)(1 + \pi_I) = W_I \tag{11.24}$$

$$\text{Sector II} \qquad (C_{II} + V_{II})(1 + \pi_{II}) = W_{II}$$

We illustrate this using some hypothetical data:

$$\text{Sector I} \qquad 100 + 50 + 50 + = 200 \tag{11.25}$$

$$\text{Sector II} \qquad 100 + 100 + 100 + = 300$$

Each of these numbers measures the total number of hours of labor used on each sector in a period of time. The total value of means of production produced is 200, and the total value of the means of subsistence produced is 300. If we continue to assume that 1 hour = \$1, then the numbers also represent dollars. Using the format of Equation (11 24) we can write:

$$\text{Sector I} \qquad (\$100 + \$50)(1.33) = \$200 \tag{11.26}$$

$$\text{Sector II} \qquad (\$100 + \$100)(\$1.5) = \$300$$

where the rates of profit in each sector are 33% and 50% respectively. Sector I total output is \$200 and Sector II total output is \$300. From this data we can infer that the prices in each sector will be proportional to the total labor embodied in production. This is the *direct price*. Recall that each sector produces diverse commodities, so we cannot divide \$200 and \$300 by the number of units produced to calculate the direct price per unit. We would be adding apples and pears. We can only do

276 Marxian and Sraffian theories of unequal exchange

this if all Sector I and Sector II output is homogenous. We can think of the price as a price index.

Note also that this is a model of a no-growth economy. The total value of the means of production produced in Sector I is entirely used up by both sectors ($100 in each sector). Similarly, workers and capitalists consume the total value of means of subsistence produced ($300). Both classes spend their entire income on means of subsistence. Marx called this situation "simple reproduction." This is an unlikely outcome, however, because of the capitalists' lust for accumulation and their drive to expand the amount of capital under their control. They are therefore unlikely to spend all their income on consumption. This is not the case with workers since they will spend their entire incomes on subsistence commodities.[5]

This model is only a first approximation. We must now account for the disparity in profit rates (33% vs. 50%). Why do the rates differ? A clue is that the organic composition of capital, β = C/V, differs. It is 2.0 (100/50) in Sector I and 1.0 (100/100) in Sector II. Sector II uses relatively more labor (C/V is smaller), so it has more opportunity to exploit currently employed workers and thus produce more profit.

If competition tends to equalize profit rates across industries and sectors, then prices must adjust to bring this about. Aggregate profits in both sectors sum to $150 (= $S_I + S_{II}$). The total cost of means of production and labor power in both sectors is $350 (= $C_I + C_{II} + V_I + V_{II}$). The average *overall* economy-wide rate of profit is $150/$350 = 42.86%. How would prices have to change so that each sector realizes a 42.86% profit rate on the capital invested?

Sector I costs of production are $150. Profit must be 42.86% of that amount, or $64.28, not $50. The total mass of value produced in Sector I, calculated using this new profit rate, will be revalued as $150 + $64.28 = $214.28. This is slightly more than the previous $200. Applying the same reasoning to Sector II results in a profit of $85.72, or 42.86% of total investment ($100 + $100). The total mass of value produced, calculated using this new profit rate, must be revalued at $200 + $85.72 = $285.72. This is slightly less than the previous $300. The new equations are:

$$\text{Sector I} \qquad (\$100 + \$50)(1.4286) = \$214.28 \qquad\qquad (11.27)$$

$$\text{Sector II} \qquad (\$100 + \$100)(1.4286) = \$285.72$$

The total economy-wide mass of value produced is the same $500 (= $214.28 + $285.72). However, prices must change in order to redistribute some profit from Sector II to Sector I. We call the new prices that bring this about *prices of production*. Using Marx's terminology we say that direct prices are "transformed" into prices of production. This occurs because the organic composition of capital varies from industry to industry, causing prices to deviate from their labor values (or, direct prices). The prices of means of production (Sector I) increase by a multiple of 1.071 while the prices of means of subsistence decrease by a multiple of 0.952. These multipliers reflect the fact that Sector I firms must receive a higher price to push

Marxian and Sraffian theories of unequal exchange **277**

their profit rate up to the average rate, while Sector II firms must receive a lower price to push their profit rate down to the average rate. We label these multipliers λ where $\lambda_I = 1.071$ and $\lambda_{II} = .952$.

As a last step we note that this solution will change in the next period. This is because, using the newly calculated prices of production, the cost of means of production in both sectors will rise and the cost of means of subsistence in both sectors will fall. This will result in a new solution for the average rate of profit and for λ. These adjustments continue to occur, period after period, until a final solution emerges. To find this final solution we need to solve the following equations:

$$(\lambda_I C_I + \lambda_I V_I)(1 + r) = \lambda_I W_I \qquad (11.28)$$

$$(\lambda_{II} C_{II} + \lambda_{II} V_{II})(1 + r) = \lambda_{II} W_{II} \qquad (11.29)$$

$$\lambda_I W_I + \lambda_{II} W_{II} = W_I + W_{II} \qquad (11.30)$$

The values for λ are the final price multipliers which, when applied to the original direct prices, will redistribute surplus value so that each firm in each sector receives an average money profit rate. We designate that money rate of profit r. The third equation simply requires that the mass of value produced in both sectors remain the same in dollar terms. Using the hypothetical data from above, the final equilibrium equations are:[6]

$$(108.56 + 47.15)(1.3944) = 217.12 \qquad (11.31)$$

$$(108.56 + 94.29)(1.3944) = 282.88 \qquad (11.32)$$

where $\lambda_I = 1.086$ and $\lambda_{II} = 0.943$. We can confirm that the total output measured with the final equilibrium prices of production still equals \$500: $(1.086) (200) + (0.943)(300) = 500$.

From prices of production to market price

There is, of course, a third kind of price: *market price*. Supply and demand determine market prices. However, market prices will closely track the above production prices. If an increase in demand pushes up the market price, then profit rates rise. This attracts new firms and induces existing firms to produce more. As a result, market supply increases which drives the market price back down to where it was before. The same occurs if demand falls. In the long run, therefore, market demand is quite irrelevant as market prices tend to equal production prices which, in turn, are determined by labor costs of production.

Our model is still quite simple because it only describes simple reproduction. More complex models assume "expanded reproduction" where capitalists reinvest their surplus value in each successive period. This continuously changes the organic

278 Marxian and Sraffian theories of unequal exchange

composition of capital C/V, causing the equilibrium prices of production and rates of profit to change continuously as well. This is how Marx described pricing:

> Under capitalist production, the general law of value enforces itself merely as the prevailing tendency, in a very complicated and approximate manner, as a never ascertainable average of ceaseless fluctuations.
>
> *(Marx, 1909: 190)*

But the main ideas remain the same: only labor creates profit; prices change continuously to reflect technological differences in the economy; these price changes redistribute the surplus created as the profit rate equalizes across sectors. And profits follow a secular downward trend.

Notes

1 This is similar to Neoclassical theory where production functions define the amount of labor, L, used to produce a unit of output without distinguishing between the various kinds of labor actually used.
2 We can assume the monetary system consists of one-dollar gold coins, each of which requires one hour of labor to produce. For a fuller treatment of this idea see Shaikh (1980).
3 To be more precise, an increase in C or a decrease in V only means that the *value* of inputs changes and not necessarily the number of machines and workers employed.
4 Although labor produces all surplus value, capitalists will distribute some of it to other businesses not engaged in production, such as financial institutions. The latter do not produce anything and therefore do not create surplus value or profit. Surplus value therefore circulates among capitalists.
5 Most Post Keynesian models differ in that they assume workers spend all their income on consumption and capitalists spend all their income on investment.
6 The solution is not easy to find because it is nonlinear. For simplicity we omit the procedure used to determine the solution.

References

Marx, K. (1909). *Capital: A Critique of Political Economy. Vol. III: The Process of Capitalist Production as a Whole*. Frederick Engels (ed.) and Ernest Untermann (trans.). Chicago: Charles H. Kerr and Company.

Shaikh, A. (1980). "Foreign Trade and the Law of Value: Part II." *Science & Society, 44*(1), 27–57.

Appendix 11B

An overview of Sraffian economics

We start with a world of two nations, each in autarky. There are only two sectors, made up of iron makers and grain farmers, neither of which produces an economic surplus. This means the economy produces exactly enough iron and grain to replace the iron and grain used up in one year, and no more. We call such an economy a *subsistence economy*. Grain is an input into its own production (consumption for grain farmers and seed for further grain production) as well as an input into iron production (consumption for iron makers). Similarly, iron is an input into its own production (iron-making tools) and the production of grain (iron farm implements). Each producer acquires the inputs it needs from the other producer through some kind of social exchange mechanism that we do not specify here.

Let us assume the following hypothetical production system.[1] The total output produced of each commodity is just equal to the aggregate input requirements of both industries. Table 11.7 describes this system. The economy's survival depends on the continued reproduction of iron and grain in exactly the proportions described. If one sector falls short by not producing enough, then the entire system will begin to collapse.

We now focus on the iron–grain exchange. Iron makers must somehow exchange their 10 tons of iron output for 2 tons of the farmers' grain output. We call this 10:2 or 5:1 ratio the *relative price* of grain (P_g); 1 ton of grain must exchange for 5 tons of iron, so $P_g = 5$. Equivalently the relative price of iron (P_i) in terms of grain is .2; 1 ton of iron must exchange for .2 tons of grain, so $P_i = .2$. Supply and demand play no role in these calculations.

We can calculate the prices of iron and grain by solving the following two equations for the unknowns P_i and P_g:

$$13P_i + 2P_g = 23P_i \tag{11.33}$$

$$10P_i + 4P_g = 6P_g \tag{11.34}$$

Since we are only interested in *relative* and not *absolute* prices, we can arbitrarily set $P_i = 1$, which then allows us to calculate the relative price of grain as $P_g = 5$. Iron

TABLE 11.7 Simple reproduction (a subsistence economy)

	Production		*Total outputs*
Iron sector	13 tons iron + 2 tons grain	→	23 tons iron
Grain sector	10 tons iron + 4 tons grain	→	6 tons grain
Total inputs	23 tons iron 6 tons grain		

280 Marxian and Sraffian theories of unequal exchange

TABLE 11.8 A surplus-producing economy with labor

	Production			Total outputs
Iron sector	13 tons iron + 2 tons grain + 10 workers		→	27 tons iron
Grain sector	10 tons iron + 4 tons grain + 10 workers		→	12 tons grain
Total inputs	23 tons iron	6 tons grain	20 workers	

in this example is the *numeraire*.[2] It is the standard used to measure all other values, and the choice of a *numeraire* is arbitrary.

Now suppose that iron makers and grain farmers are able to produce a little more iron and grain than is minimally necessary for simple reproduction. In other words, we wish to describe a *surplus-producing economy*. We also explicitly introduce labor into the system and assume each sector uses exactly 10 workers. The new production equations appear in Table 11.8. Here, iron and grain output exceeds the minimum production requirements. While iron makers produce 27 tons of iron, only 23 are required, leaving a surplus of 4 tons. Also, while farmers produce 12 tons of grain, only 6 tons are required, leaving a surplus of 6 tons. What will happen to this surplus? Who will get it?

If this is a capitalist economy, the capitalist class owns all the capital, which in this case consists of all the iron and grain. Iron and grain are capital because each are *inputs* into the production process. We make no distinction between fixed capital and raw materials; all inputs are used up in one year. The working class, on the other hand, can survive only if the capitalist class agrees to turn over to them a portion of the surplus iron and grain output. This becomes their wage. Unlike Marx's labor theory of value, both profit and wage income are paid from the economic surplus, which is a residual after all production requirements are met. In Marx, only profit is a residual after wages are paid according to the customary standard of living.

How will the surplus be distributed between the two classes? One extreme is to give the entire surplus to the capitalists, in which case workers get nothing. The other extreme is to give the entire surplus to the workers, in which case capitalists get nothing. Neither of these extremes is viable because neither class can exist without a share of the surplus. The surplus must somehow be shared, and how it is shared will determine the prices of iron and grain. To see this, let us approach the problem in the following manner.

Suppose the iron capitalists advance the iron and grain capital needed to produce iron, and then hire workers to transform these inputs into iron output. Similarly, the grain capitalists advance the iron and grain capital needed to produce grain, and then hire workers to transform these inputs into grain output. Suppose, for computational convenience only, that capitalists in each sector hire 10 workers. Also suppose that iron and grain capitalists receive the same competitive rate of return of r% on the value of the capital they advance. As in the other models discussed above, the profit rate, r, is written as a percentage of the value of the capital invested. The

Marxian and Sraffian theories of unequal exchange **281**

TABLE 11.9 Equilibrium prices with alternative wage–profit distributions

Wage per worker w	Rate of profit $r\%$	Price of grain P_g	Price of iron P_i
0.92	0.00	2.40	1.00
0.74	0.10	2.42	1.00
0.56	0.20	2.44	1.00
0.37	0.30	2.46	1.00
0.19	0.40	2.48	1.00
0.00	0.50	2.50	1.00

iron and grain workers receive the same competitive wage rate, w, which is the per worker share of the surplus. Free mobility of capital and labor between sectors guarantees this result. The aggregate profit and wage income must add up to the total surplus produced.

We can write the equations describing this new system as follows:

$$(13P_i + 2P_g)(1 + r) + 10w = 27P_i \qquad (11.35)$$

$$(10P_i + 4P_g)(1 + r) + 10w = 12P_g \qquad (11.36)$$

In each industry, the monetary value of the output (the right-hand side of the equation) equals the total costs of production (the left-hand side of the equation). Those costs of production consist of three parts: (1) the money value of the capital that is advanced, $(13P_i + 2P_g)$ and $(10P_i + 4P_g)$; (2) the money value of the profits earned on that capital, or $(13P_i + 2P_g)(r)$ and $(10P_i + 4P_g)(r)$; and (3) the money value of workers' wages (the wage bill), or 10w in each sector where w is the uniform wage rate. Relative prices, P_i and P_g, must reach equilibrium values that ensure that each sector gets enough of the other sector's output and so that the uniform profit and wage rates can be paid. If these prices do not obtain, then the system breaks down.

Let us now calculate the values for P_i and P_g. Before we can calculate these solutions, however, we must first know how the two classes will distribute the economic surplus. Once they decide on a distribution, relative prices will gravitate toward the correct equilibrium values. In Equations (11.35) and (11.36) there are four unknown magnitudes: P_i, P_g, r and w, and only two equations. We get around this difficulty as follows. First assume that $P_i = 1$. This reduces the number of unknowns to three. Because there is no theory to tell us precisely how the two classes will distribute the surplus between profits r and wages w, let us choose several possible income distributions and see what the price of grain would have to be in order to make these distributions happen. We display the results in Table 11.9. Consider the two extreme cases shown in Table 11.9. The first extreme case is when workers receive nothing (the bottom row where w = 0) and capitalists receive the entire surplus. To make this happen, the relative prices will have to be $P_i = 1$ and $P_g = 2.5$. At these prices, the value of the entire economic surplus is $(4P_i + 6P_g) = 4(1) + 6(2.5) = 19$. Recall from Table 11.8 that the iron surplus is 4

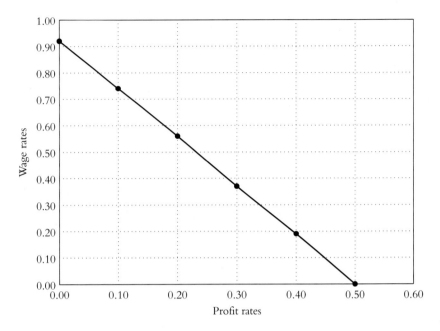

FIGURE 11.2 Wage and profit relation

tons (27 tons minus 23 tons), and the grain surplus is 6 tons (12 tons minus 6 tons). The entire surplus goes to the capitalists in this extreme scenario. At these prices the aggregate value of the combined capital advanced in both sectors is

$$(13P_i + 2P_g) + (10P_i + 4P_g) = (23P_i + 6P_g) = 23(1) + 6(2.5) = 38 \quad (11.37)$$

The rate of profit is expressed as a percentage of the capital invested or 19/38 = 50%. The other extreme case assumes workers get the entire surplus and capitalists get nothing, so the profit rate equals zero. This is described in the first row of Table 11.9. To accomplish this distribution, the iron-making sector must exchange iron for grain at a price of $P_g = 2.4$ and $P_i = 1$. In this case the value of the aggregate surplus $(4P_i + 6P_g)$ is $4(1) + 6(2.4) = 18.4$ which is then divided among 20 workers, 10 in each sector. The wage per person will then be 18.4/20 = .92, representing 100% of the surplus. Of course r = 0% in this scenario.

Varying r from 0% (the minimum profit rate) to 50% (the maximum profit rate) yields all the possible relative prices of grain shown in Table 11.9. When capitalists get a larger share of the surplus, their profit rate is higher and the workers' wage rate is lower, and vice versa. We show the negative relationship between w and r graphically in Figure 11.2.

Another way to view these relationships is to look at the percentage shares of the aggregate surplus that each social class receives. We do this in Table 11.10. The prices used to calculate the value of the aggregate physical surplus depend on the way we divide that surplus.

Marxian and Sraffian theories of unequal exchange **283**

TABLE 11.10 Percentage wage and profit shares

Value of aggregate surplus output	Profit share of surplus	Wage share of surplus
$(4P_i + 6P_g)$	(% of surplus)	
18.4	0	100.00
18.51	20.26	79.73
18.63	40.40	59.60
18.74	60.41	39.59
18.87	80.28	19.72
19.00	100.00	0

When capitalists get 100% of the surplus and workers get 0%, this translates into a 50% rate of return on capital. When workers get 100% of the surplus and capitalists get nothing, this translates into a wage rate of .92 per worker.[3]

This autarky model demonstrates a central principle: the distribution of income (i.e., surplus, or net national income) and technology determine the prices of commodities. Technology determines the input requirements, and some unspecified social conventions determine income distribution. When workers get higher wages, profits will suffer, and when capitalists get higher profits, wages will suffer. This conclusion is in line with Robinson and Kalecki.

Notes

1 This numerical example is borrowed from Braun (1984).
2 Note that the number "1" and the number "5" by themselves do not mean anything; it does not mean $1 and $5. Only the ratio of the two numbers means something. Thus, $P_g/Pi = 5/1 = 5$. We could have set $P_i = 3$ if we wished, in which case $P_g = 15$. Similarly, we could have set $P_g = 1$, in which case $P_i = .2$. Nothing would have changed in either case.
3 We could have allocated some of the surplus to other activities such as the production of consumer goods or public works, and it need not have been distributed as income to iron and grain capitalists and workers.

Reference

Braun, O. (1984). *International Trade and Imperialism*. Atlantic Highlands, NJ: Humanities Press.

12

GENDER AND FEMINIST TRADE THEORY

Introduction

In one way or another, everyone in the world is touched by international trade. However, trade affects men and women differently. Feminist trade theory tries to explain these gender differences.

To begin with, we define gender as a system of classification that separates men and women. This separation is based on social norms and customs. Society assigns to men and women specific traits, behaviors and pursuits that are considered acceptable and appropriate. These vary over time and place, and are only loosely connected to biological differences. Gender is, therefore, a social and not a biological construct. Moreover, it is also "a category of social and economic differentiation that influences the division of labor, and the distribution of work, income, wealth, productivity of inputs, and economic behavior of agents" (Grown, Elson, and Çagatay, 2000: 1147). Thus, the gender roles played by men and women ultimately determine how an economy functions.

The problem is that both orthodox and heterodox economics are mostly gender blind. They exclude women's experiences and perspectives from theoretical and empirical investigations and thus assume that men and women are identical as economic agents. This may have something to do with the fact that women have been under-represented on university faculties and in the pages of scholarly journals. Economic theory thus has been constructed by men, about men, in the ordinary business of the life of men. Women have disappeared into the black box called the household.

Things began to change in the 1960s and 1970s. Criticism of women's place in society and in the economy, together with widespread demands for justice and equal rights, became part of the 1960s revolution in social and cultural norms. This affected the economics profession as women began to demand representation, not only in the ranks of academia but also as subjects of economic analysis.[1] And they have met with considerable success. In 1972, for example, only 6% of economics faculty at all institutions were women. By 2014 that percentage rose to 15.4%. At universities with graduate PhD programs, women "quadrupled their representation amongst new PhDs to 32.9%, more than tripled their representation amongst assistant professors to almost 30%, increased their representation at the associate level more than six-fold to 23.5% and increased their representation at the full professor level five-fold to 12.1%" (The Committee on the Status of Women in the Economics Profession, 2015). Also, by the 1990s, there appeared a new professional organization (the International Association for Feminist Economics), a new scholarly journal (*Feminist Economics*), and countless books and articles in which gender is the central subject.[2]

Today, Feminist economics is a relatively new genre of scholarship that has established a legitimate presence in the economics discipline. Part of this genre is Feminist trade theory, the subject of this chapter. The overarching goal of Feminist trade theory is to figure out how world trade patterns (i.e., the volume, composition and direction of trade) affect, and are affected by, gender relations. A related goal is to answer the question of how Neoliberal trade policies (i.e., trade liberalization, trade expansion, trade openness, etc.) affect gender inequality and women's welfare. These are difficult goals to attain because gender relations are deeply embedded in economic, social, political and cultural life and are incredibly complex and difficult to unravel.

Gender relations and gender inequality also have assumed a central place on the research agendas of major international organizations. Initiatives taken in the past two decades by the United Nations, World Bank, International Labour Office and others have brought gender equality and empowerment issues to the forefront. In this sense, one might say that gender has become "mainstreamed." Despite these developments, much work still remains to be done to eliminate the masculinist orientation that continues to hold sway in the economics discipline and that continues to mute women's voices.

This chapter proceeds as follows. The next two sections define the connection between trade and gender. One section explores how gender affects competitive advantage. The key factor in this section is the role played by the unit costs of male and female labor. The other section describes the structural context of the trade–gender linkage. That context is what we might call the economic medium through which changes in trade relations affect, and are affected by, changes in gender relations. The section that follows describes global gender gaps in employment and earnings.

The chapter thus far sets the contextual background for a more detailed consideration of Feminist trade theory. We begin by examining how orthodox trade theory deals with gender. The work of Gary Becker has been instrumental in establishing the groundwork. We then proceed to an examination of heterodox Feminist trade theories. There we sample three models that address specific issues concerning gender and international trade. We end the chapter with some concluding thoughts.

The trade–gender connection: competitive advantage

Underlying international trade is the struggle among firms to gain a competitive advantage. Competitive advantage is the ability to sell a product at a lower price (and/or superior quality) than competing firms. It boils down to who can produce a good at the lowest unit cost. Gender relations influence the competitive advantage of firms by affecting male and female unit labor costs. The extent of this influence depends, of course, on how much male and female labor firms use.

Competitive advantage, or absolute advantage, is not the same as the more traditional comparative advantage. Comparative advantage is calculated on the basis of opportunity costs; competitive advantage is calculated on the basis of actual or absolute costs. A nation's resource endowments determines comparative advantage and shows why nations specialize in particular industries. Input prices and firms' competitive strategies determine competitive advantage. Competitive advantage, it is argued, is better suited than comparative advantage in dealing with gender disparities in particular countries and in particular industries.

Men and women worldwide rarely have the same employment opportunities. Nor do they earn the same wages, even if they work in the same occupations and have the same levels of education and skills. These disparities are due mainly to gender discrimination and the occupational segregation of women in the labor force. These practices are deeply rooted in cultural norms and in the distribution of power between men and women in society. One manifestation of these gender biases is that firms wishing to protect or enhance their competitive positions have an incentive to prevent women (and men) from improving their economic positions and pushing up unit costs. This is especially relevant in female-labor-intensive, export-oriented industries.

It follows from this that lying beneath the struggle for competitive advantage in international trade are national struggles between men and women over wages, employment, work conditions and social and political power.

The trade–gender connection: structural context

Feminist trade theories explain how trade relations interrelate with gender relations. In particular, these theories ask questions such as, do changes in the volume, composition and/or direction of trade improve or worsen gender disparities? Does globalization, trade liberalization and openness diminish or exacerbate employment and earnings gaps between men and women?

Before we explore these theories, however, we first need to outline the assumptions that Feminist economists make about the *structural context* to which trade theories apply. Structural context refers to the general economic environment in which men and women live, work and earn income. It includes economic and financial institutions, incentive structures, industrial structures, legal and political frameworks, educational systems, and, of course, social customs and traditions. Men and women in different countries participate in all of these in different proportions.

Gender and Feminist trade theory **287**

This means that any changes that might occur in either trade patterns or in gender relations will have different economic effects on men and women and on the macro economy.

To simplify matters, we will define the structural context of an economy to include: (1) its stage of economic development; (2) its division into market and non-market activities; and (3) its division of production into industrial, agricultural and service sectors.

Stages of economic development

There are many ways to classify nations. How we do this depends on what we intend to accomplish. A common way of doing this is to divide nations into three basic categories: industrially advanced, post-communist and post-colonial. This three-part classification is convenient in describing historical political-economic developments in the 20th century. The Feminist trade literature, however, uses a different classification system, one often found in development economics. These categories are: industrially advanced, semi-industrialized and pre-industrial (or agrarian).[3]

Industrially advanced nations have high per capita incomes, relatively low poverty rates, high levels of education and life expectancy, well-developed infrastructures and access to clean water and health resources. Their exports include capital-intensive manufactured goods that use the most advanced technologies. Semi-industrial economies lack most of the amenities and advantages of rich nations. Their export industries are less technologically advanced and use more labor-intensive production techniques. Pre-industrial and agrarian economies are lower down on the development scale. They specialize in and export cash crops and primary goods (e.g., mining and forestry products).

The economic status of women in each of these groups of nations differs considerably. One way of measuring this is the Gender Inequality Index (GII) produced annually by the United Nations Development Programme (United Nations Development Programme, 2014). This index is a composite that measures gender inequality along three dimensions: (1) reproductive health; (2) empowerment; and (3) labor markets. The index ranges between 0 and 1.0, where the higher the number, the higher the degree of inequality.

Figure 12.1 shows the average GII for six regions of the world. We can assume that Europe and Central Asia, and East Asia and the Pacific, belong to the industrially advanced category; that Latin America and the Caribbean and South Asia belong to the semi-industrial category; and that sub-Saharan Africa and the Arab States belong to the agrarian and pre-industrial categories. These are only rough approximations, however. Judging from the figure, it appears that the lower the level of economic development, the higher the degree of gender inequality.

The importance of dividing the world into categories such as these is that the gender effects of trade differ depending on who is trading with whom. Thus, trade among industrially advanced economies has different characteristics and poses

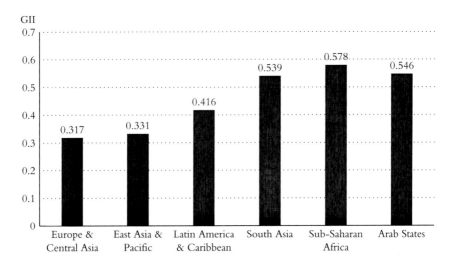

FIGURE 12.1 Gender Inequality Index
Source: United Nations Development Programme, 2014

different gender issues than trade among industrially advanced and developing nations or trade among developing countries. Therefore, any theory that explains trade–gender relations must specify the kinds of economies the theory is dealing with. A one-size-fits-all theory that propounds universal principles can explain very little.

Formal, informal and non-market sectors

Another aspect of the structural context of an economy is its division into market and non-market sectors. Market sectors are those in which exchanges of labor and commodities are influenced by supply and demand and in which all transactions consist of monetary payments. We will consider two kinds of market sectors, formal and informal. Non-market sectors are those in which transactions are not based on rational supply and demand calculations and in which work is unpaid. Each nation differs in terms of the relative size and importance of each of these sectors.

Formal market sector employment

Firms in the formal market sector function within a legal framework of taxation and business and labor regulations. They engage in commercial monetary transactions and abide by generally accepted rules of competition. Firms also tend to use technologies that are more advanced than those used elsewhere in the economy and therefore require workers to have relatively more advanced skills. The labor force is structured and disciplined and there is a measure of job security and government protections not found elsewhere in the economy. As a result, wages are higher, working conditions are better and employment is more stable. For these reasons, jobs in the formal sector are highly valued and workers here belong to the nation's labor elite. To put it simply, this is where the good jobs are.[4]

How accessible are these good jobs to women? What kinds of barriers exclude women? The ease with which women qualify for the good jobs depends on their access to education and training. It also depends on the cultural obstacles and societal expectations that exclude women from particular industries and that channel them away from the formal sector into the informal sector. The evidence suggests that countries where female employment rates are the highest also tend to have a smaller share of women working in the formal sector (World Bank, 2010). It also suggests that women are segregated into informal market sectors where pay is low and hours are long. The lower the stage of development, the greater this trend seems to be.

Informal market sector employment

Firms in the informal sector respond to market forces and compete on the basis of unit costs just as do firms in the formal market. However, firms are smaller in size and production is more labor intensive. Most jobs in this sector are unskilled and low paid, with little or no benefits, job security or formal government protections.[5] Work is irregular, often temporary, and workers are directly exposed to the risks of cyclical instability and suffer from recurrent periods of unemployment. Examples of informal market employment are "own-account workers" (e.g., waste pickers, street vendors), temporary wage laborers, paid domestic workers (e.g., maids, cooks) and paid home-based workers who take in work for businesses, typically on a piece-rate basis. Once again, to put it simply, this is where the bad jobs are.

As suggested above, women tend to be segregated into these informal jobs by social and cultural forces. Labor markets are "segmented" in the sense that women have little ability to cross over from the bad-job market to the good-job market. Informal non-agricultural employment accounts for 50% to 67% of total employment globally and is more prevalent in developing countries. Women also account for the largest share of total informal employment (ILO, 2013).

Non-market household sector employment

Household production consists of unpaid (or underpaid) labor such as family domestic services (e.g., food preparation and cleaning); subsistence farming; child rearing and nurturing; care-giving services for the sick and elderly; and volunteer services to non-government organizations, churches and other households (Levy Economics Institute, 2005). Most of this kind of labor takes place entirely within the household—and hence outside the marketplace. Market forces play no direct role in organizing household activities.

Household production is vital to the functioning of an economy. It frees up time for family members to participate in the formal and informal market

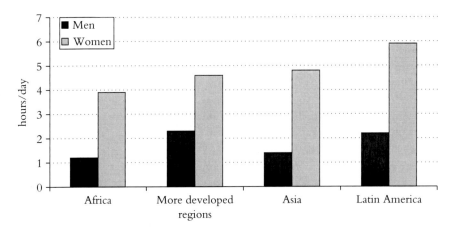

FIGURE 12.2 Time spent on domestic work
Source: United Nations, 2010: 100

sectors. And it provides subsistence for those who work outside the home. This is why many refer to household production as "social reproduction" or "social provisioning."[6]

Another way of looking at unpaid household labor is that it lowers unit labor costs because firms do not pay for the full subsistence costs of workers. Because of this, profits are higher than what they otherwise would be if firms paid living wages. Unpaid labor is therefore an indirect subsidy from households to businesses.

Because of prevailing cultural views of what constitutes proper male and female roles, household production is the domain of women. For example, time use studies indicate that women allocate twice as much time to household work as do men, and four times as much time to childcare (Duflo, 2012). Figure 12.2 shows the average time men and women spend on domestic work.

How valuable is household production to an economy? Estimating the contribution of household production to national output, and to general economic well-being, is hard to do because of the difficulty of imputing the value of household labor. However, in one study of a sample of 27 countries, Ahmad and Koh (2011) calculated that the value of non-market household labor as a percentage of GDP ranges between 30% and 70%.

Industry, agriculture and service sectors

Another way of slicing up an economy is to classify sectors according to types of output: industry, agriculture and services.[7] Women participate in different proportions in each of these sectors, depending on an economy's stage of economic development.

Worldwide, about 1/3 of women are employed in agriculture, 1/6 in industry and 1/2 in services. However, gender shares have changed since the early 1990s.

Whereas the global share of women working in industry has remained fairly constant, in industrially advanced countries the share has been cut in half as women have migrated into the service sector. And in semi-industrial and pre-industrial countries (except for East Asia) there has been a shift in female employment from agriculture to services.

Agriculture is still the most important source of income and employment for women in the developing world. In semi-industrial and pre-industrial countries, 2/3 of the female labor force is engaged in agricultural activities. Most are rural small farmers who produce food either for household consumption or for sale in local farmers' markets. Commercial and industrial agriculture, on the other hand, consists of large-scale farming. Crops are cash crops that are either exported or destined for further processing. Statistically, this is the domain of men, while small-scale farming is the domain of women (FAO, 2011).

Global gender gaps in employment and earnings

Gender disparities appear as employment and earnings gaps. These gaps vary by geographical region and by sector. In some places, women fare quite well relative to men, while in other places they suffer from systematic discrimination and acute inequality.

Employment and unemployment

Globally, the evidence suggests that the share of women in paid employment has increased substantially in the last two decades. On the other side of the coin, however, the evidence also suggests that paid work has become increasingly irregular, temporary and exposed to economic and financial cycles. Many have called this twin character of employment the "feminization of the labor force." In other words, paid work has become more like women's work.

One indicator of how women are integrated into an economy is the gender–employment ratio. This is calculated by dividing the female share of total employment by the male share in agriculture, industry and services. Ratios greater than 1.0 indicate that proportionally more women are working than men. Table 12.1 shows these ratios for a number of regions of the world for the years 1992 and 2012. With few exceptions, the gender–employment ratio in agriculture and industry has decreased during this 20-year period and increased in services. This suggests a worldwide shift in female employment into services.

Of course not all women in the labor force are employed. Figure 12.3 shows female and male unemployment rates for each of the same regions. Discrepancies between men and women are modest in most places with women having a slight advantage (i.e., lower unemployment rates) in developed economies and in East Asia, and a slight disadvantage elsewhere in Asia and sub-Saharan Africa. Female unemployment rates are substantially higher for women in the Middle East and North Africa.

TABLE 12.1 Gender–employment ratios by sector

	Agriculture		Industry		Services	
	1992	2012	1992	2012	1992	2012
WORLD	1.18	1.11	0.64	0.63	1.04	1.15
Developed economies & European Union	0.82	0.67	0.49	0.34	1.39	1.35
Central & South-Eastern Europe (non-EU) & CIS	0.90	1.07	0.61	0.55	1.37	1.29
East Asia	1.38	1.23	0.70	0.79	0.61	0.98
Southeast Asia & the Pacific	1.06	1.04	0.76	0.72	1.00	1.11
South Asia	1.37	1.56	0.70	0.67	0.42	0.48
Latin America & the Caribbean	0.56	0.43	0.53	0.48	1.57	1.51
Middle East	1.71	2.16	0.43	0.46	1.00	0.98
North Africa	1.17	1.07	0.54	0.46	1.08	1.24
Sub-Saharan Africa	1.10	1.01	0.54	0.60	0.94	1.13

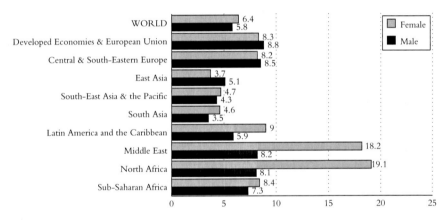

FIGURE 12.3 Male and female unemployment rates
Source: ILO, 2012: 51

Female labor force participation rates

Another dimension of the female employment experience is the female labor force participation rate (FLFPR). This is a measure of the proportion of a country's female working-age population that is working and/or looking for work.

Figure 12.4 shows how these rates vary globally. Over the past three decades the FLFPR has increased everywhere except in East Asia and the Pacific and Europe and Europe Asia. The FLFPR varies from a low of 26% in the Middle East and North Africa to a high of 64% in East Asia and the Pacific. Worldwide, the gap between the male and female participation rates has narrowed: female rates have risen from 50% to 52% while male rates have fallen from 82% to 78%. But the female–male gender gap remains high in most places.

Gender and Feminist trade theory 293

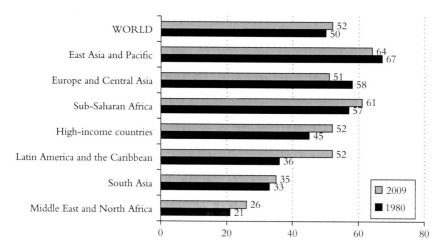

FIGURE 12.4 Female labor force participation rates
Source: ILO, 2012: 56

The FLFPR also varies with per capita income. For developing economies with low per capita income there tends to be a high FLFPR. As household incomes rise, women can afford to withdraw from the market in favor of non-market household production and so the FLFPR drops. Then, as income levels rise further, the FLFPR rises again as women gain access to better education, have lower fertility rates and can afford labor-saving household technologies.

Finally, participation rates vary by sector. From Table 12.2 we can see that, worldwide, women participate relatively more than men in agriculture and services, while men participate relatively more in industry. The female–male gap is largest in Latin America and the Caribbean with a gap of 26.2% in services and in South Asian agriculture where the gap is 24.6%. Male and female employment are fairly equal in agriculture in sub-Saharan Africa.

Wage and earnings gaps

For 40 years, from the 1960s to 2000, gender pay differentials around the world have narrowed significantly. But, after 2000, improvements in pay gaps have levelled off (Tijdens and Van Klaveren, 2012). Data on wage gaps are difficult to obtain, however, because in many countries women work in informal markets where information on female earnings is not collected.

To be sure, gender pay gaps persist. Women are paid less than men just about everywhere in the world, even if we take education and productivity into account. Women in most countries earn from 60% to 75% of men's wages. Reasons for this include the fact that women are more likely than men to engage in low-productivity activities and to work in the informal sector. They are thus less likely to benefit from legal protections and to belong to labor organizations.

Gender, orthodox economics and international trade theory

Neoclassical trade theory asserts that free trade promotes economic efficiency and hence economic growth and development. The theory admits that a move toward free trade—trade liberalization—creates winners and losers. But according to this theory a net gain would still result because the winners could compensate the losers. Accordingly, free trade is always "welfare enhancing." But women appear nowhere in this standard model. The presumption is that if increasing openness improves men's welfare, then it would equally improve women's welfare.

To their credit, orthodox economists have not remained silent about the omission of gender. There have been three main avenues of research that explicitly include gender, each with implications for international trade theory. One avenue follows the path laid out by Nobel Laureate Gary Becker (1930–2014), whose theories of the family, developed in the 1960s, suggest how economists might analyze the trade–gender linkage. The second is the theory of discrimination, which follows some of Becker's other works and which predicts that trade liberalization would reduce gender discrimination and inequality. The third avenue of research is the application of the standard Neoclassical trade theorems to the study of global gender inequality. We consider these in turn.

Becker's theory of the household and trade liberalization

Before Becker came onto the scene, the household was little more than a "black box" in a circular flow diagram. Unlike the "firm," for which an extensive microeconomic theory already existed, no one had looked inside this black box. What Becker did was to create a new microeconomic framework with which to study this previously neglected institution (Becker, 1991). His work included such topics as discrimination, marriage, fertility, the demand for children, education and human capital formation, the allocation of time and crime—all topics normally deferred to sociologists.

In Becker's theory, the household, or the family (we will use the terms interchangeably), purchases inputs in the formal and informal marketplace (e.g., food items, transportation, cleaning products, etc.) and then allocates these inputs to various productive household activities (e.g., preparing and consuming food, child rearing, educating, caring, home maintenance, leisure). Family members pool their incomes, which the husband then distributes based on his altruism. To model altruism, Becker assumes that the husband derives utility from an increase in the wife's utility. The wife, therefore, benefits from her husband's largesse. Thus, inside the family altruism prevails. Outside the family, in the marketplace, selfishness prevails. In addition, rational, utility-maximizing behavior of course plays a central role everywhere, inside and outside the family.

Each family member responds to monetary and non-monetary incentives when deciding how to use his or her time, labor and income. Family decisions then lead to an equilibrium, constrained by income and time, in which family resources

Gender and Feminist trade theory **295**

TABLE 12.2 Gender participation rates by sector, 2012

	Agriculture			Industry			Services		
	Male	Female	Gap	Male	Female	Gap	Male	Female	Gap
WORLD	32.80	36.40	1.11	25.90	16.20	0.63	41.30	47.40	1.15
Developed economies & European Union	4.50	3.00	0.67	31.30	10.60	0.34	64.20	86.40	1.35
Central & South-Eastern Europe (non-EU) & CIS	19.00	20.30	1.07	33.30	18.30	0.55	47.70	61.40	1.29
East Asia	31.80	39.00	1.23	31.40	24.80	0.79	36.80	36.20	0.98
Southeast Asia & the Pacific	42.30	44.20	1.04	21.00	15.10	0.72	36.70	40.70	1.11
South Asia	44.30	68.90	1.56	23.10	15.40	0.67	32.60	15.80	0.48
Latin America & the Caribbean	20.70	9.00	0.43	27.70	13.30	0.48	51.50	77.70	1.51
Middle East	14.00	30.30	2.16	28.10	13.00	0.46	57.90	56.70	0.98
North Africa	29.80	31.80	1.07	24.50	11.20	0.46	45.80	57.00	1.24
Sub-Saharan Africa	61.80	62.50	1.01	10.50	6.30	0.60	27.70	31.20	1.13

Source: ILO, 2012

are optimally allocated to family productive activities. This equilibrium implies a division of household labor between paid and unpaid work. Paid work involves labor performed in the market sector (formal and informal) outside the household. Unpaid work involves labor done within the household sector. This division of labor is "gendered" in the sense that men typically predominate in paid labor while women predominate in unpaid labor.[8]

We turn now to the question of how trade liberalization affects women's welfare. The household is the intervening institution through which changes in trade patterns affect the macro economy and hence the welfare of women and men. Specifically, any change in a nation's trade orientation alters employment opportunities and the structure of incentives for paid and unpaid labor. These in turn influence household allocative decisions and lead to new family equilibria. We would then witness changes in male and female labor force participation rates, employment and unemployment rates and wage rates. Trade liberalization, therefore, would have allocative and distributive consequences for families and hence for men and women.

In regions and sectors where men and women participate equally in the labor force, the effect of trade liberalization would likely affect men and women equally. This might be the case in sub-Saharan agrarian economies where the male participation rate is 61.8% and the female rate is 62.5% (see Table 12.2). If nations in this region specialize in the export of agricultural goods, then we might expect trade

296 Gender and Feminist trade theory

expansion to benefit men and women equally. In South Asia, however, the gap between male (44.4%) and female (68.9%) labor force participation rates is large. We might predict that women in this region would benefit more than men. In developed economies, on the other hand, both male and female participation rates in agriculture are very small—despite the fact that men experience a slight advantage. The effect of trade liberalization would be negligible here.

The situation is quite different in manufacturing industries, where the gender gap is larger for men in all regions of the world. The gender effects of trade expansion in advanced economies that export mostly advanced manufactured goods would likely be different than semi-industrialized economies that export less advanced manufactured goods.

Against the gender effects of export expansion we would need to calculate the offsetting gender effects on income and employment in import-substituting sectors that lose their protections due to trade liberalization. Reductions in trade protections, for example, expose domestic industries to more foreign competition, which can have deleterious effects on women.

In the end, the effect on women of trade liberalization and openness depends on the kind of commodities produced, the technologies used, the skills required and the degree to which women have access to these skills. In Neoclassical economics, these effects work through the medium of the family. In other words, it depends on the structural context of the economy in question. And, to complicate matters further, even if trade liberalization favorably affects women's employment and income, it may simultaneously squeeze the resources available for the provision of care and other unpaid family activities. We will revisit this issue later in this chapter.

Becker on gender discrimination, competition and trade liberalization

Changes in trade patterns, we know, affect men and women differently. But these differences are not due to any physical or biological differences. They are instead the consequence of discrimination in the way people and institutions deal with men and women.

Becker and others have argued that gender discrimination would not exist in perfectly competitive capitalist economies. Further, trade liberalization would alleviate, if not eliminate, such discrimination. Thus, global capitalism and free trade cannot be blamed for prejudice against women. To the contrary, discrimination is fundamentally irrational and the "adverse fate" of women is chiefly due to market imperfections or to cultural factors about which we can do nothing.

According to these economists, people have, in varying degrees, a taste for gender discrimination. These tastes are built into individual preferences. In the absence of any external pressures, employers would act on their preferences and discount the economic value of women. However, as men refuse to hire women, women's wages fall and men's wages rise. Firms will have higher labor costs and lower profits. But this situation creates opportunities for other entrepreneurs to enter the labor market and to hire women at below-market wages. With competition,

Gender and Feminist trade theory **297**

firms could reduce labor costs by hiring women, thereby increasing profits. Female wages will eventually rise until all gender-based wage disparities disappear—despite any preference or taste for discrimination. Only if women are excluded from the labor market by institutional barriers can discrimination persist.

Free enterprise and competition would therefore eliminate the practice of, if not the desire for, gender discrimination and lead to gender equality in pay and employment. It would not matter if firms refusing to discriminate do so because they are simply enlightened or because they value higher profits more than the disutility of employing women. The result—gender equality—is the same.

Applying these ideas to international economics suggests that increased competition through trade liberalization would lead to gender equality in terms of male and female wages and employment. Discrimination is costly in competitive market economies where market forces drive down profit margins. As a result, gender wage and employment gaps would diminish. Once again, free trade always improves well-being. And globalization is good for women.

All in all, research has shown that the effects on women of Neoliberal trade policies is ambiguous and the effects of these policies do not readily agree with Neoclassical predictions.

Gender, Neoclassical trade theorems and trade liberalization

In Chapter 4 we assumed two nations, A-Land and B-Land, each producing two tradable commodities, computers and wheat. There are two inputs, capital and labor. In A-Land, the price of capital, r, is relatively low because it is relatively abundant, and the price of labor, w, is relatively high because it is relatively scarce. The opposite is true in B-Land. Also, computer production is capital intensive, while wheat production is labor intensive. In autarky, computers in A-Land are cheap compared to wheat while in B-Land wheat is cheap compared to computers. Formally, $P_C^A/P_W^A < P_C^B/P_W^B$ and $r^A/w^A < r^B/w^B$.

According to the Heckscher-Ohlin theorem, a nation will have a comparative advantage in the production of those commodities that use the abundant (i.e., cheap) factors most intensively, and will export those commodities. This means A-Land has a comparative advantage in computers and B-Land has a comparative advantage in wheat. A-Land will specialize in and export computers to B-Land, lowering computer prices there. B-Land will specialize in and export wheat to A-Land, lowering the price of wheat there. This causes P_C^A/P_W^A to rise (because the denominator falls), and P_C^B/P_W^B to fall (because the numerator falls). The final terms of trade equilibrium falls somewhere between the two extremes.

The Stolper-Samuelson theorem states that a rise in the relative price of a good will cause a rise in the price of that factor of production used most intensively in the production of that good, and a fall in the other factor of production. Thus, when trade causes the relative price of computers to rise in A-Land, owners of capital benefit since computer production is capital intensive. Workers lose; wages would fall as they are less able to gain employment in the capital-intensive computer

298 Gender and Feminist trade theory

industry. In A-Land, the functional distribution of income between capital and labor shifts in favor of capital. The opposite holds true in B-Land as the relative price of wheat increases. The functional distribution of income changes in favor of labor.

Samuelson's factor–price equalization theorem states that free trade eliminates global differences in factor prices. In the above example, the return to capital equalizes globally as it rises in A-Land and falls in B-Land. Global wage differentials equalize as well because wages fall in A-Land fall and rise in B-Land. Therefore, free trade leads to the international equalization of factor prices. Capitalists around the world get the same return on their capital, and workers around the world get paid the same wage rate.

Now suppose A-Land is a rich developed country and B-Land is a poor developing country. According to the Stolper-Samuelson theorem, trade liberalization changes the distribution of income in the poor developing country in favor of labor; income inequality diminishes. According to the factor–price equalization theorem, wage rates rise in the poor developing nation to match wage rates in the rich developed country. Global wage differentials disappear. From the perspective of the developing nation, the prospects of trade liberalization are rosy indeed.

But how would these changes affect women? Let us focus on women in developing nations. This has been a major concern of Feminist trade theory.

First, if labor is homogenous, which the Neoclassical model assumes it is, then there is no difference between men and women. Both would equally benefit from rising employment and rising incomes as a result of trade liberalization. However, if the labor force is made up predominantly of men, then women would benefit from trade expansion only to the extent that men, Becker-like, altruistically share their rising incomes with women.

Second, suppose the two factors of production are skilled and unskilled labor. If we replace the capital input with skilled labor, and the labor input with unskilled labor, the theorems would predict the following. According to Stolper-Samuelson, trade liberalization benefits skilled labor in rich A-Land since computer production is intensive in the use of skilled labor. Wages of skilled labor rise and wages of unskilled labor fall; the distribution of income shifts in favor of skilled labor. In poor B-Land, the opposite holds true: the distribution of income changes in favor of unskilled labor.

According to the factor–price equalization theorem, trade liberalization eliminates global differences in factor prices. Thus, in the above example, the wages of skilled labor rises and unskilled labor falls in rich A-Land, while the wages of skilled labor falls and unskilled labor rises in poor B-Land. Therefore, trade liberalization leads to a reduction in global wage differentials for skilled labor and unskilled labor.

To the extent that women occupy mainly unskilled occupations, how would they be affected by trade liberalization in developing nations? Based on the Neoclassical predictions, women would benefit as their employment opportunities expand and their wages rise. Trade liberalization, therefore, would bring about greater gender equality in developing countries. The opposite would occur in developed countries where gender inequality rises—unless, of course, women have greater employment opportunities in skilled professions.

Some Feminist critiques of orthodoxy[9]

For many reasons, Feminist economists are critical of the orthodoxy. First, the latter pays little attention to the different structural contexts that exist around the world. The experiences of women are diverse and cannot be aptly summarized by a one-size-fits-all theory that presumes universal applicability.

Second, Feminist economists charge that orthodox trade theory is androcentric. Androcentric means that the theory is centered on male experiences and points of view and excludes those of women. This hinders our ability to build a robust, "gendered" theory of international trade.

Third, the notion that actors are always and everywhere rational maximizers leaves out important non-rational motives and behaviors that many associate with the "feminine domain." Examples are altruism, love, sympathy, emotion, caring and nurturing.[10] In the female domain, women engage in communities and families where economic interactions are chiefly non-market *and* non-rational. Traditional optimization techniques are of little use in analyzing this feminine domain.

Fourth, orthodox models of the family stereotype gender roles by designating men as dominant husbands. This glosses over the subservient, second-class position in which women often find themselves. It reflects a privileged male world view which casts men as productive agents and women as non-productive agents who play only supportive roles in the economy.

Heterodox Feminist theories of international trade

Feminist theories of international trade are by definition heterodox. The main reason is that, in order to make gender relations visible, we need to include in our models economic behaviors and activities that the standard orthodox model cannot handle. Altruism, caring, unpaid work, non-market economic relations and the like are beyond the reach of the narrow and restrictive rational economic man doctrine that is the foundation of orthodoxy. Instead, we must look to Institutionalist, Post Keynesian, Sraffian, Kaleckian and Marxian economic theories to supply us with the theoretical tools needed to deal with gender. Elements of Neoclassical microeconomic theory that do not rely on the rationality assumption are often useful as well, as we shall see. Perhaps the maxim "Whatever works" applies here.

Another reason Feminist trade models are heterodox is that, unlike the orthodoxy, they are thematic rather than universally applicable. By thematic we mean that these trade models deal with particular questions and situations pertaining to particular countries, regions and institutions. They shy away from building general models that apply to everyone, always and everywhere.

Because of the wide variety of Feminist trade models, we can only offer a small sample in this chapter.[11] We therefore select three formal Feminist trade models

300 Gender and Feminist trade theory

that incorporate elements of various heterodox traditions.[12] The first, by Osterreich (2007), has a decidedly Sraffian quality. It explores the question of how a reduction in the economy-wide gender–wage gap in a developing nation in the South affects the nation's terms of trade with the developed North.[13] The second model, by Darity (2007), analyzes the effect of export promotion policies on women's wages and women's welfare. The model assumes an agrarian economy that exports cash crops. The third model, by Blecker and Seguino (2007), examines a semi-industrial economy that exports light industrial consumer goods. It looks at how a rise in female wages relative to male wages affects the distribution of income between men and women and between workers and capitalists.

Generally speaking, these models ask whether trade liberalization and trade expansion increase or decrease gender inequality in trading nations. They divide the subject into two parts: how gender inequality affects trade, and how trade affects gender inequality. They also make different assumptions about male–female labor requirements in exporting sectors and about wage and employment gender gaps. The object of these models is to make gender relations transparent and to explain how trade and trade policies affect these gender gaps.

North–South trade: a Sraffian approach

This model assumes that a Southern country specializes in and exports to the North manufactured goods requiring less advanced technologies. The export price is P_1. The North specializes in and exports to the South manufactured goods using advanced technologies. The export price is P_2. Export production in each nation uses as inputs the nation's own manufactured goods plus the imported manufactured goods from the other nation. The terms of trade can then be defined as P_1/P_2. We use a set of Sraffa-like production equations to represent trade:[14]

$$P_1 = w^S l_1^S + (1 + r^S)(P_1 a_{11}^S + P_2 a_{21}^S)$$

$$P_2 = w^N l_2^N + (1 + r^N)(P_1 a_{12}^N + P_2 a_{22}^N) \qquad (12.1)$$

where each equation represents production in the export sector. The general economy-wide wage rates are w^S and w^N and the prevailing rate of profit is r^S and r^N. The variables l and a are the unit labor and capital requirements, respectively. Each equation says that the price of the exported product is composed of the wage bill (wl), the costs of capital ($P_1 a_{1i} + P_2 a_{2i}$) for i = 1 and 2; and the rate of return on capital (r times the total capital employed in each sector).

Note that there are two equations and six unknowns: P_1, P_2, w^S, w^N, r^S, r^N. We can reduce the number of unknowns as follows. First, assume the world profit rate equalizes so that $r^S = r^N = r$. We now have only one profit rate variable, r. Second, make the first commodity the *numeraire*. This means that the prices of all other commodities are expressed in terms of this commodity so that $P_1 = 1$. Third, we assume w^S and w^N are exogenous; we treat them as constants and can give them any

Gender and Feminist trade theory **301**

values we choose. We are now left with only two unknowns, r and $P(P = P_2/P_1)$ and two equations. Because the number of equations now matches the number of unknowns, an equilibrium solution exists.

We can obtain the terms of trade by dividing the first equation in (12.1) by the second:

$$P = \frac{P_1}{P_2} = \frac{w^S l_1^S}{w^N l_2^N} + \frac{(1 + r)(P_1 a_{11}^S + P_2 a_{21}^S)}{(1 + r)(P_1 a_{12}^N + P_2 a_{22}^N)} = \frac{w^S l_1^S}{w^N l_2^N} + \frac{(P_1 a_{11}^S + P_2 a_{21}^S)}{(P_1 a_{12}^N + P_2 a_{22}^N)} \quad (12.2)$$

We can simplify this equation by writing it in functional form:

$$P = f(w^S, w^N, l^S, l^N, \mathbf{A}) \quad (12.3)$$

where $\mathbf{A} = \begin{bmatrix} a_{11} & a_{12} \\ a_{21} & a_{22} \end{bmatrix}$ is a square matrix that represents capital requirements. This equation says that wage rates, labor requirements (or productivity) and capital requirements determine the terms of trade, P.

At this point in the model we introduce gender wage gaps. We do this by assuming men and women in each region receive different wage rates, w^f and w^m. Gender discrimination is then the ratio w^f/w^m. We can now write (12.3) as:

$$P = f\left(\left(\frac{w^f}{w^m}\right)^S, \left(\frac{w^f}{w^m}\right)^N, l^S, l^N, \mathbf{A} \right) \quad (12.4)$$

The w^f/w^m ratios represents gender discrimination in each nation. We can take this a step further by focusing on *relative* magnitudes, i.e., the gender wage gap in the South relative to that of the North and labor productivity in the South relative to that of the North. Equation (12.4) now becomes:

$$P = f\left(\frac{(w^f/w^m)^S}{(w^f/w^m)^N}, l^S/l^N, \mathbf{A} \right) \quad (12.5)$$

Empirical research by Osterreich (2007) shows that, based on a sample of North and South nations, when the gender wage gap in the South decreases (i.e., women in the South are better off), the manufacturing terms of trade also improve for the South. In other words, P_1 rises relative to P_2, implying that everyone in the South benefits when the economic position of women in that country improves.[15]

Trade in a pre-industrial agrarian economy: a Feminist-Neoclassical approach

This model describes trade with an agrarian economy that exports cash crops. Here, men work only in the cash crop export sector; they work neither in the domestic sector nor in the social reproduction sector. Women, on the other hand, work in all sectors. The model applies basic Neoclassical microeconomics. What makes

302 Gender and Feminist trade theory

it heterodox is the way it incorporates gender relations. Specifically, the model presumes men dominate women in the export sector, by influencing female labor markets and female wages.

We begin by assuming that the male and female supplies of labor are fixed at $\overline{M}$ and $\overline{F}$, respectively. Since men do not work in the domestic sector, $M_D = 0$. We now have:

$$\overline{M} = M_X \text{ and } M_D = 0$$

$$\overline{F} = F_X + F_D + F_H \tag{12.6}$$

The subscripts denote the export sector (X), the domestic sector (D) and the household sector (H). The more labor women provide to the export sector, the less they can provide to the domestic sector. However, there is a minimum amount of subsistence goods that must be produced in the domestic sector to sustain the population. There is thus a minimum amount of labor that women must perform in the domestic sector to keep the economy afloat. Thus, if F_X gets too large, and if F_D cannot fall, then women will need to devote less time to the household production and F_H must decrease. Society has fewer subsistence goods and women devote less time to crucial household activities. Export expansion can therefore have a negative effect on economic and social welfare.

Three factors determine female employment in the export sector, F_X: (1) coercion, which means men force women to work; (2) voluntary cooperation, which means women volunteer to assist working male family members, perhaps to augment family incomes; and (3) self-interest, whereby women simply seek to increase their own wage income. The female labor supply to the export sector is described by the equation:

$$F_X = kM_X^{\sigma}\left(\frac{w}{P_D}\right)^{\rho} = \text{f(coercion, cooperation, compensation)} \tag{12.7}$$

The parameter k is the male coercion parameter ($k \geq 1$). It measures the degree of male control over female labor supply decisions. If $k = 1$ then men have no control. The parameter σ measures the ease with which men can induce women to labor voluntarily without either coercing them or paying them higher wages. If $\sigma = 1$ then $M_X^{\sigma} = M_X^1$, which means that for every man working in the export sector, one woman volunteers. The higher the value of σ, the more women volunteer per male worker. Finally, the variable P_D is the domestic sector price index and w/P_D is therefore the real wage rate. The parameter $\rho (\rho \geq 0)$ measures the influence of the real wage rate on women's decisions to supply labor, F_X. If $\rho = 0$ then self-interest plays no role and women are indifferent to the wage rate.

With men making all decisions in the export sector, the economic problem is how to maximize men's income from exports. We will now elaborate on this theme by focusing on production in the export and domestic sectors.

Production in the export sector

We use a standard Neoclassical Cobb-Douglas production function to describe the output of exported cash crops:

$$X = M_X^\alpha F_X^\beta K_X^\gamma \tag{12.8}$$

The variable X is cash crop output, M_X is male employment, F_X is female employment and K_X is fixed capital input. The exponents measure how output responds to changes in male and female labor and capital inputs.[16] Production is characterized by diminishing returns so that $\alpha + \beta < 1$. Men's income (Y_M) is a residual. It equals what remains after paying women's wages. We assume a small economy so that export prices (P_X) are given by world competition. We then have an expression for men's income:

$$Y_M = P_X X - w F_X \tag{12.9}$$

This says that male income consists of the revenues from export sales $(P_X X)$ minus the female wage bill $(w F_X)$. There is, therefore, no separate variable for men's wages. Women spend all their wage income on subsistence goods (they do not save), while men spend their incomes on subsistence goods and investment in household and export production.

Substituting into Equation 12.9 the expressions for X (Equation 12.8) and F_X (Equation 12.7), we get:

$$Y_M = P_X M_X^\alpha [k M_X^\alpha (w/p_D)^\rho]^\beta K_X^\gamma - w M_X^\alpha (w/p_D)^\rho \tag{12.10}$$

The only variables in this cumbersome equation are Y_M, M_X and w. Everything else is assumed constant or given. Since men are in charge, they will choose how much to work (M_X) and how much to pay women (w). These decisions, made by men, determine their own residual income (Y_M). We omit the derivation and simply note that the equilibrium solutions are w^* and M_X^*.

Production in the domestic sector

Only women work in this sector. Output, D, is therefore only a function of the supply of female labor F_D: $D = D(F_D)$ or $D = g F_D$. Female productivity, g, depends on three things: (1) the time women spend working in the export sector (F_X); (2) female real income (Y_F/P_D); and (3) male real income (Y_M/P_D). The expression for female labor productivity in the domestic sector can be summarized as

$$g = g(F_X, Y_F/P_D, Y_M/P_D) \tag{12.11}$$

Female productivity, g, is negatively related to F_X because the more labor women supply to the export sector, the less efficient they will be in producing subsistence

304 Gender and Feminist trade theory

goods (the female workday must increase to maintain domestic output for subsistence, which reduces their efficiency). Productivity rises as female real income rises. It also rises when male real income rises because it adds to family income.

We can use the model to analyze various trade-related issues. For example, suppose there is a currency devaluation. How would this affect women? This question is relevant because many global institutions recommend this policy as a development strategy. A currency devaluation makes the cash crop cheaper for foreigners to buy. This promotes export demand, raises the price, P_X, and boosts export profits. Male income, Y_M, increases, which induces men to work more to increase output and also to increase female wage rates to attract more female labor. However, all other things remaining the same, such an expansion in exports can actually harm women because domestic subsistence production cannot be reduced. Thus, women must continue to provide subsistence at the same level as before or else social well-being is jeopardized. "It is precisely when there is a highly successful effort to promote exports through a currency devaluation that gender-specific health disadvantages are more likely to rise" (Darity, 2007: 85). This conclusion differs from Osterreich, who suggests that raising women's wages increases export prices, which in turn causes the terms of trade to improve.

Trade in a semi-industrial economy: a Kaleckian approach

In many developing, semi-industrial economies (SIEs), export sectors employ mostly women and pay them wages at or below subsistence. This is the opposite of the agrarian economy modeled by Darity in which export sectors (cash crops) employ mostly men. This reflects real-world differences in these two types of developing economies. The issue addressed in this section is whether paying women higher wages in the export sector of a semi-industrial economy (SIE) would reduce competitiveness and exports and hence dampen economic growth.

We again assume two sectors, an export sector and a domestic sector. The export sector specializes in the production of light industrial goods destined for final consumption. We assume that some of this output is sold domestically. The domestic sector, on the other hand, produces both consumer and investment goods for home use only. Further, only women work in the export sector while only men work in the domestic sector. All markets are assumed to be perfectly competitive. Finally, production in both sectors requires imported intermediate goods. We ask, what is the effect of an exogenous increase in female wage rates on national income and output and on male and female employment?

Price equations

The relevant price equations for each sector are:

$$[\text{domestic sector/male domain}] \ P_D = \tau(w_M a_D + e P_n^* n_D), \tau > 1$$
$$[\text{export sector/female domain}] \ \ P_X = \varphi(w_F a_X + e P_n^* n_X), \varphi > 1 \quad (12.12)$$

Gender and Feminist trade theory **305**

The first equation describes the domestic sector in which only men work and the second equation describes the export sector in which only women work. The parameters τ and φ are profit markups in each sector;[17] a is the per unit labor input coefficient; n is the imported intermediate input coefficient; P^* is world price of intermediate goods; e is the nominal exchange rate. The expression wa is the per unit labor cost and ePn is the per unit cost of intermediate output. The unit price of output therefore covers the costs of production plus an increment for capitalists' profits. We also impose the condition that female wages are lower than male wages so that $w_F < w_M$.

Aggregate income and output

We let D and X stand for home output and export output, respectively. Additionally, let W be aggregate male and female wage income and R aggregate profit income. Aggregate national income is therefore $(W + R)$. We now make a Kaleckian assumption that wage and profit recipients have different propensities to consume. Aggregate consumption of domestic output by male and female laborers is $P_D C_{LD}$ and the amount consumed by capitalists is $P_X C_{KD}$ where C is real consumption and P is price as determined in (12.12).

Macroeconomic equilibrium requires that national income $(W + R)$ equals aggregate expenditures. Aggregate expenditures are the sum of (1) consumption of domestic output; (2) domestic consumption of export output; (3) purchases of investment goods made at home; and (4) exports minus imports of intermediate goods (i.e., net exports). The macroeconomic equilibrium equation is:

$$W + R = P_D(C_{LD} + C_{KD}) + P_X(C_{LX} + C_{KX}) + P_D I_D + P_X E_X - eP_n^*(n_D D + n_X X) \quad (12.13)$$

When there is general equilibrium each sector will also be in equilibrium. Thus,

$$D = C_{LD} + C_{KD} + I_D \qquad (12.14)$$
$$X = C_{LX} + C_{KX} + E_X$$

Market forces will drive the economy to a general equilibrium in which $X = X_0$ and $D = D_0$ are produced in each sector.

Using this analytical framework we may now ask what the effect would be of raising the female wage rate in the X sector. The total effect can be broken into four parts: a price effect, an exchange rate effect, a gender redistribution effect and a class redistribution effect.

#1 Price effect

Look at the price equation in (12.12): $P_X = \varphi(w_F a_X + eP_n^* n_X)$. An increase in w_F causes the right side of the equation (unit costs of production) to increase. This causes P_X to rise as well as the relative price P_X/P_D. But the extent to which P_X rises depends on the value of φ, the profit mark-up. This profit mark-up can vary.

306 Gender and Feminist trade theory

If there is perfect competition in the world market then higher unit costs cannot be passed along and P_X will not rise at all. This means the profit margin, φ, will decrease. Aggregate wage income rises and profit income falls.

#2 Exchange rate effect

If the world market is imperfectly competitive then an increase in P_X due to a rise in women's wages is possible. This would cause the real exchange rate, ρ, to decrease. The real exchange rate is defined as $\rho = e P_X^* / P_X$ where e is the nominal exchange rate and P_X^* is the price of the export good measured in foreign currency. Therefore any rise in the export price brought about by higher female wages causes the real exchange rate to fall.

#3 Gender redistribution effect

Rising wages for women would cause women to spend more on consumption. This means D and X rise. Since domestic production does not use any female labor, the costs of production there remain unchanged and domestic prices, P_D, would remain unchanged as well. Thus, women's real income rises while that of men remains the same: women become better off relative to men.

#4 Class redistribution effect

If w_F rises while w_M remains the same, then aggregate wage income rises. This means aggregate profits falls. Workers benefit at the expense of capitalists. This is a decidedly Kaleckian conclusion.

Overview

What is the consequence of an increase in women's wages relative to men's wages? Osterreich's Sraffa-inspired model shows that raising women's wages in the South causes the terms of trade with the North to improve, thereby improving the welfare of everyone in the South. The second model by Darity shows that export promotion pushes up women's wages and increases their work effort. However, because subsistence cannot be reduced, women cannot also reduce their work effort in the production of subsistence goods. In other words, women must work harder, which jeopardizes their health and the well-being of families. The third model by Blecker and Sequino shows that raising women's wages improves women's position relative to men as well as workers' position relative to capitalists. This answer is very tentative, however, because it depends on the values of a wide range of parameters, including the propensities to consume out of wage and profit income, the amount of export sector output consumed domestically, the sensitivity of profit mark-ups to changes in costs, the effect of changes in profits on domestic investment, and more.

Conclusions

We conclude this chapter with three observations.

First, in terms of pure theory, contemporary Feminist trade theory is necessarily heterodox. It contains distinct traces of Institutional, Marxian and Post Keynesian ideas. Provisioning, social reproduction, non-market relations and unpaid labor are all concepts developed by Feminist Institutionalists and Post Keynesians. The latter have also pointed to gender differences in risk aversion and in propensities to consume and save and have built these into their macroeconomic theories (see Barber and Odean, 2001 and Charusheela, 2010). From Marxist Feminists we get a more radical view of international trade as a system of exploitation of workers—and of women. We also find an emphasis, central to Marxian economics, on the role of the family as the basis of the reproduction of labor power, the provider of subsistence, and the source of surplus value and capitalists' profit. These are all themes that appear in Feminist trade theory.[18]

Second, in terms of empirical research, it is not possible to make sweeping generalizations about the interaction between trade and gender. The effect of trade on gender, and vice versa, depends on the social and cultural characteristics of each trading nation. It also depends on each nation's structural context: its general stage of economic and technological development, gender employment and wage structures, the composition of export and import sectors, etc. This means that much of what we know about gender and international economics is necessarily idiosyncratic.

Third, as for the policy questions of how trade liberalization, trade expansion and trade openness affect women's welfare, research indicates that the effects are ambiguous if not negligible. Scores of econometric models, case studies, simulations and qualitative and theoretical analyses have failed to show with certainty that women benefit from these policies.

Notes

1 One consequence of these movements was the establishment, in 1971, of the Committee on the Status of Women in the Economics Profession by the American Economic Association. The Committee monitors and promotes women's status in the ranks of academia.
2 For example, Nelson (1993 and 2002); Ferber and Nelson (1993 and 2003); Kuiper and Sap (1995); Hewitson (1999); Moe (2003); Power (2004); and Van Staveren, et al. (2007).
3 To be clear on our vocabulary, we often use the word "developed" to describe the industrially advanced countries and "developing" to describe all the others.
4 The International Labour Organization calls this "Decent Work" (ILO, 2002).
5 For a detailed definition of the informal economy see Hussmanns (2004).
6 On social provisioning see Todorova (2013), Neysmith et al. (2012), Power (2004), Dugger (1996) and Nelson (1993).
7 Technically speaking, agriculture belongs to a broader category called primary goods. Primary goods consist of all natural resources. This includes, other than farm products, mineral and forest products. Female participation in the latter is low and thus rarely included in discussions.

308 Gender and Feminist trade theory

8 For a feminist critique of Becker's economic theory of the family see Bergmann (1996) and Ferber (2003).
9 For feminist critiques of orthodoxy theory see Bergmann (1996), Ferber (2003) and Nelson (2002).
10 While Becker permits altruism, this is little more than a reduction of non-rational motives to rational ones.
11 See, for example, the models introduced in the 1995 and 2000 special issues of *World Development*.
12 All three models appear in Van Staveren, Elson, Grown and Çagatay (2007). This is a seminal collection of articles on feminist trade theory.
13 The term North refers to advanced industrialized countries, most of which are located in the northern hemisphere. The term South refers to developing agrarian and semi-industrialized developing countries, most of which are located in the southern hemisphere. We can alternatively use the terms center and periphery to describe these two regions.
14 See Chapter 11, Appendix B for a review of Sraffa production equations.
15 This conclusion is similar to the Prebisch-Singer thesis reviewed in Chapter 11. That thesis suggested that North–South trade works to the advantage of the North at the expense of the South. This is because the North's manufacturing exports are sold in oligopolistic markets whereas the South's primary goods exports are sold in competitive markets. Also the demand for manufacturing goods is income elastic whereas the demand for primary goods is income inelastic. This North-South bias is intrinsic to the capitalist world trading system and is the cause of unequal exchange. Today, feminist economists would argue that the bias is due to gender discrimination.
16 For example, if $\alpha = .5$ then a 1% increase in male labor input will increase output X by .50%.
17 This is equivalent to the more conventional expression $(1 + r)$.
18 See Weeks (2011) and (Engels, 1884). Also, see the seven special issues between 1972 and 2001 of the *Review of Radical Political Economy* devoted to the political economy of women.

References

Ahmad, N., & Koh, S. (2011). *Incorporating Estimates of Household Production of Non-Market Services into International Comparisons of Material Well-Being*. OECD. Retrieved June 18, 2015, from http://dx.doi.org/10.1787/5kg3h0jgk87g-en.

Barber, B. M., & Odean, T. (2001). "Boys will be Boys: Gender, Overconfidence, and Common Stock Investment." *The Quarterly Journal of Economics, 116*, 261–292.

Becker, G. S. (1991). *A Treatise on the Family* (Enlarged ed.). Cambridge, MA: Harvard University Press.

Bergmann, B. R. (1996, Janurary–February). "Becker's Theory of the Family: Preposterous Conclusions." *Challenge, 39*(1), 9–12.

Blecker, R. A., & Seguino, S. (2007). "Macroeconomic Effects of Reducing Gender Wage Inequality in an Export-oriented, Semi-industrialized Economy." In I. Van Staveren, D. Elson, C. Grown, & N. Çagatay (Eds.), *The Feminist Economics of Trade* (pp. 91–114). London: Routledge.

Charusheela, S. (2010). "Gender and the Stability of Consumption: A Feminist Contribution to Post-Keynesian Economics." *Cambridge Journal of Economics, 34*(6), 1145–1156.

Committee on the Status of Women in the Economics Profession (2015). *Annual Report*. American Economic Association. Retrieved June 27, 2015, from https://www.aeaweb.org/committees/cswep/newsletters/CSWEP_nsltr_IssueI-2015.pdf.

Darity, Jr., W. A. (2007). "The Formal Structure of a Gender-Segregated Low-Income Economy." In I. Van Staveren, D. Elson, C. Grown, & N. Çagatay (Eds.), *Feminist Economics of Trade* (pp. 78–90). London: Routledge.

Duflo, E. (2012). "Women's Empowerment and Economic Development." *Journal of Economic Literature, 50*(4), 1051–1079.

Dugger, W. M. (1996). "Redefining Economics: From Market Allocation to Social Provisioning." In C. J. Whalen (Ed.), *Political Economy for the 21st Century* (pp. 31–43). Armonk, NY: M. E. Sharpe.

Engels, F. (1884). *The Origin of the Family, Private Property and the State*. Retrieved December 22, 2014, from https://www.marxists.org/archive/marx/works/1884/origin-family/.

Ferber, M. A. (2003). "A Feminist Critique of the Neoclassical Theory of the Family." In K. S. Moe (Ed.), *Women, Family, and Work: Writings on the Economics of Gender* (pp. 9–23). Malden, MA: Blackwell Publishing, Ltd.

Ferber, M. A., & Nelson, J. A. (Eds.). (1993). *Beyond Economic Man: Feminist Theory and Economics*. Chicago, IL: University of Chicago Press.

Ferber, M. A., & Nelson, J. A. (Eds.). (2003). *Feminist Economics Today: Beyond Economic Man*. Chicago, IL: University of Chicago Press.

Food and Agriculture Organization (2011). *The Role of Women in Agriculture*. United Nations. Retrieved July 7, 2015, from http://www.fao.org/docrep/013/am307e/am307e00.pdf.

Grown, C., Elson, D., & Çagatay, N. (2000). "Introduction." *World Development, 28*(7), 1145–1156.

Hewitson, G. J. (1999). *Feminist Economics: Interrogating the Masculiinity of Rational Economic Man*. Northhampton, MA: Edward Elgar.

Hussmanns, R. (2004). "Statistical Definition of Informal Employment: Guidelines endorsed by the Seventeenth International Conference of Labour Statisticians (2003)." *7th Meeting of the Expert Group on Informal Sector Statistics*. New Delhi. Retrieved May 20, 2015, from http://ilo.org/public/english/bureau/stat/download/papers/def.pdf.

International Labour Office (2002). "Decent Work and the Informal Economy, Report VI." *International Labour Conference*. Geneva: International Labour Office.

International Labour Office (2012). *Global Employment Trends for Women*. Geneva: International Labour Office. Retrieved June 4, 2015, from http://www.ilo.org/public/libdoc/ilo/P/09275/09275%282012%29.pdf.

International Labour Office (2013). *Women and Men in the Informal Economy: A Statistical Picture* (2nd ed.). Geneva: ILO. Retrieved June 18, 2015, from http://www.ilo.org/stat/Publications/WCMS_234413/lang--en/index.htm.

International Labour Office (2014). *Global Employment Trends 2014*. Geneva: ILO. Retrieved June 19, 2015, from http://www.ilo.org/wcmsp5/groups/public/---dgreports/---dcomm/---publ/documents/publication/wcms_233953.pdf.

Kuiper, E., & Sap, J. (Eds.) (1995). *Out of the Margin: Feminist Perspectives on Economics*. New York: Routledge.

Levy Economics Institute (2005). *Unpaid Work and the Economy: Gender, Poverty and the Millennium Development Goals*. Retrieved 18 February, from http://www.levyinstitute.org/undp-levy-conference/program_documents.php.

Moe, K. S. (Ed.). (2003). *Women, Family, and Work: Writings on the Economics of Gender*. Malden, MA: Blackwell Publishing, Ltd.

Nelson, J. A. (1993). "The Study of Choice or the Study of Provisioning? Gender and the Definition of Economics." In M. A. Ferber, & J. A. Nelson (Eds.), *Beyond Economic Man: Feminist Theory and Economics* (pp. 23–36). Chicago, IL: University of Chicago Press.

Nelson, J. A. (2002). *Feminism, Objectivity and Economics*. London: Routledge.

Nelson, J. A. (2003). "Confronting the Science/Value Split: Notes on Feminist Economics, Institutionalism, Pragmatism and Process Thought." *Cambridge Journal of Economics, 27*, 49–64.

Neysmith, S., Reitsma-Street, M., Baker-Collins, S., & Porter, E. (2012). *Beyond Caring Labour to Provisioning Work*. Toronto: University of Toronto Press.

Osterreich, S. (2007). "Gender, Trade and Development: Labor Market Discrimination and North–South Terms of Trade." In I. Van Staveren, D. Elson, C. Grown, & N. Çagatay (Eds.), *The Feminist Economics of Trade* (pp. 55–77). London: Routledge.

Power, M. (2004). "Social Provisioning as a Starting Point for Feminist Economics." *Feminist Economics, 10*, 3–19.

Tijdens, K. G., & Van Klaveren, M. (2012). *Gender Pay Gap Unchanged for 10 Years*. Brussels: International Trade Union Confederation. Retrieved June 20, 2015, from http://www.ituc-csi.org/IMG/pdf/pay_gap_en_final.pdf.

Todorova, Z. (2013). "Connecting Social Provisioning and Functional Finance in a Post Keynesian–Institutional Analysis of the Public Sector." *European Journal of Economics and Economic Policies: Intervention, 10*(1), 61–75.

United Nations (2010). *The World's Women 2010: Trends and Statistics*. Department of Economic and Social Affairs. New York: United Nations. Retrieved June 30, 2015, from http://unstats.un.org/unsd/demographic/products/Worldswomen/WW_full%20report_BW.pdf.

United Nations Development Programme (2014). *Human Development Report 2014*. New York: Oxford University Press. Retrieved July 7, 2015, from http://hdr.undp.org/en/2014-report.

Van Staveren, I., Elson, D., Grown, C., & Çagatay, N. (Eds.) (2007). *The Feminist Economics of Trade*. London: Routledge.

Weeks, J. (2011). "Un-/Re-Productive Maternal Labor: Marxist Feminism and Chapter Fifteen of Marx's Capital." *Rethinking Marxism: a Journal of Economics, Culture and Society, 23*, 31–40.

World Bank (2010). *Women's Economic Opportunities in the Formal Private Sector in Latin America and the Caribbean*. Washington, DC: World Bank. Retrieved July 9, 2015, from http://siteresources.worldbank.org/INTLACREGTOPPOVANA/Resources/840442-1260809819258/Book_Womens_Economic_Opportunities.pdf.

World Development (1995). "Special Issue on Gender, Adjustment and Macroeconomics." *World Development, 23*(11).

World Development (2000). "Special Issue on Growth, Trade, Finance, and Gender Inequality." *World Development, 28*(7).

INDEX

absolute advantage 37–8, 44–6, 56, 63, 83, 286

aggregate demand: in Classical and Keynesian open economy model 118–19, 123; in Mercantilist theory 20; in Neoclassical trade theory 69; in New Orthodoxy 90; in new open economy macroeconomics 131; in Post Keynesian economics 206, 212–13

aggregate supply: in Classical model 118, *140*, 141; in Kaleckian model 212–13

Austrian economics 144–73; anti-equilibrium 149–50; critique of socialism 170–1, 172n8, 173; human action and spontaneous order 148–9, 152–3, 158, 171, 173; praxeology 148–9, 152, 168; production chains 157–8, roundaboutness of production 159, 160–1, 172n6; voluntary action 150; *see also* methodological individualism; methodological subjectivism; subjective theory of value

autarky 79–83, 84n4; and Mercantilism 12, 31n2; in Mundell model 76–7; *see also* Neoclassical trade theory; Ricardian trade theory; taste bias model

balance of payments 121, 139, 198n10; and Austrian economics 157, 170; payments crises 38, 81; floating exchange rates 126; internal and external balances 123–5; in Keynesian model 142–3; and money supply adjustments 116;

Washington Consensus and austerity 133; *see also* current account; financial account; trade balance

bancor 231

Baran, Paul A. 234n18, 235, 241–3, 250

Baumol, William *see* Baumol-Gomory Global Conflict Model; entrepreneurship

Baumol-Gomory Global Conflict Model 99–105

Becker, Gary 285, 294, 296, 298, 308n8, 308n10; theory of discrimination 294; theory of family 294–6, 299, 308n8

beggar-my-neighbor policies *see* Robinson, Joan

Blecker, Robert A. 30, 32, 233n3, 234; and Sequino, S. 300, 306, 308

Bretton Woods 135, 139n17, 155, 167, 171, 228, 230

BOP curve 122, 125, 142–3

Bukharin, Nikolai 240

bullion 12, 17, 20, 28, 31n1, 114, 116; bullionism 17

Cambridge capital controversy 82

Cambridge Circus 200, 234

capital: capital abundance 65; capital accumulation 35, 37–9, 63, 245, 263, 267; capital controls 122, 228–9, 234; capital flight 133, 226, 227–8; capital–labor ratio 67, 75, 78, 273; capital mobility 115, 122, 135–6, 142–3, 229; human capital 294; international capital flows 76, 121, 256–7

312 Index

class conflict (struggle): in Classical economics 63; in Kaleckian economics 203, 209–10, 281; in Marxian economics 64, 236, 238, 240; in Neoclassical economics 5, 81; in Post Keynesian economics 219, 232; in Robinson 202, 205–6; in Sraffa model 204, 259; and trade 219

Classical counter-revolution 109, 112–13; microeconomic foundations of macroeconomics 113, 129; rational expectations theory 113; real business cycle theory 113; and Neoliberalism 132

Classical international macroeconomics 114–18; full employment 116–17; labor market theory 117–18; loanable funds theory 115; macroeconomic equilibrium 118; production theory 117; quantity theory of money 115–16; Say's Law 115; *see also* New Classical macroeconomics; species flow mechanism

Colbert, Jean Baptiste 15–16; Colbertism 21–22, 32

colonialism: in Smith's theory 36–7; and Mercantilism 14, 17, 22–3, 31; *see also* imperialism

community indifference curves 48, 49, 52, 76; *see also* Neoclassical trade theory

comparative advantage 7, 9–10, 28–9, 34, 61n2, 62n8; in Austrian economics 164, 171; and competitive advantage 286; critique of 58–61, 83, 159, 197; empirical evidence for 57–8; in Keynesian economics 110; in Marxian economics 238, 260; in Neoclassical trade theory 63, 72–3, 75, 82, 297; in new orthodoxy 86, 97, 105–6; in Ricardian trade theory 38, 41, 44–6, 51, 53–4, 56–7; in Smith's theory 37–8; source of 193, 286; *see also* absolute advantage

compensation principle 80; *see also* Neoclassical trade theory

competitive advantage 83, 285–6; *see also* absolute advantage

cost of production theory of value 35, 147; *see also* labor theory of value

current account: in Classical open economy model 114; defined 31n5; focus of Mercantilist thought 17; in Keynesian open economy model 121–4, 131; in Post Keynesian theory 204–5, 215; in relation to financial account 138n1,

138n13; and trade imbalances 111; *see also* balance of payments; trade balance

currency: appreciation 126; convertibility 136; depreciation (devaluation) 125, 131, 157, 161, 206, 229, 304

Darity, Jr., William A. 300, 309; women's wages in semi-industrial economies 304–6

Davidson, Paul 111, 202, 233–4; stagnation bias 229; Davidson Plan 230, 232

dirigisme 25, 30–1; *see also* Mercantilism

dependency theory 246–7, 250n2; and underdevelopment 247; world systems theory 246, 250n2

dollarization 157

East Asian Consensus 136–7

East Asian Miracle 33, 136, 139

economic liberalism 21–3, 32n6; Classical liberalism 132–3; *see also* Neoliberalism; trade liberalization

economies of scale 9–10; in Neoclassical trade theory 68, 77, 84; in New Orthodox trade theory 87–93, 95–7, 100–1, 106, 108; in Ricardian trade theory 42; and transnational corporations 190–1

effective demand 207, 212–14, 218–19, 223, 231

efficiency: in Baumol-Gomory Global Conflict Model 101; economic efficiency 4–5, 37, 78, 132; efficiency wage theory 113; and Institutionalism 194; Robinson's critique of 202, 204; and trade 41, 165, 192, 294

Emmanuel, Arghiri 252, 260, 268n4, 268; unequal exchange 256–9

entrepreneurship 4, 22; Austrian economics 158, 170–3; Baumol, William 162–6; measuring global entrepreneurship 165, *166*

equilibrium: anti-equilibrium 149–50; autarky 50–1, 70, 75; balance of payments 122, 142; disequilibrium 116, 129, 162; exchange rate 207; financial sector 122; and full employment 5, 113, 201; general 88, 107, 118, 127, 129, 143, 150, 305; in Keynesian model 210, 213; labor market 117; macroeconomic 118, 220, 305; in Neoclassical trade model 65, 68; partial 90; in Marxian production model 270, 277–8; in Sraffa model 281

European Union (EU) 25, 135, 156, 167, 169, 171, 179, *292*, *295*
Eurozone 132, 134, 156, 169
exchange rates 139, 155; and Austrian roundaboutness 161; in Classical open economy model 114–15; in Davidson Plan 230; and *dirigism* 31; exchange rate controls 12; fixed and flexible 157; in Keynesian economics 110–11, 143; in Mundell-Fleming model 125, 126–9; real and nominal 215–17, 220–1, 305–6; and trade balance 204–7, 214–17; and Washington Consensus 133, 135; *see also* Ricardian trade theory; trade liberalism

factors of production: endowments of 64–5, 69–70, 75, 81–2, 86; mobility of 77, 84, 115, 122, 135–6, 142–3, 228–9, 268n3; *see also* Neoclassical trade theory
feminist economics 284–8; *see also* Feminist trade theory
Feminist trade theory 284–310; competitive advantage 286; and categories of developing countries 287–8; gender effects of export expansion 296, 302; gender gaps 291–3; household labor 290, 295; in Kaleckian trade model 304–6; labor force participation and feminization 291–3; male and female wages 297; market vs. non-market sector 288–90; and Neoclassical trade model 297–8, 301–4; orthodox and heterodox theory 294–300; Osterreich model 300, 304–6, 310; social reproduction 290, 301, 307; in Sraffaian trade model 300–1; trade–gender relationship 286–7; unpaid labor 290, 295, 307
financial account: defined 32n5; in Keynesian open economy model 121; in Post Keynesian theory 204–6; in relation to financial account 138n1; and trade imbalances 111
financialization 224–6, 234
fiscal policy: in Austrian economics 168–9; and fixed and floating exchange rate regime 125–8; new open economy macroeconomics 128, 131; *see also* Mundell-Fleming model
free trade: alleged superiority of 79–83, 87, 91–2, 99; antidote to Schumpeterian imperialism 248, 267; in Austrian economics 167, 171; and developing economies 31; in East Asian model 27; gender and 297–8; Institutionalism and

195–6; in Keynes 29; vs. managed trade 87, 106; Marx's position on 237–8, 251–2, 256, 263; and Mercantilism 14, 22–4; in Neoclassical trade theory 64–5, 68–70, 73–7; and Neoliberalism 26, 132–5; and New Orthodoxy 106–8; and Post Keynesian economics 209; and pluralist economics 7; positive-sum game 12; Ricardian trade theory 41–2, 45, 51, 59–60; Robinson's view of 30; in Smith's theory of development 36–7, 63–4
Friedman, Milton 14, 62, 111; and Classical counter-revolution 112; positive economics 57; predictive instrumentalism 181
full employment: assumed in orthodox trade theory 5, 43, 47, 81, 110, 117; as natural state 5, 109; in Keynesian economics 28, 110–13; in Post Keynesian economics 201–5, 208–9, 231; *see also* Classical international macroeconomics; Swan-Salter model

game theory *see* New Orthodoxy
gender: defined 284; gender blindness 284; gender discrimination 286, 296–7, 301, 308n15; gender employment ratio 291, 292; gender inequality 285, 287, 294, 298–300, 310; Gender Inequality Index 287, 288; *see also* feminist economics
Gereffi, Gary 184, 198; *see also* Institutionalist international economics
global capitalism 2, 4, 24, 105, 187, 198; in Smith, Adam 36–7; in Austrian economics 171; in Marxian economics 63, 236, 239, 250, 263; and Minky's financial instability 226–7; in Neoclassical economics 64, 105, 296
Global Classicism 132–3; *see also* Neoliberalism
Global Keynesianism 134–6
gold standard 154–6
Graham, Frank 105, 108
Grossman, Henryk 252; and unequal exchange theory 255–6, 260, 269

Haberler, Gottfried 62n8, 84n2, 154, 172–3
Hamilton, Alexander 15, 22–3
Hansen, Alvin 111, 139
Hardt, Michael 246, 250
harmonization of standards: Austrian criticism of 167; labor standards 193–4
Harvey, David 233n9, 245, 250

314 Index

Hayek, Friedrich 144, 146: catallaxy 172n3; competitive currencies and free banking 156; diversity thesis 168–70; economic planning 151; fatal conceit 151; fixed exchange rates 157; Hayek Triangle 159; interstate federations 167–8; seduction of cheap money 155; spontaneous order 150

heterodox economics 3–6, 10; and Austrian economics 11n2, 165–6; compared to orthodox economics 6; diversity of 7; feminist economics 299–302, 307; *Heterodox Economics Directory* 11; Institutional economics 174, 196; Mercantilism and Neo-Mercantilism 9; New Orthodoxy 105; Post Keynesian economics 231; and Robinson, Joan 206–7; *see also* Marxian economics

Hicks, John: Hicks-Hanson IS-LM model 138; origins of Keynesian economics 111; *see also* compensation principle

Hilferding, Rudolf 240

Hobson, John A. 240–1

household production 289–90, 293, 302, 308

Hume, David 61n1; *see also* species flow mechanism

Hymer, Stephen 199; *see also* transnational corporations

imperialism: Baran and Sweezy (monopoly capitalism) 242–3; cultural imperialism 249; dependency and world systems theory 246–7; vs. globalism 248–9; Lenin, Vladimir Ilyich 241–2, 244, 251, 258; Magdoff, Harry 243–4; Mandel, Ernest (late capitalism) 244–5; Marxism and Leninism 239–42, 255; post-Fordism and empire 245–6; *see also* Bukharin, Nikolai; Hilferding, Rudolf; Hobson, John A.; Schumpeter, Joseph A.

Industrial Revolution 17, 22, 35

income inequality: economic orthodoxy 4–5, 267; flaw of capitalism 231–33; *see also* gender; trade liberalization

informal markets 288–90; *see also* feminist economics

Institutionalist international economics 174–99; characteristics of institutions 176–7; commodity chains 184–5, 187; critique of orthodoxy 174, 192–4; economic power 178–9; formalism 181; holism 180–1; instincts 177–78; instrumentalism 181–2; means-ends

dualism 182–4; methodology 175–84; network analysis 184–6; vs. New Institutionalism 175, 188, 197n2; theory of the firm 187–9; trade policy 192–6; transactions costs 177, 187–9; transnational corporation 189–92; *see also* Hymer, Stephen

insufficient aggregate demand 114, 205, 243; *see also* aggregate demand

International Confederation of Associations for Pluralism in Economics (ICAPE) 8, 11

International Monetary Fund (IMF) 24, 132–3, 139n17, 170, 179, 228–31, 246

international reserve currency 227; Keynes Solution 230–1; *see also* bancor

International Student Initiative for Pluralism in Economics 8, 11

intra-industry trade 86, 93, 105

investment 24, 26–9, 31, 35, 111, 135; in Austrian economics 150–4; in Classical open economy model 114–18; foreign direct investment 27, 76, 104, 135, 188, 190–1, 227; in Kaleckian model of semi-industrial economy 305; in Keynesian open economy model 118–22; in Marxian economics 239, 241, 243, 259, 267, 274, 276, 278n5, 303; in Mundell-Fleming model 125; portfolio investment 76, 135–6, 227–8; in Post Keynesianism 201, 205–14, 220–7, 228; source of investment funds 36; and transnational corporation 187–8, 191

Jevons, William Stanley 34, 61n1

Kaldor, Nicholas *see* compensation principle

Kalecki, Michał 200, 202; class struggle over income shares 203; degree of monopoly 203, 209–10; income distribution and macroeconomics 209–11; Kaleckian open economy model 211–22; mark-up pricing 203; spending multiplier 211, 214; *see also* effective demand; Post Keynesian economics; feminist economics

Kautsky, Karl 241

Keynes, John Maynard *see* Keynesian economics

Keynes Solution 227, 230–1

Keynesian economics: balance of payments 121–3, 126, 138–9; Classical-Keynesian synthesis 111–12, 200; floating (flexible)

vs. fixed exchange rates 125–8; involuntary unemployment 111–12, 117, 141; IS-LM-BOP model 111, 122–3, 129; Keynes and Mercantilism 27–30; Keynesian Revolution and critique of Classical theory 109–111; liquidity 111, 120, 125, 217; liquidity crisis 223–4; market imperfections 112–13; money supply and demand 120, 130; Mundell-Fleming open economy model 118–23, 125, 128–9, 139, *142*; New Keynesian economics 113–14; New Open Economy Macroeconomics 128–32; Obstfeld-Rogoff model 129–32; and Post Keynesian economics 200–02; price and wage rigidity 112; *see also* Swan-Salter model

Kirzner, Israel 145, 148, 173

Krugman, Paul 14; political economy of free trade 106–7, 107n3, 107n4, 108; *see also* New Trade Theory

labor productivity: in Classical and Keynesian international economics 117; in gendered trade models 301, 303; and imperialism and unequal exchange 243, 266; in Marxian value theory 254; in Neoclassical trade theory 64; in New Orthodoxy 86; in Post Keynesian international economics 210, 233n6; *see also* Ricardian trade theory

labor theory of value: formation of world prices, wages and profits 243, 265, 268n5; Neoclassical critique of 63–6; and objective theory of value 147; rejected in Sraffa model 280; Ricardian theory 39–40, 45, 62n8; Smith's cost of production theory of value 35; unequal exchange theory 252, 269; and source of capitalist profit 242, 243

laissez faire 5, 28–30, 34–5, 112–13, 152, 195, 232, 242, 264

Lenin, Vladimir Ilyich *see* imperialism

Leontief Paradox 74, 83–4

List, Friedrich 15; theory of mercantilism 23–4, 30

Luxemburg, Rosa 240–1

Magdoff, Harry 234n18; on New Imperialism 243–4

managed trade 87; *see also* New Orthodoxy

Mandel, Ernest: late capitalism 244–5; underdevelopment 245

marginal: cost 47, 67, 88; productivity 179,

204, 259; propensity to consume 211, 213; propensity to import 211, 215; rate of substitution 49–50, 68–9, 88–9; rate of technical substitution 46–8, 50; rate of transformation 67, 69, 88–9; utility 48, 88

Marshall, Alfred 106, 108; *see also* Marshall-Lerner condition

Marshall-Lerner condition 115, 206

Marx, Karl *see* Marxian economics

Marxian economics: centralization and concentration of capital 238, 241; class 236–8, 240–9, 259, 263, 268, 280, 282, 299, 305–6; Classical Marxism 242, 245; economic surplus in Marxian models 243, 252, 259, 260–2, 267; economic surplus in Sraffa model 279, 281; exploitation 4, 151, 197, 236–7, 240, 249–54, 257–8, 262–7, 273–4, 307; falling rate of profit 264, 269, 274; overview of Marx's theory of value and price 270–8; profit equalization 243, 256, 266; socialism 4, 170–3, 240, 250; *see also* free trade; imperialism; labor theory of value; Neo-Marxism; Sraffa, Piero; unequal exchange theory

Mercantilism 12–33; Classical Mercantilism 16; economic self-sufficiency 12; national vs. private interest 12, 18; protectionism 22–3, 25, 32; special trading privileges and rules 12; state intervention 13, 26, 30; trade surplus as goal 12, 20; *see also dirigisme*; Neo-Mercantilism

methodological individualism 145–7, 172

methodological subjectivism 145, 147–8

Minsky, Hyman 234–5; business cycle theory 224; financialization 224–7; global financial instability 222; global investment 226; money manager capitalism 225–7; output prices and asset prices 223–4; uncertainty, investment and cash flow 222–3

Monetarism 112; *see also* Friedman, Milton

monetary policy: in Austrian economics 153, 157, 169; and internal and external balances 123–5; LM curve 121; new open economy macroeconomics 128, 131; Post Keynesianism 229; and quantity theory of money 116; relative effectiveness in fixed and floating exchange rate regime 125–8; *see also* Mundell-Fleming model; Swan-Salter model

316 Index

multinational corporations *see* transnational corporations
Mun, Thomas 15, 19–21
Mundell, Robert *see* Mundell-Fleming model
Mundell-Fleming model 76–7, 118–129, 139, *142*; *see also* Keynesian economics

Negri, Antonio *see* Hardt, Michael
Neoclassical trade theory 63–85; factor abundance and intensity 66; factor mobility 76–9; factor-price equalization theorem 73, 138n9, 298; Heckscher-Ohlin theorem 72–3, 297; production possibilities frontier 66–8; putty and clay models 78, 84n5; Robinson's critique of 204–5; Rybczynski theorem 73; specific-factor model 78; Stolper-Samuelson theorem 72; terms of trade 71–78, 80; Vanek-Leamer factor content theorem 74; *see also* Feminist trade theory; free trade; marginal; taste bias model; terms of trade
Neoliberalism 23–6, 30, 133–4; *see also* economic liberalism; trade liberalization
Neo-Marxism 242–7; imperialism (Magdoff, Harry) 243–4; late capitalism (Mandel, Ernest) 244–5; monopoly capitalism (Baran, Paul and Sweezy, Paul) 242–3; post modernism and post Fordism 245–6; world systems theory 246–7
Neo-Mercantilism 23–30; East Asian model 26–7; European model 25–6; and Keynes, John Maynard 27–30; *see also dirigisme*
New Classical macroeconomics 112–13, 128; *see also* Classical counter-revolution
New Orthodoxy 86–108; Airbus–Boeing game theory model 97–99; Baumol-Gomory Global Conflict Model 99–105, 108; critique of comparative advantage 86; game theory 10, 86, 97, 106; managed trade (strategic trade) policy 87, 106; market imperfections 9–10, 83–4; monopolistic competition 94; oligopoly 97; partial equilibrium 90; payoff matrix 97–8, 106; product differentiation 93; strategic trade policy 92; *see also* economies of scale; terms of trade
New Trade Theory 10, 84, 208; alleged newness of 105–6, 208; *see also* New Orthodoxy

Obstfeld-Rogoff model *see* Keynesian economics
open economy macroeconomics 1, 10, 128
orthodox economics 6, 8–9, 60, 144, 147; atomism vs. monism 180; and Austrian economics 144, 148, 162; axiomatically based science 5–6; central principles 4–5; formalism 181; full employment as natural state 5; Institutionalist critique 174–5; instrumentalism 181; New Institutionalism 188–9; value relativism 193; *see also* feminist economics
Osterreich, Shaianne *see* feminist economics

pattern of trade 1, 56, 86–7, 108
pluralism 7–9
Post Keynesian economics 200–35: animal spirits and herd-like instincts 201; capital controls 228–9, 234; class struggle and income shares 204–5, 219, 232; endogeneity of money supply 217; flaws of capitalism 231–2; instability 202, 222–7, 234; macroeconomic foundations of microeconomics 223; psychology of expectations 222; speculation 135, 202, 205, 232; strands of Post Keynesian theory 200–4; uncertainty 201–2, 205, 222–3, 226, 230; world reserve currency; *see also bancor*; Keynes Solution; Robinson, Joan; Kalecki, Michał; Minsky, Hyman; Davidson, Paul
Prebisch-Singer thesis 265–6, 308n15
production possibilities frontier: in Neoclassical trade theory 66, *67*, *68*, 75; in New open economy macroeconomics 129; in New Orthodoxy 88; *see also* Ricardian trade theory
post-Fordism 245–6
protectionism: in East Asia model 27; export subsidization and promotion 12, 207; import restrictions 12, 17–19, 133, 206; infant industries 22–3; Marx's view of 237; Mercantilism 22–5; Neoliberal rejection of 134; non-tariff barriers 27, 187; Post Keynesianism 205, 208–9, 228; quotas and tariffs 18, 24, 26, 30, 164–5, 171, 209; regulation of capital flows 12; *see also* Mercantilism; Neo-Mercantilism; trade barriers
purchasing power parity 220, 267

reswitching 161
Ricardian trade theory 38–60; 93% labor theory of value 40; assumptions of 41–2;

autarky 45–55, 59; conclusions of model 40–1; consumption possibilities 48–9; empirical evidence 57–8; exchange rates 55–6; gains from trade 52; labor productivity 41–4, 46, 55–8; law of diminishing returns 38; monetizing the Ricardian model 54–6; necessary and surplus output 38–9; opportunity cost 42, 44–6; 62n8; population growth 36, 38; production possibilities 42, 43, 46; rent 38–9; steady state 38; subsistence wages 38–40, 47, 55–9, 61n4; weaknesses of model 58–60; *see also* community indifference curves; terms of trade

Robinson, Joan 200, 202; balance of payments and macroeconomics 205–9; beggar-my-neighbor policies 208–9, 235; critique of orthodox economics 202, 204–5; exchange rates 206–7; New Mercantilism 208–9; *see also* Post Keynesian economics; Neoclassical trade theory

Rothbard, Murray 145, 150–1, 173

Rybczynski theorem *see* Neoclassical trade theory

Samuelson, Paul 85, 111, 138n2, 139, 173, 297; *see also* Cambridge capital controversy; Neoclassical trade theory

Say's Law *see* Classical international macroeconomics

Schmoller, Gustav 16, 30, 32

Schumpeter, Joseph A. 144, 146, 154, 173; entrepreneurship 162–6, 172n7, 172n8; imperialism 247–8, 251

Seguino, Stephanie *see* Blecker, Robert A.

Shackle, G. L. S. 148, 173

Shaikh, Anwar 84n7, 85, 264–5, 269, 278n2

Smith, Adam 52, 63, theory of capitalist development 35–7

social provisioning 290, 307n6, 309–10; *see also* household production

species flow mechanism 28, 114–15

specific-factor model *see* Neoclassical trade theory

Sraffa, Piero 82, 200, 203–4, 235, 269; gendered North–South trade model 300–1; production model 279–83; unequal exchange model 259–63, 268n5; *see also* class conflict; equilibrium; labor theory of value; Marxian economics; Post Keynesian economics

Stolper-Samuelson theorem *see* Neoclassical trade theory

strategic trade policy *see* New Orthodoxy

subjective theory of value 64, 147

subsistence: economic surplus 243; household production 289–90, 302–4, 306; in Marx's value theory 253–4; means of subsistence 263, 274–7; in Sraffa production model 259; subsistence economy 279; subsistence production 236; subsistence wages 35, 38–40, 47, 55–9, 61n4, 237, 242

Swan-Salter model 123–5

Sweezy, Paul M. *see* imperialism; Neo-Marxism

stagnation: Davidson stagnation bias 229–30; in monopoly capitalism 243; Post Keynesian views on 227

taste bias model 74–6

terms of trade: Institutional economics 193; Neoclassical 71–80; New open economy theory 131; New Orthodoxy 89; Post Keynesian economics 116–7, 129, 131; Ricardian trade theory 53–8; Sraffa model 262; unequal exchange theory 257, 265

Tobin tax 136

trade balance: assumed balanced in Classical and Neoclassical theory 42, 83, 110; in Austrian theory 155; and Mercantilism 18–23, 27–9; in Post Keynesian theory 206–8, 213–21, 231; trade deficit 116, 155, 157, 215–16, 219, 229, 231, 233n3; trade surplus 12, 20, 211, 214–16, 221, 229, 230–33; *see also* balance of payments

trade barriers 112, 129, 131, 164, 171

trade liberalization 26–7, 30–1, 133n6; gender and 285–6, 294–300, 307; and trade in factors of production 77; *see also* Neoliberalism

trade openness 285, 307

transactions: arm's-length and intrafirm (non-market) 187–8; transactions costs 42, 177, 187–91

transnational corporations 2, 23, 179, 185, 189–92, 197, 197n9, 246

uncertainty: in Austrian economics 149, 153, 158, 162–3, 171; in Institutional economics 191, 197–8; in Post Keynesian economics 201–2, 205, 222–3, 226, 230

318 Index

unemployment: in Austrian economics 153–4; in Classical model 110, 233n2; and free trade 81, 83; gender gaps and 291–2, 295; in Keynesian economics 20, 28, 110–14, 117, 137, 141; in Post Keynesian economics 204–8, 224–5, 227, 229–30, 232–3, 235; and production possibilities frontier 46; in Swan-Salter model 124, 138n14
unpaid labor *see* Feminist trade theory
unequal exchange theory 237, 252–83; Emmanuel's theory of 256–9; Grossman's theory of 255–6; and Marx's economic imperialism 252–5; Sraffa's theory of 259–63

Vanek-Leamer factor content theorem *see* Neoclassical trade theory
Veblen, Thorstein 174, 198–9; economic theory 177–81
Von Mises, Ludwig 144–9, 151, 163, 172n2, 173

Wade, Robert 27, 32n7, 33, 136, 139
Washington Consensus 24, 133–6
Williamson, Jeffrey 77, 84
Williamson, John 133–4, 139
Williamson, Oliver 188, 197n2, 198n13, 199
World Bank 24, 132–6, 139n17, 167, 169–70, 184, 191, 246, 285
World Trade Organization 25, 139n17, 194